Violence, Conflict, and Politics in Colombia

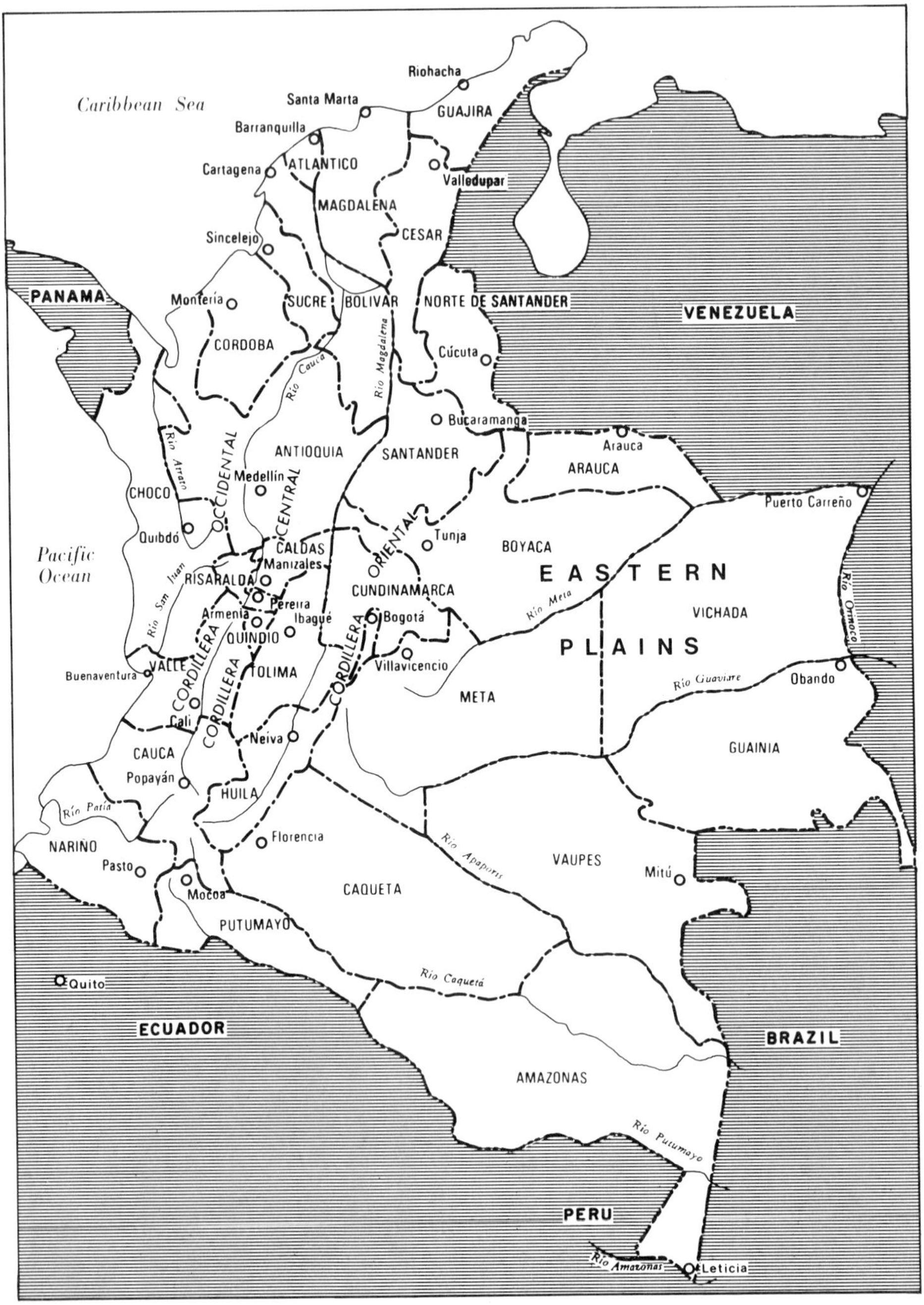

Map of Colombia adapted from a highway map published by the Mobil Oil Corporation.

Violence, Conflict, and Politics in Colombia

PAUL OQUIST

Casa de Gobierno
Managua, Nicaragua

ACADEMIC PRESS

A Subsidiary of Harcourt Brace Jovanovich, Publishers

New York London Toronto Sydney San Francisco

This is a volume in

STUDIES IN SOCIAL DISCONTINUITY

A complete list of titles in this series appears at the end of this volume.

ACADEMIC PRESS, INC.
111 Fifth Avenue, New York, New York 10003

United Kingdom Edition published by
ACADEMIC PRESS, INC. (LONDON) LTD.
24/28 Oval Road, London NW1 7DX

Library of Congress Cataloging in Publication Data

Oquist, Paul H.
Violence, conflict, and politics in Colombia.

(Studies in social discontinuity)
Originally presented as the author's thesis, University of California, Berkeley, 1976.
Bibliography: p.
1. Violence--Colombia--History. 2. Social conflict--History. 3. Colombia--Politics and government. I. Title. II. Series.
HN310.V5068 1980 303.6'09861 80-23141
ISBN 0-12-527750-4

PRINTED IN THE UNITED STATES OF AMERICA

80 81 82 83 9 8 7 6 5 4 3 2 1

To the memory of
BARBARA EDITH OQUIST

Contents

Preface

Between 1946 and 1966, the Republic of Colombia was the scene of one of the most intense and protracted instances of widespread civilian violence in the history of the twentieth century. Known in Colombia simply as *La Violencia,* this social process took at least 200,000 lives, including 112,000 in the 1948–1950 period alone.

As a case of social violence, the great intensity of *La Violencia,* its widespread and highly collective nature, the extreme length of time—over 20 years—and its differential geographical distribution within Colombia all present fundamental research problems, in addition to the basic question of what produces social violence. With regard to Colombian society, *La Violencia* represents one of the most important and traumatic social processes in the nation's history. Knowledge of this phenomenon is essential for an understanding of the dynamics of Colombia's basic economic, social, and political structures. By extension, this is, of course, relevant to the study of Latin American society, given that Colombia represents a microcosm of numerous social processes also present in some of the other countries of the region.

This book attempts to formulate an explanation of the appearance and subsequent development of *La Violencia.* What caused this violent process? What might account for its intensity, duration, and geographical distribution? These questions have guided this study. The search for answers to these queries has also led to the task of seeking a rigorous description of the phenomenon to be explained and of specifying the sociohistorical context of *La Violencia,* with regard both to previous instances of social violence in Colombian history and to the evolution of the nation's basic social structures. This book is based on the first research project to deal with all of these questions and collateral tasks in an integrated fashion. The result of this approach has been the production of an approximate explanation of *La Violencia* that differs significantly from existing interpretations. Students and laymen interested in social conflict and social violence, violence as a factor in political processes, Latin American society and politics in general, and, of course, in Colombian society and politics in particular should find this book especially relevant.

The book opens with a discussion of the general contours of *La Violencia* as well as an introduction to the basic argument of the social-structure explanation of the phenomenon presented in this work. Chapter 2 presents a summary of previous instances of social violence in Colombian history as well as a general overview of the evolution of the nation's socioeconomic and sociopolitical structures, with special attention devoted to the relationship between the state and social conflict and violence. Chapter 3 consists of a description of the immediate antecedents and general evolution of *La Violencia.* Chapter 4 contains a summary and critique of the existing explanatory literature as well as an analysis of the contribution of the social-structure explanation. The remainder of the book argues the case for this explanation: Chapter 5 presents an analysis of the view that *La Violencia* was conditioned by a partial collapse of the state, whereas Chapter 6 presents evidence for the position that *La Violencia* consisted of multiple socioeconomic and sociopolitical processes that turned violent in the same general period due to the common conditioning element of the partial collapse of the state. The diverse social conflicts associated with these processes are analyzed by means of a structural regionalization of *La Violencia* in Chapter 6.

The author is responsible for all of the translations from Spanish utilized in this work.

Acknowledgments

This research initially constituted my doctoral dissertation for the Department of Political Science of the University of California, Berkeley, in 1976. The study was undertaken in the Republic of Colombia between October 1970 and June 1975. Except for a 6-month stay in Chile during 1972, I was employed throughout the period of this research as a professor of political science at the University of the Andes in Bogotá under the auspices of the Latin American Teaching Fellowship Program (LATF) of the Fletcher School of Law and Diplomacy, Tufts University. I especially wish to express my appreciation to Fernando Cepeda of the University of the Andes and to Gary Glenn of the LATF Program for having made this project possible, as well as to the Special Career Fellowship Program of the University of California, Berkeley, which sponsored my doctoral studies.

The persons who have assisted in this research project are so numerous that a complete list is impossible. I wish to thank all of them.

I particularly wish to thank, for their collaboration in the undertaking of this project, my students at the University of the Andes who taught me Colombian history and politics in classes and seminars. I am also deeply indebted to my friends and colleagues at the Department of Political Science of the University of the Andes in general, and particularly to Dora Rothlisberger, Gabriel Murillo, Gary Hoskin (a visiting professor from the State University of New York, Buffalo), Rodrigo Losada, Christopher Abel, Israel Rivera, and Francisco Leal. Friends of great assistance have been Juan Buitrago, Jorge Leiva, Darío Fajardo, José Olinto Rueda, Ema García, Marta Isaza, Carlos Lemoine, Marco Palacios, and Margarita Ponce de Ingre.

I further wish to thank the members of my doctoral committee—Robert Ayres (chairman), Chalmers Johnson, and Arthur Stinchcombe

—for their patience with me and the inconvenience involved in long-distance advising.

A final group intimately involved in this study are the scores of persons who collaborated in interviews and contributed documentary data. They remain anonymous here and in the footnotes of the text. *La Violencia* in Colombia is recent history, and in some areas it is a potent reality to this date. It constitutes a most delicate topic whose unwise treatment could lead to violence itself. For these reasons, most of those interviewed were promised anonymity, and I prefer to extend it to all those consulted, including those who did not explicitly request to remain unnamed. This procedure has ample precedents in the literature of social science research.

Given the delicacy of the topic of *La Violencia* and the continued polarization of Colombian society with regard to its evaluations of this process, it was a distinct advantage to be a foreigner conducting this work. A Colombian researcher would immediately have aroused questions in the minds of the persons interviewed. What party does this fellow belong to? What is he after by researching *La Violencia?*

However, in other aspects I did not feel foreign to Colombia at all. The friendship, general hospitality, and life-style of the Colombian people made me feel increasingly less foreign in Colombia, as I came to identify with the country and the dramatic circumstances in which it is living. In sum, it is to all of the people with whom I was associated in Colombia that I owe great gratitude for making both this study and my prolonged residence in Colombia not only possible but also stimulating and most enjoyable.

1

Introduction: An Overview of *La Violencia*

To give the reader a broad view of the phenomenon of *La Violencia,* this chapter summarizes the principal events associated with it and presents the social-structure explanation that will be detailed throughout this work.

A Summary of *La Violencia*

The 1946–1966 violence occurred in a country whose historical context includes the Spanish conquest, the wars for independence, and the multiple civil wars that took place throughout the nineteenth century. Since the 1850s, social violence in Colombia has been closely associated with partisan rivalries between the two traditional political parties—the Liberals and the Conservatives—but, although party competition is an important element in the analysis, it cannot be stated that this factor alone caused the violence. This work will explore the various complex events and situations that culminated in the 20-year period of violence known as *La Violencia.*

The immediate twentieth-century antecedents of the 1946–1966 violence stem from the electoral violence that surrounded the 1922 presidential campaign, the transference of the presidency from the Conservative to the Liberal party in 1930 with the election of Enrique Olaya Herrera, and the various manifestations of socioeconomic violence in the 1920s, 1930s, and 1940s.

The 1930 electoral process was accompanied by violence and, despite a coalition cabinet, the postelectoral transition form Conservative to Liberal control of the executive branch of government was also violent in some areas. The period between 1930 and 1932 was marked by Liberal attempts to intimidate members of the defeated party and by the violent resistance of recalcitrant Conservatives to acceptance of the Liberal hegemony, which was being achieved in the context of the bipartisan transitional government.[1]

Forced abandonment of agricultural plots and coerced land sales at undervalue prices spurred the political conflicts. Centered principally in Norte de Santander, Santander, Boyacá, and Cundinamarca, with fewer manifestations in Antioquia, Bolívar, Tolima, and Caldas, this violence was relatively short-lived and did not assume crisis proportions.

The Liberals subsequently gained control of the Congress for the legislative period that began in 1933; the Conservatives withdrew their collaboration in the bipartisan cabinet, and a period of Liberal political hegemony ensued. The new government of Olaya Herrera, and especially the subsequent administration of Alfonso López Pumarejo, embarked on reformist projects that were radical when compared to the socioeconomic initiatives that preceded and succeeded them. Official support for labor unions and educational reform, a law to stabilize squatters' rights on unexploited land, and a reversion of unexploited land to the state (Law 200 of 1936) were highly controversial.

This period of political change was followed by the Eduardo Santos administration (1938–1942), during which the moderate wing of the Liberal party largely ended the reformist experiments. López was once again elected president in 1942, but his second administration was extremely weak because he received opposition from both the Conservatives and one wing of the Liberal party. He was forced to resign in 1945. Alberto Lleras Camargo headed an interim government, with a Liberal-controlled, bipartisan cabinet, until the 1946 elections.

With regard to violence in the period 1930–1946, only isolated incidents took place after 1932, associated primarily with party rallies and agrarian conflicts. The most notorious case of party violence was a bloody encounter in Gachetá, Cundinamarca, in January 1939. Politically, the most important coercive event was an aborted military coup in 1944 in Pasto, Nariño, where President Alfonso López Pumarejo was imprisoned by Conservative

[1] Partisan hegemonies generally required at least one transitional administration before they were consolidated. For the 1930 change of administration, consult Rafael Azula Barrera, *De la Revolución al Orden Nuevo* (Bogotá: publisher not listed [hereafter n.p.], 1956), chap. 2; Mauricio Solaún, "La Violencia: Socio-Historical Determinants of Political Violence in Colombia" (unpublished manuscript), pp. 157–159 (this source also contains an analysis of political violence in the 1922 presidential elections, pp. 128–156); Ignacio Torres Giraldo, *Los Inconformes* (Bogotá: Editorial Margen Izquierdo, 1974), vol. 4, pp. 189–197; Manuel Serrano Blanco, *La Vida es Así* (Bucaramanga: Imprenta del Departamento, 1953), chaps. 14–17; Germán Guzmán, Orlando Fals Borda, and Eduardo Umaña Luna, *La Violencia en Colombia* (Bogotá: Universidad Nacional, 1962), vol. 1, pp. 22–25.

troops. However, the bulk of the army remained loyal to the president, and the plot failed.[2]

Violence reappeared in 1946 during the electoral campaign. A Conservative, Mariano Ospina Pérez, was elected president due to a division within the Liberal party, which had presented two presidential candidates, Gabriel Turbay and Jorge Eliécer Gaitán. Gaitán, a Liberal dissident with a reformist platform, was a charismatic leader who was supported by the middle and working classes, especially in Bogotá.

In the Ospina Pérez administration, governmental power was divided initially between the two parties, with the Liberals maintaining control of the Congress, and the new president forming a bipartisan cabinet, labeled the *Unión Nacional* ("National Union"). Despite the coalition, local violence similar to that of the early 1930s recurred in various areas of the country.

Between 1946 and 1948, the violence initially, although transitorily, encompassed Nariño, while serious and long-lived manifestations were found in Valle, Antioquia, Tolima, and Western Caldas. However, the most intense violence centered precisely in those areas that had been most affected by the partisan violence of the 1930s: Norte de Santander, Santander, Boyacá, and Cundinamarca.

This local partisan violence soon became the overriding national political issue. Charges and countercharges of responsibility for the killing escalated the friction between the two political parties. An accelerated rate of inflation and numerous strikes also contributed to the general social unrest. The violence increased in intensity in early 1948, and by March the Liberal party had left the cabinet.[3]

[2] Francisco Leal Buitrago, "Política e Intervención Militar en Colombia," in *La Dependencia Externa y el Desarrollo Político de Colombia,* ed. Rodrigo Parra Sandoval (Bogotá: Universidad Nacional de Colombia, 1970), pp. 174–175; República de Colombia, Ministerio de Gobierno, *Memorias 1945* (Bogotá: Imprenta Nacional, 1945), pp. vi *ff.*, 115; Abelardo Patiño, "The Political Ideas of the Liberal and Conservative Parties during the 1946–1953 Crisis," Ph.D. dissertation, American University (Washington, D.C., 1954), chap. 2; Anthony Maingot, "The Colombia Military: A Case of Inconsistent Status," in "The Role of the Military in Latin America," ed. Lyle N. McAlister (unpublished manuscript), pp. 323–325; José María Nieto Rojas, *La Batalla Contra el Comunismo en Colombia* (Bogotá: Empresa Nacional de Publicaciones, 1956), pp. 62–64.

[3] General accounts of these events and of those subsequently described in this chapter are to be found in the following works: Mauricio Solaun, "La Violencia: Socio-Historical Determinants"; Francisco Leal Buitrago, *Comportamiento Legislativo en Colombia,* vol. 1: "Análisis Histórico del Desarrollo Político Nacional, 1930–1970" (Bogotá: Ediciones Tercer Mundo, 1973), pp. 73–148; Diego Montaña Cuéllar, *Colombia: País Formal y País Real* (Buenos Aires: Editorial Platina, 1963), pp. 170–225; Rafael Azula Barrera, *De la Revolución,* pp. 47–502; John Martz, *Colombia: A Contemporary Political Study* (Chapel Hill: University of North Carolina Press, 1962), esp. pp. 42–169; Vernon Lee Fluharty, *The Dance of the Millions: Military Rule and Social Revolu-*

It was in this explosive socioeconomic and political environment that Liberal leader Jorge Eliécer Gaitán was assassinated on April 9, 1948. Bogotá became the scene of an urban insurrection after Gaitán's assassination, with the police supporting the rioters; other cities and towns also joined in open defiance of the government. Only after a bloody military occupation of Bogotá did the government regain control of the capital.

In this emergency situation, one group of prominent Liberals led by Darío Echandía reentered the Ospina Pérez government to form a new coalition. Another important group remained aloof from this alliance and eventually began to plot the overthrow of the government.

When the Liberals sought to impeach President Ospina in 1949, the Conservative government closed the Liberal-controlled Congress, and the Liberals subsequently abstained from participating in the 1949 presidential campaign, alleging a total lack of political guarantees. Consequently, the Conservative candidate, Laureano Gómez, was elected without competition.

By this time, at least one Liberal-sponsored coup attempt had failed. Liberal guerrillas had been formed in several areas, and the Conservatives had created a politically homogenous police force to confront their opposition. The violence had become intense in all of the areas of Colombia except Nariño and the Caribbean Coast.

Based on the most reliable data available, the distribution of *La Violencia* fatalities (1946–1957) for the 10 most affected *departamentos* ("departments") is shown in Table 1.1.[4] (*Departamento* is the Colombian administrative unit roughly equivalent to a European province or a state in the United States.)

Political party violence was also associated with armed conflicts

tion in Colombia 1930–1956 (Pittsburgh: University of Pittsburgh Press, 1957), esp. pp. 86–310; Robert H. Dix, *Colombia: The Political Dimensions of Change* (New Haven: Yale University Press, 1967), esp. pp. 360–386; Guzmán, Fals Borda, and Umaña Luna, *La Violencia*, pp. 25–38; James Daniel, *Rural Violence in Colombia Since 1946* (Washington, D.C.: American University, Special Operations Research Office [SORO], 1965), pp. 35–190; James Payne, *Patterns of Conflict in Colombia* (New Haven: Yale University Press, 1968), pp. 167–182.

[4] These data are based on information from Dr. Carlos Lemoine of the Compañía Colombiana de Datos. As in most all cases of widespread civilian killing, the data on *La Violencia* are extremely weak. The most common indicator of the intensity of the violence is the statistic of the number of intentional deaths. The number of fatalities, however is a very elusive figure, and most estimates are based principally on guesswork.

An important exception to the general state of the data is the national survey research on the violence conducted by Dr. Carlos Lemoine of the Compañía Colombiana de Datos (COLDATOS). Utilizing the *municipio*-level (municipal-level) data developed by me, Lemoine drew a representative sample of *municipios* affected by *La Violencia* and included them within a national preelectoral survey that contained a battery of questions related to the violence. This national survey was administered in Aug. 1973 and analyzed during the subsequent 12-month period.

The survey findings project an estimate of 180,253 *Violencia* fatalities. This figure was obtained by the following procedure. A battery of items in the survey questionnaire ascertained the number of those interviewed who had been directly affected by *La Violencia.* Of the 5800 respondents interviewed, 15.6% had suffered deaths in their families, property losses, or migrations. Of the 874 individuals affected in this sample, half had lost one or more relatives in their immediate family (i.e., operationalized as father, mother, siblings, spouse, and children).

Thus, for each individual fatality, detailed data were collected in relation to dates, locations, and circumstances. In addition, a demographic description of the family was produced. These facts were then used to estimate the total number and distribution of *La Violencia* fatalities by means of projections based on demographic data.

The family-level demographic information, on which the projections were based, included the following items. The survey revealed that, at the time of death, the *Violencia* fatality had an average of 7.10 members in the immediate family, excluding the deceased himself. Overwhelmingly male, the average age of the victim was 25 years; 65% were single, the spouse's average age was 21, and she had an average of three children with a mean age of 3 years. The victims' fathers were alive in 53% of the cases (average age, 60 years), and the mothers were alive in 60% of the cases (average age, 55 years). The deceased had an average of 3.3 siblings with a mean age of 25 years.

On the basis of this demographic information, it was determined, using the actuary survival tables compiled by the Centro de Estudios para el Desarrollo Económico (CEDE), of the University of the Andes, that there would be a mean of 6.2 survivors in families affected by the violence at the time of the survey. For cases in which there were multiple fatalities, the mean number of survivors would be 5.2 for two *Violencia* deaths and 4.2 for three deaths.

In sum, studying the sample determined the number of surviving relatives in Aug. 1973. This was related to the number of victims and to the size of their families at the time of death, and this information was then in turn related to the population statistics for different localities at different times to project the number of total deaths in Colombia and in the various departments for the years of *La Violencia.*

This procedure might be expected to yield a minimal estimate of *Violencia* deaths. The most probable errors are in the direction of underestimating the number of fatalities.

An element of survey error might be expected in "no responses" and "contrary to fact responses" from persons reticent to discuss *La Violencia.* A source of sampling error in the nationwide survey is the number of Colombians living in Venezuela, approximately 600,000–800,000, an appreciable percentage of whom were originally *Violencia* refugees. For the Venezuela population estimate, consult Comisión Católica Internacional de Migración and Caritas Internacionalis, "Informe de Misión: Venezuela y Colombia" (Geneva and Rome: Feb. 1972).

Other minimizing factors are that multiple-victim families have less chance to figure in the sample than single-victim families. This would affect the estimates despite the allowances made in the projections for the multiple-victim cases. In addition, *Violencia*-victim families for which there are no contemporary survivors could not be added to the sample. Of these, the greatest underestimation would occur in the case of those families decimated in collective slaying during the violence (known in Colombia as *genocidios* ("genocides").

All of the aforementioned factors have the effect of minimizing the fatality estimates.

TABLE 1.1
Distribution of *Violencia* Fatalities for the Ten Most Affected Departments, 1946–1957

Department	Deaths
Caldas Antiguo	44,255
Tolima	30,912
Antioquia	26,115
Norte de Santander	20,885
Santander	19,424
Valle	13,106
Meta	5,842
Boyacá	5,363
Huila	4,111
Cundinamarca	4,033
	174,046

stemming from other causes. In addition to the partisan battles, agrarian conflicts of various types, struggles for control of local power structures, revenge raids, and banditry were common.

The social fabric of Colombia seemed to have disintegrated. Although the civil wars of the nineteenth century with their positional, battlefield warfare carried high death tolls, they were not comparable to the horror and lack of security for the entire population that resulted from decentralized battles, raids, and killings in village after village, year after year.

Table 1.2 lists the best available estimate of the number of *La Violencia* fatalities for the period 1948–1953.[5] In this situation the Gómez government mustered only a very narrow political base, facing opposition not only from the Liberals but also from the Conservative wing led by ex-

TABLE 1.2
Chronological Distribution of *Violencia* Fatalities, 1948–1953

Year	Deaths
1948	43,557
1949	18,519
1950	50,253
1951	10,319
1952	13,250
1953	8,650
	144,548

[5] The data were furnished by Dr. Carlos Lemoine of the Compañía Colombiano de Datos.

President Mariano Ospina Pérez. Seriously ill, Gómez discharged the duties of the presidency to a "designate," Roberto Urdaneta Arbeláez (there is no vice-presidency in Colombia). When Gómez resumed the presidency on June 13, 1953, to manage a crisis involving Army Commander Gustavo Rojas Pinilla, he was deposed by a military coup.

The subsequent Rojas Pinilla government enjoyed initial political backing from all partisan factions except Gómez's wing of the Conservative party and the Communist party. This support and a general amnesty for all those implicated in the violence dramatically, and almost immediately, reduced the level of fatalities. This truce, however, was short-lived. As a result of clashes between the military and civilians, particularly in the Communist-influenced areas of Eastern Tolima, the violence was rekindled.

The fatality estimates given in Table 1.3 reflect the decline and resurgence of *La Violencia* under the military government.[6]

TABLE 1.3
Chronological Distribution
of *Violencia* Fatalities, 1951–1960

Year	Deaths
1951	10,319
1952	13,250
1953	8,650
1954	900
1955	1,013
1956	11,136
1957	2,877
1958	3,796
1959	2,550
1960	2,557
	57,048

[6] The 1951–1957 data are from Dr. Carlos Lemoine of the Compañía Colombiana de Datos. The 1958–1960 figures are from police information, which began to be systematically compiled in 1958. The source is República de Colombia, Policía Nacional, *Criminalidad en 1964* (Bogotá: 1965), charts 23, 24, pp. 50–51.

Police statistics were only compiled beginning in 1955. The first attempts were very unorganized and it was only in 1958 that relatively consistent, systematized data became available; see República de Colombia, Fuerzas Armadas, Ministerio de Guerra, Fuerzas de Policía, Estado Mayor, F-2, *Estudio Criminalístico del Año 1958* (Bogotá: 1959), pp. 3–8. Previous information was so unreliable that police and military sources admit that the fatality figures for their own personnel are incomplete. See Guzmán, Fals Borda, and Umaña Luna, *La Violencia*, p. 258, citing "Resúmen Discriminado de Muertos por Causa de la Violencia Política," in *Proceso* ("Trial") No. 9223 of the "Segunda Instancia de la Jurisdicción Penal Militar," *Vista Fiscal*, No. 3848, Feb. 15, 1962 (Bogotá: Fiscalía Tercera), pp. 75–76.

The police information has numerous flaws, including compilation defects and the usual discrepancies between "real crime," "crime known to the public but unreported

The initial bipartisan support for the military government had become bipartisan opposition by the end of the regime, when a coalition of Conservative and Liberal leaders engineered Rojas Pinilla's fall from power. Rojas Pinilla was succeeded by an interim military junta in 1957 and then by the inauguration of the *Frente Nacional* ("National Front") government in 1958.

The Frente Nacional was a Conservative–Liberal coalition added to the Colombian constitution as a result of a national vote in 1957. As subsequently revised, the constitution provided for the alternation of Liberals and Conservatives in the presidency for four consecutive presidential terms (1958–1974), the equal division of ministerial positions and public administration (through 1978), and the equal division of all legislative bodies. With regard to the latter, the departmental assemblies and municipal councils were equally divided through 1972, and the National Congress was evenly split until 1974.

Despite the reduction in partisan political activities implied by the governmental coalition, the violence did not end. Given the long-term Conservative–Liberal coalition, the continued armed conflicts had less to do with traditional partisan politics than with other causes. Economic factors such as forced land abandonment, coerced land sales, crop seizures, title disputes, and other agrarian conflicts were important causes throughout the period of *La Violencia,* but they were particularly pronounced during the "late violence" of the Frente Nacional. In addition to the agrarian conflicts, nonpartisan struggles for control of local power structures, banditry, local partisan rivalries (despite the national accord), and revolutionary guerrilla activity were also present in the continuation of the violence throughout the first two administrations of the Frente Nacional.

This violence was more restricted geographically than the armed conflict of the late 1940s and early 1950s. It took place principally in the areas of Tolima, Northern Huila, Northern Valle–Western Caldas, and Antioquia, with fewer occurrences in Santander, Cauca, and Cundinamarca. Table 1.4 shows the departmental distribution of fatalities in the 10 most affected areas for the period 1958–1966.[7]

---

to the police," and "crime known to the police." One might expect that, under normal circumstances, homocide would be among the crimes known to the public and most exhaustively reported to the police, but that is not always a safe assumption with regard to the violence-ridden areas of Colombia.

Despite their defects, however, the police data remain the most complete information for a *minimal* fatality estimate for the period 1958–1966.

For further analysis of these data, consult Paul Oquist, "Una Aproximación Descriptiva del Crimen en Colombia," *Revista Cámara de Comercio de Bogotá* 3 (1973).

[7] These data are from the Policía Nacional de Colombia. The sources are República de Colombia, Policía Nacional, *Criminalidad en 1964* (Bogotá: 1965), charts 23, 24, pp. 5–51; *ibid., Criminalidad en 1965* (Bogotá: 1966), charts 6, 7, 16, pp. 3–31, 49; *ibid., Criminalidad en 1966* (Bogotá: 1967), chart 16, p. 49

TABLE 1.4
Departmental Distribution
of *Violencia* Fatalities, 1958–1966

Department	Deaths
Tolima	5,257
Valle	5,016
Caldas Antiguo	2,606
Antioquia	2,127
Huila	733
Santander	649
Cauca	457
Cundinamarca	334
Meta	166
Boyacá	142
	17,487

By 1966, the violence that had begun in 1946 had been drastically reduced; the decline in the violence was gradual but steady, as shown by the data given in Table 1.5.[8] However, a certain residual violence persists. The presence, still, of revolutionary guerrilla activity figures prominently in the political violence that continues in Colombia to date.

The combination of the two most reliable indicators of the intensity of the violence reveals a *minimum* of 193,603 fatalities in the period 1946–1966.[9] These data suggest that the actual number of deaths, including unreported homicides, exceeds 200,000. The *minimal* estimate, when compared to the 1951 census (the population statistic closest to the years of the in-

TABLE 1.5
Chronological Distribution
of *Violencia* Fatalities, 1961–1966

Year	Deaths
1961	3173
1962	2370
1963	1711
1964	972
1965	950
1966	496
	9672

[8] From Policía Nacional de Colombia; the sources are listed in n. 7 to this chapter.

[9] The most reliable indicators, as argued previously, are the Lemoine COLDATOS data for the years through 1957 and the Colombian National Police statistics for the period 1958–1966. See nn. 4 and 6 in this chapter.

tense violence), reveals that 1.56% of the total population was slain. That, in turn, amounts to 2.79% of the population aged 15 years or older.

Of the 842 *municipios* (roughly equivalent to United States counties) into which Colombia was divided during the period of *La Violencia,* 384 (33.7%) experienced violence at one point in time or another (see Table 1.6).[10] Of the total number of *municipios,* 14.82% experienced only the early violence and 6.7% only the late violence (with these being concentrated in fewer departments), whereas 12.2% suffered violence during both periods for totals of up to 20 years of violent conflict.

Although it is difficult to place these facts into an international context, in the early 1960s, when *La Violencia* had subsided, Colombia still had the highest violent death rate in the world.[11]

From the preceding discussion it is clear that the more than 200,000 estimated deaths represents one of the most intense and protracted cases of widespread collective civilian violence in contemporary history, for

[10] The sources for the identification of *municipios* affected by the "early violence" are the qualitative appraisals of the National Police and of Germán Guzmán as part of his research for the *Comisión Nacional Investigadora de las Causas Actuales de la Violencia* (National Investigating Commission on the Current Causes of Violence).

No source explicitly covers the 1954–1957 violence. However, this consisted predominantly of *municipios* also affected in the 1948–1953 period. The few cases in which this rule does not hold were overwhelmingly affected by violence after 1958 as well. In sum, the two indicators include the *municipios* for those years, with only rare exceptions.

The appraisals of the presence or absence of violence are from Guzmán, Fals Borda, and Umaña Luna, *La Violencia,* chap. 4; República de Colombia, Ministerio de Guerra, Policía Nacional, Estado Mayor, *Criminalidad Colombiana, 1959,* map no. 1 (1948–1953—Zonas Más Afectadas por la Violencia). I have reconstructed from the police maps lists of the areas considered to be most affected.

The presence of violence in the late period is based exclusively on police data. These data exist, discriminated at the *municipio* level, for the years 1958, 1959, 1962, 1963, and 1965. The sources are República de Colombia, Ministerio de Guerra, Policía Nacional, Estado Mayor, *Criminalidad Colombiana, 1959,* pp. 25–26; *ibid., Criminalidad en 1963,* maps 4–16, pp. 76–183; *ibid., Criminalidad en 1965,* map 1.

[11] In United Nations, *Demographic Yearbook,* vol. 8, 1961, item BE 50, pp. 398–471, the following intentional death rates are given:

Selected International Intentional Death Rate (per 100,000 population)

World-wide rank order	Country	Deaths	Year
1.	Colombia	34.0	1960
2.	Mexico	31.1	1958
3.	Nicaragua	22.8	1959
4.	South Africa	21.2	1959
5.	Burma	10.8	1959

TABLE 1.6
Early Violence (1948–1953) and Late Violence (1958–1964) at the Municipal Level [a]

		LATE		
		No Violence	Violence	Total
E A R L Y	No violence	558 (66.3)	56 (6.7)	614 (72.9)
	Violence	125 (14.8)	103 (12.2)	228 (27.1)
	Total	683 (81.1)	159 (18.9)	842 (100)

[a] The numbers of *municipios* (≈ counties) with incidences of violence and those with no incidences of violence are given; the values in parentheses are the percentages of the total number of *municipios* (842). $X^2 = 141.0997$; significant at .001. Degrees of freedom (*df*) = 1. Contingency coefficient = .3788.

which an explanation is sought in the remainder of this work. The basic argument of that explanation is summarized in the following section.

A Summary of the Social-Structure Explanation [12]

The initial field research conducted in different areas affected by *La Violencia* led to the notion that the phenomenon seemed to result from various sociopolitical processes rather than a single, unitary process. The standard party-rivalry explanation could not logically explain the unusual intensity of the violence or its wide geographical distribution. A second basic idea that emerged from the research was that the Colombian state had lost its efficacy during *La Violencia* to the point that one could speak of a partial collapse of the state.

[12] The social-structure analysis used in this research has no relation whatsoever to "structuralism" of either Louis Althusser or Claude Levi-Strauss or to the applications of the former to social analysis by Nicos Poulantzas. Indeed, rather than rely on a priori "structural categories" for a more often than not abstract speculation about their conditioning effect on ongoing social practice, the approach employed here requires empirical research on specific social formations, guided by a theoretical framework that conceptualizes both objective and subjective social structures and processes and that posits dialectical relationships between them. Thus which of these levels conditions the other is never an a priori or static postulate but rather an explanatory objective of research on specific social structures and processes within concrete sociohistorical contexts.

The partial collapse of the state was basically caused by intense sectarian rivalries between the Liberal and Conservative parties. These conflicts came to be expressed in more and more violent forms. The partial collapse of the state led to a further increase in the intensity of the partisan violence that had contributed to the partial collapse itself. More important, however, the partial collapse of the state conditioned an entire series of social contradictions into conflicts with a high potential for violence. A complex set of socioeconomic processes, previously structured by the state, came to be decided by the direct application of violence. The state could no longer militarily back social policies that favored some groups to the disadvantage of others, nor did the state possess the capacity to intervene as a third party in all of the disputes among groups not represented in the effective power structure of the state. Thus, conflicts given a low priority by government officials were largely left to run their violent course.

In sum, the partial collapse of the state led to violent sociopolitical processes that confronted groups with contradictory interests on multiple issues. Partisan differences were important in *La Violencia* both before and after the partial collapse of the state, but they constitute only one sociopolitical process within a complex pattern of conflicts. Indeed, partisan conflict becomes less and less important across time. After 1953 socioeconomic conflicts, which were also present before that date, became the most significant element in *La Violencia*. During the course of the violence, traditional party conflicts also decreased in importance relative to revolutionary political struggles.

A knowledge of the historical development of Colombian society is necessary in order to understand the partial collapse of the state and its impact on Colombian society of the late 1940s. A historical perspective is also necessary to appreciate fully the nature of the sociopolitical processes involved in *La Violencia* and their tendency to be expressed in violent form.

Violence has been an important and often decisive structuring process throughout Colombian history. The initial Spanish conquest and the consolidation and maintenance of the Spanish colonial social structure were largely violent processes. The Indian groups and the African slaves were subjected to violence in order to maintain the structure of domination within colonial society. Most of the social violence during the colonial period was spurred by interclass conflicts.

For the bulk of its existence, however, the colony of the Nuevo Reino de Granada was characterized by a strong state within a strong structure of social domination. Apart from the unconquered Indian groups and the rebellious slaves, the other groups in society did not generally need to be physically coerced to accept the structure of society and their place in it. Nonstate mechanisms of social control such as religion, political ideology, and paternalistic economic relations were more important than violence in structuring social relations. The state is said to have been strong because it controlled almost every facet of colonial life and was capable of easily controlling threats to continued Spanish domination.

At the end of the colonial period, the state was dramatically weakened, in large part because of Spain's declining international position vis-à-vis England. Under these circumstances, certain social contradictions matured into acute conflicts with a high potential for violence. One such process was the *Comunero* ("Commoners") Rebellion of 1782 wherein the contradictory interests of small farmers, artisans, and Indians on the one hand and the fiscal interests of the Spanish crown on the other matured into a violent conflict conditioned by the reduction of the power of the colonial state. Later, in the independence movement the same factor conditioned violent conflict between the Spanish-American *criollo* ("creole") oligarchy against the Spanish crown; the contradictory interests involved were social and economic discrimination. The end result of this armed struggle was the political independence of Nueva Granada and the rest of Spain's mainland colonies.

The first century of independence was characterized by a weak state within a strong structure of social domination. Conflicts arose primarily within the *criollo* oligarchy over questions such as the retention or reformation of the colonial socioeconomic structure, the organization of the new republican state, and which groups were going to effectively control the state. Thus, the conflicts in nineteenth-century Colombia were generally intraclass. The main exceptions to this rule were the revolts of professional military officers in the early 1830s, the diffuse popular uprising that occurred during the War of the Supremes, and the artisan–military coup d'etat of 1854, as well as the civil war that followed it.

The intraclass conflicts of the nineteenth century might be categorized as those primarily related to the formation of the republican state, those that revolved around the midcentury anticolonial reforms, and those that involved the defense of the interests of different factions of the dominant class. The nineteenth-century civil wars increasingly took on political party connotations. In turn, the wars reinforced party identification. This was particularly the case in the traumatic War of a Thousand Days, which accentuated the progressive ossification of partisan identification.

In the early twentieth century, Colombian society was the scene of rapid socioeconomic change. The availability of desirable land for colonization in the central "core" area of the country diminished; the construction of the nation's transport infrastructure, financed by massive foreign loans, was accelerated; and the process of industrialization began to have a considerable socioeconomic impact. Under these circumstances, the traditional structure of social domination began to weaken. Social movements and conflicts began to appear among such diverse groups as Indians, land colonists, and wage laborers. These interclass movements began to be violently repressed.

The Colombian state was strengthened by virtue of political reforms that accompanied the socioeconomic changes, and it also assumed a more important role in structuring the relations among the various groups that composed Colombian society. By means of both repression and reform, the state became progressively more important within an increasingly weakened total structure of social domination.

Throughout the last half of the nineteenth century and the first half of the twentieth century, factional and partisan conflicts in Colombia had been typified by exclusivistic politics. The final objective of political groups was often to construct sectarian hegemonies that could wield power for the benefit of the group in question to the exclusion of all other groups. Alliances and coalitions did occur, but they were frequently strategic or tactical moves designed to further long-run hegemonic goals.

This element of Colombian political culture persisted during the period in which the role of the state in society increased markedly. By 1946, an interventionist state apparatus had come to be a crucial factor in almost all spheres of the national economy and, indeed, in almost all spheres of Colombian life. This same process has occurred in almost every country in the course of the twentieth century, but in Colombia it took place in the context of exclusivistic, hegemonic politics. Thus, the group that did not control the state could expect only discrimination from it, whereas those persons politically connected with the party in power could expect to monopolize state decision making and the benefits to be derived from state power.

Given the increased importance of the state in Colombian life, no group within the bourgeoisie could conceive of accepting exclusion from state power and its benefits. Certain groups in both political parties attempted to advance formulas that would have implied sharing power between the traditional political parties. Their efforts failed because exclusivistic hegemonic political objectives were still an invincible political reality among the bulk of party sectarians. Thus, there occurred a tenacious conflict in the period 1946–1949 over whether the Conservative party would consolidate a political party hegemony or whether the Conservative government would fall from power and be replaced by a Liberal party hegemony. The stakes were such that the elites of both parties proved willing to accept an extremely high degree of violence. The results were a partial collapse of the state and widespread, intense violence.

The partial collapse of the state was manifested in the crisis and inoperativeness of established institutions, the loss of legitimacy of the state, the state's resort to terrorist tactics which led to a further breakdown of social relations, the physical absence of the state in large areas of the country, and contradictions within the armed apparatus of the state.

The crisis of established institutions was acutely reflected in the electoral system, in the police force and judicial institutions, and in executive versus legislative conflicts, as well as in numerous other spheres. Elections became contests of fraud and coercion more than civic debates. The Conservative party, which was an obvious minority in the country despite its control of the presidency, especially sought to keep Liberal voters away from the polls. The police and judicial institutions were highly politicized as a result of the party conflicts. In April 1948, Liberal policemen in Bogotá and other areas joined with the rioters and distributed arms among them in the wake of the assassination of Liberal party leader Jorge Eliécer Gaitán. After that event, the police force was systematically purged of Liberals. Police and judicial favoritism reached the point where certain party-backed gunmen enjoyed immunity from legal proceedings and engaged in violent acts with complete impunity. The conflicts between the executive branch of the government controlled by the Conservatives and the Liberal-controlled Congress reached the point where the constitutional structure of government was overturned. In 1949 the Liberal Congress began to attempt to impeach the president of the republic, who responded by closing the Congress. The lack of internal coherence within the state, and the sectarian politicization of the state, greatly reduced its efficacy as an institution within Colombian society.

One of the results of the institutional crisis was the loss of legitimacy of the government. Millions of Liberals began to consider the Ospina Pérez and Gómez administrations as arbitrary, dictatorial regimes. Voluntary compliance to government fiats was reduced among large and significant segments of the population, and subtle forms of noncompliance began to sabotage government policies. The Conservative authorities responded to this situation by attempting to repress the Liberals into compliance. The government, however, did not possess the means to repress the Liberals to the extent necessary to guarantee its continued power. The government resorted to terrorist tactics that included arbitrary police harassment of Liberals, Conservative counterguerrillas who served as paramilitary forces against Liberal guerrillas, and political gunmen who assassinated the leaders of the Liberal resistance, as well as some Liberals randomly. These official and semiofficial terrorist activities merely served to break down further the relations between the parties and the structure of social relations in general. Ironically, Conservative terrorism contributed to the situation of chaos in many areas, which further weakened the state that the Conservative party controlled.

An obvious manifestation of the partial collapse of the state was its physical absence from large areas of the country. In areas controlled by

Liberal guerrillas, in zones where the Conservative government could not afford to protect government officials to the extent necessary, and in areas in which active noncompliance simply overwhelmed state officials, the offices and personnel of the public administration ceased to function. In some areas alternative authority structures were constructed by rebel groups, in others local custom structured the social relations, and in still others conditions of structural anomie reigned.

One of the serious limitations of the state's ability to repress its opposition was the presence of partisan and corporate considerations within the armed forces. In this complicated matter, the Conservative government could not depend entirely on armed forces in which Liberal officers were overrepresented. At the same time, the military commands were apprehensive about taking an active role in *La Violencia* because they feared an exacerbation of internal partisan tensions and division of the armed institutions.

Liberal coup d'etat plots did not prosper because of the certainty that such a move would divide the army. Thus, crossed partisan and corporate loyalties kept the armed forces on the margin of *La Violencia* until the government was confronted with guerrilla movements that threatened its very existence. The army's effectiveness in the antiguerrilla campaigns was reduced by partisan considerations: Conservative officials acted vigorously, whereas Liberal officers often reached "live and let live" agreements with Liberal guerrillas and sabotaged the activities of the wholly Conservative police. The threat that continued combat to defend the increasingly isolated Gómez administration would lead to internal divisions was one factor that contributed to the military coup d'etat of June 13, 1953. Another factor was that the army's ineffectiveness had been accompanied by an increase in the military potential of guerrilla groups, especially on the Eastern Plains. In sum, the army's initial lack of participation in *La Violencia,* its partisan-induced lack of effectiveness once involved, and the lack of coordination between Liberal officers and the Conservative police all represent the influence of partisan conflict within the armed apparatus of the state. These conflicts, which led to a reduction of the government's repressive capacity, form still another element of the partial collapse of the state.

Collapses of state authority of varying degrees are not without precedent in Colombian history. During the nineteenth-century civil wars, divisions within the dominant class had led to drastic reductions in the efficacy of state authority. However, widespread social violence did not result from those partial collapses because the intraclass nature of the civil wars and the continued strength of the total structure of social dominations mitigated against the development of interclass conflicts. Despite the partial collapses of state authority, political control of the dominant classes was not in doubt. For example, during the War of a Thousand Days, in which the economy was ruined and the state was without power in many areas of the country, there were no popular uprisings of Indians, land colonists, sharecroppers, agricultural laborers, or port, railway, and river workers. We may conclude that there was not a large potential for social conflict or social violence among the dominated classes of society.

During the second and third decades of the twentieth century, however, interclass relations proved increasingly conflictive. Thus, when the state partially collapsed once again in the late 1940s, there was a high potential for contradictory social interests to develop into conflicts and for these conflicts to be expressed violently given the state's partial collapse. The state had collapsed in a society in which the structure of numerous social relations had come to depend on it. With the partial collapse of the state, these social relations became unstructured, highly conflictive, and prone to violence.

In different areas of Colombia, different types of contradictions, some intraclass and others interclass, developed into conflicts with a high potential for violence. The following are some of the most important of the myriad types of conflicts: partisan-guerrilla civil wars; traditional rivalries between villages with vendetta mentalities over the entire gambit of conflicts endemic to agrarian societies; conflicts over the control of local power structures; land tenure conflicts; the coerced abandonment or sale of agricultural parcels; conflicts over the appropriation of the coffee crop and other forms of banditry; and revenge violence stemming from all of the foregoing.

With the partial collapse of the state, the political resistance of the Liberals to the hegemonic objectives of the Conservatives assumed the form of organized armed struggle in many areas. A Liberal guerrilla force controlled the vast region of the Eastern Plains and had reached the point of development where alternative authority structures had begun to function. Other important Liberal guerrilla groups operated in Tolima, Cundinamarca, Santander, and Caldas. Thus, the violent partisan conflict that had led to the crisis of the state itself increased in intensity and assumed more organized forms as a result of the partial collapse of the state.

Traditional rivalries between villages also erupted into widespread violence as a result of the reduction of state power. Often identified by opposing political tendencies, many villages and hamlets of smallholders have had traditions of vendettas since the civil wars of the nineteenth century. These conflicts have little or nothing to do with national partisan conflicts despite the political identification of the towns. Questions such as land limits, water rights, transit privileges, commercial transactions, and courtship all have the propensity to develop into conflicts in such areas. Given the vendetta mentality of the towns, conflicts tend to become collectivized, and the use of violence by one group in a conflict demands as a matter of honor a collective, violent response from the other group. These vendettas have existed for years, and they still continue to occur. Under normal circumstances, the state intervenes as a third party in such conflicts to separate the factions and repress the manifestations of violence. During the period of *La Violencia,* however, these areas were given a very low priority by state decision makers, and the subsequent lack of state intervention led to the development of small wars between different villages. The absence of the state in these areas led to a policy of letting the violence run its course.

Similar to the previous violent sociopolitical processes were those that involved control of the local power structure in smallholding communities. In these localities, control of the local power structure is highly conflictive in that much is at stake for the desperately poor *minifundistas* ("small farmers"). Local political cliques tend to vie for power; they tend to identify nominally with the national political parties, but the conflicts themselves have little to do with national politics (except when there is a change in the national administration and thus of the party identification of the governors and mayors). Often, violent conflicts occur between different cliques identified with the same political party. Under normal circumstances, the state intervenes as a third party in these violent disputes. During the period of the partial collapse of the state, this intervention was absent. Highly intense violence accompanied the local disputes, and it became vital for the *minifundistas* to belong to one or another clique to protect their property and even their lives from the violence of the other cliques. This is another example of conflicts that were simply left to run their violent course as a result of the absence of the state.

In areas where land conflicts had been structured by the state in favor of certain groups to the detriment of the interests of others, violence over land accompanied the reduction of state power. In some areas, the basic structure of land tenure was maintained by the armed apparatus of the state, since significant segments of the local population did not voluntarily accept the distribution of real property. When the state collapsed in such areas, the land disputes began to be determined by the coercive capacity of the groups involved. This was particularly the case in zones in which there had been disputes over the authenticity of the land titles held by *latifundistas* ("large landowners"), in areas of intensive colonization, and in zones where Indians occupied a large portion of the land.

Another form of conflict involving land was the coerced removal of numerous landholders from the countryside, especially in the coffee-growing areas. Those removed were generally the smaller, weaker landholders.

Some farmers simply abandoned their parcels and fled to the cities never to return to their native areas, whereas others were forced to sell at undervalue prices; still others lost their land due to diffuse panic selling at absurd prices in violent areas. Given the partial collapse of the state, there was often no authority to appeal to in order to defend one's rights in some zones; worse yet, in other areas the local state authorities were participants in the land bonanza provoked by the coerced abandonments and sales.

In areas in which the state had collapsed and in which alternative authority structures had not been consolidated, property was massively distributed by violent means. The coffee bean harvest came to be as much a military as an economic activity. Exceptionally powerful coffee growers "connected" with government authorities could rely on troops and police, while others sought to protect their crops by reaching agreements with armed bands. Embezzlement, the robbery of farms, the protection racket, and highwaymen all became highly significant parts of *La Violencia* in the coffee-producing areas. Revenge violence and irrational violence also accompanied these processes, as is inevitable when there is widespread killing.

In sum, the partial collapse of the state conditioned the maturation of numerous socioeconomic and sociopolitical contradictions into intense conflict, some of which were intraclass and others interclass.

During the period of *La Violencia,* the traditional partisan conflicts decreased in importance and interclass conflicts became more important. In addition, organized revolutionary activities also appeared on the scene. Confronted with this situation, the dominant class sought to end the violence by first supporting the military coup d'etat of 1953 and the resultant military government and by next forming a coalition between the two traditional political parties. The coalition known as the Frente Nacional guaranteed that neither of the two traditional political parties nor any fraction within them would be excluded from state power or the benefits derived from it for a prolonged period of time. Thus, the bourgeoisie overcame the contradiction that had led to the partial collapse of the state. However, the coalition did not put an end to hegemonic politics: Instead of the hegemony of the Liberals *or* the Conservatives, the Frente Nacional represented the hegemony of the Liberals *and* the Conservatives.

The creation of the Frente Nacional did not end the violence. It dramatically reduced the traditional party violence, but it did not and could not resolve the myriad other types of social processes involved in *La Violencia.* The late violence (1954–1966) continually reflected more and more elements of interclass conflict. Furthermore, the state continued to have only a tenuous existence in many areas and was absent in still others. Indeed, it was necessary in the areas with alternative political structures to reimpose state relations by armed invasions. Under the Frente Nacional, the reduction of traditional party rivalries, the violent reinstatement of state authority in rebellious areas, the violent repression of violent conflicts, and the declaration of amnesties for certain rebel leaders had the end result of reducing the level of violence. However, the violence did not entirely end, and, indeed, it continues to this day in some areas of Colombia.

In addition to the continuation of previous forms of violence, new sociopolitical processes have led to violence in Colombia. Organized guerrilla movements with revolutionary objectives have appeared on the Colombian political scene. Some of these groups have their origins in the period of *La Violencia*, whereas others are the result of subsequent sociopolitical processes.

The succeeding chapters in this work develop the social-structure explanation summarized here, beginning with a consideration of violence in Colombian history (Chapter 2), which is followed by a detailed description of the origins of *La Violencia* (Chapter 3), a critical review of the explanatory literature on the subject (Chapter 4), the presentation of the evidence for, and an analysis of, the partial collapse of state (Chapter 5), and the structural regionalization of *La Violencia* (Chapter 6). A concluding note is given in Chapter 7.

2

Violence in Colombian History

Violence has been an important and often decisive social process in the structuring of Colombian society throughout the nation's history. The same, of course, may be said for almost any society. Indeed, the perennial wars of the European countries present far more frequent and intense instances of widespread violent behavior than anything to be found in Colombia or other South American nations. The presence of conflict-prone, contradictory interests, and of conditions that facilitate their violent expressions, is considered to be the structural basis of collective violence.

This chapter will explore past instances of violence in Colombia in an attempt to describe the underlying social conflicts. The role of the state as a prime conditioning agent in violent conflicts will receive special attention. This general survey will provide important elements for a more thorough understanding of the twentieth-century *Violencia* by placing it within its sociohistoric context.

In Colombia, physical coercion has been a significant structuring process in the distribution of territory among indigenous groups prior to the arrival of the Spanish, in the Spanish conquest, in the construction and maintenance of the Spanish Colonial Empire, in the Latin American independence movement, in the multiple civil wars and political conflicts of the first century of independence, and in the twentieth-century *Violencia.*

The Colony

Colonial Nueva Granada was characterized by a strong state within a strong structure of social domination.[1] This would tend to depict a very

[1] The contemporary *República de Colombia* was known in the colonial period as the *Nuevo Reino de Granada.* During the first years of independence it formed the part of

stable society, which is what Nueva Granada was for nearly three centuries. This is not to say that violence was absent or that the threat of physical coercion was not important in structuring society, but, once the conquest had been consolidated and the Spanish Colonial Empire constructed, the dominant social group (the Peninsular Spanish) managed to control the bulk of society by economic, ideological, and religious means without resorting to widespread repression to maintain the structure of society.

Violent conflicts are to be found generally during the imposition and the deposition of Spanish rule. During the imposition, the colonial state had yet to be constructed and, during the deposition, the Spanish state could not adequately respond to challenges to its authority due to a process of power deflation.

The violent conflicts of the period were primarily between different social groups. Within the dominant social group there was usually a high degree of internal coherence.

CONQUEST

The domination of the indigenous peoples of America and the imposition of Spanish authority in the continent were achieved by violence. Two types of wars were fought against the indigenous groups the Spanish found in the New World.

Wars of conquest were conducted against the more highly organized nations, such as the Incas, the Aztecs, and, in Nueva Granada, the Chibchas. These violent conflicts occurred in the sixteenth century and, from these wars, the Spanish accumulated wealth (mostly gold) as well as control of centralized economic, social, and political institutions. Onto these existing structures were grafted the mechanisms of Spanish domination.[2]

---

the *República de Gran Colombia*. Once that political unit was dissolved, the name reverted to *Nueva Granada* until 1857, when the nation was named the *Confederación Granadina*. In 1863, the name changed to *Estados Unidos de Colombia* and in 1886 to *República de Colombia*.

[2]The conquest of the Chibchas did not entail particularly intense violence. The Spanish assassinated the principal leaders, the *Zipa* of Bogotá and the *Zaque* of Tunja, and the demoralized Chibchas resisted under secondary leaders, the *Uzaques* of Tundama and Sugamuxi until 1540. Sporadic revolts continued well after that date, but they were protests against the degree of exploitation of Indian laborers that took place within the context of a Chibcha nation under the consolidated domination of the Spanish.

See Juan Friede, *Invasión del País de los Chibchas* (Bogotá, Ediciones Tercer Mundo, 1966), Ch. XVI, XVII; Indalecio Liévano Aguirre, *Los Grandes Conflictos Sociales y Económicos de Nuestra Historia* (Bogotá: Ediciones Nueva Prensa, 1954), vol. 1, p. 43; Orlando Fals Borda, *Subversión y Cambio Social* (Bogotá: Ediciones Tercer Mundo, 1968), p. 44; Alvaro Delgado, *La Colonia* (Bogotá: Editorial Colombia Neuva, 1974), pp. 8–16.

Wars of dislocation and extermination were waged, on the other hand, against the less organized and less economically developed groups. These groups were less attractive targets for conquest because they were more difficult to defeat militarily and to control politically. In Nueva Granada, wars of extermination were waged against the Pijaos, while other groups were displaced and sought refuge in inaccessible and/or undesirable areas such as the Amazon Basin, Eastern Plains, Catatumbo region, Guajira Peninsula, Pacific rain forests, and Sierra Nevada de Santa Marta. Sporadic battles and raids did occur throughout the Spanish colony and into the first years of independence; despite these forays, the displaced groups, as well as the groups already located in these areas, managed to remain on the margin of colonial society. They were a nuisance to the Spanish, but they presented no real threat to the crown's ability to control the areas the Spanish wished to be controlled.[3]

[3] Wars of extermination and dislocation were particularly important in the period 1575–1675. See Germán Colmenares, *Historia Económica y Social de Colombia* (Cali: Universidad del Valle, 1974), chap. 1, esp. the map of Indian wars, p. 17. Colmenares enumerates campaigns against the Pijaos, Carares, Sutagaos, Moanamas, Cirambiras, Sindagues, and Paeces.

Other groups subjected to such wars include the Taironas. Gerardo Reichel-Dolmatoff writes: "It took the Spanish the better part of a century to subdue the Tairona, who, after periods of uneasy peace, rebelled again and again against the foreign invader. The last great rebellion occurred in 1599 and was suppressed in 1600, after 3 months of fierce battles in which resistance was broken and the tribe ceased to exist as a unit. Spanish troops burned and sacked the villages, devastating the fields, taking prisoners all chieftains and their relatives, except those who had been able to escape into the mountain vastness." Reichel-Dolmatoff continues: "Early in 1600, when the last battle had been fought, the Governor Juan Guival Velón condemned the captive chieftains to death or exile. The chief Cuchacique, ringleader of the last rebellion was ordered . . . to be dragged by the tails of two wild colts and torn into quarters and these put on the trails and the head put in a cage." Other chieftains met similar fates. See Gerardo Reichel-Dolmatoff, *Colombia* (London: Thames and Hudson, 1963), pp. 144, 156.

The communities of the Noamamaés, Chancos, and Citaraes in Chocó were also terrorized. Germán Colmenares writes: "A little before 1680, there were numerous gold mines in existence around Negua in the Citará region exploited by residents of Antioquia utilizing Negro slaves. However, in 1684, there was an Indian rebellion in the region that led to a war of extermination. The new frontier was opened definitively by this method, but the war left behind almost insuperable supply and labor problems." See Colmenares, *Historia Económica*, p. 195.

In the Llanos Orientales (Eastern Plains), the Indian communities were dislocated by initial armed incursions, by the formation of Catholic missions in the seventeenth and eighteenth centuries, and by punitive expeditions that sought to maintain the area open to Spanish commerce and transport.

See the historical section of Bernard Ascand, "The Urgent Situation of the Cuiva Indians of Colombia" (Copenhagen: I.W.G.I.A., 1972), pp. 7 ff.

The Indian groups in the Province of Cartago (the Quimbayas in particular) were also practically exterminated. See Juan Friede, *Los Quimbayas Bajo la Dominación Española* (Bogotá: Banco de la República, 1963); Hermes Tovar Pinzón, "Estado Actual

In summary, violence was decisive in the imposition of the Spanish as the dominant social group in what is today Colombia.

FORMATION AND MAINTENANCE OF COLONIAL SOCIETY

In the New World, the Spanish faced an economic, not military, problem. The superiority of Spanish military and transportation technologies gave the conquerors great material and psychological advantages in their armed confrontations with the indigenous groups. Spain's basic problem was not how to control America but how to exploit it. The initial pillage of Indian gold quickly gave way to the need to produce wealth in the new domains. Minerals and land were abundant, and there was no problem in employing the rudimentary tools of sixteenth-century technology. The only basic economic element in critically short supply was *labor.*

The Indians were initially enslaved. However, this labor force rapidly diminished due to a first-magnitude demographic disaster. The Indian population was greatly reduced by the wars with the Spanish; unlimited exploitation of forced labor; contraction of European diseases; and by a decline in the birthrate and an increase in the mortality associated with the disintegration of the Indian communities, which resulted in a concomitant decrease in the Indians' ability to produce their subsistence.[4]

The labor shortage led to social conflicts between the Spanish in America and the Indians, and between the Spanish in America and the Spanish state. The crown, interested in the long-term productivity of the colonies, sought to stem the demographic debacle. Among the measures taken were the abolition of direct Indian slavery, the establishment of protective *resguardos de indios* ("Indian reservations"), and the regulation of the feudal-type work obligations placed upon the Indian groups. The crown sought to exploit Indian labor, not eliminate it.[5] On the other hand, the Spanish

---

de los Estudios de Demografía Historica en Colombia," in *Anuario Colombiano de Historia Social y de la Cultura,* no. 5 (Bogotá: 1970), pp. 105–111; Delgado, *La Colonia,* pp. 48–67.

[4] Jaime Jaramillo Uribe, "La Población Indigena de Colombia en el Momento de la Conquista y sus Transformaciones Posteriores," in *Ensayos sobre Historia Social Colombiana,* ed. Jaramillo Uribe (Bogotá: Universidad Nacional, 1968), pp. 91–150. See also Darío Fajardo Montaña, "La Población Indígena en el Momento de la Conquista," in *Ayer y Hoy de los Indígenas Colombianos,* ed. Departamento Administrativo Nacional de Estadística (DANE) (Bogatá: 1971), p. 4; Woodrow W. Borah, "America as Model: The Demographic Impact of European Expansion upon the Non-European World" (Berkeley: University of California, Center for Latin American Studies, n.d.); Juan Friede, *Los Quimbayas,* p. 253. The author acknowledges the assistance of Darío Fajardo on anthropological matters.

[5] For descriptions of the feudal-type work obligations (the *encomienda* and the *mita*) and the *resguardos de Indios,* consult the sources cited in this note; for the *encomienda* and the disputes that surrounded this institution, see: Darío Fajardo Mon-

in America, interested in the short-run accumulation of fortunes, sought to maximize the exploitation of Indian labor and minimize the reservations, which gave the Indians the means to subsist independently of the Spanish.

These contradictions led to violence between the Spanish in America and the Indians, and to rebellions by the Spanish in America against the authority of the crown. One such revolt was led by Alvaro de Oyón in Popayán (Nueva Granada) in 1553.[6] The Spanish state responded to the rebellions with a mixture of violent repression and compromises. These conflicts were, in sum, between both the dominant group (the Spanish) and the dominated group (the Indians), and internal within the dominant groups (the Spanish in America versus the Spanish crown). The latter represents one of the few examples of intraclass conflict in the colonial period. The results of these sometimes violent conflicts structured the socioeconomic and political relationships between the various groups involved. The Spanish in America and their descendants, the Spanish Americans, were to be clearly subservient to the Spanish on the Iberian Peninsula. Thus, the physiognomy of the institutions of colonial society was defined and the colonial state was consolidated.

Another violent conflict was produced by the labor shortage. To solve this labor problem, the Spanish introduced African slaves into the colony. The conflicts of the Spanish miners, landowners, and merchants with the slaves led to the most persistent violence of the colonial period. Slavery was the most difficult institution to maintain in colonial society, and this interclass conflict led to the most widespread repression.

---

taña, *El Regimen de la Encomienda en la Provincia de Vélez* (Bogotá: Universidad de Los Andes, 1969); Colmenares, *Historia Económica y Social de Colombia, 1537–1719;* Guillermo Hernández Rodríguez, *De los Chibchas a la Colonia y a la Republica* (Bogotá: Universidad Nacional, 1971), pp. 19–26. For the *mita* see: Milciades Chaves, *Apropiación de la Tierra y Reforma Agraria* (Bogotá: Instituto Colombiano de la Reforma Agraria [INCORA], 1965), pp. 96–99 of the version of Editorial "Una Chispa . . ."; Hernández Rodríguez, op. cit., pp. 26–30. For the *resguardos de Indios* consult: Margarita González, *El Resguardo en el Neuvo Reino de Granada* (Bogotá: Universidad Nacional, 1970); Luis Nieto Arteta, *Economía y Cultura en la Historia de Colombia* (Bogotá: Librería Siglo XX, 1941), p. 169; Tirado Mejía, op. cit., pp. 31–33; Delgado, *La Colonia*, pp. 48–61.

[6] These rebellions occurred throughout Spanish America. In 1544, the Spanish crown attempted to enforce a prohibition on the use of Indian labor for the "personal services" of the *encomenderos* (the Spanish who administered the Indian work obligations). The measure was vigorously opposed by the *conquistadores* and the clergy. In Peru, the conflict developed into a rebellion led by Gonzalo Pizarro. The viceroy was slain and for a short time Pizarro controlled Peru. A similar movement was led at the same time in Mexico by two sons of Cortés. Smaller isolated revolts over similar issues took place in Paraguay between 1535 and 1560 and in Nicaragua led by the Contreras brothers in 1542; another was headed by Aguirre in the Upper Amazon Basin in 1580. See John A. Crow, *The Epic of Latin America* (Garden City, N.Y.: Doubleday, 1952), chap. 30; Liévano Aguirre, *Los Grandes Conflictos*, vol 1, chaps.2–4.

By the end of the sixteenth century, slaves constituted the most important merchandise sent to the colonies.[7] In Nueva Granada, slaves were used in the mines, on the river boats, in the ports, and on the plantations of the low-lying valleys and coastal areas. From the very beginning, the institution proved highly conflictive. Violently brought from Africa, the slaves used violence to attempt to regain their freedom. Approximately 30% of the slaves that arrived in Panama in the sixteenth century managed to escape, and Sir Francis Drake's attack on Panama City was aided by these *cimarrones* (the Spaniards' term for "escaped slaves").[8] Escaped slaves set fire to the port of Santa Marta in 1529, and in 1598 there was a large-scale *cimarrón* rebellion in Zaragoza in the Antioquia region, which was brought under control by royal troops one year later.[9]

The most important violent conflict stemming from this contradiction occurred in Cartagena. In 1600, Dionisio Bioho, an African slave also known as Rey Benkos, organized a group of fugitive *cimarrones* that successfully resisted the attempts of their ex-owners to recapture them. This group evolved into a social movement, and large numbers of Blacks raided ranches and destroyed commerce throughout the Caribbean coastal region, but especially in Cartagena, Tolú, Mompós, and Tenerife. A permanent, fortified settlement, known as Palenque de San Basilio, was also established by these *cimarrones*.

The local governor sent two expeditions against Benkos, both of which were defeated. A new governor considered the money spent on these expeditions exorbitant, and he commissioned a peace expedition to come to terms with the inhabitants of the *palenque* of San Basilio. An agreement was reached in 1613 by which the escaped slaves and the Spanish were to leave each other in peace. However, a new slave revolt spread along the coast in 1619. Rey Benkos was found to be involved, and he was captured and hung.[10]

[7] Slave ships constituted 47.9% of all bottoms arriving in Spanish-American ports in the late sixteenth century. Cartagena in Nueva Granada was the most important slaving center in Spanish America. See Rolando Mellafe, *La Esclavitud en Hispanoamérica* (Buenos Aires: Editorial Universitario de Buenos Aires EUDEBA, 1964), p. 60

[8] Aquiles Escalante, *El Negro en Colombia* (Bogotá: Universidad Nacional, 1964), p. 112 citing I. A. Wright, *Spanish Documents concerning English Voyages to the Caribbean (1569–1580)* (London: 1932), chap. 19; Tirado Mejía, *Introducción a la Historia Económica*, (Bogotá: Universidad Nacional, 1971), p. 45.

[9] James J. Parsons, *Antioqueño Colonization in Western Colombia* (Berkeley and Los Angeles: University of California Press, 1949), p. 51.

[10] The account of Benkos and Palenque de San Basilio is from Jaime Jaramillo Uribe, "Esclavos y Señores en la Sociedad Colombiana del Siglo XVIII," in *Ensayos sobre Historia Social*, ed. Jaramillo Uribe, pp. 60–63; and Escalante, *El Negro*, pp. 114–116. The Palenque de San Basilio continued, however, and, in the eighteenth century, the Spanish once again reached an agreement with the *cimarrones* for the purpose of obtaining their labor for the construction of a road near their area. The accord stipulated that the *palenqueros* would elect their own "captain" and govern

The formation of *palenques* (which came to be the Spanish term for "settlements of escaped slaves"), often after collective slave rebellions, continued throughout the colony.[11] In the late eighteenth century, the phenomenon became increasingly important, as Jaime Jaramillo Uribe asserts:

> Rebellions, cimarronism, and slave *palenques* constituted a serious problem for colonial society in the second half of the eighteenth century. It is true that resistance to slavery and the conflicts with the Black population were frequent from the beginning of the sixteenth century, but in the eighteenth century they acquired many times the characteristics of a civil war. Above all, in the years between 1750 and 1790, the degree of conflict was such that one has the impression that there could have existed an agreement between the different nuclei of slaves to conduct a general rebellion. In effect, in this period there were *palenques* on the Atlantic Coast and in Panama, Chocó, Antioquia, the Valley of the Cauca, Cundinamarca, and the Eastern Plains. The phenomenon took place, in sum, in the entirety of the territory of the viceroyalty. The *palenques* created a permanent state of alarm among the proprietors and the colonial authorities.[12]

The evidence suggests considerable organization and coordination between the slaves of different areas. The aborted slave rebellion in Cali in 1782 and the important 1785 revolt in Cartago demonstrate these points. In the former case, court testimony revealed a large-scale, interregional conspiracy. In Cartago the slaves escaped and formed *palenques* in the upper reaches of the Upia River and above the tree line of the snow-covered Ruíz Volcano. This carefully planned movement had contacts with

---

themselves, and that no non-Black, other than the parish priest would be allowed to live in the community.

[11] In 1696 the Blacks of Caragena revolted once again, and the *cimarrones* of the present-day department of Atlántico attacked Piojó, and around 1703 an entire series of *palenques* were formed in the Santa Marta area, including one in Santa Cruz de Masinga and another in the Sierra Nevada.

In 1706, the slaves of Antioquia rebelled in Marinilla, Rionegro, and Girardota. In Cauca, a highly stable *palenque* was established at the western end of the Patía Valley. The *cimarrones* raided neighboring areas from their stronghold. The failure of several armed expeditions against the slaves led the Spanish to reach a "San Basilio-type" agreement in 1732. Peace and liberty were promised the *cimarrones*, on the condition that they no longer raided or admitted any new escaped slaves. The latter condition was never kept and, in 1745, the *palenque* was reduced by an armed expedition reenforced by a Catholic priest who convinced the Blacks to surrender.

Some areas, such as Tocaima in Cundinamarca, then a sugar cane center, were affected by slave uprisings in a chronic fashion. Tocaima was the scene of revolts in 1731, 1758, and again in 1784; Antioquia in 1774 and 1777; and the perennially affected Cartagena hinterland in 1748 and 1799.

See Escalante, *El Negro*, pp. 115–117; Parsons, *Antioqueño Colonization*, p. 51; Jaramillo Uribe, "Esclavos y Señores," pp. 65–67.

[12] Jaramillo Uribe, "Esclavos y Señores," pp. 59–60.

Cauca, Chocó, and Valle. The Spanish investigation found that the Cartago slaves had an organization that had been electing officials for over 20 years.[13]

Slave revolts and cimarronism became a serious problem for the economy because slave labor was the most important source of wealth for the Spanish and Spanish Americans in the eighteenth century. The most authoritative student of this subject states the matter in the following terms:

> The New Granadan economy of the eighteenth century was based on six activities: mining, agriculture, cattle-raising, artisan production, commerce, and domestic work. Of these, the most important in terms of their volume and place relative to private wealth were based on the work of the slave population. Gold and silver mines, cattle ranches, and plantations that produced molasses and sugar moved on the basis of slave labor.
>
> Given the rudimentary technological development of the New Granadan economy of that era, production was based on human labor to the highest degree. Of its three constituent elements—land and raw materials, techniques [instruments of production], and labor—the latter was the most critical and the most expensive, because it was the scarcest. Inasmuch as at that time the free labor market was not fully developed and had only just begun to predominate in the Colombian East once the regimes of the *encomienda* ["precapitalist relations of production"] and the *mita* were abolished, wealth was measured by the number of slaves. Land, buildings, and instruments of production represented insignificant sums in the accounting of private wealth.[14]

The very situation just described stagnated the institution of slavery and increased the interest of the Peninsular Spanish and the Spanish Americans in "free labor," a transition that led to other social conflicts, which will be described in the subsequent section on the *Comunero* Rebellion.

In sum, the formation and maintenance of Spanish colonial society were accompanied by violence. The most difficult institution to maintain proved to be slavery, which required the continual application of violence by the state. Once established, the other colonial institutions required far less repression to maintain. Most of colonial society was structured by paternalistic economic relationships, ideological domination, and religious beliefs. Thus, apart from the conflicts with the slaves and the running battles with the undominated Indian groups, there was no socially significant violence in colonial Nueva Granada until the *Comunero* Rebellion of the late eighteenth century.

[13] *Ibid.*, pp. 58–70.

[14] *Ibid.*, pp. 20–21. James Parsons concurs with this assessment: "The wealth of a *vecino* was determined by the number and quality of his Blacks. Antioquian mine owners complained that the best part of their profits were consumed by the purchase of slaves." See Parsons, *Antioqueño Colonization*, pp. 50–52.

THE *COMUNERO* REBELLION

The social conflicts involved in the social avalanche that violently shook Nueva Granada to its foundations in 1782 are clear but varied and complex. The *Comunero* Rebellion occurred in the context of the accentuation of an entire series of social contradictions, and it was conditioned by a reduction in the authority and power of the Spanish colonial state.

The contradictions that were the basis of the rebellion involved most of the groups in colonial Nueva Granada. The conflict itself was conditioned by governmental reforms which accentuated the contradictions. The violent expression of the conflicts to the point that a full scale rebellion occurred was conditioned by a deflation in the power of the Spanish colonial state.

To understand the contradictions, it is essential to review briefly the social structure of Nueva Granada in the second half of the eighteenth century. The structure of domination had become greatly differentiated since the initial conquest of the Indians by the Spanish.

Ethnically, Nueva Granada underwent a relatively fast process of racial mixture. The relatively low density of the original Indian population and the rapid decline of the same made the process of *mestizaje* ("Indian-White racial mixing") very complete. By 1750, the *Mestizos* and other mixed types such as Mulattoes and *Zambos* ("Negro–Indian"), were the most numerous components of Nueva Granadan society.[15]

The process of racial mixture was accompanied by an increasingly rigid division of ethnic groups within the structure of domination. Occupations were divided into the noble pursuits fit for persons who could prove their *limpieza de sangre* ("cleanness of blood") and ignoble, or "infamous," pursuits for those with impure (i.e., non-European) blood. Education was limited to "clean-blooded" subjects of legitimate birth, and marriages could be blocked or annulled for ethnic reasons. The social evaluation of the mixed types was obviously negative in this society, and many libel and slander suits were brought over "insults" related to ethnic origins. Exceptions to all of the ethnic rules were granted, but always after "long involved legal procedures and always as a special, exceptional grace granted by the authorities."[16]

Social differentiation was thus based on a mixed class–caste system, with ethnic considerations forming the latter criterion. The class and caste relations were closely related, although poor Whites were also found among those who lived from "ignoble pursuits."

[15] Jaime Jaramillo Uribe, "Mestizaje y Diferenciación Social en el Nuevo Reino de Granada en la Segunda Mitad del Siglo XVIII," in *Ensayos sobre Historia Social Colombiana*, ed. Jaramillo Uribe, pp. 163–203.

[16] *Ibid.*, p. 189.

The Indians generally lived on their reservations, although they were collectively subject to the precapitalist work relations of the *encomienda* and the *mita* ("obligatory form of labor"). Some had also become independent workers on *haciendas* ("a colonial agricultural productive farm"). The bulk of the hacienda labor, however, was undertaken by the *Mestizos*. The social productive relations of the haciendas were varied. Some laborers worked as sharecroppers and some as renters, others exchanged labor on the owner's land for the right to work an individual plot, others were wage laborers (with much of the wages being paid in kind), and still others combined these types of labor relations.

The activities of the Negro slaves have been described (see p. 25 ff.). The *cimarrones* added the category of free Blacks to the system of social differentiation. The *Mestizos*, Mulattoes, and poor Whites also worked as small farmers and artisans. These artisans and small farmers (with the principal cash crop being the tobacco sold to the state monopoly) were particularly prevalent in the Eastern Highlands (contemporary Santander and Boyacá), where they constituted the predominant form of economic activity.

There also existed a social difference between the Peninsular Spanish and all those subjects born in America. This distinction included the *criollos* (the prosperous Spanish-American landowners, merchants, and high clergy). They were discriminated against socially and were largely excluded from government positions, even though they were the most important economic stratum.

The Spanish officials were discouraged from private economic activity, and they were rotated from post to post to avoid overidentification with a particular region. Private Spanish immigrants did not tend to be prosperous initially.

Colonial society at the end of the eighteenth century was thus differentiated ethnically between Peninsular Spanish, Spanish Americans, Indians, Blacks, *Mestizos*, Mulattoes, and *Zambos*. The Peninsular Spanish and the Spanish Americans were divided into classes on the basis of their economic activity, which was also the case with the rest of the pure and mixed ethnic types in this class–caste system of stratification.

Various latent conflicts divided the components of colonial society. These conflicts were accentuated in the late eighteenth century by a series of reformist and emergency initiatives adopted by the Spanish state. Most of these measures are related to the policy change that resulted from the passing of the Spanish crown from the Hapsburgs to the Bourbons.

The Bourbon reformists sought to revitalize the colonial economies and increase capital transfers to Spain.[17] The new dynasty began to recognize the importance of the colonies as the source of raw materials for manufac-

[17] William Paul McGreevey, *An Economic History of Colombia* (Cambridge: Cambridge University Press, 1971), chap. 2.

turing and as a market for manufactured products.[18] The measures sought to stimulate commerce,[19] restrict the Indian reservations, control more rigorously the crown's monopolies, and increase taxes. The Spanish, however, continued the prohibition against engaging in manufacturing activities in the colonies; they wanted the colonies as taxpayers and customers, not as competitors.

Restricting the Indians' use of their reservations had been a long-standing objective of the Spanish-American landowners. The crown adopted the measure in an attempt to stimulate agriculture. The Indians were permitted to grow their own food on only a small part of their land; the rest of the land was either idle or rented to outsiders.[20] Under these circumstances it was very difficult to entice the Indians to work on the haciendas. Indeed, the Indians who had remained on the haciendas "voluntarily" after the termination of the agricultural *mita* in the 1740s received relatively high renumerations, as did their *Mestizo* counterparts.[21]

The high cost of slaves and the relative scarcity of "free" labor led the *criollos* and the crown to seek more Indian laborers by reducing the number engaged in subsistence agriculture. The restriction of the reservations served the dual purpose of "freeing" Indian land for purchase by *criollo* landowners and "freeing" Indian labor.[22] The concrete mechanism consisted of combining several reservations into one. Indalecio Liévano Aguirre writes:

> The lumping together of the population of several reservations on the land of only one produced the consequences that such lands did not manage, given the primitive methods of cultivation of the era, to supply the means of sub-

[18] Chaves, *Apropiación de la Tierra,* pp. 106–111.

[19] This objective was achieved by eliminating restrictions on the ports in Spain and in America that could be used for commerce as well as restrictions on the coasting trade and commerce between the colonies. Not all of these innovations were voluntary. Freer trade policies stemming from the Treaty of Utrecht were concessions to Great Britain.

See Chaves, *Apropiación de la Tierra,* pp. 106–111; Manfred Kossok, *El Virreynato del Río de la Plata* (Buenos Aires: Editorial Futuro, 1959), pp. 36–42; Liévano Aguirre, *Los Grandes Conflictos,* vol. 3, pp. 77–88; Tirado Mejía, *Introducción a la Historia Económica,* pp. 73–78.

[20] Luis Ospina Vásquez, *Industria y Protección en Colombia: 1810–1930* (Medellín: E.S.F., 1955), p. 7; McGreevey, *Economic History,* p. 4.

[21] The payment in kind received by the Indians (meat and corn) in addition to their wages made for a consumption of primary foodstuffs at a level far superior to the intake in contemporary Colombia for the same class of rural workers. Ospina Vásquez provides documentary evidence that the haciendas of the Sabana de Bogotá had as their *minimum* wage 14 pesos per year *plus* 1104 kg of corn and 300 kg of meat per year. Today, the farm laborer can hardly afford to eat meat at all. Ospina Vásquez, *Industria y Protección,* p. 15.

[22] McGreevey, *Economic History,* pp. 54–57; Liévano Aguirre, *Los Grandes Conflictos,* vol. 2, pp. 205–212.

> sistence necessary for this forced crowding of the population. This obliged the Indians to search for supplemental incomes, to rent their labors to the haciendas, with the conditions being decided according to the convenience of the large landowners. The abundant mass of Indian labor obliged to search for work in the haciendas in order to survive caused a reduction in salaries and permitted the *haciendas* of Cauca, the Sabana, Tunja, and principal areas of the contemporary Department of Santander to have an excess labor supply[23]

These circumstances led to heightened interclass conflicts between the Indians and both the *criollos* and the Peninsular Spanish. In 1780, these conflicts exploded in predominantly Indian Peru into the formidable Tupac Amaru Rebellion, in which an estimated 80,000 persons were killed.[24] In predominately *Mestizo* Nueva Granada, it was to form the basis of Indian participation in the 1782 *Comunero* Rebellion of *Mestizos* and poor Whites.

The increased control of the state monopolies and the augmented taxes accentuated contradictions between the crown and almost all the segments of colonial society. In the eastern region, the situation became tense when Spanish officials restricted the areas in which tobacco could be grown and then uprooted crops and confiscated produce outside of the designated areas.[25] This led to an explosive situation with the yeoman tobacco growers, who were supported by the artisans because their production was also to be affected by the new taxes. In Socorro and neighboring areas, the tobacco growers and artisans began to ignore the Spanish officials and attack the state tobacco trading shops.

Revolts over taxes or other immediate grievances were not without precedent in the colonies.[26] The Socorro movement, however, had been pre-

[23] Liévano Aguirre, *Los Grandes Conflictos*, vol. 2, p. 209.

[24] The violent conflict in the Peruvian Highlands was led by an educated Indian Chief, José Gabriel Condorcanqui, also known as Tupac Amaru. Seeking the restoration of the Incan Empire, he attracted large numbers of followers. However, the poorly equipped Indian armies were defeated by the Spanish forces and Tupac Amaru was captured and quartered. The Indian movement continued despite the initial defeats and the loss of the supreme leader. The Indians seized towns and beheaded the Spanish. They even managed to besiege La Paz for 109 days before a relief column from Argentina saved the Spanish there. Eighty thousand deaths is the most common figure given for the mortality of this first-magnitude rebellion.

See Daniel Valcárcel, *La Rebelión de Tupac Amaru* (México City: Fondo de Cultura Económica, 1965); Liévano Aguirre, *Los Grandes Conflictos*, vol. 3, pp. 39–42; Crow, *Epic of Latin America*, pp. 404–408; Torres Giraldo, *Los Inconformes* (Bogotá: Editorial Marger Izquierdo, 1973), vol. 1, pp. 59–60.

[25] Immediately before the *Comunero* Rebellion, the local officials had torn up 1500 tobacco plants in one field in Guadalupe and 600 in another. They had also confiscated 1200 bundles (*tangos*) of tobacco. See Nieto Arteta, *Economía, y Cultura*, pp. 49–50.

[26] Tunja and Quito were the scene of tax revolts in 1592. In 1765 over 400 persons were killed in a riot over the sales tax (*alcabala*) in Quito that was backed by such a powerful movement that the Spanish granted amnesty for the leaders and participants. In 1730, the Quito *criollos* formed a tax protest movement that managed to

ceded by two years of persistent social ferment over the new taxes in Nueva Granada and had reached serious proportions.[27] Furthermore, the movement took place in the context of the full-scale war against the Indians in the Peruvian Highlands and the war that Spain was waging against England. These factors tended to weaken the usually impressive power of the Spanish colonial state. Psychologically and ideologically, the Spanish were also disquieted by news of the war of independence being waged by 13 of the English colonies in North America.

Concretely, the colonial government in Nueva Granada had less repressive capability than usual inasmuch as Viceroy Flórez (who thought the new taxes were ill-advised) had taken the bulk of the troops to Cartagena to prepare for expected English attacks along the Caribbean Coast. The highest ranking Spanish official in Santa Fe de Bogotá was thus *Visitador* ("Visiting Official") Gutiérrez Piñeres, who was charged with applying the Bourbon fiscal reforms to Nueva Granada.[28]

Spain's declining fortunes in European power politics were weakening the Spanish state in America. The new taxes, which had heightened the existing social conflicts in Nueva Granada, were primarily destined to finance the war efforts (e.g., the "Barlovento" taxes which helped spark the Socorro Rebellion), and a large part of the state's armed apparatus in

---

win them the right to elect some local officials; in the Nueva Granadan town of Vélez a 1740 protest went beyond taxes and questioned the authority of local officials.

Other instances of violence include a church-led riot in México City in 1624 as part of a church–state conflict between local officials; a riot in the same city 50 years later over rationing during a grain shortage in which the city's poor partially destroyed the central district of the capital of Neuva España; rebellions by Venezuelan *criollos* in 1733 and again in 1751 against the trade monopoly that the Caracas Company enjoyed in that area; and the early eighteenth century rebellions in Paraguay, which threatened the king's authority as well as the local control of the Jesuits and in which the doctrine of popular authority was defended. In the latter case, the *criollos* and *Mestizos* that supported the revolt were defeated by Indian armies commanded by the Jesuits. The rebellion of the Paraguayan subjects was an important indicator of the crumbling of the Spanish authority system in the colonies.

See Crow, *Epic of Latin America*, pp. 319–328, 400–402; Torres Giraldo, *Los Inconformes*, vol. 1, pp. 59–60.

[27] The tax protest movement had begun in early 1780 and continued through 1781 with riots in Simacota, Mogotes, Barichara, Charalá, Onzaga, Tunja, and La Robada (today Galán). In early 1781, a Spanish official in Pasto was slain in a 2-day riot. The official had arrived to extend to that area the state liquor monopoly and to proclaim new taxes as part of the Bourbon fiscal policy. See Liévano Aguirre, *Los Grandes Conflictos*, vol. 3, pp. 28–29.

[28] The factual account of the *Comunero* Rebellion is based on information to be found in Francisco Posada, *El Movimiento Revolucionario de los Comuneros* (México: Siglo XXI, 1971); Liévano Aguirre, *Los Grandes Conflictos*, vol. 3, chaps. 16, 17; Torres Giraldo, *Los Inconformes*, vol. 1, chap. 2; Nieto Arteta, *Economía y Cultura*, pp. 49–50; Roberto María Tisnes, *Movimiento Pre-Independientes Grancolombianos* (Bogotá: Academia Colombiana de la Historia, 1962), pp. 61–82.

America had to be deployed to defend the colonies against enemy attacks. Thus, social contradictions were matured into open conflicts at the same time that the repressive capacity to deal with them diminished. Add to this the inflexible and repressive policies of Visitador Gutiérrez Piñeres, and one has the structural basis and conditioning factors of the initial successes of the *Comunero* Rebellion.

The rebels began to elect their own officials, who were known as *El Común* ("The Commons"). The elections spread from town to town as the movement gained power throughout the entire eastern region of the colony. Troops sent to crush the rebels were easily defeated, and the *Comuneros* began a march on the capital. This army of artisans, small farmers, and Indians was composed of between 16,000 and 24,000 men when it arrived at Zipaquira, 30 km from the capital. Visitador Gutiérrez Piñeres had decided to abandon Santa Fe de Bogotá, taking another brigade of royal troops with him and thus further weakening the capital's garrison. Under these circumstances, the capital was virtually defenseless.

The *criollo* oligarchy was allied with the remaining Spanish in the hopeless situation in Bogotá. The Spanish-American landowners, merchants, and high clergy initially supported the 1780–1781 tax protests, but the evolution of the *Comunero* movement led them to unanimously back the Spanish.[29] The *Comunero* march on Santa Fe was accompanied by land invasions, the proclamation of indigenous monarchs, and slave rebellions.[30] Another *Comunero* army, led by José Antonio Galán, which had been sent after Gutiérrez Piñeres, spread the most radical aspects of the revolt to the Magdalena River Valley. Galán defeated numerous Spanish garrisons and freed the slaves in all regions under his army's control. Galán's army marched under the banner of "The Oppressed against the Oppressors." What began as a local tax revolt had become a widespread movement that combined the interests of the "impure" peoples of "infamous" occupations against those with *limpieza de sangre* and wealth.[31]

29 Liévano Aguirre, *Los Grandes Conflictos*, vol. 3, p. 55.

30 The Indians of the Sabana of Bogotá proclaimed a descendant of Chibcha royalty, Ambrosio Pisco, as "Señor of Chia" and "Prince of Bogotá." Indians in Tocaima, the Eastern Plains, and Silo (contemporary Norte de Santander) proclaimed their allegiance to the Incan rather than the Spanish king. Thus, the Tupac Amaru revolt also had its repercussions in the *Comunero* revolt in Nueva Granada.

31 The José Antonio Galán column defeated the Spanish in Facatativá, Villeta, Guaduas, Mariquita, and Ambalena, freeing the slaves in all of those areas. The widespread nature of the *Comunero* Rebellion might be appreciated from the following areas, excluding the Eastern Highland, in which there occurred *Mestizo*, poor White, Indian, and slave uprisings: Tocaima, El Espinal, Purificación, Aipe, Ibagué, Honda, Chaparral, Caguán, Pasto, Barbacoas, Valledupar, Neiva, Labranzagrande, Ten, Tamara, Manaure, Cravo, Cúcuta, and Mérida (today Venezuela). See Torres Giraldo, *Los Inconformes*, vol. 1, p. 90; Liévano Aguirre, *Los Grandes Conflictos*, vol. 1, pp. 43–44; Tisnes, *Movimiento Pre-Independiente*, pp. 61–82. The latter work describes the ramifications of the movement in Antioquia, Pasto, Pamplona, and Venezuela.

Given the impossibility of a military defense of the capital, Archbishop Caballero y Góngora of Santa Fe de Bogotá, a *criollo*, was commissioned to negotiate with the *Comuneros* in Zipaquirá and to agree to anything that would gain time for the arrival of royal troops from the coast. The agreement reached, known as the *Capitulaciones de Zipaquirá*, presents the student of social conflict and violence with a rare opportunity to understand the contradictions involved in a complex, heterogeneous social movement by studying the measures that led to the disbanding of a successful rebel army.

The *Capitulaciones* stipulated (among other things) that the new taxes, which had initiated the movement, would be rescinded, that the state would abolish the tobacco monopoly and set a perpetual fixed price on the bottle of *aguardiente* ("sugar cane liquor") in its alcohol monopoly, that the sales tax was not to be applied to foodstuffs, and that the sales tax would be limited to 2% for other transactions.

In favor of the some 6000 Indians in the *Comunero* army, the *Capitulaciones* proclaimed that the salt mine taken from the Indians of Zipaquirá (the most important in South America) would be returned, that the "demolition" of the reservations would be stopped, that the reservation land that had already been sold would be returned to the Indians, and that the Indians would receive complete and unrestricted property rights to their land.

With regard to the contradiction posed by Spanish discrimination, the *Capitulaciones* dictated the following:

> In employment, within the first, second, and third categories, Americans will be given priority and preference over Europeans, inasmuch as the latter daily manifest their antipathy toward the people from here . . . . They believe, ignorantly, that they are the masters and that the Americans, all without exception, are their servants, and so that this blind state of affairs is not perpetuated, only in the case of necessity, according to their ability, and with sympathy toward the Americans, should they be equally employed. Inasmuch as all of us are the subjects of the same King and Master, we ought to live brotherly.[32]

Despite internal dissensions among the *Comuneros* over the agreement, it was accepted and subsequently sanctified at a solemn *Te Deum* mass at which Archbishop Caballero y Góngora officiated. The *Comunero* army was disbanded. The Spanish troops soon returned from their coastal preparations against the British and proceeded to violently repress the *Comuneros* and to execute the militant leaders. The *Capitulaciones* were completely ignored because the Spanish noted that they had been signed under the duress of the threat to the capital.

[32] The *Capitulaciones* are enumerated in Liévana Aguirre, *Los Grandes Conflictos*, vol. 3, pp. 58–61. The citation is from p. 60.

Spanish authority had been reasserted and the *criollo* oligarchy had been relieved of an immediate threat to its interests as a result of the outcome of this *interclass* conflict. However, the social contradictions that had led to the movement had simply been repressed; none had been resolved. The tobacco monopoly, Spanish fiscal policy, the question of the Indian reservations, slavery, the exclusion of Americans from high governmental posts, and other forms of ethnic discrimination remained intact. Many of them were to resurface in the independence movement three decades later.

The *Comunero* Rebellion also demonstrated the weakened nature of the Spanish state, due primarily to its deteriorating international position. The need to maintain troops on the Caribbean Coast to defend the state against the British allowed the movement to reach the proportions it did. However, the structure of social domination was shown to be highly resilient due to the continued strength of ideological and religious domination. With regard to ideology, the rebels shouted "Death to the bad officials" and "Long live the king." With regard to religion, the archbishop's word was capable of achieving what the state apparatus could not—the defeat of the rebel army.

The loyalty of the *criollos* and the lack of leadership among the *Comuneros* proved to be factors in favor of the Spanish. This was not to be the case in 1810, when the cream of the well-educated *criollo* oligarchy became the vanguard of the subversive forces.

THE INDEPENDENCE MOVEMENT

The crucial contradiction that led to the armed conflict for independence was between the Peninsular Spanish and the Spanish-American oligarchy (the *criollos*). This contradiction was based on divergent economic interests and discrimination against the Spanish Americans. Apart from the church and the state, the *criollos* were the most powerful economic group in the colony. However, given the situation of imperialist domination, they were deprived of political power. The achievement of political power by the *criollo* oligarchy was the major outcome of the conflict.

The conflict was conditioned by Spain's continued demise as a world power, particularly in relation to England. Independence itself was obtained when the Spanish state collapsed as a result of the French invasion of the Iberian Peninsula. Intense violence occurred when the Spanish state attempted to reimpose its authority and reverse the forms of self-government that the *criollo* oligarchy had devised.

The aforementioned elements of this violent interclass conflict will now be examined, beginning with the basic economic contradictions.

The commercial and industrial restrictions placed on the colonies by the Spanish were increasingly considered by the *criollo* oligarchy to fetter their development. There were no contradictory interests between the *cri-*

ollo merchants and the Bourbon reformists with regard to the expansion of metropolis–colony commerce. However, there were the following contradictions: Spain's inability to monopolistically supply the colonies; Spain's subsequent role as a price-increasing yet unproductive middleman in selling to the colonies manufactured goods from more industrially advanced nations [33]; and the dramatic increase of contraband under these circumstances. The latter was facilitated by Spain's loss of control of the sea.

Combining unparalleled industrial production, low prices, and naval hegemony, Spain's archenemy, England, became a prime commercial power *within* the American colonies. Spain's commitments to European power politics further weakened her position. At the end of the eighteenth century, free trade flourished as Spain opened her American ports to all neutral ships in an attempt to break the British blockade of Spanish bottoms. These ships, however, tended to bring the enemy's goods.[34]

Contraband exports were another contradiction inasmuch as gold was the overwhelming export and the Spanish had a 20% tax *(el quinto real)* on its production.[35] In sum, the mercantilistic policy of maintaining a monopoly on both exports and imports in America had become untenable. Thus, the attempt to reimpose the monopoly after the end of the British blockade produced conflict. This was expressed in the merchants' guild of Cartagena, where free-trading *criollo* businessmen engaged in bitter controversies and disputes with their Spanish colleagues. The crown's countermeasures were simply repressive. Coastal traffic was forbidden, and the Atrato River was closed to commerce, with violators being executed. Nonetheless, illegal commerce exceeded its legal equivalent.[36]

Neither tariffs nor armed repression were to prove to be as important in conditioning the patterns of international commerce as a "stream of cost reducing innovations in the English textile industry." [37]

[33] Tirado Mejía, *Introducción a la Historia Económica,* p. 74 citing French documents analyzed by Henry See.

[34] Liévano Aguirre, *Los Grandes Conflictos,* vol. 3, pp. 77–86.

[35] Ospina Vásquez, *Industria y Protección,* p. 38.

[36] Liévano Aguirre, *Los Grandes Conflictos,* vol. 3, pp. 77–86. Criollo losses as a result of the repressive restrictions were large. Consider, for example, the following letter from José Acevedo y Gómez to Antonio Villavicencio, both leaders of the conspiracy that led to *criollo* power in Santa Fe de Bogotá on July 20, 1810:

> One hundred twenty thousand pesos, the fruit of twenty years of work, fatigue, and danger, the government made me lose at the beginning of the war with England because there was no means by which the Viceroy would admit even the coasting trade, and in three years the quinine was lost and the cotton which the peninsular monopoly obliged me to sell in Cádiz fell into the hands of a powerful enemy on the sea. I willingly will lose my fortune and the twenty thousand pesos which remain of it in Cádiz and Barcelona, if only my fatherland cuts the chain that ties it to that peninsula, perennial spring of tyrants. (Cited in Arturo Abella, *El Florero de Llorente* [Bogotá: Editorial Antares, 1960], p. 104)

[37] McGreevey, *Economic History,* p. 48.

In a very real sense, the *criollo* merchants were at war with the metropolis well before the declaration of formal hostilities. This is an important point because production for export and import–export commerce were the main sources of wealth in Nueva Granada. Ospina Vásquez writes of colonial society: "The comfortable, important, and influential class was not that of the landlords but rather that of the functionaries and merchants." [38]

Criollo wealth stemmed primarily from commerce because, as Spanish Americans, they were forbidden to hold political posts, domestic artisan production was subject to stringent regulations, and genuine industry was prohibited. Domestic production of foodstuffs could hardly lead to much capital accumulation in an overwhelmingly rural country; in addition, large landholdings tended to accumulate to the church, either by purchase or by bequest, from which they never returned to civilian control due to the system of mortmain. Agricultural products with a domestic commercial potential—tobacco and liquor—were closely controlled crown monopolies. In sum, mining and, to a lesser extent, agricultural production for export were the main cash producers, and the wealth they generated was appropriated and accumulated by the import–export merchants, who were the most important faction of the *criollo* class.

The exclusion of the economically powerful *criollos* from political power ended with the Napoleonic invasion of the Iberian Peninsula and the French capture of Fernando VII. The formation in Spain of *cabildos* ("assemblies of notable citizens") to confront the crisis presented by the collapse of the national state set an example soon followed in the colonies, much to the chagrin of the Peninsular Spanish officials in America. Thus, effective local political authority was soon in the hands of the *criollo* oligarchy in different areas of Spanish America. It was highly localized, however, because there was little coordination among the *cabildos*, and, in some cases, there were even conflicts between them.

Very illustrative of the criollo attitudes of the period is the *Memorial de Agravios* ("Memorial of Grievances") that Camilo Torres sent to the Junta de Sevilla in Spain; the memorial protested the frank discrimination against *criollos* perpetuated by the Supreme Junta, which allowed each Spanish province two deputies while allowing the extensive kingdoms in America but one each: "The Naturals [the Indians] conquered and subject today to Spanish domination are very few or none, compared to the sons of Europeans that today populate these rich lands." [39]

Torres's lack of sociological precision is balanced by a crystalline political clarity. The "cause" is that of the *criollo* oligarchy and not that of the other classes of Spanish-American society. This was also apparent in the

[38] Ospina Vásquez, *Industria y Protección*, p. 12.
[39] Liévano Aguirre, *Los Grandes Conflictos*, vol. 3, pp. 109–110.

July 20th conspiracy in which the *criollo* oligarchy of Santa Fe maneuvered carefully to stage a limited popular uprising that would serve their interests.[40]

Ideologically, the American Revolution and the French Revolution were important because they provided historical examples of success, justifications for rebellions and antimonarchical sentiment, and models for alternative systems of social and political organization. These historical antecedents had, of course, limited applicability to Spanish America, but they were highly significant to the *criollo* oligarchy, the effective leaders of the movement. The doctrines of equality (for all gentlemen of means and the "proper" ethnic background), unhampered economic relations, and limited government combined very well indeed with the principal *criollo* grievances.

More important, the British supplied free trade doctrine, the goods for free trade itself, support for Spanish-American conspirators (such as Miranda), the British Legion of troops and supplies, and harassment of Spain's long naval supply lines. The subversion of the Spanish capacity to govern her American colonies was greatly facilitated by Britain's determination to open Spain's imperial domain in America to British influence.[41] Once independence was achieved, the diplomatic recognition of the British crown and the commercial relations established served to inhibit further efforts at reconquest on the part of Spain and her Holy Alliance partners.

The *criollos,* of course, were not completely unified behind the republicans. The slave-owning landowners of the South initially tended to remain loyal to the Spanish. This was also the case with the predominantly Indian peasant population of the South, which feared further encroachments on the reservations in the event of a *criollo* victory. Thus, the pro-Spanish guerrillas of Agustín Agualongo and José María Obando proved highly effective in this region. The eventual adhesion to the republican cause by many key southern leaders proved to be an important element in the final Spanish-American victory.[42]

The other groups were generally divided. The slaves fought for whoever

[40] *Ibid.,* chap. 20.

[41] Mario Arrubla, "Esquema Histórico de las Formas de Dependencia," in *Estudios sobre el Subdesarrollo Colombiano,* ed. Arrubla (Bogotá: El Tigre de Papel, 1971), pp. 73–81.

[42] The landlords generally conceived independence in the narrowest of terms. It was conceptualized as consisting of the departure of the Spanish and their replacement in government by the creole oligarchy, in addition to the end of the Spanish commercial monopoly. The rest of the socioeconomic structure of society was to remain intact. Indalecio Liévano Aguirre provides evidence to the effect that some landlords, especially in the South, sought independence to avoid the possibility of being ruled by a French emperor given the antislavery and anticlerical positions of Napoleonic France. See *Los Grandes Conflictos,* vol. 3, pp. 111–112.

promised them freedom, something the royalists often did before the republicans.[43] Both armies consisted of the *Mestizo* peasant masses, who were forcefully conscripted into one or the other army in most cases.[44] With regard to the artisans, there is disagreement among historians as to their participation. There is no disagreement, however, as to the oligarchical basis of the movement or of the importance of *criollo* commercial interests in its genesis.[45]

Despite internal differences within the independence movement (discussed in a subsequent section on the formation of the republican state), the *criollos* enjoyed initial victories, largely due to the confused situation in Spain. However, the crumbling of the Napoleonic Empire and the restoration of Fernando VII to the throne temporarily resolved the political situation on the peninsula. The Spanish began the reconquest of the col-

[43] José María Samper, *Ensayo sobre las Revoluciones Políticas* (Bogotá: Universidad Nacional de Colombia, 1969), p. 159.

[44] In terms of the forceful conscription of *Mestizo* peasants, David Bushnell quotes Francisco de Paula Santander as follows: "On the other hand, our soldiers are not like those of Europe. The latter have education, they know the cause they defend and they know the laws to which they are subjected. With the former, the contrary is the case. Their ignorance is well known, *they are regularly not informed as to whom they are fighting for* [emphasis added] and for all one teaches them the legal dispositions, very few come to understand them." David Bushnell, *El Régimen de Santander en la Gran Colombia* (Bogotá: Coediciones Tercer Mundo–Universidad Nacional, 1966), pp. 283–284. The quotation is from *Mensaje de Santander al Ministro de lo Interior, para que sea Transmitido al Congreso de Cúcuta,* 7 de Diciembre de 1821.

[45] The questions of the role of the artisans in the independence movement is very controversial. Nieto Arteta maintains that a small group of artisans sought to destroy the colonial economic regime by aiding the independence movement. See his *Economía y Cultura,* p. 45. Indalecio Liévano Aguirre describes the role of the artisans and other groups as follows:

> At the same time that the merchants and landowners judged advantageous this rupture [with Spain], understanding that it would permit the establishment of free trade, the liquidation of the Indian *resguardos,* and the adoption of political institutions, like the Anglo-Saxon ones that are admirably designed to guarantee a monopoly of power for an economic oligarchy, in the popular strata of the population there were notorious doubts, because the Indians had more than sufficient motives to look with fear at the capture of the State by the big *criollo* proprietors and the artisans did not hide their alarm before the perspective of a future hegemony by the merchants that imported foreign manufactures. Only thus may one understand the profound reasons which led to the popular strata of the American societies combatting, in the first phases of the War of Independence, so decidedly in defense of the Crown. (*Los Grandes Conflictos,* vol. 3, pp. 97–98.)

Tirado Mejía, like all of the authors, considers the commercial interests within the oligarchy to have been the vanguard of the independence movement. He argues that the landlords increasingly supported the movement with the passage of time, that the slaves fought on both sides, and that the rest of the population was dragged into the struggle alternatively by the *criollos* and the Spanish. See *Introducción a la Historia Económica,* pp. 100–103.

onies, and the New Granadans were defeated by Spanish General Morillo. Nueva Granada experienced the most intense violence during the reconquest. The *criollo* movement was reduced to isolated areas, such as the Eastern Plains (Llanos Orientales), while important independence leaders were executed in the cities. During the two years of intense fighting the situation proved so favorable to the Spanish that the viceroy of Nueva Granada returned to Santa Fe in March 1817.

Two years later the Spanish were completely defeated in Nueva Granada. The rapid demise of the Spanish was due to the crown's inability to reimpose the Spanish colonial state. Despite their battlefield victories and mass executions, the old structure of domination no longer functioned for the Spanish. Basic elements of Spanish-American society were in opposition, and the Spanish state had lost in good measure its ability to elicit voluntary compliance to its fiats. The guerrillas, backed by the British Legion, were a constant threat to Spanish hegemony. The viceroy attempted to govern by repression but, given the vastness of Nueva Granada and the extensiveness of the opposition, it was impossible to repress to the extent necessary.

The guerrillas of the Llanos Orientales evolved into genuine armies; in 1819 they climbed the Andes and defeated the Spanish in several decisive battles. At this juncture many ex-royalists joined the republican cause, and the Spanish were expelled from Nueva Granada. Spanish authority was reduced to the southern region of the continent, and the Nueva Granadans proceeded to help guarantee their independence by sending troops to participate in the Peruvian campaign that terminated the last vestiges of the Spanish Empire on the South American continent.

In sum, the *criollos* formed the social basis of the independence movement. As a class, they were dominated by the Spanish state and the Peninsular bureaucracy, whose mercantilistic economic interests sacrificed *criollo* commercial and industrial opportunities. The *criollos* were also subject to social and political discrimination despite their position as the most important economic class in the colonies. The commercial faction of the *criollos* was the most important group economically, and they also formed the vanguard of the Spanish-American independence movement. This faction was well educated, cosmopolitan, and sensitive to the new economic and ideological currents of the Western world.

The *criollos* achieved initial independence as a result of the collapse of the Spanish state on the peninsula. The subsequent war to consolidate their autonomy was conditioned by Spain's weakened international position, especially vis-à-vis England, but the final victory was a product of Spanish-American arms and a decline in the support afforded the Spanish by previously royalist elements of the population.

The outcomes of the violent conflict included the *criollos'* assumption of political power, the establishment of open trade, England's replacement of Spain as the main commercial and financial partner, and little else. The war constituted a revolution for the *criollos*, who became the dominant class, but the basic socioeconomic relations between this class and the other classes in Nueva Granada society remained basically unchanged. Thus, many of the same socioeconomic conflicts of colonial society continued unresolved into the republic, accompanied by new contradictions that evolved from the social and political structures of the new republican society of Gran Colombia.

The First Century of the Republic

There were 13 important periods of violent political conflict in Colombia during the first century of independence: 1810–1814, 1827–1832, 1839–1841, 1851, 1854, 1858–1863, 1876–1877, 1885, 1895, 1899–1902, 1905, 1922, and 1929. These conflicts were generally associated with intraclass contradictions with a few highly significant exceptions. The contradictory interests underlying the conflicts varied, and each period thus requires independent analysis. However, in very broad terms, it is possible to identify recurrent conflicts (*a*) over the formation and transformation of the republican state, (*b*) over the retention of the colonial socioeconomic structure or its replacement by social forms of a more capitalistic nature, and (*c*) over which groups within the dominant class would control the national state. These types of conflicts were usually highly interrelated.

The conflicts frequently escalated because, in the first century of independence, Colombia was characterized by a weak state within a strong structure of domination. It is hypothesized that religious and ideological beliefs, paternalistic economic relationships, the emergence of intense loyalties to *criollo*-led political parties, and directly applied local power and violence were far more important than the national state, including its armed apparatus, in structuring social relationships. Local and regional power structures also appear to have been more important than their national equivalent.

The weakness of the state may be largely attributed to divisions within the dominant class. The frequent intraclass conflict reached the point where the national state may be said to have practically collapsed on several occasions. Despite these radical reductions of state authority and power, the *criollo* class did not experience, with rare but significant exceptions, serious challenges to its dominant position. This would seem to indicate that interclass contradictions generally had not matured to the point of conflict. It is also a fact that underscores the strength of the total structure of social domination despite the weakness of the state.

FORMATION OF THE REPUBLICAN STATE

The *criollos* did not inherit the Spanish colonial state, despite continuity in the legal superstructure. On the contrary, new power and authority relationships had to be created, and this proved to be a very conflictive process. Conflicts among different groups of *criollos,* and occasionally between the *criollos* and other groups, led to political violence during the first years of independent government.

Indeed, the first civil wars occurred even before independence was consolidated. In 1810, the *criollos* formed *cabildos abiertos* ("town halls") that initiated self-government in light of the Napoleonic invasion of the Iberian Peninsula and the French capture of the Spanish king, Fernando VII.

Various areas of Nueva Granada simply began to govern themselves. However, there was no centralized authority, and the phenomenon of the *criollos* of a province assuming the tasks of government soon spread beyond the regional level to local communities. Thus, not only did Cartagena separate from Spain, but Mompós separated from Cartagena. Likewise, Sogamoso decided to determine its destiny independently of the provincial capital of Tunja; Cali separated from Popayán, Quidbó from Novita, Girón from Pamplona, Vélez from Socorro, and Ibagüé as well as Tocaima from Mariquita. Inasmuch as there was no generally accepted means of resolving this unprecedented situation, some of these disputes led to violent encounters.[46]

Most of the provinces were quickly reconsolidated; the crucial conflict was between Bogotá and its immediate hinterland, which formed the *Estado de Cundinamarca* ("State of Cundinamarca") and the more important provinces organized into the *Provincias Unidas de la Nueva Granada* ("United Provinces of New Granada"). The former was organized along centralist lines and the latter federally. This division within the *criollo* class over what would replace the Spanish state led to the situation of two different state organizations within Nueva Granada. Conflicts between the two led to a civil war that included a full-scale battle for Bogotá in January 1813. These conflicts persisted through 1814 and, combined with confrontations between *criollo* military leaders over strategy, they greatly facilitated the Spanish reconquest of Nueva Granada.[47]

[46] Liévano Aguirre, *Los Grandes Conflictos,* vol. 3, chap. 23; Torres Giraldo, *Los Inconformes,* vol. 1, p. 151.

[47] Bogotá was the commercial and bureaucratic center of the country, and the groups associated with these activities sought to maintain a centralized regime with the preeminence of Bogotá. The most important economic group in the provinces was the large landowners, who sought local control of government. See Fernando Guillén Martínez, "El Poder: Los Modelos Estructurales del Poder Político en Colombia," mimeographed (Bogotá: Universidad Nacional, Centro de Investigaciones del Desarrollo [CID], 1973), pp. 121–132; Torres Giraldo, *Los Inconformes,* vol. 1, pp. 156–180;

The civil strife of the period 1810–1814, known in Colombia as the *Patria Boba* ("Foolish Fatherland"), ended with the reconquest of Nueva Granada by Spanish General Pablo Morillo. With the subsequent elimination of Spanish control, the *criollos* attempted once again to organize themselves politically.

The Congress of Angostura (1819) and the Congress of Cúcuta (1821) proclaimed the formation of the *República de la Grán Colombia,* a unitary republic consisting of contemporary Colombia, Venezuela, Ecuador, and Panama. The Cúcuta Congress elected Simón Bolívar as president and Francisco de Paula Santander as vice-president. The latter was the effective chief executive through 1826 due to Bolivar's participation in the Peruvian campaign against the Spanish. The continuation of the wars and the fear of a Spanish return to Nueva Granada provided a relatively high degree of cohesion to a population that had suffered the severe repression of the Spanish reconquest after the *Patria Boba.*

The basic question of the political structure of society had not been decided, however, by the proclamation of the congresses. The effective definition of the new nation state itself was not even consolidated. From the very beginning of the new republic, important groups in Caracas favored the independence of Venezuela.[48] The political structure of the new state, who was to govern, and what socioeconomic policies were to be adopted were all unsolved questions. They began to assume the forms of political conflicts once the essentially negative coalition against the Spanish commenced to break down as a result of decisive Spanish-American military victories and the diplomatic recognition of England.

The differentiation of the opposing groups within *criollo* society occurred gradually, and the positions adopted were subject to frequent changes.

For example, the debate over centralism versus federalism was undogmatic and closely linked to political tactics.[49] Political sentiment had not yet ossified into the formal Conservative–Liberal fissure of later years.

The two basic groups that emerged were the *Santanderistas* and *Bolivianos,* to use the political terminology of that era. The Santanderistas, or

---

Arturo Abella, *El Florero de Llorente* (Medellín: Editorial Bedout, 1968), pp. 139–176; Arturo Abella, *Don Dinero en la Independencia* (Bogotá: Ediciones Lerner, 1966). The Federalists were defeated in their attempt to conquer Bogotá in 1813. Complex political negotiations followed, and another Federalist march on Bogotá proved successful in 1814.

Conflicts over strategy are illustrated by Bolívar's siege of Cartagena from La Popa after the Spanish-American commandant of that plaza refused to grant him reenforcements and authority.

[48] Bushnell, *El Régimen de Santander,* pp. 319–324; Joaquín Posada Gutiérrez, *Memorias Histórico-Políticas* (Medellín: Editorial Bedout, 1971), vol. 1, p. 25.

[49] See Posada Gutiérrez, *Memorias Histórico-Políticas,* vol. 1, chap. 4.

Constitucionalistas as they were also called, tended to be identified with laissez-faire, free trade, and the 1821 constitution.[50] Thus, they tended to favor departures from the colonial socioeconomic and political status quo, although their reformists achievements when in power were very modest indeed when compared to their ideological stance. Merchants and financiers (practically the same thing in this period) and lawyers were very prominent in these groups.

The Bolivianos (frequently referred to by contemporary historians as *Bolivarianos*) sought to maintain a centralized regime under the "authority of the liberator." Continuity in socioeconomic policy and strong authoritative government were the basic political goals of this group, which included many traditional landowners, clergymen, and that part of the military that sought to maximize the interests of officers as a social stratum.[51] The Boliviano ranks were reenforced late in the war by the adhesion to the republican cause of many previously royalist elements. A certain amount of opportunism might be suspected in these shifts, but in some influential cases, such as that of Bishop Rafael de la Vega of Mérida, the successful Spanish liberal movement of 1820 made conservative sentiment in America genuinely proindependence.

The economic and political contradictions between the two groups emerged into systematic, open conflict in the year 1826. The existing contradictions were accentuated by Bolívar's assumption of exceptional powers after his return from Peru and by his subsequent granting of autonomy to Venezuela when he named General Páez *Jefe Supremo* ("Supreme Chief") of that region.[52] The concessions to the Venezuelan military and the institution of an authoritarian regime in Venezuela marked the final break between the Santanderistas and the Bolivianos.

The utilization of violence in the conflicts began gradually, with other forms of struggle retaining a greater importance for two years. A military revolt in Guayaquil in January 1927 in "defense of the Colombian constitution" was crushed, but it prompted Bolívar to resign in search of a vote of confidence in Congress.[53] Some Santanderistas attempted to accept it, but they could muster only a few votes. Politically strengthened, Bolívar complained that he lacked sufficient power to deal with the critical situation that the nation faced and he proposed a "Great Convention" in Ocaña in 1828 to restructure the constitution. The Santanderistas in the 1827

[50] Bushnell, *El Régimen de Santander*, pp. 154–158, contains a discussion of the laissez-faire ideology of this group.

[51] Posada Gutiérrez, *Memorias Histórico-Políticas*, vol. 1, pp. 128–129; Nieto Arteta, *Economía y Cultura*, pp. 81–82, cites the description of the Bolivianos of José María Samper.

[52] Posada Gutiérrez, *Memorias Histórico-Políticas*, vol. 1, pp. 68–77; Bushnell, *El Régimen de Santander*, pp. 378–383.

[53] Bushnell, *El Régimen de Santander*, pp. 383–386.

Congress vigorously opposed the measure, but it passed with the support of Nueva Granadan Bolivianos, joined by the representatives of Venezuela and Ecuador.

At Ocaña, the local elections of representatives to the "Great Convention" had favored the Santanderistas, who, in alliance with certain independent groups, were able to muster consistent majorities. The Bolivianos reacted to this correlation of forces by abandoning the convention en bloc, thus depriving the deliberations of a quorum.[54]

Some Santanderista delegates nonetheless remained in Ocaña to plan their future political strategies, which were now of a conspiratorial nature.[55] Another armed outbreak had already occurred, this time in Cartagena between Santanderista Admiral Padilla and Boliviano General Montilla, with the former suffering arrest.

A political impasse had been reached, and the next step in the breakup of the political coherence of the *criollo* class occurred on June 13, 1928, when the *Intendente* ("Governor") of Cundinamarca, General Pedro Alcántara Herrán, convened an assembly of prominent citizens that proclaimed Bolívar the holder of absolute power. Dictatorial pronouncements followed Bolívar's supporters throughout the country. The institutional impasse was broken by a decree known as the *Arreglo Provisorio* ("Provisional Arrangement"), by which Bolívar assumed absolute powers on August 27, 1928. Thus, the Santanderistas had their worst fears fulfilled and the Bolivianos their political aspirations realized.

A civil war situation had evolved in a political arena that did not go far beyond the "respectable" *criollo* class. The principal exceptions to this were the lower class military officers who enjoyed considerable political power. The economic and political contradictions between the previously described groups and the lack of mutually accepted mechanisms to resolve peaceably the resulting conflicts led to a situation with a high potential for violence. There simply was no agreement on the institutions that were to organize the state in the new republic.

The division in the *criollo* ruling class was so deep that, when the Santanderistas in Bogotá attempted a coup d'etat on September 25, 1828, one of the military objectives was the assassination of Bolívar.[56] Both the assassination attempt and the coup were unsuccessful. As a result, the most prominent Santanderistas were exiled, jailed, or executed. Santander was exiled, as were other important leaders such as Vicente Azuero and Francisco Soto.

Although the Santanderistas were crushed in Bogotá, this was not the

[54] José María Obando, *Apuntamientos para la Historia* (Medellín: Editorial Bedout, n.d.), chap. 8; Florentino González, *Memorias* (Medellín: Editorial Bedout, 1971), p. 129.

[55] José Hilario López, *Memorias* (Medellín: Editorial Bedout, 1969), pp. 215–219.

[56] González, *Memorias*, pp. 142–147.

case in the departments. In Popayán, José Hilario López and José María Obando arose in arms but soon retreated to Obando's strongholds in the Patía Valley and Pasto. To further complicate matters, Peru had invaded the southern departments (contemporary Ecuador) in a conquest attempt. Generals Sucre and Flóres fought Peruvian General (and President) Lamar in the South. Bolívar attempted to march to aid the southern Ecuadorian forces, but he could not arrive due to the strength of the rebels in Pasto. Bolívar came to terms with the rebels, offering them complete amnesty and acceding to their demand for the realization of the Constituent Congress planned for January 1830.[57] However, despite the lack of reenforcements from the North, Sucre defeated the Peruvian forces at Portete de Tarqui, and Lamar signed a peace treaty at Girón.

During this period Bolívar entertained the following ideas about the political situation and future, as transmitted by General Posada Gutiérrez:

> Since the Liberator heard the news that Marshall Lamar was breaking the Girón agreement, that he was not surrendering the Department of Guayaquil, and that he was preparing for war, he advised the Council of Ministers to privately and confidentially manifest to the ministers of England and the United States the few hopes he had that the Spanish-American states could consolidate a tolerable government; that the probabilities were that they would cut each other up, and themselves up, in civil wars and revolutions, if a powerful nation did not intervene in their differences and take them under its protection.[58]

The Council of Ministers undertook, on its own initiative, negotiations with a representative of the House of Orleans, M. Bresson, and with the English minister over the possibility of a constitutional monarchy in Gran Colombia. This project became public knowledge, and it proved to be politically explosive. The Council of Ministers was ridiculed and the Santanderistas began to gain force for the first time since their political–military demise. Bolívar was forced to disown his own Council of Ministers, and the Bolivianos even suffered political losses in their own ranks.[59] The "monarchy project" exacerbated the perennial separatist sentiment in Venezuela, and it led to an armed rebellion in Antioquia.[60]

The Santanderistas supported the Venezuelan movement inasmuch as it was a tremendous blow to Bolívar. Liberals attempted to influence the Constituent Congress by passing civic resolutions urging that no armed action be taken against Venezuela.

[57] López, *Memorias*, pp. 248–255.

[58] Posada Gutiérrez, *Memorias Histórico-Políticas*, vol. 1, p. 301.

[59] José Manuel Restrepo, *Historia de la Revolución de la República de Colombia* (Bogotá: 1942–1950); Posada Gutiérrez, *Memorias Histórico-Políticas*, vol. 1, pp. 326–327.

[60] Posada Gutiérrez, *Memorias Histórico-Políticas*. vol. 1, p. 385; López, *Memorias*, pp. 256–260.

Bolívar's situation continued to deteriorate. The Boyacá battallion sent to the border with the Venezuelan departments as a threat to the separatists passed over to Maracaibo and joined en masse the Venezuelan army, asking to be considered "an integral part of the Liberal banners."[61]

The Constituent Congress was convened on January 20, 1830, with a Boliviano majority. However, Bolívar was now the recipient of the negative political effects of the now chronic economic crisis and of Venezuelan and Ecuadorian regional dissatisfactions. The view that the Bolivarian dictatorship was the panacea for the nation's problems had dissipated in his diminished group of followers. The Boliviano delegates to the Congress advised against the presentation of the Liberator's name for president.

The Congress produced a republican constitution and elected as president the moderate Boliviano Joaquín Mosquera and as vice-president Domingo Caicedo. Relieved of power and exhausted, Bolívar left Bogotá for the Caribbean Coast. His departure was dramatized by the mutiny the same day of two Venezuelan military units that demanded back pay and then marched to Venezuela.

The separatist decision of Venezuela was followed by Ecuador, which left the Bogotá government only in charge of Nueva Granada. The moderate Boliviano government began a political alliance with the Santanderistas, a policy stimulated in part by an uprising of pro-Santander forces in Cúcuta. Not only were the Santanderista exiles allowed to return, but some of them even began to play major roles in the new administration.[62]

Bolívar's demise and the closing of ranks among the *criollos* affected the interests of the pro-Bolívar military stratum that had played such an important role in the formation and maintenance of the Boliviano political faction. The new *criollo* alliance left many high-ranking military officers, mostly Venezuelans, politically isolated. National finances were also in a disastrous state, which led to the reduction of military expenditures to the point that the military payroll itself became chronically precarious. Furthermore, the government suppressed the military *fueros* (the set of privileges that separated the military from civilian authority). Thus, the new government represented not only the antithesis of the ideology with which the military had backed Bolívar but also a concrete threat to the interests of the military as an important social stratum.

This combination of interests and ideology led to the rebellion of the Callao battalion, which sparked a coup d'etat. The Mosquera–Caicedo government attempted a military defense in August 1830, but it was defeated. Mosquera left the country and Caicedo retired from the capital while General Rafael Urdaneta (Bolívar's minister of war) assumed the presidency.

[61] Posada Gutiérrez, *Memorias Histórico-Políticas*, vol. 1, p. 380.
[62] González, *Memorias*, p. 173.

The military coup was rapidly seconded by praetorians throughout the country. However, a civil war ensued as resistance arose in the Casanare and in Popayán, where José María Obando and José Hilario López formed an opposition army. The military faced an increasingly potent coalition of opponents that included most of the moderate, primarily civilian Bolivianos and all of the Santanderistas.

The military, not insensitive to their increasingly isolated political position, ceased to struggle in May 1831. Urdaneta signed the *Capitulaciones de Apulo,* which permitted the military officers to leave the country for Venezuela. Obando subsequently assumed an interim presidency that expelled the remaining Venezuelan officers and purged the army of Bolivianos.[63]

The purged officers created a problem for the subsequent administration of Santander. In 1833, a group of these officers led by General Sardá attempted a coup d'etat known as the "23rd of July plot." A law passed in June 1833 had decreed the death penalty for conspirators, and 17 leaders were executed, whereas 2 others, Sardá and Mariano París, were killed while escaping.[64]

The net effect of the Urdaneta military government, its fall, and the Sardá plot was the elimination of the Boliviano military machine that had liberated South America from the Spanish. The battle against the military usurpation, with all of the class and power connotations that it involved, had unified the *criollo* landowners, clergymen, lawyers, and merchant–financiers.

The economic conflicts of an intraclass nature had become secondary to the common political interests of the ruling class as a class. Out of the chaos, the *criollo* civilians had firmly decided on republican institutions and the elimination of the military. The national territory had also finally been definitively delimited (save for the partition of Panama at the end of the century).

In terms of the dispute over who would govern, the Constitutional Convention of 1832 elected Santander as president and the moderate Boliviano Márquez as vice-president. Santanderistas and ex-moderate Bolivianos are indistinguishable in this period. The identifying terms themselves began to lose relevance. The political status quo was unquestioned by the *criollo* ruling class and the economic contradictions that had previously animated internal political struggles were ignored in a conservative reaction that sys-

[63] The purge was massive. It affected 17 generals, 49 colonels, 58 lieutenant colonels, and 158 officers of the line of lower graduations. Also taken off the military rolls were 13 militia colonels and 151 militia officers of lower rank. See Posada Gutiérrez, *Memorias Histórico-Políticas,* vol. 2, p. 392.

[64] Milton Puentes, *Historia del Partido Liberal Colombiano* (Bogotá: Editorial Prag, 1961), p. 103; Posada Gutiérrez, *Memorias Histórico-Políticas,* vol. 2, chap. 44; López, *Memorias,* p. 352.

tematically postponed economic controversies. Aníbal Galindo describes this period as follows:

> Upon the reconstruction of Nueva Granada as an independent state, the natural reaction was against the immense disorder of the central administration of Colombia, and against the anarchy that had captured the republic since 1826, and this led to profoundly conservative government in all spheres, but particularly with regard to national finances, upon which the existence of the state itself depended.[65]

By 1833, the economic, social, and political conflicts that had led to violence among the *criollo* ruling class had been eliminated or reduced to latent contradictions. These conflictive and frequently violent sociopolitical processes had been highly significant in determining the initial structure of the nineteenth-century republic.

THE WAR OF THE SUPREMES

The high degree of cohesion within the *criollo* ruling class permitted the advent of mutually accepted political norms. This made possible the use of elections as a means of presidential succession in 1837.[66] The Márquez administration elected in that year continued the comfortable administration of the status quo that had marked Santander's second government, although it was even more conservative. The opposition was mild and largely restricted to parliamentary tactics in this era in which politics resembled a gentlemen's club.

Thus, the civil war that began in June 1839 and lasted through 1841 caught the *criollo* ruling class by surprise. Indeed, Francisco de Paula Santander had introduced a bill in Congress that month to reinstate on the army's reserve rolls the Boliviano military officers who had been dismissed by Obando in 1832. When presenting the measure, Santander noted: "The actual state of Nueva Granada permits the adoption of the proposed measure, for the reason that one does not find any elements in the nation other than order, tranquility, and general happiness." [67]

The civil war that erupted that same month and lasted through 1841 is known as the *Guerra de los Supremos* ("War of the Supremes")[68] or as

[65] Cited in Nieto Arteta, *Economía y Cultura*, p. 110.

[66] The franchise was highly restricted by property and literacy requirements and mediated by an electoral college plus the provision that, if no candidate received a majority in the electoral college, the election reverted to the Congress. The 1837 election went to the Congress. See Puentes, *Historia del Partido Liberal*, pp. 105–106.

[67] Cited in Posada Gutiérrez, *Memorias Histórico-Políticas*, vol. 3, pp. 6–7.

[68] A reference to the many declarations of rebellion issued by "Supreme Commands," "Supreme Leaders," etc., of the different movements that participated in the war.

the War of the Convents. This series of armed conflicts presents one of the more complex cases of violence as a sociopolitical process in Colombian history.

It began with a seemingly innocuous law, passed in June 1839, which eliminated small convents in Pasto at the request of the bishop of Popayán. This measure led to an insurrection by the deeply religious *Pastusos* under the leadership of a popular, ascetic priest, Francisco Villota.[69]

Politically, the Pasto movement was led by close associates of General José María Obando, who subsequently joined the rebels in the South. Obando was subject at the time to persecution on the part of central governmental authorities, who had revived an old allegation that he was the intellectual author of the assassination of Marshall Sucre in 1830. Obando was a genuinely popular leader in the South and one of the few national political figures who could independently muster large armies of Indians, slaves, and *Mestizos.*

The size of the movement in the South presented a serious threat to the central government. It also incapacitated the government to deal with an entire series of subsequent rebel movements that arose throughout the country. In Vélez and Socorro there were several insurrections, with one being led by Governor González of Socorro. A column from this area seriously threatened the capital for a time. In Antioquia, Salvador Córdova captained the rebels to control of that department. The Atlantic Coast also became independent of the Bogotá government for a time as the result of a movement led by General Carmona.[70]

The different rebel movements were independent, there was little contact and no coordination between them, and they were defeated one by one by the central government. The most important movement, led by Obando in the South, was crushed when General Flóres, the president of Ecuador, led an army from the South while the Nueva Granadan army attacked from the North.

A nearly totally united *criollo* ruling class backed the government throughout the conflict. Obando was practically the only national political figure involved in the rebellion. The whole *criollo* ruling class felt that the war was greatly prejudicial to their interests. This sentiment is reflected in José María Samper's summary of the conflict:

[69] This contradiction had been long-standing. A law passed in the 1820s ordered the closing of all convents with less than eight members. Pasto was intentionally excluded from the application of that law so as to maintain order and aid in the pacification of that heavily royalist area. See Bushnell, *El Régimen de Santander*, pp. 245–247.

[70] For accounts of the "War of the Supremes" consult the following sources: José María Obando, *Apuntamientos para la Historia* (Medellín: Editorial Bedout, n.d.),pp. 275–460; Posada Gutiérrez, *Memorias Histórico-Políticas*, vol. 3, pp. 5–342; Chaves, *Apropiación de la Tierra*, pp. 164–168; Torres Giraldo, *Los Inconformes*, vol. 2, pp. 35–50.

> Never has this land seen such an unmotivated revolution, nor one as popular and general, delayed and disastrous, as that which sadly began in 1839 and finished in 1841 . . . . The elements of that cruel struggle were simply the fanaticism of a few monks and of superstitious and ignorant Indians; the personal persecution, hateful in every sense, declared against General Obando; and the resentment that Liberals felt for the loss of power and the change of policies of Dr. Márquez.[71]

This vastly oversimplified assessment reflects the *criollo* oligarchy's lack of explanation for a war that did not fulfill the concrete aims of any group within the *criollo* ruling class. It was thus seen as the epitome of irrationality.

The importance of the dominated groups of society in the war was notorious. Indians from Pasto and Tierradentro, slaves from Barbacoas and Cauca, and *Mestizo* small farmers from the Patía Valley, Socorro, Ocaña, and Antioquia were prominent in the origin and execution of the war.[72]

In the South, religious and reactionary (even royalist) support was to be found for the rebels. The bulk of the movement was based, however, on Indian anti-*criollo* backing, Black antislavery support,[73] and *Mestizo* anti-oligarchical sentiment. These forces were channeled by secondary, provincial political leaders who formed the organizational backbone of the various movements. Thus, regional interests and those of low-level politicians dovetailed with the aforementioned popular groups in a revolt against the closed political control of the *criollo* oligarchy. The federalist banner was the most important common denominator in the maze of "causes" for which the popular groups fought in this extremely complex conflict.

The popular elements in the war were highly inarticulate as to their objectives and uncoordinated in their actions. The lack of unified strategies and actions allowed the government to defeat the various movements separately. The popular aspects of the war were, however, an indicator of increased social ferment in a relatively stagnant political environment.

[71]Cited in Nieto Artera, *Economía y Cultura*, p. 111.

[72] Torres Giraldo, *Los Inconformes*, vol. 2, pp. 35–55; Posada Gutiérrez, *Memorias Histórico-Políticas*, vol. 3, pp. 23, 29–30, 33, 183.

[73] After the war, repressive measures were taken in regard to some of the social contradictions that had proved highly conflictive during the fighting. For example, a slave law was approved that was reminiscent of colonial legislation. It provided for drastic penalties for escaped slaves and their accomplices. The law was passed due to the participation of rebellious slaves in the War of the Supremes. The conservative political actor General Joaquín Posada Gutiérrez states that the law was passed due to "the excesses of those slaves that General Obando and Sarría excited to rebellion in the revolution of 1841." He continues: "Resisting a return to slavery, they burned the haciendas, they remained in rebellion in the country-side, they followed and threatened their owners, not wishing to tranquilly work under the protection that the law provides, but rather to live by pillage, with no brake and without law" [Posada Gutiérrez, *Memorias Histórico-Políticas*, vol. 3, pp. 357–358].

THE WARS OF THE MIDCENTURY REFORMS

Violent political processes occurred in 1851 and 1854, and between 1858 and 1863 as a result of conflicts over the basic socioeconomic structure of society. These conflicts were principally intraclass, with one highly significant exception in 1854. The de facto weakness of the state within a generally strong structure of domination that marked nineteenth-century Colombia also became legally institutionalized at the end of this period.

The dominant classes in Nueva Granadan society emerged from the War of the Supremes with less cohesion than in the 1830s. Contradictory interests developed into conflicts over long-postponed issues. The basic question in dispute was whether the colonial socioeconomic structure was to be modified. The reformists tended to be merchants, manufacturers, artisans, and those whose agricultural interests were linked to the market economy in general and the export sector in particular. Owners of traditional haciendas, with the church being the largest landowner and the leader of this group, tended to oppose the trend toward capitalistic modes of production and liberal institutions.

In the late 1840s, the ideological divisions that ran along the lines described in the preceding paragraph began to develop organizational coherence, and the Liberal and Conservative parties were effectively founded in this period.[74]

The 1841 presidential election demonstrated a sharp polarization within the dominant class of society (the only group to enjoy the franchise). The bulk of the votes were split between the victorious Conservative, General Pedro Alcántara Herrán, and the Radical Liberal, Vicente Azuero.[75] The Conservatives elected Tomás Cipriano de Mosquera president in 1845, but his initially conservative administration became increasingly reformist with the passage of time. Mosquera was succeeded in the presidency by the reformist José Hilario López due to a Liberal electoral victory in 1849.

The Liberal anticolonial reforms enacted in the late 1840s and early 1850s included the adoption of a free trade policy with the replacement of the protective tariff by one of a strictly fiscal nature, the abolition of the state tobacco monopoly (at the time that this product was beginning to boom as the nation's leading export product), and a fiscal reform that included decentralization and the widespread replacement of indirect by direct taxes.[76] Other measures reformed the agrarian structure: the aboli-

[74] Eduardo Santa, *Sociología Política de Colombia* (Bogotá: Editorial Iqueima, 1955), pp. 33–45; Francisco Leal Buitrago, "Social Classes, International Trade and Foreign Capital in Colombia: An Attempt at Historical Interpretation of the Formation of the State," Ph.D. dissertation, University of Wisconsin (Madison, 1974), pp. 78–90; Gerardo Molina, *Las Ideas Liberales en Colombia: 1849–1914* (Bogotá: Ediciones Tercer Mundo, 1970), pp. 13–16.

[75] Puentes, *Historia del Partido Liberal*, p. 115.

[76] Nieto Arteta, *Economía y Cultura*, chaps. 10, 13, 14; Ospina Vásquez, *Industria y Protección*, pp. 197–214; Tirado Mejía, *Introducción a la Historia Económica*, pp. 124–

tion of slavery; the dissolution of the Indian reservations by permitting their free alienation; the elimination of public use lands, called *ejidos*, which encircled cities and towns and provided pasture lands for the urban poor; and the restriction of precapitalist tributes on land and agricultural production, such as the *censos* ("perpetual leins on land") and the *diezmos* ("titles on land and produce").[77] Other reforms consisted of the separation of church and state, the expulsion of the Jesuits, the establishment of civil marriage and divorce, and the adoption of universal, secret suffrage.[78]

The net effects of these measures were the stimulation of international commerce,[79] a tobacco boom that was to last 25 years,[80] the ruin of domestic manufactures and a concomitant increase in Nueva Granada's dependency on foreign powers in general and Great Britain in particular,[81] a growth in purchasable land and the availability of inexpensive wage labor,[82] the entrance of new groups into politics, the near-absolute identification of the Catholic Church with the Conservative party, the maturation of many social contradictions into conflicts, and the violent expression of these conflicts.

The conflicts between the capitalist reformists and the traditional factions within the *criollo* class led to a search for political allies outside of that class. The Radical Liberals, influenced ideologically by the European revolutions of 1848, began to organize support among the urban working class, which meant independent artisans in mid-nineteenth-century Nueva Granada. The highly intellectual Radical Liberals (known as *Gólgotas* in the political parlance of the era) were instrumental in advancing the existent, nascent organizations of the artisans. The result was a national movement known as the *Sociedades Democráticas* ("Democratic Societies"). The

---

128; Eduardo Peña, *Origen y Desarrollo de la Burguesía Colombiana* (Barranquilla: Tipografía Dovel, 1971), pp. 27–52; McGreevey, *Economic History*, chap. 4.

77 Nieto Arteta, *Economía y Cultura*, chap. 11; McGreevey, *Economic History*, chap. 6; Tirado Mejía, *Introducción a la Historia Económica*, pp. 123–147; Chaves, *Apropiación de la Tierra*, pp. 170–193; Ospina Vásquez, *Industria y Protección*, pp. 196–197; Peña, *Origen y Desarrollo*, pp. 27–34.

78 Puentes, *Historia del Partido Liberal*, p. 158.

79 McGreevey, *Economic History*, p. 104.

80 Nieto Arteta, *Economía y Cultura*, chap. 17; Luis Fernando Sierra, *Tabaco en la Economía Colombiana del Siglo XIX* (Bogotá: Universidad Nacional de Colombia, 1971).

81 McGreevey, *Economic History*, p. 97; Nieto Artera, *Economía y Cultura*, chap. 13; Ospina Vásquez, *Industria y Protección*, chap. 14.

82 The elimination of the Indian reservations in the central area of the country made available choice Indian lands, which the *criollos* had sought since the colony. Combined with the abolition of slavery, it also increased the supply of cheap wage labor while deteriorating the bargaining position of renters and sharecroppers. See Ospina Vásquez, *Industria y Protección*, p. 196; Comité Interamericano de Desarrollo Agrícola (CIDA), *La Estructura Agraria: Formas de Tenencia* (Washington, D.C.: CIDA, 1966), p. 68.

Conservatives attempted to counter this movement with Jesuit-organized *Sociedades Populares* ("Popular Societies," also known as Catholic Societies). The latter were never a significant political force. The same cannot be said for the Sociedades Democráticas, which soon possessed some 200 chapters.[83]

The political environment became increasingly tense as the accelerated social reforms of the new government matured long-standing social contradictions. By early 1851, there were frequent violent conflicts between members of the Conservative party and groups from the Sociedades Democráticas. Slavery was abolished in May 1851, and that same month a civil war broke out with Conservative slave owners and Catholic priests in the vanguard of the rebellion. This proslavery, antiseparation of church and state movement was defeated by the government in the course of the year. Its demise served to consolidate the major reforms temporarily.[84]

Given their military defeat and allegations of coercion with regard to the 1849 presidential vote, won by the Liberals, the Conservatives abstained from the 1853 presidential elections. Nonetheless, there was an electoral contest inasmuch as the Liberals were divided into two factions. One, the Gólgotas, or Radicals, represented the interests of the commercial bourgeoisie of Bogotá and the coastal areas. The other, the *Draconianos*, or Progressives, consisted of old-line Santanderistas, Liberal landowners, and the professional military. The victorious Draconiano candidate General José María Obando enjoyed the support of the López movement and of the artisan's Sociedades Democráticas. This group had grown and had become increasingly important due to the official support proffered the artisan's organizations by the López government. The *Democráticos* had

[83] Gustavo Vargas Martínez, *Colombia 1854: Melo, Los Artesanos y el Socialismo* (Bogotá: Editorial Oveja Negra, 1972); Miguel Urrutia, *Historia del Sindicalismo en Colombia* (Bogotá: Ediciones Universidad de Los Andes, 1969), pp. 33–42; Orlando Fals Borda, *Subversión y Cambio Social* (Bogotá: Tercer Mundo, 1967), pp. 79–83; Torres Giraldo, *Los Inconformes*, vol. 2, pp. 34–137.

[84] The war was concentrated in the main slave areas: Barbacoas, Cauca, Antioquia, Chocó, Mariquita, and Neiva. It began in Pasto, led by Julio Arboleda (one of the largest slave owners) and Manuel Ibáñez, and it enjoyed the support of the Ecuadorian government. After a major military defeat at Buesaco, the Conservatives reverted to guerrilla tactics. The movement in Antioquia was led by Eusebio Borrero, and it adopted federalism as one of its banners. The war in Cundinamarca was centered around Guasca, the political stronghold of Pastor and Mariano Ospina.

The Conservatives alleged the "excesses of the Democratic Societies" as the immediate case of the war, whereas Liberal Salvador Camacho Roldán adduced three causes: "a) the party spirit exalted to dementia; b) the interests of the slave-owners; and c) and the exaltation of the Catholic clergy against the reforms, that is to say, the religious fanaticism of an ignorant people who were made to believe that religion was going to be destroyed." See Salvador Camacho Roldán, *Memorias* (Medellín: Editorial Bedout, n.d.), pp. 199–224, esp. 207–208; Posada Gutiérrez, *Memorias Histórico-Políticas*, vol. 3, pp. 385–387.

broken with their initial mentors, the Gólgotas, over the issue of free trade, which was rapidly ruining the artisan's economic position.[85]

The Obando government faced vigorous opposition from the Congress, in which a majority coalition was formed by the Gólgota faction of the Liberals and the Conservatives. This parliamentary alliance produced the 1853 constitution, which called for radical decentralization; it shelved an artisan-backed Draconiano bill to raise tariffs and substituted in its stead a further tariff reduction; and it passed a bill to drastically reduce the army.[86]

Political violence erupted between the Sociedades Democráticas and the Gólgotas in addition to the protracted series of killings and beatings in conflicts between artisans and Conservatives. The institutional stalemate within the state (Draconiano control of the executive and Gólgota–Conservative majorities in Congress) further conditioned the high potential for sociopolitical conflict. On April 17, 1854, the commander of the army, General José María Melo, staged a coup d'etat backed by the Sociedades Democráticas. The presidency was initially offered to the incumbent Obando. He refused to accept, and Melo took charge of the government.[87]

The viability of the military–artisan regime was clearly tenuous. Despite initial military successes against the Gólgotas in Zipaquirá and Tiquiza, the new government in Bogotá faced the armed opposition of a coalition of Conservatives and Gólgotas as well as anticoup Draconianos supported by foreign embassies (particularly the United States and Great Britain).[88] The Melo regime effectively controlled only Cundinamarca, while the constitutionalist coalition assembled armies in the remainder of the country. In November 1854, the government fell after a military defeat in Bogotá. Subsequently, the Sociedades Democráticas were crushed and 200 artisan leaders were imprisoned in Panama; Melo was exiled, and the national army was purged and reduced to an authorized strength of 400 officers

[85] Germán Colmenares, *Partidos Políticos y Clases Sociales* (Bogotá: Universidad de Los Andes, 1968), pp. 155–188; Nieto Arteta, *Economía y Cultura*, pp. 206–209; Vargas Martínez, *Colombia 1854*, pp. 33–68; Urrutia, *Historia del Sindicalismo*, pp. 33–70.

[86] Torres Giraldo, *Los Inconformes*, pp. 82–85; Oscar Rodríguez Salazar, "Las Constituciones del Siglo XIX y su Contenido de Clase," unpublished thesis for degree of Licenciado, Universidad de Los Andes (Bogotá, 1972), pp. 46–47; Indalecio Liévano Aguirre, *El Proceso de Mosquera ante el Senado*, (Bogotá: Editorial Revista Colombiana, 1968), pp. 37–38.

[87] Vargas Martínez, *Colombia 1854*, pp. 59–80; Urrutia, *Historia del Sindicalismo*, pp. 64–72; Francisco Leal Buitrago, "Política e Intervención Militar en Colombia," in *La Dependencia Externa y el Desarrollo Político de Colombia*, ed. Rodrigo Parra Sandoval (Bogotá: Universidad Nacional de Colombia, 1970), pp. 160–161.

[88] Vargas Martínez, *Colombia 1854*, pp. 113–126; Guillén Martínez, *El Poder*, p. 184.

and men.[89] The *criollo* class, despite its factional differences, united to defeat a challenge to its dominance of the state.[90]

The end result was the elimination of the artisans from the political scene, the practical abolition of the professional military, and the ascendancy of the Conservative faction of the *criollos.* An interim bipartisan government headed by Conservative Manuel María Mallarino finished Obando's term (with two Conservative and two Liberal ministers.) In 1857 elections were held in which the victorious candidate was orthodox Conservative Mariano Ospina Rodríguez. He defeated the Gólgota Liberal candidate, Manuel Murillo Toro, and the candidacy of Tomás Cipriano de Mosquera, backed by Draconiano Liberals (both *Obandistas* and *Melistas*) and a group of dissident Conservatives.[91]

The 1857 presidential election, conducted by the bipartisan Mallarino administration, was the first in Colombia to employ universal manhood suffrage, which was later revoked. The election was also probably the fairest in the course of the entire century. The results showed that the Conservatives held a clear majority in Nueva Granada. The Liberals recognized this fact, and they considered that the adoption of universal manhood suffrage had been a strategic mistake since the peasant masses were easily manipulated by the vehemently pro-Conservative clergy.[92]

[89] Vargas Martínez, *Colombia 1854*, pp. 97–110, 129–141; Torres Giraldo, *Los Inconformes*, vol. 2, pp. 85–90; Guillén Martínez, *El Poder*, p. 185; Anthony P. Maingot, "The Colombian Military: A Case of Inconsistent Status," in *The Role of the Military in Latin America*, ed. Lyle N. McAllister (Gainesville: University of Florida Press), pp. 277–279. The latter gives data showing that the military's budget was reduced from 548,924 pesos in 1853 to 184,941 pesos in 1857, a 75% reduction in 5 years.

[90] The leadership of the Constitutionalists was a coalition of *Gólgotas,* anti-Melo Draconianos, and Conservatives. Among them figure Tomás Herrera, Pedro Alcántara Herrán, Tomás Cipriano de Mosquera, Joaquín París, Julio Arboleda, and Joaquín Posada Gutiérrez.

[91] Puentes, *Historia del Partido Liberal*, p. 195.

[92] Manuel Murillo Toro explicitly recognized this reality, as did almost all of the Liberal politicians of the era. Murillo Toro considered universal suffrage to present a clear "danger" to the Liberal party given the huge Conservative majority in nineteenth century Colombia. See Puentes, *Historia del Partido Liberal*, p. 296. Perhaps the most explicit recognition of the Liberal's position and the nature of nineteenth century partisan politics may be seen in a speech delivered to the Assembly of Cundinamarca by Francisco Eustaquio Alvarez during the period of Liberal hegemony that followed the Conservative defeat in the 1858–1863 civil war:

> Having the Conservatives as they have, an immense numeric majority, and in addition great influence in the country, there has been no other method but fraud to impede them from recovering by elections the power that they lost by battles. The great error of the Liberal party consisted of organizing the country after its armed triumph in such a way that the Conservatives were conceded political rights, inasmuch as this led to the necessity of fraud and violence, to the discredit of the prevailing institutions and legality in order to make the Conservative's votes void.

The Conservative-controlled Congress in 1858 adopted a new constitution that formed the *Confederación Granadina,* a federal republic. This charter was strongly federalist in that the states obtained legislative attributes and the right to elect their own presidents.[93]

The net effect of the introduction of federalism was to transfer the political arena of the conflicts over the anticolonial reforms (and the civil wars associated with them) from the national to the regional level. Thus, there began a series of local civil wars in 1858, which evolved into a national civil war that lasted until 1863. The first local civil war began in the State of Santander, whose president was Radical Liberal Murillo Toro, who instituted a vigorous package of anticolonial reforms. The Conservatives arose in arms (aided indirectly by the Confederal government), but they were quickly defeated. A Conservative invasion of Santander followed from Boyacá, which was also overcome.[94]

In April 1859 the Conservative Congress modified the constitution. A new electoral law gave the Confederal president the power to replace state presidents and to intervene in questions of public order, and the Confederal legislature was given the faculty to judge state elections and review state laws. General Mosquera, the president of Cauca, resisted this measure. The Liberals were once again divided, this time over what strategy to adopt in the political struggle with the Conservatives. The Draconianos tended to advocate resistance and civil war while the Gólgotas sought compromises. Mosquera, in alliance with José María Obando, rebelled in the South, and in June 1860 the Confederal government invaded the State of Santander, which was at peace at the time, in an apparent attempt to guard its rear flank by gaining control of that Liberal department before confronting the rebellion in the South. This invasion had the effect of unifying the Liberals, and the civil war thus became national.[95]

After a year of fighting the Liberals entered Bogotá, having won a battle for the capital city. Mosquera assumed control of the government and immediately proceeded to dictate a package of anticolonial reforms, aimed primarily at the backbone of the Conservative party, the Catholic

---

And void they had to be, in that no one is so stupid to lose by means of pieces of paper what he has won with arms. We the Liberals have never pretended to govern Colombia by virtue of greater numbers; we govern by virtue of intelligence and force, both of which we have needed to vanquish the Conservatives. (Cited in Indalecio Liévano Aguirre, *Rafael Núñez* [Lima: Editora Latinoamericana, n.d.], pp. 126–127)

[93] Rodríguez Salazar, "Las Constituciones del Siglo XIX," pp. 43–47; Puentes, *Historia del Partido Liberal,* pp. 176–177, 196. For an overview of the constitutions of the nineteenth century, consult Manuel Antonio Pombo and José Joaquín Guerra, *Constituciones de Colombia* (Bogotá: Biblioteca Popular de Cultura Colombiana, 1951).

[94] Puentes, *Historia del Partido Liberal,* pp. 196–201.

[95] *Ibid.,* pp. 199–200.

Church. The most significant was the declaration of the desamortization of mortmain land. By virtue of this measure the state expropriated the lands of the religious communities, which by colonial custom were inalienable and held perpetually. This land had accumulated in the church's hands across the centuries and, according to estimates of the era, it constituted nearly a third of the real estate holdings in the country.[96] All agricultural land thus became commerciable. Along with the laws that abolished slavery, reduced the previously inalienable Indian reservation land, and eliminated colonial taxes, this measure constituted a frontal attack on the colonial socioeconomic structure and laid the foundation for capitalistic economic relations and the strengthening of the bourgeoisie.

The desamortization of mortmain land and the other reforms decreed[97] could not immediately be placed into effect universally inasmuch as the Bogotá government did not control the entirety of the national territory. Indeed, the antichurch measures fueled the resistance of the Conservative cause.[98] With multiple battles, including two for Bogotá itself, the war lasted through 1862, and it did not entirely end in the South until mid-1863.

Thus ended a chain of civil wars that had begun in 1858. These civil wars were a continuation of the conflicts that had emerged from the contradictory interests involved in the anticolonial reforms initiated in the late 1840s, which previously had led to the civil wars of 1851 and 1854. The Liberals emerged victorious from the war, whereas the Conservative party ended the conflict in absolute disarray. The end result was the political consolidation of the anticolonial, procapitalistic reforms enacted in midcentury Nueva Granada.

Violence had once again proved to be a significant and often decisive social process within the complex political processes that reformed the socioeconomic structure of Colombian society at midcentury.

THE WARS OF THE CLASS FACTIONS

Between 1863 and 1902, there were periods of major, national political violence in 1876–1877, 1885, 1895, and 1899–1902. In addition, there

[96] Indalecio Liévano Aguirre, *El Proceso de Mosquera ante al Senado* (Bogotá: Editorial Revista Colombiana, 1966), p. 49.

[97] Other reforms included the licensing of Catholic priests by the government and the reexpulsion of the Jesuits (they had been readmitted during the previous Conservative period). See Torres Giraldo, *Los Inconformes*, vol. 2, pp. 102–103; Puentes, *Historia del Partido Liberal*, pp. 207–208.

[98] The church attempted to convert the conflict into a religious war. Those associated with the expropriation of church lands, including the secretary of the Treasury, Rafael Núñez, were excommunicated. See Indalecio Liévano Aguirre, *Rafael Núñez* (Lima: Editora Latinamerica, n.d.), pp. 87–90.

were civil wars, insurrections, coup d'etats, and other forms of political violence on the provincial level at various points in time.[99]

Political violence in this period tended to be almost exclusively intraclass in nature. Different factions of the dominant socioeconomic class of society vied for state power in order to secure and to maximize their position in society. The political expression of the contradictory interests that divided these groups tended increasingly to be political party factions rather than the political parties themselves. The working classes in Colombian society participated in politics principally as cannon fodder during the civil wars, in which they were recruited as soldiers, often violently, for the different armies of the propertied classes whose interests were at stake. The working classes were not politically organized during this period. After the experience of the 1854 artisan–military coup, the propertied

[99] Space limitations inhibit all but the mention of the most important instances of local violence that occurred throughout the nineteenth century but which were most frequent in the period 1863–1885. This was due to the Federalist political institutions of that epoch. Urrutia states that, in that era, there were "more than fifty insurrections or armed revolts of an exclusively local or state nature" (*Historia del Sindicalismo*), p. 77).

Rafael Núñez, cited by Guillén Martínez (*El Poder*, p. 20), lists both the major national and local wars of the period:

> Since 1860 when there began a struggle between the old national parties, a struggle which, as is known, ended with the complete triumph of Liberalism at the beginning of 1863, the republic hasn't had, until now, the enjoyment of a presidential period in complete peace.
>
> Between 1864 and 1866 there were three revolutions: one in Cundinamarca, one in Cauca and another in Panamá.
>
> Between 1866 and 1868 there was the coup d'etat of General Mosquera, the counter-revolution headed by General Acosta and various local disturbances related to these two events.
>
> Between 1868 and 1870 there was one revolution in Cundinamarca and another in Panamá.
>
> From 1870 to 1872 one or two revolutions in Boyacá and Cundinamarca.
>
> From 1872 to 1874, there were a series of disturbances in Panamá and great agitation in Boyacá.
>
> Between 1874 and 1876 there was agitation and disturbances in the entire republic.
>
> From 1876 to 1878 there was a general civil war.
>
> From 1878 through 1880 there were disturbances in Panamá, Antioquia, Cauca, Magdalena and Tolima as well as general agitation.

Núñez omits from his list the highly significant provincial civil war in Antioquia in 1864.

Maingot ("The Colombian Military" p. 256) lists the following civil wars by regions for the nineteenth century: Antioquia, 5; Bolívar, 5; Boyacá, 5; Cauca, 5; Cundinamarca, 6; Magdalena, 6; Panamá, 15; Santander, 2; Tolima, 3; for a total of 52 violent conflicts.

See also Ospina Vásquez, *Industria y Protección*, p. 233.

classes did not attempt again, for the remainder of the nineteenth century, to seriously seek allies and organize support among the workers.[100]

The factionalism within the political parties was due to the progressive ossification of party identification within a society that was undergoing socioeconomic change. The recurrent civil wars themselves might be hypothesized to be an important element in the ossification of party identification.[101] Consider, for example, that, in the United States of America, a single civil war (of great intensity, to be sure) precluded the effective organization of the Republican party in the South for nearly a century. In Colombia, two generations of party civil wars led to a situation in which partisan identification came to be inculcated in offspring in a manner similar to religious belief.

The second half of the nineteenth century was a period of socioeconomic change in Colombia. As the society became more varied, different socioeconomic interests emerged within each party. Some of these interests proved to be incompatible, and party factions became distinguished. On occasion this led to the existence of equivalent factions within the Liberal and Conservative parties that were more similar to each other than their respective opposing faction within the same party. This led to complex politics in which interparty alliances were sometimes formed to advance common interests and/or to weaken the opposing party and/or to improve the situation of the faction in question in the power structure of its

[100] The general opinion would appear to be similar to that of Conservative leader Posada Gutiérrez, who thought that "it is dangerous to let party discussions and passions penetrate the last strata of society" (*Memorias Histórico-Políticas*, vol. 3, p. 395).

[101] The 1859–1863 civil war would seem to be important in the initiation of this process. The killing of escaped Liberal political prisoners in Bogotá and the execution of Conservatives in Bogotá after the Liberals captured the capital were significant changes in the "rules of the game." Consider, for example, the civil war of 1851. The rebels were promptly given amnesty and they returned to active politics, including the most important leader, Julio Arboleda. The war that ended in 1863, however, led to bitter recriminations and the exclusion of the Conservatives from representation in the subsequent constitutional convention. The tone of the era might be appreciated from the message sent by President Ospina to Governor Giraldo of Antioquia: "All of us understand that it is necessary to exterminate the opposing party at all cost; this is what reason advises, what the public conscience expects" (cited in Lievano Aguirre, *El Proceso de Mosquera*, p. 41). See also Puentes, *Historia del Partido Liberal*, pp. 201–202; Torres Giraldo, *Los Inconformes*, vol. 2, pp. 97–98; Lievano Aguirre, *El Proceso de Mosquorra*, pp. 41–44.

Nonetheless, certain party factions continued to change their party identification in the course of the century. The final ossification of party identification would appear to have occurred as a result of the War of a Thousand Days (1899–1902), in which an estimated 100,000 Colombians died. From then until the 1960s there was extremely little change in family-based party identification and practically none in the partisan orientations of party factions.

own party. It also led occasionally in the nineteenth century to the fusion of factions of opposite parties to form new political forces. The same pattern, except for the fusions, continued into the twentieth century, and, indeed, to a certain extent it continues to this day. All of the foregoing refers to elite-level politics, although the masses were also subject to the increase in the intensity of party identification and its subsequent ossification. Examples of all of these types of political relationships are to be found in the history of the period 1863–1902, to which we now turn.

The Gendarme *State*

The victorious Liberals assembled after the end of the 1858–1863 civil war in the Antioquian town of Rionegro. There, in 1863, they proclaimed the formation of the *Estados Unidos de Colombia* ("United States of Colombia"). The constitution that resulted from this meeting extended individual liberties to a maximum, reduced the functions of the state to a minimum, separated church and state, and organized the country around a radical federalism that considered the states to be "sovereign and independent" although joined in a "perpetual union." The executive branch of government was to be weak vis-á-vis the legislative branch, and the presidential term was limited to two years with the president not being allowed to succeed himself. The independence of the states was such that the federal government was not supposed to intervene in their internal affairs even in the event of local civil wars.[102]

The Constitution of Rionegro is frequently regarded as a collection of experiments compiled by reformists heavily influenced by the ideological currents of European liberalism. This is a generally accurate depiction. However, with regard to the radically federalist tenents of the constitution and the extremely limited powers afforded the national state, the Rionegro constitution merely institutionalized what already existed in Colombia, that is, a weak state within a strong structure of domination. Genuine centralism had died with the Spanish colony. The economic and sociopolitical structures and superstructures of the republic were decentralized from the beginning. The *criollo* class was divided along regional lines with the local power structure being of greater importance than the distant government in Bogotá for the determination of the structure of society. Even the national army was generally of no importance in political calculations after

[102] For descriptions of the Constitution of Ríonegro and discussions of it, consult: Rodríguez Salazar, "Las Contituciones del Siglo XIX," pp. 57–84; Manuel Antonio Pombo and José Joaquín Guerra, *Constituciones de Colombia* (Bogotá: Biblioteca Popular de Cultura Colombiana, 1951), pp. 89–170; República de Colombia, *Actos Legislativos de la Constitución de Ríonegro* (Bogotá: Imprenta Nacional, n.d.); Camacho Roldán, *Memorias*, pp. 269–326; Liévano Aguirre, *Rafael Núñez*, chap. 6; Eduardo Santa, *Sociología Política de Colombia* (Bogotá: Editorial Iqueima, 1955), pp. 54–61.

1831. Far more important were the *criollo*-generaled and peasant-soldiered ad hoc armies that were the main military protagonists of the civil wars.

The 1886 constitution, which sought to lay the basis for a strong, centralized state, is a much more "reformist" measure, interpreting this term to connote departures form existing reality.

The radical federalism once again transferred political attention and many political struggles from the national to the local level. Acute political conflicts became localized, as did the civil wars. The most important of the regional civil wars was that which occurred in Antioquia in 1864. The Conservatives of that sovereign state revolted (with the aid of arms and money from Conservatives throughout Colombia) and militarily defeated the Liberal government. In the decisive battle, Liberal State President Pascual Bravo was slain. The national government headed by President Murillo Toro, a Radical Liberal, accepted the decision reached on the battlefield, and Antioquia under the leadership of General Pedro Justo Berrío became a Conservative stronghold. Murillo Toro and the faction of the "Radical Liberals" began to collaborate with the "*Berrío*" faction of the Conservatives and even conceded this same faction control of the sovereign State of Tolima. The other major faction of the Liberals, the "*Mosqueristas,*" opposed the conciliatory policy by which the Radicals sought Conservative allies.[103]

The results of the 1866 elections led to the rotation of the presidency from the leader of the Radicals, Murillo Toro, to the head of the Mosqueristas, Tomás Cipriano de Mosquera. However, the Radicals, along with their Conservative allies in Antioquia and Tolima, retained control of Congress. A series of disputes over economic and international policy, as well as over the limits of national governmental power, arose between the executive and legislative branches of government. This political battle led to a decree by Mosquera that closed Congress in April 1867 for the remainder of that year and to a bloodless coup one month later by means of which the Radicals, with the passive compliance of the Conservatives and the active support of the army, deposed Mosquera and transferred the presidency to the chief of the army, General Santos Acosta.[104]

The Radical Olympus (with the support of its Conservative allies) had become clearly hegemonic in a majority of the sovereign states and in the national government, with the former being the most important power base. The defeated "Mosqueristas" and other Liberal dissidents organized under these circumstances what later came to be known as the "*Independiente*" (Independent) faction of the party. In April 1869, this faction signed a formal alliance with the majority Conservative faction headed by

[103] Torres Giraldo, *Los Inconformes*, vol. 2, pp. 111–115.

[104] Liévano Aguirre, *El Proceso de Mosquera*, pp. 49–120; Puentes, *Historia del Partido Liberal*, pp. 244–248.

Carlos Holguín. Thus, each of the two warring factions of the dominant Liberal party had its group of Conservative allies.[105]

The Radical Olympus was composed of the most important commercial interests in Colombia, those most directly involved in the import–export sector, and those that initiated the institutionalization of finance capital in Colombia. The Independientes were a more heterogeneous group, but they clearly tended to include those Liberals most closely related to the principal power base of the Conservative party. The exception to the relationship between landholding and the Conservative party was Antioquian conservatism.[106] It was closely related to gold mining and commerce.

Disputes between the Radicals and their factional rivals within the Liberal party, first the Mosqueristas and later the Independientes, as well as between the Radicals and the Conservatives, ranged over a wide variety of issues. The Conservatives were particularly concerned over church–state relations, while both they and the Independientes opposed Radical policies with regard to land distribution, the public debt, and credit.

With regard to land, Mosquera had originally sought to gradually distribute the mortmain land taken from the church. This would maintain the land's market value, allow the issuance of treasury notes backed by the land for state finance, and allow *latifundistas* ("large landowners") to participate in the land auctions by providing easy terms. The Radicals, however, passed a law in 1865 that provided for the auction of all church land to the highest bidder within one year. This measure depressed auction prices and immensely favored the merchant–financiers, whose great liquidity, vastly expanded by a tobacco boom, allowed them to take advantage of the land bonanza. Furthermore, many of the land sales were canceled and depressed government obligations issued to cover the chronic government deficit. Thus, the merchant–financiers often enjoyed a double speculation. They purchased at low prices government obligations that were then used to acquire land at discount prices.[107] Mosquera's third government decreed an investigation into these land transactions in August 1866, which threatened to revert to the state those sales in which the state had

[105] Torres Giraldo, *Los Inconformes*, vol. 2, pp. 115–117.

[106] The differences between Antioquia and Colombia's other regions is a much treated subject that goes beyond the purview of this historical overview of violence as a structuring process in Colombian history. Discussions and information may be found in: Parsons, *Antioqueño Colonization, passim;* Alvaro López Toro, *Migración y Cambio Social en Antioquia en el Siglo XIX* (Bogotá: CEDE, 1968); T. Lynn Smith, *Colombia: Social Structure and the Process of Development* (Gainesville: University of Florida Press, 1967), pp. 338–339; Chaves, *Apropiación de la Tierra*, pp. 121–151; Tirado Mejía, *Introducción a la Historia Económica*, pp. 148–150; McGreevey, *Economic History*, chap. 8; Eduardo Santa, *Arrieros y Fundadores* (Bogotá: Editorial Cromos, 1961).

[107] Law 47 of May 22, 1865. See Leal Buitrago, "Social Classes," p. 103; Peña, *Orígen y Desarrollo*, pp. 57–58; Liévano Aguirre, *El Proceso de Mosquera*, pp. 57–58.

suffered "enormous lesions, having considered the value of the credit papers given as payment by the auction buyers and the effective value of the farms auctioned."[108] After the coup d'etat in May 1867, the Radicals definitively revoked the investigation order at the very first session of the reconvened Congress.[109] Thus, the distribution of an estimated one-third of the real estate in the country was undertaken in a manner that favored more the merchant–financiers than the traditional *latifundistas.* This formed an important intraclass contradiction during the period of the Radical Olympus.

Another conflictive issue was the financing of the national debt. The merchant–financiers in control of the state used public finance mechanisms to regressively redistribute wealth to the financial sector. Indeed, in the *gendarme* state of the Estados Unidos de Colombia, the internal debt was the state's main expense. The *Guardia Colombiana* (as the national army was known) never exceeded 1500 men in times of peace, there was no national police force, public works were rare, and little was spent on education, but there was a bureaucracy and an increasingly mammoth public debt whose service was government's principal expenditure. Table 2.1 shows the importance of this item for selected years as compared to other expenses.

Consistently over half of governmental expenditures were devoted to tax collection and the service of the national debt. This benefited the Radical's power base, but obviously not the other segments of society whose wealth was redistributed via the state to the merchant–financiers.

With the protection and support of the Radical governments, commercial capital began to be transformed into financial capital and the latter came to be institutionalized. The end result of this process was an increase in the concentration of wealth, which benefited the merchant–financiers, while it placed the other sectors of society at a disadvantage. The crux of these political conflicts was the control of credit in Colombian society.[110]

Mosquera in his presidency of 1862–1864 attempted to avoid state dependence on finance capital by issuing treasury notes, backed by the desamortized church land. The Radical government of Murillo Toro by means of Law 14 of 1864 recalled the treasury notes, began to pay government

[108] Presidential decree of Tomás Cipriano de Mosquera, August 11, 1866, Article 1, cited in Liévano Aguirre, *El Proceso de Mosquera,* p. 65. Some of the land was sold at one-tenth or one-twentieth of its value; see McGreevey, *Economic History,* p. 129 citing Academia Colombiana de Historia, *Historia Extensa,* vol. 15, "Economía y Hacienda" (by Abel Cruz), p. 45.

[109] Liévano Aguirre, *El Proceso de Mosquera,* p. 91.

[110] Nieto Arteta, *Economía y Cultura,* pp. 257–309; Ospina Vásquez, *Industria y Protección,* pp. 238–244; Tirado Mejía, *Introducción a la Historia Económica,* chap. 13; McGreevey, *Economic History,* chap. 5; López Toro, *Migración y Cambio Social,* passim.

TABLE 2.1
Selected Budgets of the Estados Unidos de Colombia (in pesos by fiscal years)

Department	1864–1865	1867–1868	1871–1872
Interior	363,254	168,982	208,543
Justice	70,360	26,660	27,060
Foreign Relations	106,200	69,475	69,436
Public Works	9,000	53,000	73,154
Tax Collection	*475,504*	*477,566*	*569,755*
Treasury	38,362	143,758	115,718
National Debt	*760,200*	*3,184,159*	*2,267,632*
Army and Navy	723,111	247,870	462,819
Mail		101,367	138,398
Development		183,000	471,056
Education		23,000	141,840
Welfare		20,000	74,400
Miscellaneous			26,625
	2,545,991	4,698,837	4,646,436

Source: "Constitución y Leyes de los Estados Unidos de Colombia Expedidos en los Años 1863 a 1875" (Bogotá: Editorial Medardo Rivas, 1875), pp. 53, 95, 215, 356, 450, 541, 612, 717, 812, 863, 967. Cited in Rodríguez Salazar "Las Constituciones del Siglo XIX," p. 75. The totals have been corrected.

expenses in metallic currency, and authorized the *Banco de Londres y América del Sud* the privilege to issue bank notes, manage treasury funds, collect public income, and pay state expenses. State finances were to be in private, foreign hands. Once again in power in 1866, Mosquera was authorized to found the *Banco de los Estados Unidos de Colombia,* a semi-official bank that would emit metallic backed federal notes that would be obligatory legal tender for all public debts. The coup d'etat of 1867 blocked the formation of this forerunner of a national bank.[111]

The Radical Liberal commercial–financial interests finally began to found their own banks. The first Colombian bank was the *Banco de Bogotá,* which was organized in 1871, and the second was the *Banco de Colombia,* which was founded in 1874.

Despite the increase in financial capital and the ease of its access due to its institutionalization in banks, interest rates did not fall. This was due to the export of much of Colombia's gold currency. Silver was demonetized in European financial circles in the 1870s, and its price as a commodity declined sharply thereafter. A Colombian fiscal law of 1873 retained, however, the traditional ratio of silver to gold at 15½ to 1. It thus became very profitable to export Colombian gold for cheap silver, with which the mer-

[111] Liévano Aguirre, *El Proceso de Mosquera,* passim.

chants could in turn purchase gold in Colombia at 15½ to 1. In the total period 1867–1885 Colombia exported more metallic currency than it minted, thus reducing the monetary supply[112] in a country in which paper money was only beginning to circulate to a limited extent.

The Radicals became both increasingly prosperous and politically isolated across time, and their situation deteriorated very rapidly with the advent of an economic crisis. The continual export of gold money had flooded the country with silver money that was continually devalued. The European economic crisis of 1873 also came to be felt in Colombia. Exports began to fall in 1876, and they sharply declined after 1881. Colombia lost its European tobacco markets and was affected seriously by the crash of the indigo and quinine booms. The resulting depression became chronic and did not hit bottom until the period 1883–1885.[113] The economic crisis accentuated the contradictory interests in Colombian society and debilitated the political position of the governing Radicals.

Politically, the Radicals were confronted by increased opposition within the Liberal party. In 1875, the group that came to be known as the Independents presented the presidential candidacy of Rafael Núñez, while the ruling Radicals nominated Aquileo Parra. Controversies over railway construction on the Atlantic Coast and the problems presented by economic reverses also led to the defections of some prominent Radicals to the Independents. To complicate matters, the minister of war and the commander of the Guardia Colombiana, General Ramón Santodomingo Vila and General Solón Wilches, respectively, favored the candidacy of Núñez. The Radical president, Santiago Pérez, proceeded to dismiss both of them and to employ the Guardia to ensure the support of recalcitrant states for the Radical candidacy.[114] This policy led to an invasion of the pro-Núñez State of Magdalena by the Guardia Colombiana, which was resisted by the state government. The local forces lost the single and decisive battle of the conflict in which the state president was slain.[115] Thus, Magdalena was assured for the candidacy of Parra. Pressure and deals were also very apparent in the electoral decisions of other states. As in all of the elections of this period, fraud was rampant.[116] The Independents, backed by some Conservatives, launched the slogan of "Núñez or war," and the political environment acquired a belligerent atmosphere accompanied by violent in-

[112] Darío Bustamante, "Efectos Económicos del Papel Moneda Durante la Regeneración" (Bogotá: Universidad Nacional, CID, 1973), p. 10.

[113] *Ibid.*, pp. 1–14; Ospina Vásquez, *Industria y Protección*, p. 283; Nieto Arteta, *Economía y Cultura*, pp. 283–300; Rodríguez Salazar, "Las Constituciones del Siglo XIX," p. 95 (dates the Colombian depression from 1874 due to the gold exports); McGreevey, *Economic History*, chap. 7.

[114] Puentes, *Historia del Partido Liberal*, pp. 302, 306–308.

[115] Liévano Aguirre, *Rafael Núñez*, p. 137.

[116] *Ibid.*, pp. 131–139.

cidents, including tense street confrontations between supporters of Parra and Núñez in the capital.[117]

The Liberal division had reached the point where the Conservatives, who had also presented a candidate in 1875 (winning the states of Antioquia and Tolima), decided to reconquer power. The "ideological motif" of the conflict was religious and the war was spearheaded by the clergy. The church, deprived by the Liberals of its lands and aggrieved by the separation of church and state, launched a holy war against the Liberals. Malcolm Deas has termed the church "the electoral arm of the Conservative Party." [118] In 1876, the church was the recruiting office of the Conservative insurrectional armies. The church from 1863 onward (and as we shall subsequently see as recently as the late 1940s) advised that "Liberalism was sin: The Colombian pastoral letters were intense and insistent about this point." [119]

The Conservative strategy was to convert Antioquia with its strong army into the Prussia of the Estados Unidos de Colombia. It was also thought that the pro-Núñez Liberals would begin to join the Conservatives once they had achieved decisive victories.[120] The strategy of dividing the Liberals in the course of the war was potentially viable. Núñez, as governor of Bolívar, was quietly sitting the war out, and one of his supporters, the ex-war minister, Santodomingo Vila, even attempted a Liberal uprising on the Atlantic Coast.[121] What the Conservative political strategy lacked were military victories. When the Conservatives offered Núñez the presidency in return for his support, he replied, "I do not embark on sinking ships." [122]

The Conservative defeat led to sanctions against the church figures who had been conspicuous in the leadership of the rebel movement. The bishops of Santa Fé de Antioquia, Medellín, Popayán, and Pasto were exiled, and the church was subjected to stricter state control.[123]

The Radicals won the holy war of 1876–1877, but they lost their battle. If the war had temporarily united the Radicals and the Independents, and thus ended the Independents' dissidence, it had also made the Radicals dependent on the Independents for their political power. The presidential succession in 1878 went to the Liberal war hero General Julián Trujillo, who formed a mixed Independent–Radical cabinet, with the former group occupying the most important positions. The Independents, with the in-

[117] Puentes, *Historia del Partido Liberal,* p. 264.

[118] Malcom Deas, "Algunas Notas sobre el Caciquismo en Colombia," *Revista de Occidente,* no. 127 (1973), p. 130.

[119] *Ibid.,* p. 130.

[120] Torres Giraldo, *Los Inconformes,* vol. 2, p. 155.

[121] Puentes, *Historia del Partido Liberal,* p. 307.

[122] Liévano Aguirre, *Rafael Núñez,* p. 145.

[123] Puentes, *Historia del Partido Liberal,* pp. 331–332.

creasing support of the Conservatives, gained control of more and more states. With the tolerance of the national government, armed coups in Magdalena and Cauca destroyed the Radical governments in those states and prepared the way for the presidential succession in 1880 of the leader of the Independent Liberals, Rafael Núñez.[124]

The attainment of power by the Independent Liberals signified a fundamental change in government policies. With the merchant–financiers no longer in control of the state, a national bank was founded (Law 39 of 1880) and a protectionist trade policy was adopted (Law 40 of 1880). As a result of the founding of the national bank, private finance capitalists faced a competitive source of liquidity and lost their monopoly on emissions, their control over governmental finances, and their principal depositor because government funds were transferred to the new entity.[125] The new trade policy, which consciously sought to encourage domestic manufactures, struck at what the Radicals thought to be the core of Liberal thought, free trade, which was also the main source of capital accumulation for the merchant–financiers.[126]

Politically, those merchant–financiers who had abandoned the Radicals in 1875 to support the Independents quickly moved back to the prime political expression of their factional interests.[127] The Radicals began an active political opposition and the merchant–financiers sought to boycott the new national bank.

The Radical–Independent competition placed the country on the verge of civil war in 1884. The presidential elections were contested, with Núñez being the Independent candidate with Conservative support and Solón Wilches being the Radical candidate. A victorious Núñez attempted to defuse the explosive situation by forming a "National Union" cabinet composed of three Independents, two Radicals, *and two Conservatives.* This unaccustomed example of partisan pluralism was viable in that the economic crisis which had begun in the mid-1870s was touching a desperate bottom in the period 1883–1885.

Within the coalition, however, the Independent–Conservative alliance became continually strengthened at the expense of the interests of the

124 Torres Giraldo, *Los Inconformes,* vol. 2, pp. 165–168.

125 Bustamante, "Efectos Económicos," pp. 11–29; Rodríguez Salazar, "Las Constituciones, del Siglo XIX," pp. 99–105; Liévano Aguirre, *Rafael Núñez,* chap. 4.

126 Liévano Aguirre, *Rafael Núñez,* p. 170.

127 Important examples of this group consist of Miguel Samper and Salvador Camacho Roldán. Initially Radicals, they supported Núñez but later returned to the Radical fold to attack Núñez with all of the fury of deceived apostates. Samper was an executive of the Banco de Bogotá and president of the Chamber of Commerce of Bogotá, and Camacho Roldán was the principal founder of the *Banco de Colombia.* See Liévano Aguirre, *Rafael Núñez,* pp. 175–178; for an exposition of the Anti-Núñez position, see Miguel Samper, *La Miseria en Bogotá y Otros Escritos* (Bogotá: Universidad Nacional de Colombia, 1969), "La Protección—1880," pp. 195–291.

Radicals. The situation remained tense throughout 1884, with local-level violence in several states, including a regional civil war in Santander. By January 1885, these conflicts had evolved into a full-scale national civil war between the Radicals and the Independent–Conservative coalition. During the conflict, the government distributed arms to the Conservatives, who decidedly backed the Núñez government.[128]

The Radicals were defeated on the battlefield. Their military demise marked the end of the Estados Unidos de Colombia, that *gendarme* state controlled and exploited by the commercial–financial faction of the dominant class.

The Regeneration

In September 1885, after several decisive victories over the Radicals, Núñez proclaimed that "the Constitution of Rionegro has ceased to exist." In a political process known as *La Regeneración* ("The Regeneration"), the Independent Liberal–Conservative coalition began to restructure the state. With the vanquished Radicals barred from the proceedings, a new constitution was drafted in 1886, which formed the *República de Colombia.* Still in effect, this constitution contemplates a strong centralized state. The constitution was supplemented in 1887 by a concordat with the Vatican, which defines close relations between church and state. In addition, the church was granted a perennial indemnification to compensate it for the damages received as a result of the desamortization of mortmain land in 1861. Thus, the *gendarme* state constitution of 1863, federalism, and the separation of church and state were all buried by the Regeneration movement of 1886.[129]

The Radicals had been defeated and the basic tenets of Radical Liberalism had been erased from the constitution. The *latifundistas* and the church had returned to consolidated power for the first time in nearly a quarter of a century. Protectionist trade policies were followed, state monopolies were eventually reestablished, and the national bank was authorized to issue paper money that was to serve as obligatory legal tender for all public and private debts. In addition, the private banks were deprived of the right to conduct emissions.

La Regeneración government consciously attacked finance capital on all

128 Torres Giraldo, *Los Inconformes*, vol. 2, pp. 178–203; Puentes, *Historia del Partido Liberal*, pp. 345–353; Liévano Aguirre, *Rafael Núñez*, pp. 200–246.

129 Rafael Núñez, *La Reforma Política* (Bogotá: Editorial Imprenta de la Luz, 1882); Miguel Antonio Caro, *Estudios Constitucionales* (Bogotá: Editorial Biblioteca Popular, 1951); Jaime Jaramillo Uribe, *El Pensamiento Colombiano en el Siglo XIX* (Bogotá: Editorial Temis, 1964); Gerardo Molina, *Las Ideas Liberales en Colombia, 1849–1914* (Bogotá: Tercer Mundo, 1973), pp. 131–155; Liévano Aguirre, *Rafael Núñez*, pp. 268–298, 314–339; Nieto Arteta, *Economía y Cultura*, pp. 412–430; Rodríguez Salazar "Las Constituciones del Siglo XIX," pp. 110–141.

fronts. The manager of the *Banco Nacional,* Felipe Paul, wrote that the government should "increment the Banco Nacional, with the principal aim of lowering interest rates and giving activity to capitals, which today are destined almost exclusively to usury, and stimulate anonymous companies [corporations] by buying stock and making concessions in loans." [130] Rafael Núñez was a firm believer in cheap money plus protectionism to encourage industry.[131] The end result was an entire series of monetary measures that added numerous economic setbacks to the political defeat of the Radical Liberals.

Of 42 banks that existed in Colombia in 1881, there were only 14 left in 1892 as a result of the economic crisis and the monetary policies of *La Regeneración.* Financial and commercial capital were also adversely affected by an accelerated inflationary spiral and by the rapid devaluation of Colombian currency. These measures made all but short-term lending hazardous and greatly increased the price of imported goods.[132]

If commercial and financial capital were damaged by *La Regeneración,* industrial and agricultural activities were stimulated. The state subsidized new industries and the construction of railways. The government also reestablished state monopolies as a source of official revenues.

The devaluation of the 1890s also stimulated exports. The most important item in this regard, and the economic basis of the consolidation of *La Regeneración* itself, was coffee.

Coffee had long been grown in Colombia, but it was not until a dramatic increase in world coffee prices in the late 1880s that exports boomed. The devaluation of the peso also contributed to the boom in that transport and labor costs were kept low by inflation while the peso income of the exporters increased. The real income of financial and import commercial capital decreased, as did the real income of wage labor, whereas capital accumulation was principally concentrated in the agricultural export sector.[133]

Coffee planting during *La Regeneración* (unlike in later years) was overwhelmingly a commercial activity undertaken on large plantations.

In other policies, *La Regeneración* generally sought to restrict the press and political activities, which it considered "subversive." That definition was frequently extended to all Radical activity and sometimes to the activities of Conservative opponents of *Le Regeneración.*

Politically, the Independent Liberals and the Conservatives fused into

[130] Cited in Guillermo Torres García, *Historia de la Moneda Colombiana* (Bogotá: Banco de la República, 1945), p. 184.

[131] Liévano Aguirre, *Rafael Núñez,* pp. 299–313.

[132] Ospina Vásquez, *Industria y Protección,* p. 278.

[133] Bustamante, "Efectos Económicos," pp. 46, 56; Liévano Aguirre, *Rafael Núñez,* p. 373; William Paul McGreevey, "The Economic Development of Colombia," Ph.D. dissertation, Massachusetts Institute of Technology (Cambridge, 1965), appendix.

what became known as the *Partido Nacional* ("National Party"). The Independents, however, suffered continual political reverses and defections. In the end, the Independents became but a small, weak part of the Partido Nacional, which itself became a faction within the Conservative party.

Rafael Núñez was named president for the period 1886–1892, but he did not exercise day-to-day power. Retiring to his native Cartagena, Núñez left the duties of the government to the vice-president, Eliseo Payán, an Independent Liberal. Payán's policies, which sought to attract the support of the Radicals, created a crisis within the Partido Nacional which resulted in his replacement by the Conservative leader Carlos Holguín, who was the acting chief executive from 1888 through 1892. Núñez, however, remained the ultimate power behind the throne.[134]

By the time of the 1892 presidential elections, factional differences had arisen in Conservative ranks. The Nationalists proposed Núñez for president and Miguel Antonio Caro for vice-president. The Antioquian Conservatives and their allies proposed a Núñez–Marceliano Vélez ticket. Núñez chose Caro as his running mate and thus as the effective chief executive given his continued semiretirement. The dissidents, who were known as the "*Históricos*" ("Historic Conservatives"), proceeded to launch their own unsuccessful presidential candidate in the person of Vélez. The Históricos were based principally on the traditional Antioquian mining–commercial interests, which had become more and more oriented toward commerce with the advent of the coffee boom. The Histórico faction was also important in Bogotá, where there existed another group of commercially oriented Conservatives. The Históricos demanded monetary stability, freer international trade, an end to state monopolies, administrative decentralization, freedom of the press, and generally less repressive policies. After 1892, the Históricos began an aggressive opposition, and the "*Nacionales*" redoubled political repression.[135]

The Liberal party had regrouped during *La Regeneración* around the Radical faction. Discrepancies arose among the Liberals, however, as to what strategy to adopt to oppose *La Regeneración*. The factional terms utilized in the 1890s were "*Civilistas*" ("Civilists") and "*Revolucionarios*" ("Revolutionaries"). The former were composed of the old-line Radicals who controlled the official party apparatus and were led by ex-Presidents Santiago Pérez and Aquileo Parra. The "Civilistas" proposed negotiations with the Conservatives in the hope that concessions for political participa-

[134] Liévano Aguirre, *Rafael Núñez*, pp. 345–352; Torres Giraldo, *Los Inconformes*, vol. 2, pp. 228–230; Puentes, *Historia del Partido Liberal*, p. 399.

[135] Charles Wylie Bergquist, "Coffee and Conflict in Colombia 1886–1904: Origins and Outcome of the War of a Thousand Days," Ph.D. dissertation (Stanford University, Stanford, Calif., 1973), p. 63; Liévano Aguirre, *Rafael Núñez*, pp. 409–417; Jorge Orlando Melo, "Colombia 1880–1930: La República Conservadora," mimeographed (Cali: Universidad del Valle, 1964), p. 9.

tion might be obtained. Charles Bergquist characterizes the Civilista elite as composed of rich, old merchants, mostly from Bogotá, who had enjoyed political power during the Estados Unidos de Colombia. The merchant–financiers had soured on civil wars as early as 1885, when many of them were nearly ruined. During the 1890s (a period of relative prosperity for the bourgeoisie due to the coffee boom), the Civilistas sought to avoid war at all costs.[136]

One reason for their reticence to war was that, during the civil wars, and especially during the period of the wars of the class factions, the expropriation of the enemy's goods became increasingly common. Rafael Núñez once observed:

> In the 1876–1877 civil war there was already apparent a tendency to convert the upheavals into opportunities to dispossess the property of the defeated for the benefit of the victors. From then, until now, this tendency has become even more pronounced and, judging from various local disturbances, life runs less of a risk than property. . . . So many examples of expropriations, authorized by the governments, have had the effect of relaxing the notions of "yours" and "mine" and awakening appetites for communism.[137]

One of the most important "direct" economic aspects of the party faction wars was the tendency to finance the conflicts with the funds of the opposing faction. In the war of 1885, forced loans were raised from the prosperous merchant–financiers in progressively larger amounts with only weeks between such levies. The Liberal-owned *Banco Central Hipotecario* had to close its doors after the government began to levy contributions from its vaults.[138]

The prowar Revolucionario faction of the Liberals would seem to have a significant generational difference with the Civilistas. They were mostly younger men who had not experienced state power. Many of them were also very much related to the coffee boom of the 1880s and 1890s.

Coffee planting was undertaken to a large extent by Liberals during *La Regeneración*. Part of the reason for this would appear to be the large-scale entrance of commercial capital into coffee at the beginning of the boom.[139] Another reason is expressed by Luis Ospina Vásquez: "At a certain point in time, in the last years of the past century, many of the most prominent men amongst the Liberals, having no opportunity for public life given the systems of *La Regeneración*, dedicated themselves to coffee

[136] Bergquist, "Coffee and Conflict," p. 178; Gerado Molina, *Las Ideas Liberales en Colombia: 1849–1914*, (Bogotá: Ediciones Tercer Mundo, 1972), pp. 173–193.

[137] Rafael Núñez, *La Reforma Política* (Bogotá: Imprenta La Luz, 1888), p. 108.

[138] Eduardo Santa, *Rafael Uribe Uribe* (Medellin: Editorial Bedout, n.d.), pp. 86–88; Torres Giraldo, *Los Inconformes*, vol. 2, p. 196; Puentes, *Historia del Partido Liberal*, pp. 369–370.

[139] Bustamante, "Efectos Económicos," pp. 55–58.

planting."[140] The leader of the Revolucionarios was Rafael Uribe Uribe, the owner of one of the largest coffee plantations in Antioquia, "Gualanday," and the manager of the largest in Cundinamarca (the properties of De la Torre in Viotá).[141]

The Liberals and the Histórico Conservatives criticized the lack of civil liberties and the economic policies of *La Regeneración*. One of the complaints was the "state socialism" of the Nationalists, a reference to state intervention in the economy. The opposition strongly attacked the reimposition of the state tobacco monopoly, and those with coffee interests vehemently protested the impending imposition of an export tax on the grain.

Rafael Núñez's death in 1894 led to renewed opposition activity as *La Regeneración's* opponents assumed that the Nationalists would soon lose their internal coherence.

Under these circumstances the "*Histórico–Nacionalista*" division within the Conservative ranks acquired new fury. Encouraged by these political trends, one sector of the Revolucionario Liberals led by coffee baron Eustaquio de la Torre Narváez began to plot. Despite the fact that the initial leaders were jailed, some groups of Liberals, including Rafael Uribe Uribe, took to the battlefields in 1895. Their situation was very poor in that the Históricos supported the Nacionalistas in face of the Liberal uprising and the Civilista Liberals also opposed the adventure. The war lasted but two months and was mainly confined to Cundinamarca and adjoining departments. Despite their defeat, the Revolucionarios were not dissuaded from advocating the armed route to power. They pointed out that the government had been forced to mobilize almost all of its forces to defeat the small faction of Liberals who had taken to the fields.[142]

Political controversy continued to be heated after the war as the Liberals and the Históricos uncovered countless political scandals. They were mostly related to the government's mismanagement of its monopolies, the government's allocation of protected private monopolies to individuals as a development strategy, and the government's subsidizing of private activities (including the English-owned railways), in addition to *La Regeneración's* continuation of the century-long scandal of the allocation of government land grants to political supporters.[143]

The political exclusion of the Liberals continued throughout the period. Only one Liberal representative, Rafael Uribe Uribe, was admitted to the

[140] Ospina Vásquez, *Industria y Protección*, p. 245.

[141] Bergquist, "Coffee and Conflict," pp. 84–87.

[142] Torres Giraldo, *Los Inconformes*, vol. 2, pp. 234–240; Puentes, *Historia del Partido Liberal*, pp. 439–443; Chaves, *Apropiación de la Tierra*, p. 156; Bergquist, Coffee and Conflict," pp. 83–89.

[143] A summary of some of the industrial scandals is to be found in Guillén Martínez, *El Poder*, pp. 213–222. The question of land in the nineteenth century civil wars is surveyed in Tirado Mejía, *Introducción a la Historia Económica*, pp. 162–167.

Chamber of Representatives (out of a total of 60 members), while none reached the Senate. The Histórico Conservatives, however, led an active parliamentary opposition and the Nacionalistas were weakened because many prominent Conservatives passed over to the "Histórico" camp led by Marceliano Vélez and Rafael Reyes.

The most unstabilizing factor for *La Regeneración* was an impending financial crisis. Coffee prices were progressively falling from year to year while inflation within Colombia continued to regressively redistribute wealth. The coffee bourgeoisie was initially protected from the price decline by accelerated devaluations, which increased the domestic price of the grain despite the international tendency. In 1898 the price drop amounted to an acute crash after five years of steadily declining prices.[144]

The coffee situation provoked a general economic crisis and the near bankruptcy of state finances, and it most directly affected many of the Revolucionario Liberals who were dedicated in large measure to coffee planting. Charles Bergquist observes that many of the Revolucionario or "War" Liberals felt that their opportunities for economic and social mobility were unacceptably limited by the political exclusiveness of the governments of *La Regeneración*.[145] During the 1890s, this group had formed the backbone of the national economy inasmuch as they contributed the bulk of the export product during the coffee boom, yet they were nearly totally excluded from political power. At the end of the decade, this circumstance was aggravated by the drastic decline of coffee prices, which greatly jeopardized their principal economic base.

The Civilista or "Peace" Liberals also contained groups in the coffee trade, but their interests were more diversified in that they also possessed old-line import operations, financial interests, and other types of agricultural holdings. These interests would be adversely affected by a war. Torres Giraldo writes: "From a class point of view, the interests and aspirations that the 'Civilistas' represented did not lead, voluntarily and of their own accord, to war, but to 'political compromises on the basis of mutual and honorable concessions'."[146] The latter is a reference to the conclusions of the 1897 Liberal Convention in which the Civilistas maintained control of the party.

The political situation was further complicated by the Históricos' negotiations with all of the other factions: the Nationalist government, the "Civilista Liberals," and the "Revolucionario Liberals." Uribe Uribe, as the only Liberal in Congress, attempted to work with the Históricos who controlled the Senate, in order to achieve a political program that included the rescinding of a new government tax on coffee exports, the restriction of the state monopolies, freedom of the press, political pardons, a new census

[144] McGreevey, "Economic Development," appendix.

[145] Bergquist, "Coffee and Conflict," pp. 186–187.

[146] Torres Giraldo, *Los Inconformes*, vol. 2, p. 246. With regard to the commercial interests of the "Civilistas," see Bergquist, "Coffee and Conflict," pp. 184–187.

to determine electoral districts, and electoral reform. The Revolucionarios were particularly adamant for the electoral reform measure, and they coined the political slogan of "reform or war."[147]

Widespread, open electoral fraud and violence in the 1896 congressional and 1898 presidential elections combined with the inability to extract from *La Regeneración* an electoral reform weakened the position of the "Civilistas" in the eyes of their younger, Revolucionario party brethren.[148] Reform hopes were also dashed when the Conservative division began to diminish. In 1898, the new Conservative president was the elderly Manuel A. Sanclemente, a Nacionalista, and the vice-president was José Manuel Marroquín, a candidate acceptable to many Históricos. In 1899 four leading Históricos, including Rafael Reyes, also entered the cabinet.[149]

In February 1899, the Revolucionario faction of the Liberals meeting in Bucaramanga decided to go to war that same year, and in October the War of a Thousand Days was begun. The Civilista directorate of old-line Radicals repudiated the movement and refused to support the armed conflict. Thus, the Liberals entered the war divided. However, the Histórico–Nacionalista division continued to produce contradictions within the government. This reached the point at which the Históricos on July 31, 1900, deposed Sanclemente and the Nacionales from power by means of a coup d'etat in the midst of the war. The pro-Histórico vice-president Marroquín assumed the presidency as a result of this movement. In September 1901, a plot to stage a countercoup to reinstate Sanclemente and the Nacionales was led by the minister of war, Pedro Nel Ospina. The plan was discovered and Ospina and other high-ranking officials were exiled. Ospina alleged widespread corruption and war profiteering to justify his coup attempt. Quite obviously, both the reticence of the Civilista Liberals to support the Revolucionario Liberals and the plots and coups within the government reduced the military efficacy of each of the two groups in conflict. The lack of internal coherence in both the Conservative and Liberal camps probably contributed to the protraction of the three-year war.[150]

Another factor conducive to the prolongation of the war was profiteering. During the War of a Thousand Days, speculation in the commodity-scarce, inflation-ridden war economy centered on making acquisitions with recently printed paper money in real estate, beasts of burden, cattle, military rations, and clothes. Rodríguez Piñeres reports that:

> In Bogotá there arose a class of people who did business with the war, and who contemplated "peace with all of its horrors" in that it would end their

[147] Torres Giraldo, *Los Inconformes*, vol. 2, pp. 248–250.

[148] Bergquist, "Coffee and Conflict," pp. 160–258.

[149] Torres Giraldo, *Los Inconformes*, vol. 2, p. 251.

[150] Bergquist, "Coffee and Conflict," pp. 302–306, 363–368; Puentes, *Historia del Partido Liberal*, pp. 515–516.

> means of enrichment at the expense of the blood, the suffering, and the ignorance of others. . . . They tended to form partnerships between some guerrillas and the chiefs of government forces to divide the buzzards' rewards.[151]

The deposed war minister, Pedro Nel Ospina, in his accusations against President Marroquín and the Históricos after the aborted coup attempt of 1901 charged that war speculation reached the very highest level of the state:

> Related to the war and its continuation are large and active interests, whose influence . . . is felt in the highest spheres of government. There is no other way to explain that Señor Marroquín twice frustrated my projected plans to conduct operations in Viotá and Cunday, currently active centers of the war and of complex speculations based upon the war and insecurity.[152]

The Liberals enjoyed early successes on the battlefield, but their chances for victory were diminished after a decisive defeat in the Battle of Palonegro. Nonetheless, the chances for victory for the Conservative government were not good either, especially after Liberal General Benjamín Herrera achieved military success in the strategic Department of Panamá.[153]

Neither the Liberals nor the government could decisively and absolutely defeat their opponent in the course of the conflict. The war ended by means of separate pacts reached with the most important Liberal generals (Rafael Uribe Uribe and Benjamín Herrera) as well as with the various Liberal guerrilla groups. The war resulted in a draw, and the Conservatives retained power.[154] The political situation, however, was traumatic after the profuse bloodletting and property destruction of 37 months of armed conflict. This situation was further complicated in 1903 when a rebellion in the Department of Panamá was backed by the United States. The imperialist intervention in that political conflict is best summarized by Theodore Roosevelt's cryptic "I took Panama" statement.[155] Colombia thus lost a department and one of its brightest long-run economic prospects, given the potential for a transoceanic canal.

[151] From the essay "Por el Reinado del Derecho" cited in Eduardo Santa, *Rafael Uribe Uribe* (Medellín: Editorial Bedout, n.d.), p. 241.

[152] Román, *La Vida del General Pedro Nel Ospina,* p. 202.

[153] Bergquist, "Coffee and Conflict," pp. 259–406; Santa, *Rafael Uribe Uribe,* pp. 155–312.

[154] Accounts of the War of a Thousand Days are to be found in Joaquín Tamayo, *La Revolución de 1899* (Bogotá: Editorial Cromos, 1938); Lucas Caballero, *Memoria de la Guerra de Mil Días* (Bogotá: Editorial Aguila Negra, 1939); Eduardo Rodríguez Piñeres, *Diez Años de Política Liberal: 1892–1902* (Bogotá: Editorial Antena, 1945); Bergquist, "Coffee and Conflict"; Santa, *Rafael Uribe Uribe;* Carlos Adolfo Urueta, *Documentos Militares y Políticos Relativos a la Campaña del General Rafael Uribe Uribe* (Bogotá: Imprenta de Vapor, 1904).

[155] Eduardo Lemaitre, *Panamá y su Separación de Colombia* (Bogotá: Banco Popular, 1973); Samuel Flagg Bemis, *The Latin American Policy of the United States* (New York: Harcourt, Brace and World, 1943), chap. 9.

The estimated 100,000 deaths, economic chaos, and national dismemberment resulting from the War of a Thousand Days put an end to the series of wars between the various factions of the dominant class. Fought to defend the particularistic interest of different socioeconomic groups, these wars had led the country to a state of political exhaustion.

Twentieth-Century Partisan Violence

Partisan violence did not end with the War of a Thousand Days. What did end was a modality of warfare. Armed conflict in Columbia ceased to be a matter of ill-equipped rebel armies of peasants confronting ill-equipped government armies of peasants. Beginning in 1907, with the definitive founding of the National Military Academy, the army became progressively professionalized, and it also began to acquire the artifacts and know-how of twentieth-century war technology.[156]

There were no civil wars in the period 1902–1930, although there were factions within the opposition party at almost any point in time that seriously considered armed uprising as a route to power. The main dissuasion from attempting such adventures was the slight chance of success against professional armed forces. The new military circumstances gave great advantages to the groups in power. Under these conditions, partisan violence in the twentieth century assumed the forms of street riots, isolated clashes between civilians and government authorities, local violence between civilians, coup d'etat attempts, and guerrilla warfare. Apart from *La Violencia,* which began in 1946, major instances of traditional party violence occurred in 1909, 1922, and 1929 and in the period 1930–1934. In addition, isolated violent events took place at various points in time, and there were coup d'etat plots in 1905, 1925, and 1944.

Party conflicts after the War of a Thousand Days were complicated by the completion of the process by which party identification in Colombia had become progressively ossified. In the course of the civil wars of the nineteenth century, and especially during the 37 months of military combats and civilian clashes of the War of a Thousand Days, Colombians became irrevocably identified with one or another of the two national political parties. From the beginning of the century until the 1960s party identification was inculcated in offspring in a fashion resembling religious belief. During this period most Colombians are said to be "born" Conservatives or Liberals.

The extreme sectarianism made the primordial and near invariable objective of each party the construction and maintenance of hegemonies by which they could control power to the exclusion of the opposing party.

[156] Francisco Leal Buitrago, "Política e Intervención Militar en Colombia" (México: paper presented to the 9th Congress of Latin American Sociologists, 1969); Maingot, "The Colombian Military."

Even most of the interparty coalitions and alliances must be viewed as strategic and tactical moves designed to further hegemonic goals. The coalitions were often related to factional conflicts within the political parties.

Accelerated economic changes in Colombian society in the first half of this century altered the social structure of the nation. The ossification of partisan identification within the context of socioeconomic change led to an increasing heterogeneity within the parties. The distinctions between the parties on the basis of class factions, which were important in nineteenth-century politics, became increasingly blurred with the passage of time. In the twentieth century, each party has its important segment of almost every class, faction, and stratum in Colombian society. There were and are important sociological differences between the parties, to be sure, but the salient fact of the multiclass nature of the parties is undeniable. This situation led to the expression of heterogeneous interests by means of different factions within the parties.

Thus, at almost any point in time, the Conservative and Liberal parties were divided into rival factions. The competition between them was often as intense as that between the different parties. The parties themselves often appear to be no more than alliances between different political groups joined in the last analysis by a principally ascriptive characteristic. That characteristic was family political party identification. In a very real sense it is a misnomer to speak of Colombian politics as being traditionally a two-party system given the constant proliferation of factions within the parties.

Despite the factionalism and the tenuousness of party identification as an expression of basic interests, partisan conflicts increased in importance in the twentieth century. Sectarianism in the form of political favoritism on ascriptive grounds combined with the exclusion of the opposing party from power led to party identification becoming an important sociopolitical fact of life in and of itself. Important conflicts began to arise over the conflicting interests represented by ascriptive party identification. These conflicts, as well as factional disputes, had a high potential for violence at certain junctures in the political history of this century.

All of the aforementioned relations will be illustrated in the following two sections, which give overviews of these sociopolitical conflicts.

CONCORDIA NACIONAL AND *UNION REPUBLICANA*

After the War of a Thousand Days, the Liberal party was in complete disarray. The Conservative party continued in power, but the divisions within its ranks were bitter. This was demonstrated in the campaign to choose a president for the period 1904–1910. Two Conservative candidates competed in this hotly contested, highly fraudulent, and extremely close electoral debate. The victorious candidate was Rafael Reyes, who was backed by his old wing of the Histórico Conservatives and by the Liberals (Reyes had remained outside of Colombia throughout the War of a Thousand Days). His opponent was Joaquín F. Vélez, who was supported by the Antioquian Históricos and by elements previously identified with *La Regeneración.*

The Reyes government was a Conservative-led, bipartisan coalition known as the *Concordia Nacional* ("National Concord"). Initially, it was supported by the near entirety of the Liberal party. The most important opposition to the Reyes government came not from the Liberals but rather from the competing faction within the Conservative party. Disaffected by the postwar coalition cabinet with the Liberals and by the economic policies of the National Concord, a majority of the Conservatives in Congress opposed Reyes's legislative measures. The president reacted by closing Congress in December 1904 and by sending to concentration camps a prominent group of opposition Conservatives.[157]

Reyes replaced the Congress with a National Assembly selected by the executive, which was two-thirds Conservative and one-third Liberal. One year later, Conservative elements led by Vice-President Ramón González Valencia and First Designate Joaquían F. Vélez (Reyes's electoral opponent) planned a coup d'etat. Known as the "Christmas Plot," this conspiracy was discovered and aborted. Those involved were vigorously repressed and the already dictatorial nature of the regime became even more accentuated. Another escalation in repression followed an unsuccessful assassination attempt against Reyes led by General Pedro León Acosta in 1906.[158]

The Reyes government soon lost most of its Liberal support as the majority wing of the party led by General Benjamín Herrera and Nicolás Esguerra became critical of the administration. Another wing of the liberals, led by Rafael Uribe Uribe, backed the Concordia Nacional throughout its existence. Thus, both the government and the opposition wings of the dominant Conservative party had their respective group of Liberal allies. Class factional differences, similar to those of late nineteenth-century politics, led to discrepancies over economic policies among these groups. The government was characterized by interventionist, centralist, and protectionist policies.[159]

[157] For the Reyes period consult Torres Giraldo, *Los Inconformes,* vol. 3, pp. 25–56; Jorge Orlando Melo, "Colombia 1880–1930: La República Conservadora," Leal Buitrago, "Social Classes," pp. 183–191; Puentes, *Historia del Partido Liberal,* pp. 557–561; Ospina Vásquez, *Industria y Protección,* pp. 322–345. Biographies include Eduardo Lemaitre, *Biografía de un Gran Colombiano: Rafael Reyes* (Bogotá: n.p., 1967).

[158] Torres Giraldo, *Los Inconformes,* vol. 3, pp. 25–56; Puentes, *Historia del Partido Liberal,* pp. 19–21.

[159] Guillén Martínez, *El Poder,* pp. 222–225; Ospina Vásquez, *Industria y Protección,* pp. 329–330; Leal Buitrago, "Social Classes," pp. 183–189; Francisco Restrepo Plata, *Memoria de Hacienda, 1912* (Bogotá: n.p., 1913).

Agricultural interests, particularly those related to coffee, tended to support the government. Such was the case of the Uribe Uribe faction of the Liberals. Commercial, financial, and some industrial groups opposed the government.[160]

The Reyes regime entered into crisis in 1908 when it incurred political opposition within its own power base. Reyes's policies of administrative centralism and government monopolies to improve the state's fiscal situation led to the nationalization of previously *departamento*-controlled tobacco, liquor, and match monopolies. Important regional, *latifundio*-backed caudillos such as General Manjarrés in Magdalena and Dr. Charry in Huila opposed this policy and achieved the return of the monopolies to the *departamentos.* The government's political weakness in its own ranks was capitalized on by the opposition. For example, a petition signed by 300 prominent Antioquians forced Reyes to undertake a cabinet shift. In Antioquia, merchant–financiers and some industrialists led by Medellín Banker Carlos E. Restrepo formed a bipartisan opposition block known as the *Unión Republicana* ("Republican Union"). Reyes took this group seriously enough to offer the ministry of *hacienda* ("Treasury") to Restrepo, but the Conservative leader of the Unión Republicana refused the post when Reyes would not accept the condition that the government's productive monopolies be disbanded.[161]

The Unión Republicana began to organizationally coalesce the diffuse opposition forces. Important in this process was the support of Liberal leaders Benjamín Herrera and Nicolás Esguerra. Political conflicts between the Concordia Nacional and the Unión Nacional (each led by Conservatives and each with the backing of a Liberal faction) led to street rioting in the capital on March 13, 1909. Two months later Reyes left Colombia for Europe. With a minimum of violence and a maximum of political positioning, the Reyes regime had been toppled from power.[162]

After two caretaker governments, a Republican-controlled National Constituent Assembly was called in 1910. It modified the 1886 constitution, named Carlos E. Restrepo president of the republic for the period 1910–1914, and passed a series of laws. The legal measures adopted included the prohibition of unbacked paper money and the abolition of direct taxes and forced government loans. The Republican government tended to be much more free trading and much less interventionist than the government that preceded it. The government was characterized by a comfortable administration of the status quo backed by a coffee boom. The by

[160] Rafael Uribe Uribe, *El Socialismo de Estado* (Bogotá: Editorial Stella, n.d.); Molina, *Las Ideas Liberales*, pp. 249–262; Santa, *Rafael Uribe Uribe*, pp. 313–339.

[161] Deas, "Algunas Notas," p. 131; Christopher Abel, "Conservative Politics in Twentieth Century Antioquia 1910–1953," Occasional Paper No. 3 (Oxford: St. Anthoney's College, Latin American Centre, 1973), p. 13.

[162] Melo, "Colombia 1880–1930," p. 21.

now *Partido Republicano* linked the political heirs of the old Antioquian Histórico Conservatives with the heirs of the old "Radical" Liberals. Within the latter, Bogotá's commercial and financial groups were very prominent.[163]

Opposition to the government was undertaken by one wing of the Conservative party, commanded by Marco Fidel Suárez, and by the faction of the Liberal party known as the *Bloque Liberal,* led by Rafael Uribe Uribe. The latter group advocated interventionist measures, protectionism, and a fiscal policy based on direct taxes. Thus, when the Republican party presented a Liberal Republican, Nicolás Esquerra, for president in 1914, the Bloque Liberal preferred to support the orthodox Conservative candidacy of José Vicente Concha rather than the Republican Liberal, whose policies the Bloque Liberal vigorously opposed. Concha won the elections.[164]

The Concha government initially contained two Liberal ministers. The assassination of Bloque Liberal leader Rafael Uribe Uribe on October 15, 1914, by two newly unemployed Republican laborers greatly weakened the Liberal supporters of Concha.[165] The Liberal representation in the government rapidly declined in importance, and it soon ended. The Concha administration thus marked the reconsolidation of the Conservative hegemony that had been weakened as a result of the profound crisis that followed in the wake of the War of a Thousand Days and the loss of Panama.

THE CONSERVATIVE REPUBLIC

The general political environment of Colombia began to change during World War I. Beginning with the Concha administration, rapid socioeconomic change and concomitant interclass conflicts led to new sociopolitical processes, which will be dealt with in the following chapter.

In 1918, the official Conservative party nominated Marco Fidel Suárez to replace Concha in the presidency, while a Conservative dissident group, animated by Laureano Gómez, backed the unsuccessful candidacy of Guillermo Valencia. The Liberals, led by General Benjamín Herrera, supported Valencia. The Suárez administration continued the policy of completely excluding Liberals from executive power.[166]

Excluded from government, a highly united Liberal party decided to

[163] Abel, "Conservative Politics," pp. 13–15; Molina, *Las Ideas Liberales,* p. 284; Leal Buitrago, "Social Classes," p. 212; Puentes, *Historia del Partido Liberal,* pp. 562–563.

[164] Molina, *Las Ideas Liberales,* pp. 290–294; Puentes, *Historia del Partido Liberal,* p. 564; Torres Giraldo, *Los Inconformes,* vol. 3, pp. 89–90; Santa, *Rafael Uribe Uribe,* pp. 335–347.

[165] Santa, *Rafael Uribe Uribe,* pp. 347–350.

[166] Melo, "Colombia 1880–1930," p. 24; Torres Giraldo, *Los Inconformes,* vol. 3, pp. 109–110; Puentes, *Historia del Partido Liberal,* p. 566.

present a presidential candidate in 1922. They were encouraged by the discontent manifested in the various social movements under way in the country (discussed in Chapter 3) and by the continued divisions within the Conservative party. The latter had been exacerbated by scandals in the Suárez administration. Vigorously attacked by the Gómez dissidents, President Suárez had been forced to resign, and the party had been further divided by a multiplicity of presidential aspirants. The Liberals named Benjamín Herrera as their presidential candidate for 1922. This was the first Liberal candidacy without a coalition since 1884. In light of the Liberal challenge, the Conservatives united and named Pedro Nel Ospina as their standard bearer.[167]

The campaign was fraudulent and violent. The Ospina candidacy was backed, according to the Liberal newspaper *El Tiempo,* by official favoritism and ecclesiastical support.[168]

Malcolm Deas succintly summarizes the 1922 elections in the following manner: "In 1922 the Conservative divisions were exploited by an independent coalition of Liberals and the situation was saved by use of local force and a general recourse to fraud." [169]

After the elections, war fever was apparent at the 1922 Liberal convention in Ibagué. War of a Thousand Days veteran General Bejamín Herrera answered the war advocates with the simple slogan: "Never." The assassination in 1924 of the prominent Liberal leader Justo L. Durán also increased pressures within the Liberal party for armed action.[170] The belligerent wing of the party did not prosper principally because the majority of Liberals did not think that they could win a civil war.[171] The Conservatives, however, denounced a coup d'etat plot in the army in March 1925 and proceeded to discharge several lower ranking officers.[172] Supposed army plots were not limited to the Liberals inasmuch as in December 1925 some Conservative generals were also alleged to be plotting a coup d'etat.[173]

167 Melo, "Colombia 1880–1930," p. 27; Torres Giraldo, *Los Inconformes,* vol. 3, pp. 150–154; Puentes, *Historia del Partido Liberal,* pp. 567–568.

168 *El Tiempo,* Jan. 1, 1922, and Jan. 1, 1923. Voting irregularities and violence were also particularly acute in the localities of Santa Rosa, El Líbano, Briceño, Coyaima, Chicoral, San Antonio, Vallecito, Florida, Natagaima, and San Antonio. Tolima was the principal center of the violence. See Mauricio Solaún "La Violencia: Socio-Historical Determinants of Political Violence in Colombia," unpublished manuscript (Bogotá: University of Los Andes), pp. 151–155. In "Algunas Notas," p. 133, Deas mentions the government's distribution of arms to Conservatives in Santander.

169 Deas, "Algunas Notas," p. 130.

170 Torres Giraldo, *Los Inconformes,* vol. 3, pp. 153–154; Puentes, *Historia del Partido Liberal,* p. 568; *El Tiempo,* Feb. 7, 1942.

171 Deas, "Algunas Notas," p. 130.

172 *El Tiempo,* Mar. 13, 1925. The officials accused in "La Regadera" conspiracy were defended by Jorge Eliécer Gaitán. See *El Tiempo,* Nov. 3, 1925.

173 *El Tiempo,* Dec. 4, 1925.

Electoral incidents in the municipal campaign of 1925 led to the Liberal minority temporarily retiring from Congress in protest.[174] In 1927, the Liberals adopted a policy of total electoral abstention.[175]

The Conservative hegemony entered into crisis in the years 1928 and 1929. Corruption, administrative inefficiency, the squandering of millions of dollars of foreign loans, and bloody incidents stemming from the increase in interclass conflict and government repression led not only to augmented Liberal opposition, but also to divisions in Conservative ranks. The government sought to restrict civil liberties and to repress the labor and agrarian movements as well as belligerent sectors of the Liberal party.[176]

Violence erupted in June 1929 when the government sought to repress street demonstrations in Bogotá that protested municipal government scandals. The death of a student in these demonstrations further discredited a government that had massacred striking United Fruit banana workers the year before in the Department of Magdalena.[177]

In July 1929 there occurred a badly organized armed insurrection in various parts of the country. Coordinated by the *Consejo Central Conspirativo* (CCC, "Central Conspirative Council") of the *Confederación Obrera Nacional* (CON, "National Workers Confederation") and the *Partido Socialista Revolucionario* (PSR, "Revolutionary Socialist Party"), this rebellion involved socialists and belligerent Liberals associated with labor and agrarian movements, as well as veteran Liberal guerrillas from the War of a Thousand Days. After initial battles for the control of some towns, the movement quickly reverted to guerrilla tactics. The main areas of operations were Tolima, Santander, Cundinamarca, and Valle. The government captured some of the movement's leaders and others simply aban-

174 *El Tiempo,* Oct. 4–6, 1925.

175 *El Tiempo,* May 9, 1927. For an interesting summary of the 1922 campaign, the military plots of the period, and the periodic electoral violence, consult the article by Alejandro Hernández Rodríguez, "Relieves de la Administración Ospina," *El Tiempo,* Aug. 7, 1926.

176 Melo, "Colombia 1880–1930," pp. 29–31. For the polemics over the law that sought to restrict civil liberties and the street demonstrations and violence that accompanied the debate, see *El Tiempo* for the month of Oct. 1928.

177 *El Tiempo,* June 6, 10, 1929. The demonstrations underscored the weakness of the Conservative regime. The Abadía Méndez government negotiated with a *Junta de Notables* (Board of Leading Citizens) and agreed to the resignation of the minister of war (Ignacio Rengifo), the minister of public works (Arturo Hernández), and the chief of the national police (General Cortés Vargas). Rengifo and Cortés Vargas had also been the prime official protagonists of the massacre in the banana zone. In addition, the governors of Cundinamarca and Santander also lost their posts in the aftermath of the scandals and demonstrations. See also Torres Giraldo, *Las Inconformes,* vol. 4, pp. 137–142.

doned the poorly coordinated, politically weak, and militarily isolated movement.[178]

The crisis of the Conservative regime was further complicated by the presentation of two presidential candidates in 1930, Guillermo Valencia and General Alfredo Vásquez Cobo. Under ordinary circumstances the Catholic Church would have proved decisive in determining which of the two would be the official Conservative party candidate. However, the church hierarchy vacillated between the two candidates and, in the end, it also was divided.

Given the Conservative division, the Liberal party decided to present a candidate. Several names were discarded for fear that they would unite the Conservatives. Finally, Enrique Olaya Herrera was chosen. An ex-Republican, Olaya Herrera had been a lawyer for certain United States oil companies, and he had undertaken diplomatic posts for Conservative administrations, including the representation of Colombia at the 1928 Pan American Conference in Havana. The candidacy was supported by a small Conservative dissident group oriented by ex-President Carlos E. Restrepo. Many ex-Republicans were prominent in the campaign. The ticket was named the *Concentración Nacional Patriótica* ("National Patriotic Concentration").[179]

Olaya Herrera won a simple majority in the election while the two Conservative candidates divided an absolute majority of the vote. The outgoing Conservative president, Miguel Abadía Méndez, transferred control of the executive branch of the government to Olaya Herrera in an unprecedented peaceful change of party control of the presidency. The Conservatives retained control of the Congress, and the National Concentration cabinet was formed of half Liberals and half Conservatives.

[178] This movement was initially to have been coordinated with a rebellion against the Juan Vicente Gómez regime in Venezuela. This coordination would have given the Venezuelan rebels a strong position in western Venezuela and the Colombian rebels a greater opportunity to control the Santanderes. When the Venezuelan movement was postponed, most of the Colombians involved likewise postponed their plans, but some due to bad information, and others due to blind faith in sparking a mass insurrection, carried out the revolt's plans on July 28, 1929. That day there were battles for El Líbano, Tolima; La Dorada, Caldas; and "La Gómez," Santander. The rebels immediately reverted to guerrilla groups that briefly operated in the "Murillo" district and in Lérida, Ambalema, and Armero (all in Tolima); San Vicente, Santander; and La Palma and Yacopí in Cundinamarca.

See Torres Giraldo, *Los Inconformes*, vol. 4, pp. 152–159; Ignacio Torres Giraldo, *María Cano: Mujer Rebelde* (Bogotá: La Rosca, 1972), pp. 142–143.

[179] For the 1930 elections and the change of administration, consult: Rafael Azula Barrera, *De la Revolución al Orden Nuevo* (Bogotá: n.p., 1956); Mauricio Solaún, "La Violencia," pp. 157–159; Torres Giraldo, *Los Inconformes*, vol. 4, pp. 189–197; Manuel Serrano Blanco, *La Vida es Así* (Bucaramanga: Imprenta del Departamento, 1953), chaps. 14–17.

However, the subsequent effort to consolidate a Liberal party hegemony to replace the absolute Conservative hegemony that had existed since 1914, and the continuous Conservative control of the state that had existed since 1886, proved to be a highly conflictive, and often violent, process. This subject is described and analyzed in Chapter 3.

Summary and Conclusions

Violence has been an important and often decisive social process in the structuring of Colombian society at various junctures in the nation's history.

The expansion of Spanish domination to America was undertaken by both wars of conquest and wars of extermination. The definition of the social position of the conquered indigenous groups and of the Spanish in America vis-à-vis each other as well as their relations with the crown, also proved to be a violent process. During the colonial period, violence erupted as a result of conflicts between the Spanish and undominated Indian groups and conflicts between the Spanish and the African slave population. Toward the end of the colonial period, contradictory interests matured into conflicts between the Peninsular Spanish and the Spanish Americans. Such conflicts turned violent in Nueva Granada during the *Comunero* Rebellion and during the wars for independence. The former found the Spanish, eventually allied with the Spanish-American oligarchy, confronted with artisans, small farmers, Indians, and slaves. The independence movement, on the other hand, was led by the Spanish-American oligarchy with the *criollo* commercial interests playing an especially important role in the rebellion.

Colonial society was characterized by a strong structure of domination and by a strong state. Religious, ideological, and economic domination, as well as the strength of the state, led to a highly stable society for nearly three centuries. The erosion of Spanish control was the result of a decrease in the power of the state. The independence movement itself gained full force due to a collapse of the Spanish state as a result of the Napoleonic invasion of the Iberian Peninsula. The most intense violence accompanied the Spanish attempt to reimpose the colonial state. Although the Spanish initially achieved control of most of the territory of Nueva Granada, they were unable to reerect the previously formidable state apparatus. Under these conditions, the *criollo* guerrillas expanded into full-fledged armies that eventually expelled the Spanish from Nueva Granada.

Most of the conflicts that led to violence in colonial Nueva Granada were interclass in nature. The conflicts were between the dominant groups in society and the Indians, slaves, small farmers, and artisans. Exceptions to this general pattern are the initial conflicts between *conquistadores* ("conquerors") and the crown over the degree of exploitation of Indian labor and the independence movement against the politically dominant Spanish, led by the economically dominant *criollo* oligarchy, the latter being only a partial exception, given that the *criollos* were politically dominated.

The nineteenth-century republic may also be characterized as having a strong structure of domination. The *criollo* oligarchy, which was the dominant socioeconomic and political group in the new republic, inherited the mechanisms of social control of colonial society save the state. The new state organization was exceedingly weak when compared to its colonial predecessor. Socioeconomic and political disputes, which divided the regionally based *criollo* oligarchies, greatly debilitated central governmental power.

Internal conflicts within the dominant class arose over the retention or reformation of the colonial socioeconomic structure, over the form the new republican state was to assume, and over who was to control the new state apparatus. Particularly persistent in the course of the century were divergent interests between the commercial and agricultural export interests on the one hand and the traditional *latifundistas*, the Catholic Church being the most important, on the other. Thus, most of the conflicts were intraclass.

Exceptions to this general pattern are to be found in the defiance of the political power of the *criollo* oligarchy staged by Bolivarian military officers in 1832; in the War of the Supremes, which contained elements of diverse forms of mostly diffuse class conflict (the most prominent element being the participation of rebellious slaves and Indians in the insurrection); and in the artisan–military coup d'etat of 1854 and the subsequent civil war, from which a united *criollo* oligarchy regained control of Bogotá. Apart from these exceptions, interclass conflicts were generally not significant in the course of the nineteenth century. This was so much the case that, even during the intense civil wars that disorganized the state and social relations in general, there were no popular uprisings against the dominant groups in society.

The intraclass conflicts that led to numerous civil wars may be divided into several periods. First, there were the conflicts associated with the formation of the republican state (which also contained conflicts over socioeconomic structure); second, there were conflicts over the midcentury reforms, which successfully eliminated an entire series of colonial institutions; third, there were the wars of the class factions, who vied with each other in the last third of the century to control the state and advance their particular socioeconomic interests.

During the first three decades of the twentieth century, the class factional conflicts continued, complicated by relatively intense socioeconomic change, by a concomitant further differentiation of factional interests within each party, and by the emergence of significant interclass conflict. Although no civil wars occurred in this period, largely due to the professionalization of the military and the subsequent increase in the repressive capacity of the state, the pattern of highly conflictive and sectarian partisan politics, which emerged from the nineteenth-century civil wars, persisted. The basic political objective of each party continued to be the construction of exclusivistic political party hegemonies.

3

Origins of *La Violencia*

The socioeconomic and sociopolitical processes that immediately preceded *La Violencia* and some of those that constitute the phenomenon itself are examined in this chapter. First, attention is devoted to the emergence of interclass conflicts in twentieth-century Colombian society, both in the agrarian sector and with regard to the formation of the labor movement. Second, political conflict and violence in the Liberal Republic (1930–1946) are described. Finally, attention is given to the partial collapse of the state in the Second Conservative Republic (1946–1953) and to the role of both interclass and partisan conflicts in this process.

Socioeconomic Change and Interclass Conflict

Colombia underwent rapid processes of socioeconomic change in the first decades of this century, especially beginning with World War I. Many of these processes proved to be highly conflictive, and some proved to have a potential for violence. Thus, in addition to the continuation of partisan violence in the twentieth century, there also emerged patterns of violence related to socioeconomic conflicts between different social classes. These interclass processes might be analytically divided between *agrarian conflicts* and those related to the formation of the *labor movement.*

AGRARIAN CONFLICTS

The reemergence of agrarian conflicts in twentieth-century Colombia must be analyzed against the backdrop of a lack of mature social contradictions within the Colombian countryside during most of the nineteenth century. Even given the collapses of state authority during the civil wars, interclass conflicts did not generally emerge. Of course, the state was less important than other institutions in structuring nineteenth-century social relations, as was previously argued, but it would also appear that there were simply less intense contradictions in the countryside in the nineteenth as compared to the twentieth century.

To attempt to explain the lack of social conflicts, one might make use of a modified "frontier thesis." Large tracts of unexploited land were susceptible to colonization during the nineteenth century. Displaced peasants and those who did not desire to remain on the highland haciendas as peons or sharecroppers had the option to *tumbar monte* ("clear the land"). The massive colonization of virgin land took place on state lands dedicated for this purpose, on public domain land not intended for colonization, and on lands to which private individuals held title. Many of the large, unexploited tracts were held by the recipients or heirs of the massive political land grants of the nineteenth-century.

The colonization movement was generally from the high Andean altitudes toward the lower slopes. This migratory tendency was accentuated enormously once the coffee export economy was consolidated. Most of the colonists lacked legal title to the land they occupied. However, this was also the case of most of the holdings of the haciendas, which tended to expand gradually into public domain land. Almost all of the rural holdings in Colombia were based on claims of de facto occupation inasmuch as most of them lacked clear and unblemished legal titles.[1]

Private landlords did not discourage the entrance of colonists upon their lands inasmuch as they cleared the virgin forests and vastly enhanced the value of the land. Indeed, many of the settlers were actively recruited by the landlords. On occasion, the land would be sold to the colonists (as was the case of Quindío), and sometimes the colonists would be run off the land once the landlord saw fit; however, most frequently, agreements were reached by which the colonists would pay rent to the landowners or enter into sharecropping agreements with them. A variant of the latter arrangements consisted of colonists who were given plots of land that they cleared and lived off until the land was finally "clean." At that point in time, the land would revert to the hacienda and the colonists would be given another plot to work.[2]

[1] Even those with legal titles tended to lack a clear definition of their boundaries. See Hermes Tovar, *El Movimiento Campesino en Colombia* (Bogotá: Ediciones Libres, 1975), pp. 39–41; T. Lynn Smith, *Colombia: Social Structure and the Process of Development* (Gainesville: University of Florida Press, 1967), pp. 80–105.

[2] For examples of these precapitalistic forms of social productive relations, see: Absalón Machado, "Estudio de la Economía Cafetera de Colombia," mimeographed (Medellín: Centro de Investigaciones Económicas, Universidad de Antioquia, 1975); Darío Fajardo Montaña, "Tenencia de la Tierra y Producción en el Valle de Chisaca," mimeographed (Bogotá: Centro de Investigaciones para el Desarrollo [CID], Universi-

The most significant migratory pattern of nineteenth-century Colombia was the movement of farmers from Antioquia, Cundinamarca, Santander, and Boyacá toward the uncultivated lower slopes of the Andes.[3]

In sum, the availability of land for colonization and the emergence of a cash crop to sustain this movement served to diminish social and economic contradictions within Colombian society. At different points in time in different localities, but generally in the first two decades of this century, choice land for colonization in the central "core" region of the country began to become scarce. This was particularly the case in the Andean altitude between 800 and 2000 m, which was most suitable for coffee cultivation. The end of the period of relatively easy colonization in the central "core" region (where coffee beans could be profitably transported to market) marked the accentuation of contradictions within the countryside. As a consequence, pressure to obtain Indian land and the last central core increased, and colonization areas were marked by acute conflicts as colonists vied with other colonists and with landlords for control of the land. Even geographically marginal colonization areas became conflictive. Indeed, in twentieth-century Colombia, "colonization area" is synonymous with chronic conflicts and high degrees of violence. In the nineteenth century, they were one of the basic elements in the lack of interclass conflicts.

To take but one example, the Sumapaz region was one of the last colonization areas in the central core area of Colombia. In the 1920s, peasants who paid rent to landowners with vast stretches of land in the Alto Sumapaz began to claim that the lands were actually public domain and that they should be declared *colonos* ("colonists") rather than renters. Led by Erasmo Valencia, Guillermo Rodríguez, Jorge Eliécer Gaitán, and later by Juan de la Cruz Varela, peasant organizations in the area fought political and legal battles. Armed confrontations with the landlords who sought to evict the rebellious peasants also ensued. Beginning in 1932, many of the legal battles were won, the land was declared public, and it was subsequently parceled out among the peasants.[4]

The increase in the pressure to obtain Indian lands was important in

---

dad Nacional, 1974); Malcolm Deas, "Una Finca Cundinamarquesa entre 1870 y 1910" (Bogotá: CID, 1974).

[3] James Parsons, *Antioqueño Colonization in Western Colombia* (Berkeley and Los Angeles: University of California Press, 1949); Alvaro López Toro, *Migración y Cambio Social en Antioquia en el Siglo XIX* (Bogotá: CEDE, 1968); Medardo Rivas, *Los Trabajadores de Tierra Caliente* (Bogotá: Biblioteca Popular de Cultura Colombiana, 1946); José Fernando Ocampo, *Dominio de Clase en la Ciudad Colombiana* (Medellín: La Oveja Negra, 1972).

[4] Annie Caputo, "Las Luchas Agrarias del Sumapaz," unpublished *Licenciatura* thesis, Universidad de Los Andes (Bogotá, 1974). Similar conflicts also occurred in the municipalities of Icononzo and Cabrera, where landlords engaged in intense direct repression of peasants who claimed to be homesteaders rather than renters.

the South. The colonial and mid-nineteenth-century attacks on the reservations had destroyed all but isolated and undesirable Indian holdings on the Eastern Chain of the Andes. In the southern area of the Central Chain of the Andes, where the Indian population was and is the largest and densest in Colombia, the reservations survived. The increased pressure for Indian land met with resistance. The Indians were mobilized within the structure of their traditional tribal organizations to resist further incursions and to reclaim land that had been lost. The leader of this movement in Cauca was a self-educated Indian, Manuel Quintín Lame, who managed to combine the activities of several previously disperse indigeneous groups. Violence ensued between *latifundistas* and Indians and colonists (often sent by *latifundistas* to take the land). The movement reached its height in the period 1914–1916. The departmental and national governments began a systematic repression of the Indian movement, which included jailing the Indian leaders. The Cauca movement soon lost strength, although it continued in attentuated form until the 1970s, when it reappeared with renewed belligerency.

In the 1920s and 1930s, Indian movements took place in Southern Tolima and Northern Huila. One movement was Communist-oriented under the leadership of the Indians José Gonzálo Sánchez and Eutoquio Timoté (the Communist party's 1934 presidential candidate). Another movement, with traditional orientations, was led by Manuel Quintín Lame. They had in common the objective of recovering land. The de facto invasion of haciendas and government land was the most common tactic.[5]

For example, in Southern Tolima, Indians invaded the town of Coyaima and several haciendas of the region. In 1931, they were attacked by landlords and paramilitary vigilante groups in Llanogrande, where 17 died and 37 were wounded. In 1938, there was a massive wave of Indian land invasions in Ortega, Coello, and Saldaña; in 1939, they reestablished the reservation of Ortega and part of that of Chaparral despite a lack of official recognition. The Indians managed to retain permanent control of the land in the Yanguara area of Chaparral.[6]

[5] Darío Fajardo Montaña, "Los Sectores Indígenas en el Desarrollo del Capitalismo en Colombia," in *Indigenismo y Aniquilamiento de Indígenas en Colombia*, eds. Juan Friede, Nina S. Friedmann, and Darío Fajardo (Bogotá: Universidad Nacional, 1975), pp. 33–50; Gonzalo Castillo Cárdenas, "Introducción: Manuel Quintín Lame," in Manuel Quintín Lame, *En Defensa de mi Raza* (Bogotá: La Rosca, 1971), pp. xv–xxviii; Diego Castrillón Arboleda, *El Indio Quintín Lame* (Bogotá: Tercer Mundo, 1973). The ideological orientation of Lame is to be found in his aforecited work and in Manuel Quintín Lame, *Las Luchas del Indio que Bajó de la Montaña al Valle de la Civilización* (Bogotá: La Rosca, 1973). The background of the indigenous movements of the Central Cordillera is examined in Juan Friede, *El Indio en Lucha por la Tierra* (Bogotá: Editorial La Chispa, 1972).

[6] *El Tiempo*, Jan. 19, 1938; Gonzalo Castillo Cárdenas, "Introducción: Manuel Quintín Lame, Luchador e Intelectual Indígena," in Manuel Quintín Lame, *En Defensa*

The conflicts over land were closely related to conflicts over work relations in the countryside. The types and terms of rural productive relations became conflictive questions in the 1920s, especially with regard to renting and sharecropping. These conflicts were conditioned by a scarcity of cheap labor in the Colombian countryside at that time.

The shortage of cheap labor was in turn related to the economic boom that Colombia experienced in the 1920s. In 1921, Colombia and the United States ended the dispute over the United States' role in the separation of Panama from Colombia by virtue of a treaty that contemplated a compensation from the United States to Colombia of $25 million.[7] This arrangement also led to an expansion of United States private investment in Colombia (mostly in oil) from $30 million in 1920 to $280 million in 1929 and to a dynamic expansion of New York bank credit for Colombia public entities.[8] Combined with the indemnifiation, credits during the 1920s amounted to more than $200 million,[9] most of which entered the country in the period 1925–1928. Known as the "Dance of the Millions," this investment and credit boom were channeled mostly into oil operations and public works projects designed to improve the country's import–export infrastructure. Thus, roads and railways were constructed that were designed to connect different areas of the country with the fluvial routes to the sea. The expansion of Colombia's various, isolated railway lines from 1481 km in 1922 to 3262 km in 1934,[10] in addition to massive road construction, implied the employment of tens of thousands of unskilled wage laborers. In addition, business in general was stimulated by this influx of funds. An observer of the period wrote:

> The cause, and the basis, of this national economic crisis has its root exclusively in the undertaking of multitudes of private and public enterprises throughout the republic, sustained by copious national, departmental, and municipal loans; by the millions of the coffee crops; and by the easily obtained bank credit and lowering of interest rates produced by the abundance of liquidity. Oil exploitations that are intensified day to day, construction of the oleoduct, multiplication of the banana plantations, increase in the transport enterprises, advance of the railway, highways, and roads to the departments,

---

de mi Raza, pp. xxv–xxvii; Pierre Gilhodes, *Las Luchas Agrarias en Colombia* (Bogotá: La Carreta," 1972), p. 43; Absalón Machado, "Estudio de la Economía Cafetera de Colombia" (Medellín: Universidad de Antioguia, CIE, 1975), p. 28.

[7] Samuel Flagg Bemis, *The Latin American Policy of the United States* (New York: Harcourt, 1943), pp. 148–151.

[8] J. Fred Rippy, *The Capitalists and Colombia* (New York: Vanguard Press, 1931), p. 152.

[9] Tirado Mejía, *Introducción a la Historia Económica de Colombia* (Bogotá: Universidad Nacional, 1971), pp. 232–234.

[10] William Paul McGreevey, *An Economic History of Colombia* (Cambridge: Cambridge University Press, 1971), table 32, p. 256.

intendances, and "rural wards," construction of palaces, urban works, and buildings dedicated to housing, banking, and commerce in many cities and towns, the organization of large cattle ranches in the Intendency of Meta, the organization and development of new industries, among which we should mention the extractive ones, and the exodus of colonists to the jungles in search of rubber which once again has a high price have set a colossal demand for labor, for which we were not prepared. And, inasmuch as the firms backed by foreign capital and the official works can and do pay elevated wages, Colombian agriculture cannot resist the competition for manpower, and for this reason it has been left without even an indispensable minimum of workers.[11]

The real wages of agricultural workers increased by 30% in the period 1924–1927.[12] Agricultural interests, which had foreseen the impending increase in the wages of rural laborers, began to demand governmental action to facilitate cheap labor.[13] They also began to take steps in the countryside to prop up the institutions that guaranteed a supply of cheap labor and to attack those that lessened the availability of manpower.

Debt peonage, tax peonage, and physical coercion were some of the mechanisms used to keep laborers tied to a given hacienda or area. The Liberal newspaper *El Tiempo* in 1925 described the situation of the peasants in Boyacá:

> And if there is a section of the country in which the situation is even graver, it is Boyacá, in which the exploitation of the peons is iniquitous. The unpaid servant of all of the municipal powers, of the mayor, of the political boss, and of the parish priest, the peasant spends at least half of his work time repairing roads over which the landlords transit, serving as unpaid policeman, and working on the construction of the house of the Lord.[14]

In Boyacá, there existed the *servicio personal subsidiario,* which was a tax paid by the poor in the form of labor on roads. Peasants in arrears (most of them) were prohibited from leaving the *municipio* to which they were endebted. Debt peonage to landlords was also backed by local authorities in many areas of Colombia. During the 1920s jailings and violence were employed against peasants who rebelled against these circumstances,

[11] Cesáreo A. Pardo, "La Sociedad de Agricultores y el Problema de los Trabajadores," *El Tiempo*, Feb. 17, 1926.

[12] Salomón Kalmanovitz, "Evolución de la Estructura Agraria Colombiana," *Cuadernos Colombianos*, no. 3, pp. 355–363.

[13] As early as 1920 the *Sociedad de Agricultores de Colombia (SAC)* had requested the government to allow the free immigration of Japanese agricultural workers to offset the effects of increased construction and industrial expansion. See *El Tiempo*, Feb. 17, 1920. In 1926, the SAC requested the government to hire European and United States railway workers so as to return Colombian labor to the fields. Other measures included agricultural interests achieving free transport for workers traveling to labor-short areas on the Pacific Railway. See *El Tiempo*, Feb. 8, 1926.

[14] *El Tiempo*, Apr. 24, 1925.

especially in Boyacá and Cundinamarca. To facilitate the free mobility of wage labor toward the public works projects, the government introduced legislation in 1927. Defending the move, Minister Antonio Montalvo wrote in the preamble of the law:

> Events that have occurred recently with regard to the mobilization of masses of laborers from one region to another, which have been disturbed by both official and private entities, indicate the convenience of dictating legal measures which guarantee the absolute right of transit for workers who seek higher wages and better working conditions.[15]

Given the labor shortage, landlords began to attempt to evict unwanted colonists from remote areas of their haciendas and from neighboring government land. The lack of freely available land had led to an increase in "illegal" colonists. These small farmers were largely independent, especially when they possessed coffee or cacao plants, and they did not need to sell their labor to survive. Likewise, landlords attempted to stop the cultivation of cash crops on the individual plots of their sharecroppers and renters. They wanted these workers to plant only foodstuffs while deriving most of their cash income by working on the plots of the landlords. These socioeconomic processes led to acute conflicts and violence between landlords and colonists and between landlords and sharecroppers. Jailings, house burnings, crop destruction, and killings occurred in several areas, but especially in Western Cundinamarca.[16]

During the 1920s sharecropping was much more important than wage labor on the large coffee plantations. This institution entered into a profound and conflictive crisis as a result of the capitalistic boom of the 1920s. Sharecroppers began to demand larger shares of the joint produce and the right to plant cash crops on their own as well. In Cundinamarca especially, where the conditions of the sharecroppers were worse than those of most of the rest of the country,[17] strong social movements arose among the sharecroppers. In Viotá, Quilipe, La Mesa, El Colegio, Anolaima,

[15] *Anales del Senado*, Sept. 1, 1927, as cited in Oscar Rodríguez, *Efectos de la Gran Depresión en la Industria Colombiana* (Bogotá: n.p., 1974), p. 16. Apart from violent incidents, the Departmental Assembly of Boyacá had passed a resolution requiring a safe conduct pass for peasants seeking to leave the department to work in other areas. See Kalmanovitz, "Evolución de la Estructura Agraria," pp. 355–368.

[16] *El Tiempo*, June 11, July 31, Aug. 6, 1925. See also Alvaro Tirado Mejía, "La Tierra en Colombia," *Revista de Divulgación Popular de la Universidad Nacional*, no. 7 (Dec. 1970), p. 147; *Ministro de Gobierno 1933*, p. 4.

[17] *El Tiempo*, July 31, 1925. In the article entitled "La Triste Situación de los Campesinos de Cundinamarca" ("The Sad Situation of the Peasants of Cundinamarca"), the ex-minister of the Treasury, Jesús del Corral, enumerated debt peonage backed by local mayors who jailed errant sharecroppers and allowed forced labor for landlords, obligatory rural police tasks without remuneration for the municipality, and abuses against female peasants.

and San Antonio, sharecropper strikes at harvest time proved successful, given the scarcity of agricultural labor.[18]

Foreign loans, massive public works projects, and the "Dance of the Millions" in general all abruptly ended in 1929, as a result of the advent of the world depression in the United States. A new social contradiction emerged in the countryside, as unemployed workers returned from the cities and towns. The peasant movements that had been initiated and consolidated under the condition of labor shortage did not disappear under these new circumstances in those areas in which they had acquired high degrees of organization. Such was the case in the Sumapaz region, in Viotá, and in Quilipe; the Indian movement in Southern Tolima and Northern Huila and the peasant movement in parts of Tolima also did not subside. In areas with lesser levels of peasant organization, numerous conflicts were quickly repressed either by the government or directly by the landlords.[19]

The highly organized, and often politicized, peasant movements in Cundinamarca and Tolima were confronted by the government with a mix of repression and reform. In areas with protracted conflicts and in which the peasants had resisted repression, the governments of the 1930s resorted to limited local land reforms. The haciendas with conflicts were purchased by the government and parceled out among the peasants, who were to pay for the land across the years at easy terms. These reforms were undertaken on a case-by-case basis. They were designed to solve the "social problems" of specific haciendas and *municipios.*

An important example of this process is the lower Sumapaz region, near the city of Fusagasugá, where peasants on the hacienda "El Soche" organized to resist the conversion of the hacienda from agricultural sharecropping to extensive grazing, which would result in their eviction from the land. The resistance was successful, the landowners eventually sold the hacienda to the Department of Cundinamarca, and it was subsequently parceled out to the peasants. In the neighboring hacienda "El Chocho," the peasant movement began in 1929, when an organization was formed to demand changes in sharecropping agreements both from the landlords and from the government. By 1933, the peasants were well organized under the political auspices of Jorge Eliécer Gaitán's *Unión Nacional de Izquierda Revolucionaria* (UNIR, "National Union of the Revolutionary Left"). In 1933 groups of colonists invaded portions of the hacienda that they claimed to be government land, and they began to clear fields from the forest. The following rapid succession of events then occurred: 300 police-

[18] Machado, "Estudio de la Economia Cafetera," p. 26; Gilhodes, *Las Luchas Agrarias en Colombia,* p. 35.

[19] Apart from Cundinamarca and Tolima, weaker and less successful movements occurred in Santander, Santander del Norte, and Antioquia. For examples of the failures of these movements and their repression, see *El Tiempo* for the months of Sept. and Oct. 1933.

men were sent to the area; several other haciendas were invaded by colonists; the peasants marched on Fusagasugá in January 1934; there was an armed clash with the authorities, with 5 dead and 25 wounded; and, finally, several haciendas of the region, including "El Chocho," were parceled out among the peasants.[20]

In Viotá, Cundinamarca, peasants organized by the Communist party refused to pay rent to landowners, and they engaged in successful strikes that coincided with the coffee harvest. After years of protracted conflict and many violent incidents, several large holdings were divided among the renters and sharecroppers.[21] In Quilipe, Cundinamarca, a highly organized strike by coffee sharecroppers at harvest time in 1934 achieved improvements in working conditions.[22]

On the hacienda "Tolima," near the departmental capital of Ibagüé, sharecroppers who resisted an eviction clashed with the Guardia Civil del Tolima in 1934. The result was 14 peasant and 3 Civil Guard deaths.[23] After street demonstrations of protest in Ibagüé, which led to mass arrests, the Liberal Directorate of Tolima wrote the minister of government:

> Given the most delicate situation created by the imprudent sacrifice of the peasants of this municipality, on the hacienda "Tolima," as a means to solve the social conflicts that have emerged between capital and labor, we believe that this situation should be resolved with the highest regard for social justice, and we affirm the discontent of the Liberal masses of Tolima.[24]

The solution reached was to parcel the land and sell it to the sharecroppers with payments to be made over a 20-year period at low interest.[25] Throughout 1934, 1935, and 1936, the peasant movement continued to be a national political question. Renewed strikes in Quilipe and land disputes in El Colegio led to the parceling of some haciendas in those areas of Cundinamarca in 1936. Conflicts with sharecroppers continued throughout the country.

[20] *El Tiempo,* Aug. 1, 10–12, 19, Oct. 5, Dec. 7, 10, 16, 1933, and February 5–6, 1934; Tovar, *El Movimiento Campesino,* pp. 66–72, 76–86.

[21] *El Tiempo,* May 19, 1931, Feb. 3–4, 19, 24, March 1, 1932, and Jan. 27, Sept. 13, 1934. In 1932 violent incidents between peasants and police in Viotá led to an armed clash, with 4 deaths and 25 wounded. See Machado, *"Estudio de la Economía Cafetera,"* p. 26. In 1934, the Secretary of Government of the Department of Cundinamarca, Carlos Lleras Restrepo, organized a *Junta de Acción Social* (Social Action Board) to resolve the chronic agrarian conflicts of the region; see *El Tiempo,* Jan. 27, 1934.

[22] Partido Comunista de Colombia, *Treinta Años de Lucha del Partido Comunista en Colombia* (Bogotá: Ediciones Paz y Socialismo, 1960), pp. 24–26; *El Tiempo,* Dec. 1, 3–4, 1934; Tovar; *El Movimiento Campesino,* pp. 74–76.

[23] *El Tiempo,* Aug. 15, 1934; Tovar, *El Movimiento Campesino,* pp. 72–74.

[24] *El Tiempo,* Aug. 16, 1934.

[25] *El Tiempo,* Oct. 6, 1934.

Absalón Machado characterizes the period as one of "strikes, confrontation, the eviction of families from the haciendas, attacks on haciendas by groups of peasants, the burning of homes, and invasions of the haciendas."[26]

The crisis provoked by widespread agrarian conflict and violence led to Law 200 of 1936, by which the government of Alfonso Lópoz Pumarejo abandoned the case-by-case approach and attempted to deal with the agrarian problems on the national level. The law specified the social function of property, demanded that rural property be exploited, and specified the conditions by which colonists, renters, and sharecroppers might obtain legal title to the land they worked. The net effects of the law included clearing up the confusion and anarchy with regard to legal titles to land holdings in Colombia, political opposition to the government by both Liberal and Conservative *latifundistas,* the eviction of large numbers of sharecroppers and renters from the haciendas because the landowners feared they might qualify for legal title to the plots, and the conversion of many haciendas from labor-intensive agriculture to low-labor, extensive cattle grazing as a means of avoiding labor conflicts. The passage of the law also had the effect of diminishing, but not eliminating, agrarian conflicts because the peasants began to wait for a legal agrarian reform that never materialized.[27]

In summary, beginning in the mid-1910s, agrarian conflicts became an important factor in Colombian political life. This marked a sharp departure from the second half of the nineteenth century in which there was very little interclass conflict in the countryside. At that time, the countryside was characterized by the stability of existing socioeconomic insitutions. The renewed interclass conflict in the countryside led to the increasing importance of the state in structuring conflictive, agrarian relations. This is important in the "partial collapse of the state" hypothesis because, when the state suffered a severe power deflation, it ceased to structure these

[26] Machado, "Estudio de la Economía Cafetera, p. 27.

[27] Discussions of Law 22 of 1936 and its impact in the agrarian conflicts of the period are to be found in: Alonso Tobón, *La Tierra y la Reforma Agraria en Colombia* (Medellín: La Oveja Negra, 1972), pp. 34–40; Machado, "Estudio de la Economía Cafetera," chap. 3; Kalmanovitz, "Evolución de la Estructura Agraria," pp. 363–368; Smith, *Colombia: Social Structure,* pp. 247–252; Estanislao Zuleta and ANUC, *La Tierra en Colombia* (Medellín: La Oveja Negra, 1973), pp. 63–66, 80, 95; Zuleta and ANUC, "Consideraciones sobre la Lucha en el Campo Colombiano," in *La Tierra en Colombia,* pp. 105, 108; Gilhodes, *Las Luchas Agrarias,* pp. 41–43; Darío Mesa, *El Problema Agrario en Colombia: 1920–1960* (Bogotá: El Tigre de Papel, 1972), pp. 53–103; Alvaro Tirado Mejía, *Introducción a la Historia Económica de Colombia* (Bogotá: Universidad de Colombia, 1971), pp. 259–264.

Despite the law, some agrarian conflicts continued in Cundinamarca, Tolima, Caldas, Antioquia, Bolívar, and Magdalena. For examples, see *El Tiempo,* Jan. 3, 17, 21, Feb. 2, 4, 6, 7, May 1, July 3, 1937, and Jan. 11, 19, 25, 28, 29, Mar. 31, Apr. 9, 1939.

relations efficaciously, and the contradictory interests of the agrarian sector evolved in many areas into social conflicts with high potentials for violence.

THE LABOR MOVEMENT

Colombia's industrial infrastructure, with few exceptions, only began to develop at the beginning of the century. World War I increased national industry only very modestly, but in the 1920s the country's general economic boom was accompanied by a rapid expansion of industry.

Darío Mesa asserts that Colombia never has had a period of faster modernization than that which occurred in the period 1925–1930.[28] Oscar Rodríguez presents convincing evidence that the country's industrial base was consolidated in this period and then expanded during the Depression and World War II.[29]

The process of industrialization, as well as the concomitant capitalist modernization of other sectors of the economy, led to social change and social conflict in Colombian society. Notable are the further reduction of artisan production and the emergence and growth of the proletariat.

The Colombian proletariat, apart from disperse rural wage laborers, was born in the coastal and fluvial ports and on the riverboats of the Magdalena. Both the construction and operation of railroads further enlarged the number of wage laborers. The massive railway and road expansion of the "Dance of the Millions" in the 1920s led to another increase in the number of peasants subjected to the new capitalist modality of social productive relations. The development of industry and of the tertiary sector of the economy also added to the numbers of proletarians and to the stability of this social class.

Labor organizations of artisans and of transport workers began to develop at the beginning of the century. There were a few isolated strikes undertaken by these weak and ineffectual groups.[30] The year 1918 marked

[28] Darío Mesa, "Treinta Años de Historia Colombiana," in *Colombia: Estructura Política y Agraria* (Bogotá: Edición Estrategia, 1971), p. 22.

[29] Rodríguez, *Efectos de la Gran Depresión*, passim. See also Luis Ospina Vásquez, *Industria y Protección en Colombia (1810–1930)* (Medellín: E.S.P., 1955), pp. 456–457.

Other works concerning industrialization and related topics include: Mario Arrubla, ed. *Estudios sobre el Subdesarrollo Colombiano* (Bogotá: Tigre de Papel, 1971; Carmenza Gallo," Hipótesis de la Acumulación Originaria de Capital en Colombia" (Medellín: Editorial La Pulga, 1974); Tirado Mejía, *Introducción a la Historia Económica*, chap. 18; Centro de Estudios Anteo Quimbaya, "Formación del Capitalismo en Colombia," *Revista Estudios Marxistas*, no. 4 (Sept. 1974), pp. 43–97; J. Fred Rippy, *El Capital* *Revista Estudios Marxistas*, no. 4 (Sept. 1974), pp. 43–97; J. Fred Rippy, *El Capital* *Norteamericano y la Penetración Imperialista* (Medellín: La Oveja Negra, 1971), passim. Jesús Bejarano, *El Capital Monopolista y las Inversiones Privadas Norteamericanas en Colombia* (Bogotá: Circulo Rojo Editores, 1972), passim. Salomón Kalmanovitz, "Sobre Algunas Teorías del Imperialismo en Colombia," *Ideología y Sociedad*, no. 10 (April–June, 1974), pp. 39–74.

[30] The history of organized labor in Colombia is examined in the following works: Ignacio Torres Giraldo, *Los Inconformes: Historia de la Rebeldía de Masas en Colom-*

the beginning of increased organizational activity, labor unrest, and recourse to the strike as a means of struggle. That year port and railway strikes in Barranquilla, Cartagena, and Santa Marta led to riots, to the declaration of the "state of siege" along the Caribbean Coast, and to substantial wage increases for the strikers.[31] Artisan protests in 1919 over the importation of military uniforms led to a bloody clash in the Plaza Bolívar in Bogotá.[32] During the period 1919–1920, there was a wave of strikes, the most important being those of railway workers in Cundinamarca, in El Dorado, and on the Caribbean Coast, the strike of gold miners in Antioquia, and the strike of female textile workers in Bello, Antioquia.[33] The success of these movements in obtaining wage increases of up to 40% led to strikes in other sectors as well. The wave of labor organization and strikes in the city and countryside was unprecedented for Colombia. *El Tiempo* editorialized: "It is impossible to continue the state of insecurity and anxiety produced by the constant outbreak of strikes in different parts of the country, some explicable by too low salaries, and others occasioned by excessive demands.[34]

There was less strike activity in the period 1921–1923. One reason for this was that the Liberal party, which had supported the rise of the labor movement, channeled labor's energies into the partisan battle associated with Benjamín Herrera's 1922 presidential campaign. The tense, warlike atmosphere after the Liberal's defeat also reduced activity.[35] A new wave of organizational effort and strikes began in 1924.[36] In that year the First Workers' Congress was held, and one year later the second congress founded the *Confederación Obrera Nacional* (CON, "National Workers' Confederation"). This labor organization was a coalition of socialists, anarchists, and Liberals.[37]

---

bia (Bogotá: Editorial Margen Izquierdo, 1973–1974, vols. 3–5; Edgar Caicedo, *Historia de las Luchas Sindicales en Colombia* (Bogotá: Editorial Suramérica, 1971); Miguel Urrutia, *Historia del Sindicalismo en Colombia* (Bogotá: Universidad de Los Andes, 1969); Daniel Pecaut, *Política y Sindicalismo en Colombia* (Bogotá: La Carreta, 1973); Ignacio Torres Giraldo, *María Cano: Mujer Rebelde* (Bogotá: La Rosca, 1972).

[31] Urrutia, *Historia del Sindicalismo*, pp. 88–89.

[32] Rodríguez, *Efectos de la Gran Depresión*, pp. 6–7

[33] *El Tiempo*, Jan. 3, Feb. 14, 16, 18, Mar. 3, 6, 1920. See also Torres Giraldo, *Los Inconformes*, vol. 3, pp. 119–127. The Bello strikers won a 40% raise, the promise of no reprisals, and the right to wear shoes (previously denied them because the owners thought that the poor became "uppity" when they put shoes on).

[34] *El Tiempo*, Feb. 22, 1920.

[35] Torres Giraldo, vol. 3, pp. 150–153, 184–185.

[36] *El Tiempo*, Apr. 10, 29, June 16, Oct. 8, 16, Nov. 6, 15, 1924, and Jan. 1, 1925. Torres Giraldo, *Los Inconformes*, vol. 3, pp. 193–209; Urrutia, *Historia del Sindicalismo*, pp. 123–126.

[37] *El Tiempo*, May 1, 5, 16, 1924. Torres Giraldo, *Los Inconformes*, vol. 3, pp. 176–179, 220–225.

In 1925, railway strikes in Cundinamarca, especially the successful strike of the Ferrocarril del Pacífico in Valle, led to an increase in the strength of the labor movement. In 1926, the Third Workers' Congress formed the *Partido Socialista Revolucionario* (PSR, "Revolutionary Socialist Party"). This party began to coordinate the labor movement. Thus, in 1927, a strike against the Tropical Oil Company in Barrancabermeja proved to be highly effective. The government reacted by declaring the oil-producing port city to be under a state of siege. The labor movement responded with secondary strikes throughout the nation's transport infrastructure. To break the strike, the government clashed with strikers (four dead, three wounded) and massively jailed labor leaders throughout the country.[38]

The most belligerent strikes were directed against foreign enclave production, such as the 1924 and 1927 strikes against the Tropical Oil Company in Barrancabermeja and the 1924 and 1928 strikes against the United Fruit Company in the banana-producing region of the Department of Magdalena. The principal demand of the 30,000 banana workers was to be recognized as employees of the United Fruit Company. The company hired laborers through small labor contractors in order to avoid Colombian labor legislation. United Fruit was particularly vulnerable because early in 1928 *El Tiempo* had published an exposé of how the company controlled local officials in the Department of Magdalena.[39] Local merchants supported the strike since one of the demands was to end payment in script redeemable only in merchandise at company stores.[40] Furthermore, the Colombian national government was in conflict with United Fruit over the refusal of the company's railway to transport the bananas of independent Colombian producers to the port of Santa Marta. The 1928 *Memoria* of the minister of industry states: "The government recognizes the right of private banana producers to industrial independence from the United Fruit Company and should extricate them from the circle of iron [with] which the American Company has surrounded them." [41]

United Fruit was also in conflict with the Colombian government over the latter's attempt to regulate water usage in the zone that would end the company's unlimited use of irrigation waters.[42] In sum, different phases of

[38] *El Tiempo*, Dec. 5, 1926 (Platform of the Partido Revolucionario Socialista). For the oil strike, see *El Tiempo*, Oct. 11, 1926, Jan. 20, 22, 23, 25, 27–28, 31, Feb, 2–4, 6, 15, 24, 1927. See also Torres Giraldo, *Los Inconformes*, vol. 4, pp. 3–12, 19–35; Urrutia, *Historia del Sindicalismo*, pp. 126–127

[39] *El Tiempo*, Apr. 13, 1928.

[40] Camila Botero and Angela Gómez de Martínez, "La Huelga de las Bananeras," unpublished essay, Universidad de Los Andes (Bogotá, 1972), p. 9.

[41] United States, Department of State, *Papers Related to the Foreign Relations of the United States 1928* (Washington, D.C.; United States Government Printing Office, 1943), vol. 2, pp. 596–597.

[42] *El Tiempo*, Mar. 24, 1928. See also United States, Department of State, *Papers Related to Foreign Relations 1928*, vol. 2, pp. 635–637.

United Fruit's absolute control of its enclave were under attack from different sectors of Colombian society.

The strike developed in November and December 1928. The Colombian government labor inspector sent to mediate the dispute was jailed by local officials obligated to the United Fruit Company after he issued a report favorable to the worker's position. United Fruit subsequently arranged for government support at the highest level in Bogotá. Nonetheless, the strike proved surprisingly effective. The strikers impeded the introduction of new laborers to cut the bananas and blocked the railway lines with their bodies.

The Colombian government sent troops to the region. Isolated incidents occurred between the army and the strikers. Over 400 leaders were jailed, but the powerful movement persisted. The local power structure of the Caribbean coastal region began to demand stern government action, partly because they feared United States military intervention. Only months before, United States Marines had reentered Nicaragua for the third time for the stated purpose of "defending American lives and property," both of which were progressively in greater jeopardy as the violent incidents of the banana strike escalated. Finally, the Colombian army fired on strikers assembled for a demonstration on December 6, 1928, at Ciénaga, and for days thereafter there were running battles between troops and strikers throughout the banana zone. The government categorized the violence as the initiation of the communist revolution that Conservative officials had warned about when urging legislation to restrict civil liberties. The banana worker's strike was violently repressed and the Colombian labor movement suffered a serious setback. In the wake of the defeat, most of the labor and socialist leaders in the country were jailed. The Conservative government, however, also lost strength because it was discredited in subsequent months for the "Massacre of the Banana Zone," whose unknown death toll was estimated in the hundreds.

In sum, in the period 1918–1939 an increasingly organized and belligerent union movement channeled interclass labor conflicts. Thus, a further set of social contradictions matured into a sociopolitical situation already characterized by acute agrarian conflicts and the continuation of political party violence, a topic to which we now turn.

Political Conflict and Violence in the Liberal Republic

The 1930 elections were accompanied by violent incidents.[43] Much more violent, however, were the subsequent years in which the nearly totally

[43] In the nineteenth century, the massive division of the ruling party from top to bottom would have presented conditions propitious for an attempt by the opposition party to gain power by the force of arms. The 1930 switch from the Conservatives to

Conservative public administration became "liberalized." In the period 1930–1934, Liberals and Conservatives engaged in a major power confrontation. Electoral contests became highly violent as both parties vied for exclusivistic power. In the simple and direct terms of an official document of the period: "Each party aspires to exercise the totality of power to the exclusion of its adversary." [44]

In the light of intense violence prior to the 1931 local elections, the Liberal daily *El Espectador* editorialized:

> We are in the presence of facts that it is not convenient or possible to hide: The political parties undertake their electoral activities with revolutionary impetus and open disobedience toward the authorities and the law, and they do this under the pretext that the former are inefficacious in effectively protecting their right to vote. . . . The government, for its part, limits itself, in most cases, to objecting timidly to this arbitrary thesis, and to demanding as a favor of the political directorates and the electoral agents that they voluntarily observe the evangelical precept that all creatures should love each other mutually. By this road and by these procedures, we will arrive within two weeks [the date of impending local elections] to the final catastrophe, whose tragic characteristics are already visible.[45]

The 1931 local elections were accompanied by accusations of political interventions by the clergy,[46] electoral violence,[47] and widespread recourse to fraud. On occasion, fraud was mutually accepted, and it served as a mechanism for eliminating violence. For example, in several municipalities of the Department of Bolívar, local politicians negotiated pacts between

---

the Liberals and the 1946 shift from the Liberals to the Conservatives marked dramatic changes in the rules of the political game.

The new rules would seem to indicate that a party that was divided from top to bottom, with that division being verified by an electoral process, lost its right to govern.

There was a conflict-prone lack of unanimity with regard to these new rules. As an indication of the survival of sectarianism in Colombia despite the violence and the subsequent Frente Nacional, one of the three most important Conservative leaders in Colombia told me during a 1973 interview that Miguel Abadía Méndez "must have been crazy to have given up power to the Liberals in 1930."

For the 1930 elections, see: República de Colombia, Ministerio de Gobierno, *Memorias* (Bogotá: Imprenta Nacional, 1931), pp. v–vi. (This annual series of official reports by the minister of government to the Congress will henceforth be cited *Ministro de Gobierno* with the appropriate year.) Electoral violence was particularly acute in Chinquinquirá, Coyaima, Lebrija Cocuy, and Anolaima.

44 *Ministro de Gobierno 1930*, p. xi.

45 *El Espectador*, Jan. 13, 1931.

46 For examples of these accusations, see *El Espectador*, Jan. 2, 7, 1931.

47 Over 100 persons were killed in the violence that accompanied the local elections of 1931; see *Ministro de Gobierno 1931*, pp. ix, x. The most affected areas were Montería (10 deaths, 20 wounded), Capitanejo, Cucutilla, Sogamoso, Espinal, and La Cité; see *El Tiempo*, Feb. 1, 2, 9, 25, 1931.

the two parties prior to the elections by which the results were predetermined; both parties then conspired to produce the desired electoral return fraudulently.[48]

In the entire period between 1930 and 1946, as was also the case with the previous Conservative Republic, no one in Colombia denied the existence of widespread electoral fraud and coercion. Indeed, it was accepted as a political fact of life. For example, the minister of government in 1933 stated that, despite the efforts of the government, the elections of that year "registered scandalous frauds." [49] The official report then continued: "The political parties that wish to win seek to defeat the adversary, be it by means of fraud, coercion, or violence." [50] The official panacea at that point in time was to implement a law that required all citizens to obtain a *national* identification card (*cédula de ciudadanía*), which would be demanded of prospective voters. The minister of government was of the opinion that this was "the only mechanism which could avoid fraud and assure a pure suffrage." [51]

The end result of the application of this measure was that in subsequent years accusations of fraud revolved less around the counting of votes and more around the issuance of, or failure to issue, national identification cards.[52]

Party violence, as well as violence conditioned by other factors, con-

[48] *Ministro de Gobierno 1931*, pp. xxvii, c.
[49] *Ministro de Gobierno 1933*, p. vi.
[50] *Ministro de Gobierno 1933*, p. xi.
[51] *Ministro de Gobierno 1933*, p. 45.
[52] Disputes over identification cards and violence to keep opponents away from the polls were politically important throughout the 1930s and 1940s. In a letter to Eduardo Santos on the day before his assumption of the presidency, the National Conservative Directorate observed:

> In the popular elections that have been undertaken since 1934 the Conservative party has not been able to participate due to invincible physical obstacles. On the one hand, it has lacked electoral identification cards for the vast majority of its voters, and, on the other hand, the environment of violence which predominates in many regions of the country, with unquestionable majorities belonging to our party, have made null and void the right to vote for even the few Conservatives with the electoral identification card. (*El Siglo*, Aug. 7, 1938)

The ministers of government of the period generally alleged that it was impossible to control the widespread phenomenon. For example, in 1935, the minister of government complained that the Conservative delegates named to electoral commissions did not accept the posts due to their party's abstention, the Office of Identification (*Cedulación*) was incapable of controlling fraud, there was complete impunity with regard to electoral crimes, sectarian officials were given promotions, and there were departments such as Boyacá in which the Conservatives did not have identification cards (*cédulas*); see *Ministro de Gobierno 1936*, pp. xxvii–xxviii. In 1942, the official in charge of elections wrote that "the Office of Identification does not have the means to impede or invalidate the abundant issuance of identification cards to minors. . . . The identification cards in circulation exceed reality and the electoral census is inflated" (*Ministro de Gobierno 1942*, pp. 103–104).

tinued and intensified during 1931[53] and reached a peak in 1932. The minister of government, Agustín Morales Olaya, summarized the 1932 situation:

> Despite there not having been any electoral contest in the course of the year being considered, there have occurred extremely sensitive bloody incidents, centering in Norte de Santander, the García Róvira province in the Department of Santander, and the western region of Boyacá. The pretext of these savage events is politics and the struggle between two old parties, to take for themselves even the lowliest of official positions, relegating the opposite party to the most absolute exclusion. But if it is certain that the political misunderstanding between those who seek an exclusive political predominance is important in these unfortunate events, it is no less true that, with the aid of party passions, vengeances of other varieties are executed, in which there are mixed old family quarrels and disputes over land boundaries between small and large proprietors.[54]

Land disputes, traditional village rivalries, and conflicts over control of the local power structure began to develop into violence in 1932. Local power struggles were frequent in western Boyacá (Saboyá, Briceño, Pauna, and Maripí).[55] Notable among the village rivalries was that between the Conservatives of San Andrés and the Liberals of Guasca, which led to full-scale battles.[56] Forced land abandonments and coerced land sales accompanied the violence. The lands of those who migrated out of the violent areas were exploited by others, with conflicts often arising over who would take such land in usufruct. In Palmito, Bolívar (today Sucre), the widespread burning of houses (often of partisan opponents) led to land abandonments.[57] The intense violence in Norte de Santander involved most of the aforementioned varieties of sociopolitical violence.[58]

[53] Violence occurred with particular intensity in Piedacuesta (Sabanata), the entire province of García Rovira in Santander, Saboyá, Ciénaga de Oro, Chinquinquirá, Capitanejo, Pacho, and Pamplona; see *El Tiempo*, Mar.–Dec. 1931. In Piedacuesta, the violence assumed the form of a general, but local, uprising against the authority of the government with the men of the municipality taking to the mountains; see *El Tiempo*, Sept. 1, 3, 1931. In Chiquinquirá, the assassination of Conservative leader Arcadio Supelano Medina led to military occupation of the city, and, in Bogotá, Conservative members of Congress protesting the Chinquinquirá killing ceased to attend sessions temporarily; see *El Espectador*, Mar. 30, 31, 1931.

[54] *Ministro de Gobierno 1932*, p. iii.

[55] *El Tiempo*, Jan. 8, Mar. 24, 30, May 23, 1931. In neighboring Guachetá, Cundinamarca, a coal-mining center, the local violence became characterized by dynamite attacks; see *El Tiempo*, Jan. 5, 18, 1932.

[56] *El Tiempo*, Mar. 31, Apr. 1, 5, 1932. Such attacks were repeated throughout García Rovira and in neighboring Boyacá between neighboring *veredas* ("rural neighborhoods").

[57] On one occasion, 38 homes were burned, and 25 more within a month, in the same municipality of Palmito; see *El Tiempo*, Jan. 9, 16, 1932.

[58] See *El Tiempo* for the year 1932. Principal centers of violence in this department were Arboledas, Cucutilla, Chinacota, Mutiscua, Ragonnalia, Pamplonita, Pamplona, and Ocaña.

The government sent troops, extra police, and special judges to these violent areas.[59] It also abolished the "*guardias civiles*," the often highly partisan local police who were the prime protagonists of violence in some localities.[60] The government also took other steps that recognized socioeconomic factors in the conflicts. For example, work was intensified on the Northern Highway for the purpose of creating jobs in the García Rovira province of Santander; this step was explicitly announced as a measure designed to aid in the pacification of the region.[61]

Violence decreased in intensity in most areas during 1932. The only exception to this rule was Norte de Santander, where it not only increased but also became more organized. In Arboleda and Cucutilla, the police were violently run out of town and army troops had to occupy those localities. In Chinacota, there were armed confrontations between Conservative and Liberal civilians.[62]

Violence abruptly ended in 1933, and the Liberal hegemony was consolidated. An important factor in both events, as well as in postponing the maturation of interclass conflicts in the countryside, was a border war with Peru. Incidents in the Amazon Basin and especially in the Leticia region led to battles against the Peruvians. The Colombian army was commanded in the conflict by Conservative General Alfredo Vásquez Cobo, and the country experienced an intense national mobilization in order to prepare for its first international conflict since the Gran Colombia period. However, what appeared to be an impending full-scale war was aborted and settled by diplomatic means. The conflict's domestic effect was largely to halt the partisan conflict for political hegemony, the violence related to it, and agrarian struggles in the countryside.[63]

[59] *Ministro de Gobierno 1932*, pp. iii–v, 4 ff.

[60] The Conservatives controlled some Guardias Civiles. Their principal complaint in the Santanderes was that the departmental police controlled by the Liberals acted in an arbitrary, partisan fashion; see *El Tiempo*, Apr. 1, 1932. The Liberals, on the other hand, complained that army troops sent to García Rovíra were partial to the Conservatives; see *El Tiempo*, Apr. 2, 1932. For the abolition of the Guardias Civiles, see *El Tiempo*, Mar. 18, 1932.

[61] *Ministero de Gobierno 1932*, pp. iii–v; *El Tiempo*, Jan. 28, 1932.

[62] *El Tiempo*, Jan. 22, Feb. 6, 1933.

[63] *El Tiempo*, 1933. The conflict reached crisis proportions in Jan., diplomatic relations were broken and battles began in Feb., and hostilities were ended in May. The conflict would appear to have been closely related to domestic Peruvian as well as Colombian politics. On Apr. 30, 1931, the Peruvian dictator Sánchez Cerro was assassinated in Lima, and in the course of the subsequent month hostilities were ended; see *El Tiempo*, May 1, 1933. Diplomatic negotiations continued for the remainder of the year, with the most important being the visit to Peru in December of the Liberal party's declared choice to succeed Olaya Herrera in the presidency, Alfonso López Pumarejo; see *El Tiempo*, Dec. 14, 1933.

The importance of the Peruvian conflict in Colombian politics may be appreciated from the following summary of declarations given by Olaya Herrera when analyzing

Electoral returns in 1933 demonstrated clear Liberal majorities for the first time in the century. After the October 1933 elections, the Conservative party announced its future abstention from national electoral contests, alleging massive fraud. The Conservative party leadership was declaring its defeat in the struggle to stem the implementation of a Liberal party hegemony, and it was adopting the defensive opposition strategy that the Liberals had previously employed in the 1920s. The Liberal political hegemony had been consolidated and the transition in control of the public administration had been achieved.[64]

The last instances of "transitional" violence occurred in January 1934. In the Norte de Santander municipalities of Arboledas, Cucutilla, and Sardinata, there occurred movements that the government and the Liberal press described as banditry. In Arboledas, groups of Conservative guerrillas entrenched in nearby *veredas* ("rural neighborhoods") confronted army

---

his administration for the press (*El Tiempo*, July 12, 1934: "Transcendental Resumen de la Labor de su Gobierno Hizo el Doctor Olaya"). He stated that in 1930 there did not exist parties based on doctrines, but rather personalistic factions and a complete lack of ideas, and that, had it not been for a new factor that entered on the political scene, the situation would have degenerated into a new civil war. From 1930 to 1932 the economy was on the floor. Unemployment, bankruptcies, lack of credit, and fiscal and economic crises threatened here, as everywhere in the world, to destroy everything. But in the remaining 2 years Colombia reacted favorably, and today Colombia is envied by many countries. He stated that the international conflict with Peru had occupied all of the country's resources and energies and that "today we are a nation despite all of the predictions to the contrary."

[64] Violence still accompanied the elections in some localities. In the Murillo district of the municipality of Líbano in Tolima, police sent to inspect the election and the local Conservative community engaged in battles in which there were several deaths; see *El Tiempo*, Feb. 5, 1933. In both the Feb. and Oct. elections the Liberals claimed victories, including majorities in the previously Conservative departments of Boyacá, Norte de Santander, and Magdalena; see *El Tiempo*, Feb. 6, Oct. 2, 1933. In Oct., the Liberals gained control of 366 municipal councils to the Conservatives' 185; *El Tiempo*, Oct. 3, 1933. Within Liberal ranks, talk began of the Liberal Republic, and within Conservative spheres talk was of total electoral abstention. See, for example, the following editorial in *El Tiempo* for the "flavor" of the political environment on election day, Feb. 11, 1934:

> Today's elections have the virtue of being the first genuinely Liberal manifestation to indicate to the country the decision of the Left to take upon its shoulders the integral responsibility of the public administration. There is no reason to hide that Liberalism seeks to direct the country's business with the aim of introducing substantial modifications in Colombian life. . . . The Liberal Republic did not spring forth from conspiracies or military coups, but rather from elections. It is the capitalization of half a century of hopes and fatigues. . . . The electoral abstention of the Conservatives has not been the fruit of indignation but rather of a lack of will. . . . Today the reinforced minorities of '99 [the year the War of a Thousand Days began] prepare to occupy power under their entire responsibility, within the theory of hegemonic government.

troops sent to dominate them. The struggle there had become an open rebellion.[65] In the García Rovira region of Santander, a group of Conservative peasants estimated at 200 men attacked the Liberal community of Guasca,[66] and in wholly Conservative Boavita, Boyacá, some 300 Conservatives attacked the Liberal-controlled city hall.[67] With reference to the rebellion in Norte de Santander, the National Conservative Directorate issued a statement signed by Laureano Gómez, Abel Carbonell, and Augusto Ramírez Moreno to the following effect, as quoted in *El Tiempo:*

> The Conservative party upon its retirement from power in 1930 passed on the departments of Santander and Santander del Norte in peace; then came the Liberal government and there were constant outrages committed by the authorities against the peasants of the aforementioned departments; and the directorate of the party as well as the Conservative press pointed out to the government what consequences these outrages might bring.
>
> In light of the events that have occurred in the department of Norte de Santander, the supreme directors of the party declare that it is not a question of banditry, as has been alleged, but rather of peasants defending themselves against outrages against life and property committed by the local authorities with the compliance of the current Liberal national government.[68]

The Conservative revolts were dominated and the Conservatives retired to an abstentionist opposition. One effect of the electoral abstention of the Conservatives was to reduce campaign and election-day violence.[69] Isolated incidents of partisan violence continued across the years. The most important was the attack by departmental customs officers (*Resguardo de Cundinamarca*) against a Conservative meeting in Gachetá in 1939.[70] Electoral violence increased somewhat in 1939, when the Conservatives began once again to participate in some electoral contests. Politics, however, occurred within the context of the consolidated hegemony of the Liberal party.

[65] *El Tiempo*, Jan. 3, 5, 6, 7, 9, 1934; *El Espectador*, Jan. 5, Feb. 26, 1934; *Ministro de Gobierno 1934*, pp. xxxiii–xxxvii, 32.

[66] *El Espectador*, Jan. 10, 1934.

[67] *El Tiempo*, Jan. 17, 18, 1934.

[68] *El Tiempo*, Jan. 10, 1934.

[69] This peace was referred to by the minister of government in 1934 in the following terms: "These electoral debates demonstrate the civic disposition of the people and the firm political stability of the country" *Ministro de Gobierno 1934*, p. xxiv). This observation was made despite the nearly total Conservative abstention.

[70] *Ministro de Gobierno 1939*, p. xxiii; *El Siglo*, Jan. 9, 10, 11, 1939. A similar, but smaller, incident involving departmental customs officials had occurred in La Uvita, Boyacá, in 1934; *El País*, Dec. 29, 1934. In 1939, the removal of troops from Arboledas, Norte de Santander, led to a new attack on the police, the siege of the town, and a return of the troops; *El Espectador*, Jan. 3, 1939. Electoral violence in October 1939 led to deaths in Pendamó, Cauca, and in Mutiscua, Norte de Santander; *El Siglo*, Oct. 2, 1939.

Factionalism was important in the dominant Liberal party throughout the Liberal Republic. In the end, internal divisions weakened the party to the point that it lost power. The social reformist government of Alfonso López Pumarejo (1934–1938) met with the opposition of large landowners who felt threatened by the government's agrarian policy and the opposition of the Catholic Church, which opposed moves toward secularization.[71] In a step toward unity, the Liberals chose Eduardo Santos to succeed López. The Santos government was much less reformist. The campaign to reelect Alfonso López Pumarejo in 1942 led to a formal rift within the party and to the dissident presidential candidacy of Carlos Arango Vélez. The Vélez candidacy was overwhelmingly supported by the Conservatives. Indeed, the municipal distribution of the 1942 Vélez vote correlates strongly with the municipal distribution of the Conservative vote in 1948 ($r = .768$).[72] López won the elections (which were reputedly fraudulent) and, although his second administration was much less reformist than his first, he faced strong opposition not only from the Conservatives but also from important segments of the Liberal party. These are some of the elements that led to the military coup attempt of 1944, the resignation of President López in 1945, and the division of the Liberal party for the 1946 presidential elections.

In July 1944, López Pumarejo was captured during a visit to Pasto and detained by army units commanded by Colonel Diógenes Gil. Other Conservative-commanded troops also joined the plot, including one unit from Santander that began to march on Bogotá but stopped in Boyacá. In the capital, First Designate Darío Echandía assumed the presidency, achieved the allegiance of the garrisons in Bogotá, and politically defeated the weak and badly coordinated coup attempt. After this incident, the López government removed several Conservative officers from the army and temporarily suspended civil liberties.[73]

[71] Dissident Liberals attempted unsuccessfully to oppose López by means of a political organization known as the *Asociación Patriótica Económica Nacional* (APEN; "National Patriotic Economic Association"). The opposition of the church to the government was vigorous. The church opposed, among other things, a constitutional amendment that would permit freedom of faith. Ismael Perdomo, the archbishop of Bogotá, declared: "The state that would adopt the liberty of cults . . . with a 99% Catholic population would be gravely lacking in its duties with God and would renounce a very efficacious means to reconcile the obedience and veneration of its citizens" (República de Colombia Senado, *Anales del Senado*, nos. 126–127, Nov. 12, 1935). See also *El Tiempo* and *El Siglo* for the period Oct. 1935–Mar. 1936.

[72] Paul Oquist, "Las Elecciones Presidenciales, 1930–1970," in *Boletín Mensual de Estadística*, ed. República de Colombia, Departamento Administrativo Nacional de Estadística (DANE), nos. 268–269 (Nov.–Dec. 1973), p. 71.

[73] República de Colombia, Presidencia de la República, *Documentos Relacionados con la Reuncia del Presidente López y el Orden Público* (Bogotá: Imprenta Nacional, 1945), "Los Sucesos de Pasto Relatados por el Presidente Alfonso López" (a letter of

The Conservative opposition to López Pumarejo, Liberal dissensions, and a series of scandals in the administration involving the president's family reached the point where López resigned from the presidency in 1945.[74] Alberto Lleras Camargo served out the remaining year of the presidential term. Badly divided, the Liberal party presented two candidates, Gabriel Turbay and Jorge Eliécer Gaitán, in the 1946 presidential elections. Turbay was backed by the bulk of the official party apparatus, whereas Gaitán represented dissident middle-sector politicians who had long been postponed within both the party and Colombian society itself, due to tight upper class control of politics. The Gaitán movement found support among the middle stratum and among urban workers, especially in Bogotá and on the Caribbean Coast.

The debility of the Liberal Republic and the division of the Liberal party led to the victory of Conservative candidate Mariano Ospina Pérez in the 1946 presidential elections. Thus, there began another period of party transition. The change, as in the 1930s, began with a coalition, this time known as the *Unión Nacional* ("National Union"). Despite the bipartisan cabinet, partisan competition began to reignite violence somewhat similar to that of 1922 and very similar to the violence of the period 1930–1934.

Partisan violence had changed in the course of the twentieth century. Full-scale civil wars were replaced by more localized and less systematic forms of violence. A vitiated electoral process was itself a source of violence rather than an alternative to it. The violent conflicts were based on contradictory interests arising from the attempts of each party to construct political party hegemonies and rule to the exclusion of its partisan adversary. This survival into the twentieth century of hegemonic poiltics and

---

July 18, 1944, to General Germán Ocampo), pp. 169–183; Francisco Leal Buitrago, "Política e Intervención Militar en Colombia," in *La Dependencia Externa y el Desarrollo Político de Colombia*, ed. Rodrigo Parra Sandoval (Bogotá: Universidad Nacional de Colombia, 1970), pp. 174–175; interview with the son of one of the officers involved in the coup plot outside of Pasto, *Ministro de Gobierno 1944*, pp. vi ff., 115; Abelardo Patiño, "The Political Ideas of the Liberal and Conservative Parties during the 1946–1953 Crisis," Ph.D. dissertation, American University (Washington, D.C., 1954), chap. 2; Anthony Maingot, "The Colombian Military: A Case of Inconsistent Status," in *The Role of the Military in Latin America*, ed. Lyle McAlister, unpublished manuscript; José María Nieto Rojas, *La Batalla Contra el Comunismo en Colombia* (Bogotá: Empresa Nacional de Publicaciones, 1956), pp. 62–63.

A prior coup plot was alleged by the government in June 1936. The government at that time briefly arrested a group of Conservatives, including General Amadeo Rodríguez; *El Tiempo*, June 20, 24, 1936; *El Siglo*, June 21–26, July 5, 1936.

[74] República de Colombia, Presidencia de la República, *Documentos Relacionados*, *passim;* Eduardo Zuleta Angel, *El Presidente López* (Medellín: Ediciones Aibón, 1966); Plinio Mendoza Neira and Alberto Camacho Angarita, *El Liberalismo en el Gobierno* (Bogotá: Prag, n.d.).

partisan violence occurred within the context of a country that had undergone basic socioeconomic and political changes. This is an important element for an understanding of *La Violencia.*

The Partial Collapse of the State in the Second Conservative Republic

In the late 1940s, particularly in the year 1949, the Colombian state was acutely subject to a reduction of power, which reached the point where it may be termed a partial collapse of the state. In this section a description is given of the complex processes that conditioned the crisis in state authority and power. In Chapter 5, an explanation is offered for this phenomenon, and concrete manifestations of the partial collapse of the state are enumerated.

In late 1945 and early 1946, interclass conflicts were accentuated as a result of an abrupt change in official policy toward salaried workers, and partisan conflicts were renewed as a result of impending presidential elections. Violent incidents began to occur in 1946, accelerated in 1947, and reached crisis proportions in 1948. The violence corresponded to both interclass and partisan contradictions.

INTERCLASS CONFLICT

Organized labor suffered a sharp defeat with the resignation of President Alfonso López Pumarejo in 1945. López, who had protected and expanded as well as controlled the labor movement, was forced to resign as the result of vigorous opposition from both "Moderate" Liberals and Conservatives.[75] His replacement, Alberto Lleras Camargo, adopted an entirely different policy with regard to organized labor. The new government sought to limit the strength of the labor federation (CTC) and break the power of the most belligerent unions.

Lleras Camargo, speaking before the *Asociación Nacional de Industriales* (ANDI, "National Association of Industrialists") in August 1945, stated:

> A people (*pueblo*) with little ambition does not find sufficient stimulus in the betterment of their conditions, and, instead of augmenting their capacity to work, in order to take advantage of better renumeration, they augment their capacity to rest. . . . Although it may appear a bit strange, I am going

[75] For summaries of the measures that benefited organized labor (and increased governmental control over the unions) during the second López Pumarejo administration, consult: Torres Giraldo, *Los Inconformes*, vol. 5, pp. 254–256; Pecaut, *Política y Sindicalismo*, p. 197.

> to take advantage of this occasion to address from this platform the workers of Colombia to formulate a most zealous call to change, while it is still possible, the conduct that leads to the circumstance that when the worker, urban or rural, obtains better salaries, achieves the right to overtime pay, and receives protection against work hazards, illness, and unemployment: Production begins to diminish its rate, without any other cause than deficiencies in the realization of tasks. . . . This has to end and it should end voluntarily with the categoric warning to the Colombian people (*pueblo*) that what is guaranteed by the Constitution is the right to work and not the right to not work. . . . We have struggled, as a government, for many years against the abuses of the owners, and it would be painful and absurd, when there is just beginning to vaguely appear a better situation for our people, to have to begin to struggle against the abuses of the proletariat.[76]

In November 1945, the most powerful union in Colombia, FEDENAL, which controlled all workers involved in fluvial transport on the Magdalena River, struck for higher wages.[77] This occurred in the context of widespread labor unrest. Most of the major unions in the country were considering strikes as a result of wartime and postwar inflation, which had greatly debilitated the real purchasing power of the working classes.[78]

Other strikes were prolonged because the government had ceased to intervene in most labor disputes, a fact that worked against the bargaining possibilities of the unions. The shipping companies termed the FEDENAL strike "revolutionary," and the government immediately declared it illegal. The day after the strike began President Alberto Lleras Camargo, in a nationwide radio broadcast, stated: "In this country there is only one government, mine. . . . If the workers do not return to their labors today, they will receive exemplary sanctions. . . . It cannot be permitted that there are two governments, one on the river and another in the rest of the country." [79]

On November 26, the *Confederación de Trabajadores de Colombia* (CTC; "Workers' Confederation of Colombia") undertook the first nationwide work stoppage in Colombian history to pressure government support for the workers of FEDENAL and other ongoing strikes. The CTC sought government support for unions and wage increases. The national strike

[76] República de Colombia, Presidencia de la República, *Un Año de Gobierno, 1945–1946: Discursos y Otros Documentos* (Bogotá: Imprenta Nacional, 1946), "Discurso Pronunciado por el Presidente de la República (Alberto Lleras Camargo) el 31 de Agosto, 1945, en Homenaje Ofrecido por la ANDI," pp. 48–52, 53–54.

[77] FEDENAL was the only labor group in Colombia to enjoy a union shop contract (all employees on the riverboats and wharves were required to be union members). It was also the most strategic union in that the Magdalena River was the backbone of the nation's transport system between the Caribbean Coast and the interior of the country.

[78] Pecaut, *Política y Sindicalismo*, p. 205.

[79] Torres Giraldo, *Los Inconformes*, vol. 5, p. 268; Urrutia, *Historia del Sindicalismo*, p. 204.

was weak in Medellín, but impressive in Cali and Bogotá. The government responded to this situation by sending troops to the Magdalena River to protect scab laborers and by dismissing numerous striking river workers. The great battle ended during the first days of 1946. FEDENAL received a decisive defeat from which it never recovered, and the CTC was seriously debilitated due to the demise of its most important union.[80]

The subsequent administration of Mariano Ospina Pérez continued the policy of weakening the belligerent unions. A new labor central, the *Unión de Trabajadores de Colombia* (UTC; "Workers' Union of Colombia") was founded in June 1946, and it became the favored labor instrument of the Conservative government. Organized by Jesuits, backed by many industrialists, and with the support of the new government, the UTC prospered at the expense of the CTC. The labor movement was thus divided by the creation of a compliant parallel federation.[81]

In late 1946, the Ospina Pérez government declared a series of strikes in Cali to be subversive. The strike movement spread throughout the Valle de Cauca, clashes between troops and strikers occurred, and the government declared a state of siege in the region.[82]

The Cali confrontation led to a decision by the CTC to stage a nationwide, 1-day, general strike in May 1947 as a protest against the policies of the Ospina Pérez government. The CTC strike resolution stated:

> The Colombian union movement and the workers in general are becoming victims of the most treacherous and unbelievable violations of their rights as citizens and their constitutional guarantees by the government and its agents in various areas of the republic, such as restriction of the right to strike by terroristic and repressive means, violation of the right to petition by using the armed forces, checking the right of assembly by means of intervention and search by the secret police in workers meetings, curtailment of the freedom of press, abominable surveillance of the union leaders in their public and private lives by the native variety of the gestapo, armed assault upon union buildings by employees of known criminal record, and treacherous assassinations with official arms of defenseless workers.[83]

[80] For the FEDENAL strike, see *El Tiempo* and *El Siglo*, Jan. 2, 1946, and *El Tiempo*, Jan. 3, 1946. See also Torres Giraldo, *Los Inconformes*, vol. 5, pp. 267–270; Pecaut, *Política y Sindicalismo*, pp. 204–297; Caicedo, *Historia de las Luchas Sindicales*, pp. 78–79; Diego Montaña Cuéllar, *Colombia: País Formal y País Real* (Buenos Aires: Editorial Platina, 1963), pp. 169–170; Urrutia, *Historia del Sindicalismo*, p. 204.

[81] *El Tiempo*, June 7, 1946; *El Siglo*, May 2, 1947; Urrutia, *Historia del Sindicalismo*, chap. 12; Caicedo, *Historia de las Luchas Sindicales*, pp. 79–96; Pecaut, *Política y Sindicalismo*, pp. 219–226.

[82] *El Tiempo*, Oct. 18, 1946 (which states that there were 150 labor disputes pending in the Valle of Cauca at the time); *El Siglo*, Nov. 5 ("El Gobierno Afronta El Paro de Cali como un Delito de Subversión"), 8, 9, Dec. 1, 1946. See also Torres Giraldo, *Los Inconformes*, vol. 5, pp. 286–287.

[83] *Semana*, May 17, 1947, as cited in Mauricio Solaún, "*La Violencia*, Socio-Historical Determinants of Political Violence in Colombia," unpublished manuscript, (Bogotá: 1974), pp. 325–326.

The government interpreted the strikes as a Liberal plot to overthrow President Ospina Pérez and it vigorously opposed the movement, as did the Catholic Church. The archbishop of Bogotá and primate of Colombia, Ismael Perdomo, issued a circular that stated that the proposed strike "could be classified as an attempt to upset public order and society." [84]

The strike turned out to be a colossal failure. The FEDENAL and the May 1947 strikes had demonstrated the weakness of the labor movement when it did not enjoy government backing. The latter strike, furthermore, completely broke relations between the government and the CTC. The fate of the most important labor organization thus became inextricably linked to the partisan struggle of the Liberal party to block the formation of a Conservative political hegemony.[85]

The increase in conflicts between management and government, on the one hand, and labor, on the other, is important for an understanding of partisan conflicts during the period 1945–1948. The alienation of rank-and-file workers from the "official" wing of the Liberal party enhanced the political viability of the Liberal dissident group led by Jorge Eliécer Gaitán.[86] It also might help explain the resistance of Gaitán and his followers to compromise with the majority wing of the Liberals in the name of party unity. The rhetoric of struggle against the oligarchy had an even stronger appeal than usual under the circumstances of unaccustomed, runaway inflation, a lack of government support for compensatory wage increases, and government policies designed to retract prior labor conquests and break the strength of the unions.[87] The strike-breaking labor policies of the Lleras Camargo government identified the moderate Liberals with these processes as much as the Conservatives.

PARTISAN CONFLICT

The violent incidents accompanying the 1946 presidential campaign were just as often between supporters of the two Liberal candidates, Gaitán and Turbay, as between Liberals and Conservatives.[88]

[84] Solaún, "*La Violencia*," p. 326. Government member Rafael Azula Barrera terms the movement a "frustrated coup d'etat attempt"; see his *De la Revolución*, pp, 269–283.

[85] *Semana*, May 17, 1947, as cited in Mauricio Solaún, "*La Violencia*," p. 130.

[86] *El Tiempo*, May 8, 10, 12, 14 ("El Gobierno Suspendió por Tres Meses la Personería Jurídica de la CTC"), 22, 27, 1946; *El Siglo* May 13–15, 1946; Torres Giraldo, *Los Inconformes*, vol. 5, p. 88; Pecaut, *Política y Sindicalismo*, pp. 215–218; Urrutia, *Historia del Sindicalismo*, pp. 208–210; Rafael Azula Barrera, *De la Revolución al Orden Nuevo* (Bogotá: n.p., 1956), chap. 16.

[87] With the exception of unionized Medellín, and the partial exception of Cali, Gaitán's greatest electoral strength was precisely in the nation's most unionized areas, i.e., Bogotá, the Magdalena River, and the Caribbean Coast.

[88] Both the Conservative and the Liberal newspapers of the period were alarmed by the inflation, which they considered to be the country's most serious problem. See

As was the case in 1930, electoral violence itself was insignificant when compared to the violence that accompanied the subsequent struggle for power in the basic institutions of Colombian society.[89] After 16 years of Liberal rule, Conservative Mariano Ospina Pérez assumed the national presidency. Ospina Pérez governed with a bipartisan "National Union" cabinet, and the Liberals controlled Congress. The situation was thus practically identical to 1930, with the parties reversing their roles.

Transitional party violence erupted in the areas most affected by the 1930–1934 struggle for partisan hegemony; the Santanderes and Boyacá. In addition, Nariño became a center of violence.[90] Incidents increased in the course of 1946 and further intensified in the months preceding the March 1947 local elections. Accusations of massive electoral fraud were posed by both the Liberals and Conservatives.[91] Under these circumstances, the National Union coalition began to lose support among rank-and-file members of both parties.[92]

El Siglo, Mar. 4–6, 12, Aug. 20, Sept. 10–11, 1946; *El Tiempo*, May 20, Aug. 1, 15, Sept. 11, Oct. 13, Dec. 6, 1946.

[89] *El Tiempo* and *El Siglo*, Jan.–May, 1946; see particularly *El Siglo*, Feb. 10, Mar. 3, 16, Apr. 12, 22, 1946. Violent incidents were particularly common in Boyacá, Cundinamarca, Santander, Norte de Santander, Tolima, and Bolívar.

[90] Immediately after the 1946 presidential elections, there was rioting by Liberals in Bucaramanga, which required army intervention; see *El Siglo*, May 8, 16, 1946 and *El Tiempo*, May 8, 1946. See also Manuel Serrano Blanco, *Las Viñas del Odio* (Bucaramanga: Imprenta del Departamento, 1949), pp. 128–131.

Violent incidences in Saboyá, Tuquerres, Duitama, Ocaña, Chiquinquirá, Capitanejo, Tocaima, Carcasí, and other areas are to be found in *El Siglo* and *El Tiempo* for the months July–Nov. 1946.

[91] The perennial charges of fraud by both parties once again made elections a source of violent conflict rather than a mechanism for conflict resolution. For the more significant controversies, consult *El Tiempo*, July 5, 12, 1947; *El Siglo*, Mar. 3, Apr. 9, 12, 26, 30, 1946, Mar. 10, Apr. 1, 7, June 6, July 12, Oct. 9, Dec. 6, 1947. An example of the polemics between the Liberal and Conservative Press and the two parties may be found in Laureano Gómez's accusations of double and triple issuance of national identification cards to Liberals (*El Siglo* July 12, 1947) and *El Siglo's* comment 3 months earlier:

> *El Tiempo* in its Holy Thursday Edition takes into account the last elections, but it is getting out of its field. The end of all this is to prepare the environment so that the electoral organisms systematically do not recognize the popular will and methodically dispossess the parliamentary seats that Conservatism won by honest effort. (*El Siglo*, Apr. 7, 1947)

[92] *El Tiempo*, Apr. 4, 1947, "La Crisis Conservadora," and *El Tiempo*, Feb. 6, 1947. In the latter article, Liberal leaders in the Department of Bolívar cabled the National Directorate the following message:

> The National Union is a myth. A tragedy is imminent. The Liberals respect the law but the authorities do not guarantee their rights, nor do they attend to the clamours of a persecuted and down-trodden people. It is better to die in a brave struggle than to continue living in slavery.

The 1947 political environment was further agitated when former presidential candidate Carlos Arango Vélez returned to Colombia from his ambassadorship in Rome. He declared at that time that a Liberal plot existed to employ the party's congressional majority to impeach President Ospina and replace him with a Liberal.[93] President Ospina, however, reiterated his decision to continue the coalition government. His administration also seized upon some of the more important violent incidents to symbolically demonstrate its firmness in the face of violence.[94]

The party directorates and the press alternatively sensationalized the violence and minimized it. The minister of government stated at one point that the 1947 violence would simply disappear if it were not for the yellow press.[95] The ignorance of those with blind party passions divorced from ongoing political processes, the yellow press, and lower level political figures were blamed for the violence by both the Liberal and Conservative press in the capital.[96]

Gradually, however, the partisan and press interpretations took on the overtone of the impending struggle for partisan hegemony. This was particularly the case after June 1947, when the division in the Liberal party was overcome by the naming of Jorge Eliécer Gaitán as the undisputed leader of the National Liberal Directorate.[97] At that time it became obvious that the 1950 presidential elections would match Conservative Laureano Gómez with Liberal Jorge Eliécer Gaitán. However, doubts began to arise over whether those elections would be acceptably fair or whether they would be held at all. It was in this environment of impending party

93 Solaún, "*La Violencia*," p. 321. It will be recalled that Arango Vélez led the 1942 Liberal dissidency against Alfonso López, which enjoyed massive Conservative support. Arango Vélez had also denounced a "Liberal plot" to upset public order in November 1946; see *El Siglo*, Dec. 4, 1946.

94 The Ospina Pérez government vigorously investigated a shooting by Custom's Agents in Duitama, Boyacá. The president energetically denounced the incident, and the Conservative governor resigned in the midst of the scandal. Ospina Pérez declared that it was necessary to create an environment of swift justice so as to "detain for once and for all the sectarian intransigence that establishes a dangerous state of agitation and of political hatreds which lead to these deplorable events" (*El Tiempo*, Feb. 11, 1947). See also *El Siglo*, Feb. 11, 1947. Ospina reiterated his support for the *Unión Nacional* in another speech to be found in *El Siglo*, May 1, 1947.

95 *El Tiempo*, March 11, 1947.

96 For examples of these interpretations from different newspapers, consult *El Espectador*, Jan. 2, 1947; *El Siglo*, Jan. 3, Feb. 1, 1947; *El Tiempo*, March 11, 1947.

97 *El Siglo*, June 14, 19, 1947. Once Gaitán had been named the undisputed Liberal leader, *El Siglo* began to attack him vigorously. This contrasted with the 1946 presidential campaign in which Laureano Gómez's newspaper gave respectful and tacit approval to Gaitán's dissident candidacy. In late 1947 and the first 3 months of 1948, *El Siglo* described Conservative *Violencia* deaths as having been perpetrated by "Gaitanistas" or "Gaitanista Hordes."

confrontations between two united parties that the violence increased in intensity in late 1947 and early 1948.

In a rapid spiral of events, electoral violence accompanied the October 1947 municipal elections, and Liberal headquarters in Cali were violently attacked that same month. In November, Minister of Government Montalvo stated that he would defend the National Union government and the president by "blood and fire." In January 1948, the violence dramatically intensified in Boyacá and the Santanderes, and Laureano Gómez stated that the country was in a state of civil war.[98] On January 27, 1948, Jorge Eliécer Gaitán, as the leader of the Liberal party, issued a *Memorial de Agravios* ("Bill of Grievances") that included a long list of localities affected by the violence.[99] On February 7, 1948, he led a large silent demonstration. As the sole orator before the silent crowd, he gave his most famous speech:

> Mr. President, we do not demand economic or political goals. We just ask that our country not follow the path that shames it before its own people and foreigners. We ask for the goals of piety and civilization. . . . We ask you to impede the persecution of the authorities. . . . Impede, Mr. President, the violence. We only ask of you the defense of human life, which is the very least that any people can ask.[100]

A parallel demonstration by Liberals in Manizales the same day was violently repressed by the police, with a total of 14 deaths. On February 28, 1948, a Liberal document that analyzed the competition for power announced the withdrawal of the Liberals from the National Union cabinet:

> Months after the presidential elections, with the Liberal party still divided and under the presidency of Ospina Pérez, legislative elections were held, in which the Conservative party participated using the same electoral identification cards within the same electoral regime that was their instrument

[98] *El Tiempo* and *El Siglo*, Oct. 1947, Jan. 1948.

[99] Germán Guzmán, Orlando Fals Borda, and Eduardo Umaña Luna, *La Violencia en Colombia* (Bogotá: Tercer Mundo, 1963, 1964). The localities mentioned were: *Nariño*—Samaniego, Sandoná, Linares, Gualmantán Túquerres, Guaspud, Tambo, Córdoba; *Boyacá*—Chita, Moniquirá, Ráquira, Jéricó, Soatá, Belén, Pauna, Zetaquirá, Saboyá, Chiquinquirá, Tota, Guateque, Sutamarchán, Chiscas y Ramiriquí; *Tolima*—Guamo, Roncevalles, Natagaima, Icononzo; *Norte de Santander*—Pamplona, Arboledas, Villa del Rosario, Sardinata, Cúcuta, Concepción, Durania, Teorama; *Santander*—Molagavita, Cité, Charalá; *Bolívar*—Sahagún, Sincelejo, Ovejas; *Caldas*—Anserma; *Valle*—Ginebra; *Antioquia*—Ebéjico, Abejorral, Maceo, Santo Domingo, El Penol; *Magdalena*—El Banco; *Choco*—Quibdó; *Cundinamarca*—Yacopí, Machetá, El Peñón, Pasca, Sequilé, Junín.

[100] Cited in Dirección Nacional del Liberalismo, *El Liberalismo Colombiano Frente a la Dictadura* (Bogotá: n.p., June 23, 1951) "A Report Given by the National Liberal Directorate to the Party's Convention," p. 11.

> and guarantee in the presidential elections. But the Conservative leadership learned then that not even the loss of power, nor the division that still existed in the Liberals ranks, impeded our collectivity from obtaining victory.
>
> Up until that moment, the violence that took place was sporadic and localized, understandable, for causes that reason accepts, although does not justify. Since that moment, the violence has been converted into a political system that pursues, without vacillation, the sole end of modifying by terror the volume of the parties respective electoral strengths.
>
> Thus, we arrive at the eve of the municipal elections [October 1947]. The tacticians of the Conservative party, well trained in the text of antidemocracy, concentrate the violence in those areas of the country that for their weaker social defenses appear to be the most susceptible to surrender to terror. Then there occurred the atrocious killing of Nariño and Boyacá and the outrages of Western Caldas.
>
> Without the perspective of an immediate electoral contest and with the intimate doubt that the violence might be insufficient to dominate the fervor of the Liberal party and break its discipline, official Conservatism proclaims by the mouth of its chief [Laureano Gómez] that the origin of the violence is nothing else but electoral fraud, represented by 1,800,000 false electoral identification cards. This subversive thesis attempted at the same time to lend support to the terrorism and set the precedent for ignoring our juridical order, as had already been announced by writers and orators of the Conservative party.[101]

The National Union Coalition was dead, and the parties were confronted in a direct conflict for party hegemony. The political situation obviously had a high potential for violence. A little over a month later, on April 9, 1948, the undisputed chief of the Liberal party and the hero of its popular urban bases, Jorge Eliécer Gaitán, was assassinated in downtown Bogotá. That city immediately became the scene of one of the most massive urban insurrections in the history of the twentieth century.

The Ninth of April[102]

Known as the *Bogotazo* outside Colombia and simply as the *Nueve de Abril* in Colombia, this insurrection destroyed much of downtown Bogotá. Infuriated mobs grew in number in the course of the day and attacked

[101] Declaration of the Junta of Liberal Parliamentarians issued February 29, 1948. Cited in Dirección Nacional Liberal, *El Liberalismo Frente a la Dictadura*, pp. 7–8.

[102] The extensive literature that deals with Gaitán's assassination, the *Nueve de Abril*, and its aftermath includes: Azula Barrera, *De la Revolución al Orden*, chaps. 16, 17; John D. Martz, *Colombia: A Contemporary Political Study* (Chapel Hill: University of North Carolina Press, 1962), chap. 4; Fluharty, *Dance of the Millions*, chap 7; Miguel Angel Gaitán, *El Porqué de un Asesinato y Sus Antecedentes* (Bogotá: Editorial Minerva, 1949); Enrique Cuéllar Vargas, *Trece Años de Violencia* (Bogotá: Ediciones Cultura Social Colombiana, 1960), chaps. 2–4; Joaquín Estrada Monsalve, *Así fue la Revolución* (Bogotá: Ediciones Sudamérica, 1973); Partido Comunista, *Treinta Años de Lucha*, pp. 82–91; Gonzalo Canal Ramírez, *9 de Abril de 1948* (Bogotá: Canal Ramírez, n.d.); Dirección Nacional Liberal, *Quince Meses de Política Liberal*, "Anexos: Documentos de 1948," pp. 33–69; Joaquín Estrada Monsalve, *El Nueve de Abril en Palacio: Horario de un Golpe de Estado* (Bogotá: Editorial ABC, 1968); Francisco

symbols of Conservative power, such as newspapers, churches, and the homes of the leaders of the government party. In a fashion somewhat similar to the urban insurrections by Blacks in the United States, the largely leaderless mobs soon began to concentrate on looting and arson. The police did not confront the rebellious mobs; indeed, numerous Liberal policemen joined the rioters and even distributed arms among them. Army troops successfully defended the presidential palace, and troop reenforcements restored order on subsequent days by indiscriminately shooting all those found on the streets. The survey data employed in this research indicate a minimal death estimate of 2585. The massive carnage and the destruction of the downtown section of the capital and largest city placed the whole of Colombian society in a state of crisis.

Violent incidents also occurred outside the capital. There were confrontations between Liberals and Conservatives in Barranquilla, Montería, and Bucaramanga. In Barrancabermeja, Puerto López, and numerous localities of Western Caldas and Northern Valle, there occurred mini-coup d'etats. The Conservative authorities were jailed or run out of town, often with the collaboration of the Liberal police, and on occasion after battles with Conservative officers.[103]

Fandiño Silva, *La Penetración Soviética en América y el Nueve de Abril* (Bogotá: Editorial ABC, 1949); Ignacio Gómez Dávila, *Viernes Nueve* (México, D. F.: n.p., 1953); Pedro Gómez Lorena, *El Nueve de Abril* (Bogotá: n.p., 1951); Alfonso López Michelsen, *Cuestiones Colombianas* (México, D.F.: n.p., 1955); Ramón Manrique, *A Sangre y Fuego* (Barranquilla: n.p., 1948); Alberto Miño H., *Antecedentes y Secretos del Nueve de Abril* (Bogotá: Editorial Pax, 1949); Gonzalo Orrego Duque, *El Nueve de Abril Afuera de Palacio* (Bogotá: Editorial Patria, 1949); Abraham Osorio, *Porqué Mataron A Gaitán* (Bogotá: Editorial Iqueima, 1948); Humberto Plaza, *La Noche Roja de Bogotá* (Buenos Aires: Editorial López, 1949); Luis Carlos Pérez, *Los Delitos Políticos: Interpretación Jurídica del Nueve de Abril* (Bogotá: Editorial Iquima, 1948); Roberto Restrepo, *Nueve de Abril: Quiebra Cultural y Política* (Bogotá: n.p., 1948); Julio Enrique Santos Forero, *Yo Vi Huir al Verdadero Ase sino de Jorge Eliécer Gaitán* (Bogotá: Gráficas Atenas, 1959); Luis Vidales, *La Insurrección Desplomada* (Bogotá: Editorial Iqueima, 1948); folder, *Así Fue el Nueve de Abril* (Bogotá: n.p., 1974); Gilberto Vieira, *Nueve de Abril: Experiencia del Pueblo* (Bogotá: Ediciones Sudamericana, 1973).

[103] Detailed information of several movements in Caldas is to be found in República de Colombia, Policía Nacional, *Criminalidad en 1958, "Orígenes de la Violencia."* See also Gilberto Vieira, *Nueve de Abril: Experiencia del Pueblo* (Bogotá: Ediciones Sudamérica, 1973), passim; United States Department of the Army, *U.S. Army Handbook for Colombia* (Washington, D.C.: GPO, 1961), pp. 189–190. The National Police document, *Criminalidad en 1958*, pp. 16–17, relates an armed struggle between a revolutionary junta, backed by rebel Liberal police, and loyalist forces for control of the city of Armenia. With the support of an artillery unit, the loyalists won. However, Liberal rebel groups managed to gain control of nearby localities, including Calarcá, Montenegro, and Tebaida. In Tolima the Conservatives alleged that the governor and the police led the revolutionaries in Ibagué (see *El Siglo*, Apr. 9, 1949). A Communist-led revolt in Barrancabemeja controlled that city for 8 days (see *El Siglo*, Apr. 10, 1949).

In the capital the political situation was obviously critical. The presence in Bogotá of the delegates of the soon to be inaugurated Ninth Pan American Conference (George Marshall among them) made the situation potentially delicate internationally. President Ospina Pérez received the National Liberal Directorate, which then asked for his resignation and a constitutional succession to the presidency by Eduardo Santos. The army suggested a military junta to restore order. To one suggestion that he leave the country, Ospina replied that it was better to have a dead president than a fugitive president. Ospina resisted the political pressures to resign, but he named a new National Union Cabinet with Liberal Darío Echandía as minister of government and with the commanding officer of the army, General Ocampo, as minister of war.[104]

The leadership of the Liberal party was as preoccupied as the Conservatives over the events that followed Gaitán's assassination and the revolutionary potential they seemed to entail. Even after the arson and looting subsided, there remained a nationwide strike by most of the Liberal and Communist unions, and, in many communities, local power was still wielded by rebel groups. On March 14, Carlos Lleras Restrepo, as leader of the National Liberal Directorate, asked via national radio that the strike be stopped, and he spoke again on March 15 to express his gratitude for the "discipline, wholesomeness, and patriotism" with which the labor movement had responded to his call.[105]

Meanwhile, the new minister of government, Darío Echandía, acted to return to government control those areas held by rebellious Liberals. A formal political truce was signed between the two parties on April 18. The Ninth of April had shaken the dominant groups in Colombian society regardless of their party persuasion, but, despite this fact, the struggle for partisan hegemony remained between them. Important groups within both the Liberal and Conservative parties opposed the post-Bogotazo coalition, and some Liberals favored lengthening the general strike and attempting a coup d'etat.[106]

Many Conservatives sought to violently repress the *Nueve Abrileños*

[104] Dirección Nacional Liberal (D.N.L.), *Quince Meses de Política Liberal: Informe de la D.N.L. a la Convención Nacional del Partido Reunida en Bogotá el 3 de Julio de 1949*, Annex: "Texto de las Declaraciones Publicadas por la Dirección Nacional Provisional del Liberalismo, el Día 12 de Abril de 1948," pp. 33–69; Martz, *Colombia*, pp. 84–88.

[105] See "Texto de la Alocución Radial Leída por Radio, en la Noche del 14 de Abril de 1948, por el Doctor Carlos Lleras Restrepo" and the same for Apr. 15, 1948, annexes published in Dirección Nacional Liberal, *Quince Meses*.

[106] Dirección Nacional Liberal, "Informe de la D.N.L. a la Convención Nacional del Partido Reunida en Bogotá, el 3 de Julio de 1949," in *Quince Meses*, pp. 5–28; interviews by me with conspirators (one of whom later led a coup d'etat attempt, and the other joined the guerrillas in the Eastern Plains); interview by me with ex-army colonel.

("participants in the Ninth of April riots,") a term soon used by the Conservatives when referring to the Liberals in general. The police were purged of Liberals, and the National Police soon joined the already belligerent *Policía Política* ("Political Police") in the violent repression of Liberals in many areas and their harassment everywhere.[107]

The police, civilian para-military organizations, and ad hoc groups of civilians (often under the influence of alcohol) frequently led incidents of random terror. Many of *La Violencia* anecdotes of this period revolve around shots being fired at red cars, persons being forced to eat red neckties, etc. (red being the symbolic color of the Liberal party).[108] In some areas, especially in Northern Valle and Western Caldas, genuine "Liberal hunts" were organized by *pájaros* (literally, "birds"; figuratively, "political henchmen with official protection"). Liberals would be taken from their homes or places of employment and sometimes randomly picked up off the streets or out of bars to be harassed, beaten, and sometimes shot. Union officials and organizers and Communist party members were particularly vulnerable to these forms of terrorism, especially in the smaller localities. In the prime areas of *pájaro* activity (such as Sevilla, Caicedoma, and Armenia), local Liberal leaders and randomly selected Liberal citizens were ostentatiously murdered in town in broad daylight by killers who did not even bother to hide their identities. Often the places chosen for these collective slayings were highly symbolic (for example, in front of the house of a prominent Liberal leader, in front of the Liberal newspaper, or in the patio of a union hall). Another terrorizing effect in numerous localities was the periodic appearance of bodies, often mangled, at the same site or floating in rivers after having been thrown regularly from the same bridge.[109]

Violence spread throughout the departments of the central core region of the country after the Ninth of April, and violent incidents in one place or another became a daily occurrence.[110] The undeclared civil war evolved to more organized forms in 1949 with the appearance of Liberal "Resistance Committees" and Liberal guerilla forces.

The Critical Year of 1949

Politically, 1949 marked the final rift between the Liberals and the Conservatives and the breakdown of the existing institutional structure. On

[107] United States, Department of the Army, *U.S. Army Handbook for Colombia*, p. 390.

[108] Numerous interviews with victims, witnesses, and authorities.

[109] Numerous interviews with victims, witnesses, and authorities. Official terrorism of the type described were uncovered in field research literally by the hundreds of cases. A particularly pathetic case involved a teenage girl who was permanently traumatized because she witnessed the mass slaying of 14 persons, including an uncle, on the corner of the block of her family home in Northern Valle, on her way home from school.

[110] See *El Tiempo* and *El Siglo* for 1948 and 1949.

May 21, the Liberals once again retired from the National Union government. Lleras Restrepo stated that the Conservatives had converted the coalition into a farce. The Conservatives accused the Liberals, in both 1948 and 1949, of divorcing themselves from the public administration, disauthorizing collaboration with the government, and undertaking "rude and crude opposition."[111] The Liberal Directorate in turn accused the Conservatives of sectarian repression:

> Liberal collaboration made no sense at all nor had any justification except to the extent that impartial government could be obtained as well as equal rights for all citizens. If the facts were to prove, as they have proved, that despite the mixed composition of the government the Conservative authorities practiced or protected violence and unjustified coercion over the Liberal electorate, without the president of the Republic adopting efficacious measures to avoid it, cooperation would lose its raison d'etre and could not serve for more than covering with a deceitful blanket of legitimacy the crimes and outrages of which Liberalism was victim.[112]

Congressional elections were held on June 5, 1949, and the Liberal party retained a majority of 130,000 votes. The Liberals spoke of a great victory despite official coercion, and the Conservatives spoke of massive fraud perpetrated with irregular electoral identification cards. Both before and after the elections, each side continually accused the other of fraudulent activities.[113] In his 1949 report, the National Registrar stated that the elections were vitiated by the registration of minors, double registration, inscription errors, a lack of official guarantees, a lack of punishment for electoral crimes, and the intromission of the authorities and the police.[114] The National Liberal Directorate analyzed the June 1949 elections as follows:

[111] For the Lleras Restrepo statement consult *El Tiempo*, May 28, 1949. For an example of Conservative analysis, see Serrano Blanco, *Las Viñas del Odio*, p. 154. Darío Echandia was the principal defender of the coalition in Liberal ranks. He had stated as soon before the rift as early Apr. that elections would be impossible without the coalition; see *El Tiempo*, Apr. 9, 1949. For the break itself, consult *El Tiempo*, May 22–23, 28, 1949; *El Siglo*, May 7, 9, 22–24, 29, Nov. 9, 1949.

[112] Dirección Nacional Liberal, *El Liberalismo Colombiano Frente a la Dictadura: Informe que Rinde la Dirección Nacional del Liberalismo a la Convención del Partido* (Bogotá: n.p., June 23, 1951), p. 19.

[113] These accusations are to be found in *El Tiempo*, Jan. 23, Feb. 23, March 14, Apr. 17, 28, May 1, 2, 9, 15–19, 23, June 2–4, 8–12, 18, July 4, 6–7, 18, Aug. 3, 1949. See also *El Siglo*, Feb. 21, 23–24, Apr. 18, May 3, 5, 11–16, 19–20, June 1, 8–12, 17–20, 22, 24, 1949.

[114] República de Colombia, Registraduría General de la República, *Informe del Registrador 1949* (Bogotá: Imprenta Nacional, 1950), pp. 24, 112. *El Tiempo*, June 7, 1949, reports 19 violent deaths due to partisan conflicts on election day. Another serious electoral anomaly was the assassination of local electoral registrars. This occurred in the departments of Caquetá, Boyacá, Casanare, and Santander in the period 1949–1951; see *Informe del Registrador 1952*, p. 17.

> How expensive was this victory. Not only because the violence had already caused in many departments horrible wreckage, but also because with the defeat which they [the Conservatives] had to accept, after attempting by all means to alter the legitimate results, Conservatism definitely decided to generalize the violence in the entire country, without limits and without scruples of any sort.[115]

The Liberal party's continued control of Congress led to the expression of the protracted struggle for power as an institutional battle between the executive and legislative branches of government. The symbol of the struggle for power, and an element not without substantive impact in the fight itself, was a Liberal proposal to advance the date of the impending presidential elections from June 1950 to late 1949. In acrimonious debate, this issue crystallized and summarized the battle to retain or obtain hegemonic power. The law passed the Congress with the vote running along strict party lines. Ospina vetoed it, alleging a technicality that the Supreme Court later rejected. Thus, there began a presidential campaign in 1949 with Laureano Gómez as the Conservative candidate and Darío Echandía as the Liberal candidate.[116]

In September 1949, a gunfight erupted in the House of Representatives with one Liberal congressman, Gonzalo Jiménez, slain while several other members of Congress were wounded. That same month Liberal candidate Darío Echandía and his entourage were shot at in downtown Bogotá, and Echandía's brother was killed.[117] In October, the National Liberal Directorate announced the withdrawal of its candidate and its total electoral abstention. Liberal candidate Darío Echandía stated that the party would not participate in a "bloody farce. . . . It is for to the party to wage a total battle for liberty. . . . We swear that we will not prove to be unworthy of the heroic traditions of our collectivity, even if it costs us our lives."[118] The Conservative daily, *El Siglo,* berated Echandía for "lowly attacks" on Ospina Pérez.[119] The political events were leading to a total break within the political elite in the tensest situation since the period after the 1922 elections.

The Liberal party abandoned the strategy of attempting to obtain the presidency by electoral means and adopted the abstentionist policies it had

[115] Dirección Nacional Liberal, *El Liberalismo Colombiano,* p. 24.

[116] For discussions of the electoral law controversy, consult Abelardo Patiño P., "The Political Ideas of the Liberal and Conservative Parties during the 1946–1953 Crisis," Ph.D. dissertation, American University (Washington, D.C.: 1954), pp. 151–263; Cuéllar, *Trece Años,* chaps. 6, 7; Martz, *Colombia,* pp. 121–124; Dirección Nacional Liberal, *Quince Meses,* pp. 25–40.

[117] Juventudes del Movimiento Revolucionario Liberal, *Plataforma Política: Porqué Liberal, Porqué Revolucionarios, Porqué ni un Paso Atrás* (Bogotá: Ediciones Voces Liberales, n.d.), p. 21.

[118] *El Tiempo,* Nov. 8, 1949.

[119] *El Siglo,* Nov. 8, 1949.

employed in the 1920s and that the Conservatives had applied in the early 1930s.[120] The virulence of the party conflict may be appreciated from Conservative attacks that consistently linked the Liberal party to international communism[121] and from the following words, which the leader of the Liberals, Carlos Lleras Restrepo, pronounced in Congress on October 28, 1949:

> Having practically suppressed the more popular and democratic aspects of electoral propaganda, having expelled by the violence a great number of electoral registrars, being in full effect with the implacable backing of police and custom's officers a terrorist policy that nothing detains, and with local authority in the hands of the most sectarian officials that can be found, . . . nothing remains but continued violence, designed to increase the vote for some and diminish or eliminate the vote for others.
>
> Under these conditions we believe it is our duty, the clearest and the most necessary of duties, not to participate in the organization of an electoral contest operating on these bases.
>
> Doctor Laureano Gómez is approaching the zenith of his career in a form predictable from his antecedents, his character, all that he has signified in the life of the republic. He could not crown his life in any other manner. He has represented for many years the impossibility of national accord, an anarchy of spirit in the country, and chaos in mind and conscience; he has controverted all values; he has confused in his accusations honorable and guilty to apply to both identical epitaphs; and he has formed, in a campaign of decades, the spirit of hate that today is coming to the surface. It is only natural that, when this spirit of hatred finally bursts forth violently, when it ceases to be expressed simply by libelous attacks on the pages of newspapers and is converted into massacre, into the flames of fires, into destruction, into assassinations, and into forced exiles, it is then that Dr. Laureano Gómez understands that the hour of his destiny has arrived.[122]

[120] The new strategy, however, also included active resistance to the government that was to be elected without Liberal participation. Francisco Leal writes: "The Liberal groups in the legislature declared their lack of recognition of the future presidential elections and they formulated threats of violence so as to impede the possession of power of the new president. The background of the threat was based on the nascent organization of guerrilla groups on the Eastern Plains, encouraged by directive officers of the party" (*Análisis Histórico*, pp. 78–79). Likewise, Antonio García observes:

> After the death of Gaitán, Liberalism decided to support the government of the National Union, but later, from the Congress, it decided to accept the challenge of violence unleashed by the Conservatives and lance itself into the partisan struggle. The Congress was closed and the violence arrived at its most bloody stage. (*Gaitán y el Problema de la Revolución* [Bogotá: Editorial M.S.C., 1955], p. 317)

[121] Solaún, "*La Violencia*," p. 344. For other examples, see *El Siglo*, Mar. 9, Apr. 3, May 8, 1949.

[122] Carlos Lleras Restrepo, "Discurso Pronunciado en el Senado de la República, en la Sesión del 28 de Octubre de 1949," reproduced in Lleras Restrepo, *De la Democracia a la Dictadura* (Bogotá: Ediciones Agra, 1955), pp. 203–204, 211.

The Liberals began to attempt to impeach President Ospina Pérez. The president in turn termed the conduct of the Congress subversive, and he issued a series of decrees on October 9, 1949, by which Congress was closed, press censorship was initiated, and a state of siege was declared.[123] The latter was to last for over 10 years. On November 27, Laureano Gómez was elected president of the republic, unopposed. Two days before, the Liberals had staged a nationwide protest strike.[124] The original plan had been for a military coup d'etat attempt. The strike by the CTC was a last-minute change. An air force unit in Villavicencio went ahead with the original plan in the hope that other units would join the movement and that popular uprisings might be sparked. The unit led by Captain Alfredo Silva, with the collaboration of Hernando Durán Dussan (the emissary of the National Liberal Directorate in the coup plot), captured the city of Villavicencio after a short battle with Conservative police. The movement collapsed, however, due to a lack of support from other units.[125] The Villavicencio affair gave impetus to the Liberal guerrilla groups that were already forming on the Eastern Plains, as well as in other areas.[126]

The Conservatives had proclaimed the entire chain of events that began with the general strike of the CTC in May 1947 to be subversive attempts to overthrow President Ospina Pérez and impede their full exercise of power. Liberal–Communist collusion was argued to be behind these events. The Nueve de Abril was considered to be a Communist effort to disrupt the Ninth Pan American Conference and create a social revolution in Colombia. In some versions, Rafael Betancourt and the Venezuelan political party *Acción Demócrata* were also considered to be involved. The presence of Fidel Castro in Bogotá has also frequently been cited as evidence in recent years. The formation of Liberal "Resistance Committees," the appearance of Liberal guerrilla groups, and rumors of political consultations by Liberal army officers were all cited as subversive threats to the stability of the Ospina Pérez government and to Laureano Gómez's possibilities to accede to the presidency. The Liberals were depicted as hating Gómez with a vengeance that had matured by their falling again and again into his elaborate political traps.[127]

[123] Martz, *Colombia*, pp. 127–128; Solaún, "*La Violencia*," p. 344. See also *El Siglo*, Nov. 4, 10–12, 1949; *El Tiempo*, Nov. 9–17, 23, 1949.

[124] *El Siglo*, Nov. 12, 16, 23–25, 1949.

[125] Interview with a leading conspirator; also *El Tiempo*, Dec. 1, 1949.

[126] Guzmán, Fals Borda, and Umaña Luna, *La Violencia*, vol. 1, pp. 62–64.

[127] Interviews with three top-rung Conservative politicians who were active in the period under consideration, with two younger Conservative politicians, and with a wide cross section of Conservative citizens. For written accounts, consult: Directorio Nacional Conservador, *Los Programas Conservadores 1849–1949* (Bogotá: 1952); Azula Barrera, *De la Revolución al Orden Nuevo*; Serrano Blanco, *Las Viñas del Odio*;

With reference to the violence, on July 20, 1951, President Laureano Gómez stated:

> No one can say that we are dealing with spontaneous banditry. It has been stimulated by subversive publications and clandestine radio broadcasts, whose origin and financing are no longer a mystery to anyone. They cause a horrible evil and supreme mortification due to the loss of innocent lives and the wreckage of the properties of the humble, and for the horror that one feels in the presence of the needless cruelty. But no one can believe that, with the repetition of these infamous acts, the overthrow of the institutions or a change of regime may be achieved.[128]

Conservative documents consistently used religious themes (the party enjoyed the open support of the church) and equated Liberalism with Communism. For an example of the latter, consider the following part of a speech pronounced by Gómez's minister of war and replacement in the presidency when Gómez was incapacitated by a heart attack. Roberto Urdaneta Arbeláez stated, on July 26, 1951:

> Do not think that these acts [the violence] are out of orbit. On the contrary, they obey a plan. There you have the famous "Plan A" of Liberalism, which has an unmistakable communist style and which has as its objective to destroy the national economy and plunge the country into chaos.
>
> I have said that this plan and this state of mind are of a communist style and flavor. And thus it is. In countries like Colombia, which are to be found only in the second stage of economic evolution and in which frank affiliates of communism are scarce, the tactic consists of undercover penetration. It seeks by any means to disorganize the country, to produce what they call the bankruptcy of the bourgeois economy. With the centers of banditry, it is clear that they do not seek to overthrow the government. But they attempt to impede national progress, obliging the government to spend huge sums to reconstruct the country.[129]

Attempts were made prior to the total breakdown of relations between Liberals and Conservatives to avoid the split, and peace negotiations also succeeded the rift. Such efforts, however, invariably failed.[130] Sectarianism

---

Estrada Monsalve, *El Nueve de Abril en Palacio* (Bogotá: ABC, 1968); José María Nieto Rojas, *La Batalla Contra el Comunismo en Colombia* (Bogotá: Empresa Nacional, 1969).

128 Laureano Gómez, "Alocución del Excelentísmo señor Presidente de la República," in República de Colombia, Presidencia de la República, *Un Año de Gobierno (1950–1951)* (Bogotá: Imprenta Nacional, 1952).

129 Roberto Urdaneta Arbeláez, "Exposición del señor Ministro de Guerra, Roberto Urdaneta Arbeláez, pronunciada el día 26 de Julio de 1951," in *Un Año de Gobierno*, pp. 180–181.

130 A bipartisan peace offensive took place in early 1952. A conspicuous leader was ex-President Alfonso López Pumarejo, who traveled to the Eastern Plains to seek an

consistently carried the day. Indeed, in September 1952, after funerals of police officers killed by violence, a Conservative mob, unchecked by the government, burned the Liberal newspaper *El Tiempo* as well as the homes of Alfonso López Pumarejo and Carlos Lleras Restrepo.

These and other Liberal leaders sought diplomatic asylum and later abandoned the country. The National Liberal Directorate ceased to function on a regular basis in Bogotá[131]

In sum, beginning in 1946, the Liberal and Conservative parties were engaged in a classic struggle for party hegemony. With the unification of the Liberal party in 1947, the struggle acquired a new intensity, which eventually led to the retirement of the Liberals from the first National Unity government. With increased violence, the struggle further intensified in the course of 1948. Gaitán's assassination and the massive popular insurrection that followed temporarily reunited the elite groups that controlled Colombia's two traditional political parties. The threat of a popular revolution soon proved illusory, and the struggle for power was promptly renewed. The Liberals remained in the second National Union Cabinet through May 1949, despite widespread Liberal–Conservative violence in the countryside, because their strategy was to maintain sufficient power to assure an electoral victory in the campaign to choose a president for the period 1950–1954. The definition of the conditions of that electoral contest, which was to decide a consolidation of a Conservative hegemony or a reversion of power to the Liberals, marked the final break between the two political parties.

All of these struggles represented a reduction in the real power of the Colombian state. The events of 1948–1949 represent such a severe reduction in power that one may speak of a partial collapse of the state, as will be argued in Chapter 5. However, before examining the hypothesis of the "partial collapse of the state" and presenting the "structural regionalization of the violence," analytical attention is first given to the diverse explanations in the literature forwarded to explain *La Violencia* (Chapter 4).

---

agreement with Liberal guerrillas. There were also numerous meetings of the "Pro-Peace Movement." See *El Tiempo*, Jan. 21, Feb. 9, 10, 22, Mar. 5, Apr. 20, May 6, 11, 12, June 8, 10, 12, July 3, Sept. 4, 1949; see also *El Siglo*, April 27, May 3, Sept. 4, 5, 1952.

[131] These events occurred on Sept. 6, 1952. See Martz, *Colombia*, pp. 170–179; Patiño, *Las Ideas Políticas*, p. 325, *El Siglo*, Sept. 7–10, 14, 1952; *El Tiempo*, Sept. 12–14, 1952. *El Siglo*, Sept. 7, 1952, maintains that the police and others returning from the funeral were fired upon, sparking the riot.

4

Explanations of *La Violencia*

Most interpretations of *La Violencia* posit partisan political rivalries as the initial cause. They may be classified according to the different reasons given for the partisan conflicts that divided the political elite. These range from stylistic and educational differences to confrontations between reformist and reactionary forces for control of society.

Other explanations are fundamentally based on socioeconomic factors. These are divided between *intraclass* conflict positions and those that give preponderance to *interclass* socioeconomic struggles. The latter group differs in turn over the question of the structural significance attributed to class conflict. Some perceive only banditry, conceived as a diffuse form of social protest, while others see primitive forms of social protests; still others consider *La Violencia* to have been an aborted social revolution.

Another set of authors attributes the phenomenon to a series of institutional breakdowns. A final group proposes psychological, cultural, and racial interpretations.

Obviously, these different types of explanations are not necessarily mutually exclusive, and, indeed, many authors combine different elements. The review of the literature that follows is organized into the foregoing categories for heuristic purposes. It is hoped that the basic issues that divide students of *La Violencia* are highlighted by this procedure. Where pertinent, commentaries are made in the course of the exposition; however, a general appraisal of the different approaches is presented only at the end of this section.

Political Causes

Most of the general literature on the violence varies in content according to different partisan perspectives. Thus, the political interpretations of the origins of *La Violencia* tend to assign responsibilities for the phenomenon.

For example, Conservatives assert that the violence began as a result of Liberal party attempts to overthrow the constitutionally elected government of Mariano Ospina Pérez, reenforced later by Liberal efforts to prevent Laureano Gómez from assuming the presidency. A variant on this central theme conceptualizes combined Liberal–Communist subversion, as manifested in the political conflicts and labor disputes of the 1946–1949 period. The Ninth of April riot in Bogotá is commonly depicted as a revolutionary armed insurrection directed by "international communism."[1] Local-level violence between Conservative and Liberal *veredas* ("rural neighborhoods or wards") is seen as the result of the hereditary hatreds of past conflicts. In instances where Conservative peasants attacked Liberals, the acts were viewed as vengeance for the Conservative dead of the 1930–1932 violence.[2]

According to the Liberals and some Marxists, the violence was the product of a government bent on intimidating the opposition in order to ensure Conservative party control of the state despite its minority position. The argument runs that it was impossible for the Conservatives to conceive of consolidating political hegemony unless the Liberals were kept from the polls. The method used to accomplish this was physical coercion. The Liberals formed guerrillas to defend themselves from these attacks and to depose the Conservatives from power. The situation rapidly evolved to the point that violence constituted an undeclared civil war for state power.[3]

Germán Guzmán presents a summary of these political interpretations from a Liberal perspective:

> The rationality is monstrous, but of macabre simplicity: The Conservatives support the government and the government supports the violence; therefore, they should be annihilated. The Liberals plot revolutions against the Conservative government; therefore, they should be annihilated.
>
> It was war to the death.

[1] For Conservative accounts, consult the following sources: Rafael Azula Barrera, *De la Revolución al Orden Nuevo: Proceso y Drama de un Pueblo* (Bogotá: n.p., 1956); José María Nieto Rojas, *La Batalla Contra el Comunismo en Colombia* (Bogotá: Empresa Nacional de Publications, 1956); Joaquín Estrada Monsalve, *Así fue la Revolución del 9 de Abril al 27 de Noviembre* (Bogotá: n.p., 1950); Joaquín Estrada Monsalve, *El Nueve de Abril en Palacio: Horario de un Golpe de Estado* (Bogotá: Editorial ABC, 1968); Alberto H. Niño, *Antecedentes y Secretos del 9 de Abril* (Bogotá: n.p., 1949); Francisco Fandiño Silva, *La Penetración Soviética en América y el Nueve de Abril* (Bogotá: Editorial ABC, 1949).

[2] Mauricio Solaún, "*La Violencia:* Socio-Historical Determinants of Political Violence in Colombia," unpublished manuscript (n.p., n.d.), p. 158. Solaún comments that the 1930–1932 violence may also be related to the 1922 electoral violence in terms of the desire for revenge in areas in which acute political violence had previously occurred. This is especially the case in Norte de Santander, Boyacá, and Santander.

[3] Eduardo Santa, *Sociología Política de Colombia* (Bogotá: Ediciones Tercer Mundo, 1964), pp. 64–70, presents a typical Liberal interpretation. Another account is to be found in Guillermo Hernández Rodríguez, *La Alternación Ante el Pueblo como Constituyente Primario* (Bogotá: Editorial América Libre, 1962), pp. 88–89.

> In reality it consisted of an operation to expand electoral strength by weakening the enemy; but in the mechanics of achieving this goal no limit was placed upon the means employed.[4]

Turning now to the social science literature, a strictly political account of the violence is presented by James Payne. He denies the importance of other factors:

> The conflict took place not between the rich and the poor, peasant and landowner, employee and employer, but between two heterogeneous political parties. Socioeconomic issues were not raised with particular urgency; instead it was the political claims and political fears of one party against the other that characterized the demand context. The issue was, essentially, which party would gain permanent control of the Government.[5]

Within the political interpretations, the question of why a violent break occurred between the Liberal and Conservative leadership is crucial. Factors mentioned include stylistic differences, mistrust of the opposition, spoils, ideological conflicts, and struggles between groups with different interests relative to social change.

Darío Mesa provides an example of an account based strictly on stylistic factors:

> The bourgeois sectors of both parties were basically in agreement in regard to management of the economy, of foreign policy, of religious matters, etc., but differences of personality, including here educational factors, and the influence of vigorous leaders separated the Conservative bourgeoise from its Liberal equivalent, despite efforts to avoid this division on the part of the most alert leaders. Of course, the separation was only transitory and merely political, but it did aggravate the violent conflict for control of the state to the point of physical annihilation.[6]

If one accepts the foregoing interpretation, the explanatory question then becomes why a conflict between two groups with the same interests, divided only by stylistic questions and aggressive leaders, could "aggravate the violent conflict for control of the state to the point of physical annihilation." This point of view reveals little if not accompanied by an

[4] Germán Guzmán, Orlando Fals Borda, and Eduardo Umaña Luna, *La Violencia en Colombia* (Bogotá: Tercer Mundo, 1963, 1964), vol. 1, p. 88. This book is divided into sections written by the various authors. Germán Guzmán wrote the passage cited.

[5] James L. Payne, *Patterns of Conflict in Colombia* (New Haven: Yale University Press, 1968), p. 160.

[6] Darío Mesa, "Treinta Años de Historia Colombiana (1925–1955)," in *Colombia: Estructura Política y Agraria*, eds. Darío Mesa *et al.* (Bogotá: Ediciones Estrategia, 1972), pp. 41–42.

analysis of Colombian politics and society to explain why such relatively trivial matters could lead to such drastic consequences.

Mistrust between political leaders is basic to James Payne's notion that the violence was a "defensive feud." This concept refers to a sort of political vendetta in which each side "recognizes the existence of a mutually acceptable solution less costly than fighting, but that solution cannot be reached." [7] The lack of a settlement in the Colombian case is attributed to each side's fear that the opposing group would exclude one's party from government and mistrust of the contender's ability to control his rank-and-file members.

Another cause proposed to explain the rift in the political elite centers on political spoils. In an interpretation similar to Payne's and largely based on the same, Eric Nordlinger argues:

> Between 1946 and 1953 Colombia's Liberals and Conservatives killed each other by the thousands each year in a more than active scramble for economic rewards and appointments to governmental positions. The conflict groups were based upon political loyalties of a personal variety and the desire for economic rewards stemming from governmental control. The violence degenerated into banditry and the settling of personal vendettas for another ten years after 1953.[8]

The view of violence as a struggle for the spoils of the state is elevated by Fernando Guillén Martínez to the level of a comprehensive theory of Latin American political conflict, the state, and social structure. Guillén maintains that Latin American social structure is based on a centralized bureaucracy supported by semiservile rural labor. This centralized, interventionist state is viewed as a historical constant for the past two and one half centuries, and the endemic political conflicts and civil wars have been over who would win the right to enrich himself by managing the public treasury. The armed struggles of *La Violencia* were at first no different from the traditional battles for control of the State, although Guillén qualifies this by asserting that other characteristics did emerge in the course of the violence.[9]

Ideological elements suggested to explain intraelite conflict have included a polarization of the ruling class in Colombia as a result of the

[7] Payne, *Patterns of Conflict*, p. 161. The concept "defensive feud" is discussed on pp. 161–182.

[8] Eric Nordlinger, "Conflict Regulation in Divided Societies" (Cambridge: Harvard University, Center for International Affairs, Occasional Papers in International Affairs, January 1972), no. 29, p. 76. The banditry argument is an important complement to Nordlinger's position inasmuch as the partisan violence largely ended in 1953. Thus, he must explain why the violence continued after that date.

[9] Fernando Guillén Martínez, *Raíz y Futuro de la Revolución* (Bogotá: Ediciones Tercer Mundo, 1963).

Spanish Civil War,[10] a "dysfunctional" identification between the Roman Catholic Church and the Conservative party, which made political conflicts at all levels of society a battle between "orthodox" and "heretical" groups,[11] a struggle between totalitarian and democratic ideologies,[12] and an attempt to implant Falangist doctrines in Colombia.

Ignacio Torres Giraldo expresses the latter idea in the following terms: "From 1948 to 1957, the country lived a decade of official political violence organized and directed by Falangist Conservatives from the top positions of power. In the beginning this was accomplished by a formula of combined right-wing civilian and military forces and later by an open military dictatorship." [13]

At this point the political interpretations in the literature merge with the socioeconomic accounts. The battle for the state is conceptualized in these explanations as a conflict between reformist and reactionary groups for control of socioeconomic power.

Socioeconomic Causes

Orlando Fals Borda posits that *La Violencia* was an attempt by some elite groups to maintain the socioeconomic status quo. Antireformist forces used violence as an instrument of repression to the point that it became institutionalized. Certain sectors of the Liberal party responded to this violence in an attempt to topple the reactionary groups from power. This intraelite conflict was accompanied by a revolutionary popular uprising without ideology that proved to be emotional, cruel, and unorganized.[14]

Diego Montaña Cuéllar presents an account along the same lines with the difference that he emphasizes interclass conflicts in addition to intraclass discrepancies. After describing the minority position of the Conservatives, he writes: "Then, in a systematic manner and by means of an ad hoc political police recruited among assassins and prisoners, the government initiated terrorist actions designed to destroy the leadership and the electoral contingents of the opposition." [15] In the most backward areas of

[10] Azula Barrera, *De la Revolución*, chap. 4.

[11] Solaún, "*La Violencia*," pp. 22–64.

[12] Abelardo B. Patiño, "Political Ideas of the Liberal and Conservative Parties during the 1946–1953 Crisis," Ph.D. dissertation, American University (Washington, D.C., 1954), pp. 76–119.

[13] Ignacio Torres Giraldo, *Síntesis de Historia Política de Colombia* (Bogotá: Editorial Margen Izquierdo, 1972), pp. 79–94; quotation from p. 88.

[14] Orlando Fals Borda, "Violence and the Breakup of Tradition in Colombia," in *Obstacles to Change in Latin America*, ed. Claudio Vélez (London: Oxford University Press, 1965), pp. 188–203; Orlando Fals Borda, *La Subversion en Colombia* (Bogotá: Tercer Mundo, 1967), pp. 155–205.

[15] Diego Montaña Cuéllar, *Colombia: País Formal y País Real* (Buenos Aires: Editorial Platina, 1963), p. 183.

the country, the government closely copied fascist techniques to intimidate and assassinate the political opposition as well as dispossess them of their lands and force them to migrate. This attempt to implant fascism in Colombia corresponded to the ascendancy of finance capital. The period of the violence was marked by the highest rate of return on investments that Colombia had ever experienced. Rampant inflation redistributed income regressively while the economic advances that the working classes had achieved since the 1930s were reversed as the fascist policies of the government crushed the militant labor unions and their strikes. Furthermore, the increasing political strength of the proletariat, channeled through Jorge Eliécer Gaitán, was similarly repressed. In sum, the violence consolidated the position of finance capital in the country.[16]

Camilo Torres also conceptualized *La Violencia* as an interclass conflict: "The violence was unleashed as a sectarian instrument to fulfill the functions of reenforcing the conformism of the ruled class and of guaranteeing structural stability for the ruling class. . . . Thus, violence did not occur, among the ruling class but rather among the peasant masses." [17]

Antonio García holds essentially the same position, but his exposition is more complex. He sees the violence as the product of a counterrevolutionary strategy elaborated by the dominant groups in Colombian society to crush a mass movement that threatened the basic legitimacy of the prevailing institutions. Moreover, "The violence not only has been the product of a counterrevolutionary plan to utilize the apparatus of force, but also a consequence of the nihilist psychology that blooms in all wrecks of an order. The violence has been promoted by the absolutistic *caudillos* of the parties and stimulated later by social decomposition." [18] The Conservatives were the most aggressive nucleus of the counterrevolutionary process, but important Liberals were also involved. The dismemberment of the popular movement took place in three stages: [19]

[16] *Ibid.*, pp. 181–190.

[17] Camilo Torres Restrepo, "La Violencia y los Cambios Socio-Culturales en las Areas Rurales Colombianas," in *Cristianismo y Revolución* (México: Era, 1970), pp. 227–268 (the quotation is from p. 264). Charles W. Anderson, "La Violencia in Colombia," in *Issues of Political Development*, eds. Charles W. Anderson, Fred R. Von Der Meliden, and Crawford Young (Englewood Cliffs, N.J.: Prentice-Hall, 1967), p. 113, considers that the lack of violence within the political elite itself was due to a "Gentlemen's Agreement" not to let the partisan struggles damage their private world. In any event, both are wrong because violence was directed against the political elite of the dominant classes, especially in provincial areas. In the capital, the Ninth of April attacks on Conservative newspapers and homes, the 1949 attack on Darío Echandía, the gunfight the same year in Congress, and the 1952 burning of Liberal newspapers and homes are but few of the most important examples.

[18] Antonio García, *La Dialéctica de la Democracia* (Bogotá: Ediciones Cruz del Sur, Colombia, 1971), p. 116.

[19] *Ibid*, p. 151.

1. The probing of the capacity to resist followed by an offensive against the most powerful unions, and popular organizations (the provisional government of Alberto Lleras)
2. A systematic offensive by means of the massive unleashing of violence and an implacable annihilation of popular leadership, including the assassination of Gaitán (government of Ospina Pérez and Laureano Gómez)
3. The establishment and consolidation of oligarchical support structures with the application of a formula of economic liberalism and political absolutism.

García identifies three basic types of violence: (1) the counterrevolutionary violence that used the state as the prime instrument of repression; (2) survivals of the traditional confrontations between Liberals and Conservatives; and (3) a confusing, conflictive process of combined popular resistance and social decomposition.

Estanislao Zuleta proposes another interclass interpretation of the violence that centers the conflicts in the agrarian sector of Colombian society. He argues:

> The violence is the exact dimension assumed in Colombia by the neocolonial process of the capitalist decomposition of the peasantry. Pushed by the ideological domination, either of the Liberal bourgeoise or of the landowners entrenched in the Conservative party, large masses of exploited and impoverished peasants were confronted in a severe battle which bled them from 1948 until the beginning of the 1960s. Its immediate effect took the form of the large-scale expulsion of small, peasant proprietors to the cities and, indeed also of medium-sized owners, with the conversion of these important peasant masses into exploited, pauperized proletarians. On the ruins and spoilation of these peasant masses, there occurred the most substantial capitalist development of the agrarian sector.[20]

[20] Estanislao Zuleta, *La Tierra en Colombia* (Medellín: Editorial La Oveja Negra, 1973), pp. 108–109. John A. Booth argues that agrarian conflicts best explain the persistence of the violence into the period of the Frente Nacional. In a factor analysis of the relations between selected socioeconomic variables and the Colombian *Violencia* (utilizing the *departamento*-level violence data of Guzmán, Fals Borda, and Umaña Luna, *La Violencia*), Booth states the following as one of his conclusions:

> That which most predominately appears to have determined the persistence of the violence after the year 1958, however, is what might be interpreted as a syndrome of rural economic development and social disorientation–socioeconomic change. The coffee producing regions of Colombia, those with the highest level of rural economic development and which therefore enjoy a higher overall standard of living both in monetary terms and in terms of educational advantages (but also those in which more people tend to be in insecure tenancy arrangements—a partial function of increasingly capitalistic agricultural systems), are those in which the violence has lasted longest. (See Booth, "Rural Violence in Colombia: 1948–1963," *Western Political Quarterly*, no. 27 (1974), pp. 657–679.)

Francisco Posada offers a combination intraclass–interclass conflict hypothesis that differs drastically from Zuleta's position. Posada considers that it was not the capitalist developers who were favored by the violence but rather their more traditional adversaries. The Colombian attempt at bourgeois revolution that had begun in the 1930s was blocked and repressed by an alliance between the large landowners, the parasitic commercial interests, and the industrial monopolies that have traditionally benefited from the country's underdeveloped economic structures.

Posada argues that the development of agrarian capitalism was a highly localized phenomenon. The salient process was that the traditional *latifundistas* regained rather than lost power as a result of the violence. The spoliation of peasant lands was a most important factor, but it led to a new "semifeudal redistribution of the land" and not to agrarian capitalism.[21]

Peasants who left the countryside did not benefit from capitalism either, because they were far in excess of the capacity of industry to employ them and even far superior in number to the size of industrial reserve army necessary to depress wages and maintain weak unions.

In sum, Posada considers that the violence was not a step in capitalist development but rather a reaction by the most backward groups in the dominant class that slowed rather than accelerated the development of the country.

One of the most important drawbacks of the Fals Borda, Montaña Cuéllar, and Posada interpretations is that they do not clearly identify the groups and leaders that correspond to the different sociopolitical interests and positions mentioned. That task is not simple inasmuch as the traditional Colombian political parties are very heterogeneous. Given the largely "hereditary" nature of party identification, finance capitalists, large landowners, industrial capitalists, small peasants, and industrial workers, to name only a few groups, are to be found in both parties.

Reduction of the intraelite party struggle to differences between socioeconomic factions of the dominant class is thus very difficult. When Ospina Pérez was the Conservative president closing the Liberal-controlled

[21] Francisco Posada, *Colombia: Violencia y Subdesarrollo* (Bogotá: Universidad Nacional, 1968). Other interpretations on this same matter are to be found in Alonso Moncada Abello, *Un Aspecto de la Violencia* (Bogotá: Promotora Colombiana de Editores y Revistas Ltda., 1963), pp. 25–35; Alonso Tobón, *La Tierra y la Reforma Agraria en Colombia* (Medellín: La Oveja Negra, 1972), pp. 45–46. Moncada posits that the rapid transit from a paternalistic, agrarian society to an industrial, capitalist environment left the peasant without the protection that, "for better or for worse," he was receiving in the previous semi-feudal organization of society. Tobón proposes that it was only the small peasants who were expropriated by the violence inasmuch as the large landowners had the protection of the armed forces. He concludes that the party violence was the manifest conflict but the latent process was the intentional decomposition of the peasantry.

Congress, alleging that it was subversive, and Carlos Lleras Restrepo was National Director of the Liberal party plotting military coups with Liberal officers and supporting Liberal guerrillas in the Eastern Plains, what socioeconomic interests divided them? Did not both represent finance capital? Did not both have the support of some coffee growers, some bankers, some industrialists, some cattlemen, some peasants?

Zuleta and García do not face the difficulty of identifying which groups of the dominant class benefited from the violence and which did not because they posit that the entirety of the bourgeoisie, as a class, had a kindred interest in the violence. This only leads to a more serious problem because they conceptualize the intraelite, party competition as only a secondary factor. It may be appreciated from the exposition of the violence undertaken to this point that to ignore party conflicts as a basic element of the violence is a most untenable position.

In sum, determining the reasons for the intense intraelite political competition is a most complex problem. The socioeconomic bases offered for this conflict in the literature, as well as the other versions previously described, all leave much to be desired.

The socioeconomic explanations have the further difficulty of designating the relative weight of political as compared to socioeconomic factors and of intraclass as opposed to interclass conflicts. Another question has to do with the "structural significance" of the class conflicts.

Banditry is the most common example of violent redistribution of wealth without structural changes. Eduardo Santa describes various forms of such activities:

> Political motives began to disappear gradually among the authors of the official violence, inasmuch as many of them discovered that violence directed against defenseless persons could reap considerable economic dividends. Police detectives, and *pájaros* [literally, "birds"; figuratively, "hired political henchmen"] in the service of political party committees or sectarian *caciques* (bosses), found it lucrative to rob haciendas and small farms, take the coffee crop, or buy urban and rural property at reduced prices from defenseless victims threatened with death. . . . Thus the beneficiaries of the violence were established, and it was not infrequent for local political leaders to sponsor the violence due to the economic advantages derived from it.[22]

In addition to the "official crime" described by Santa, independent urban entrepreneurs of illicit wealth also arose. In a Colombian army study, one of the consequences of the violence is held to be the appearance of new bourgeosie who accumulated wealth as a result of the violence.[23] In the countryside, the inability of many farm owners to visit their parcels due

[22] Santa, *Sociología Política*, p. 65.

[23] República de Colombia, Ejército, Octava Brigada, *De La Violencia a la Paz* (Manizales: Imprenta Departamental, 1965), pp. 32–33.

to the violence led to a great increase in the wealth of many *mayordomos* ("farm foremen"). They and other farmhands consistently began to take a portion, if not all, of the coffee crop. Roving groups of bandits arose, many of them composed of peasants dislocated by the violence.[24]

Eric Hobsbawn considers some of these types of banditry to be primitive forms of social rebellion. The case of the *mayordomos* on the coffee farms is particularly thought to have class overtones.

Elements of class struggle are described by Darío Mesa, who views the dominant groups of society as taking the initiative in such battles:

> The political violence seems to have hidden class struggles but the latter, in reality, often assumed the form of the former. . . . The violence in the cities and in the rural regions might have had electoral ends in the beginning; but later the ends became more complex, and in this complexity it was possible to perceive, in some provinces, the war of the landlords against the sharecroppers, squatters, and poor peasants, and, in the agrarian exploitations of the capitalist type, the persecution of the owners against the labor organizations.[25]

Other authors attempt to give a more "bilateral" interpretation of class violence. Charles Anderson writes that for many the violence represented a popular uprising against an oppressive and unjust social order. Thus, the violence is seen as the inevitable result of a system characterized by extreme inequality. The other side of the argument conceives of the violence as a subversive campaign inspired and directed by communist elements. Anderson maintains that both explanations shed some light on the issue, the first more than the second. He holds that without a doubt there were elements of social discontent, of revolution, and of class struggle in the violence.[26]

Some authors carry the class struggle aspect of the violence to the point of depicting it as a popular social revolution. Fals Borda describes the class

[24] Enrique Benalcázar Saavedra and Gilberto Martínez Rave, "La Violencia en Colombia," *Proceedings of the 12th International Course in Criminology* (Jerusalem: Conference on the Causation and Prevention of Crime in Developing Countries, 1963), vol. 2, part 2, pp. 358–370.

Posada, *Colombia: Violencia y Subdesarrollo*, p. 149, writes of the creation of companies specialized in violence-related speculation, robbery, and commerce.

See also: Robert H. Dix, *Colombia: The Political Dimensions of Change* (New Haven: Yale University Press, 1967), p. 364; Captain Antonio Valencia Betancourt, "Causas y Soluciones de la Violencia en Colombia," *Revista de la Policía Nacional de Colombia*, no. 86 (March–April 1961); Gustavo González Ochoa, *Frente a la Violencia* (Medellín: Editorial Bedout, 1960); Guzmán, Fals Borda, and Umaña Luna, *La Violencia*, vol. 1, pp. 129—188; T.C.N. Gibbens and R. H. Ahrenfeldt, *Cultural Factors in Delinquency* (London: Tavistock, 1966), p. 70; Eric Hobsbawn, *Rebeldes Primitivos* (Barcelona: Ediciones Ariel, 1968), p. 229.

[25] Darío Mesa, "Treinta Años," pp. 52–53.

[26] Anderson, "La Violencia in Colombia," pp. 109–113.

struggles in the violence as a popular uprising without leadership or ideology. This vision of an aborted revolution is also shared by Vernon Fluharty and Eric Hobsbawn. Vernon Fluharty considers the Ninth of April insurrection in Bogotá to have been a veritable social revolution that was defeated due to lack of organization. L. A. Costa Pinto, on the other hand, considers the violence to have been a very "sophisticated expression of class struggle" utilized by the dominant groups in Colombian society, designed precisely to keep the masses unorganized.[27]

Related to political and socioeconomic explanations are those interpretations that approach the violence by analyzing the basic institutions of Colombian society.

Institutional Causes

Another group of interpretations of the violence posits institutional factors as being extremely important. In structural–functionalist terminology, Orlando Fals Borda has analyzed the violence as a grave disequilibrium attributable to an entire series of dysfunctional institutions. The roles of the society were deformed as part of widespread structural cleavages in Colombian society. For example, the police, rather than being the guardians of order, became the agents of disorder and crime.

The principal dysfunctions were the following: impunity in the judicial institutions, poverty and lack of land in the economic institutions, rigidity and fanaticism in the religious institutions, and ignorance in the educational institutions.[28] The crux of the conflict, according to Fals Borda, was the attempt "to impose mutually exclusive values within a situation of scarcity of positions and resources, with the objective being to influence the conduct of groups and thus determine the direction of social change within them." [29]

[27] Fals Borda, "Violence and the Breakup of Tradition," p. 197; Eric Hobsbawn, *Rebeldes Primitivos*, chap. 10; L. A. Costa Pinto, *Voto y Cambio Social* (Bogotá: Ediciones Tercer Mundo, 1971), pp. 33–53; Vernon Lee Fluharty, *Dance of the Millions: Military Rule and Social Revolution in Colombia, 1930–1956* (Pittsburgh: University of Pittsburgh Press, 1957), pp. 100–117.

[28] Education and violence are discussed in: República de Colombia, Ministerio de Educatión Nacional "Primer Seminario sobre la Educación en las Zonas de Violencia" (Ibague, 1963); *Ibid.*, "Segundo Seminario" (Cali, 1963).

Another institutional factor is mentioned by the majority of the authors that have studied the violence and by anyone who has read the Colombian press of the period of *La Violencia*. The communications systems are depicted as having exacerbated the conflict by partisan reporting that portrayed the opposing bands as assassins and their own dead as "martyrs." An article devoted to this question is "La Publicidad de La Violencia" (unsigned) in *Revista Javeriana*, vol. 53, ff, no. 261 (1960).

[29] Guzmán, Fals Borda, and Umaña Luna, *La Violencia*, vol. 1, chap. 13 (written by Fals Borda), pp. 361—381, with the direct quotation from p. 370.

An institutional explanation of the violence stressing political factors is presented by Mauricio Solaún. He asserts that in the course of this century social violence in Colombia has principally been the product of an insufficient institutionalization of democratic norms. Periods of violence are highly associated with two events: electoral competition and changes in party control of the presidency. Solaún emphasizes that the first is a produce of democratic practices and the latter, given determinate electoral outcomes, is a requirement of the Colombian constitution. Thus, the violence is very much associated with failures in democratic institutions.

Solaún further argues that variations in political violence have been conditioned by the degree of elite competition. With minimal elite rivalry, violence remains sporadic, while moderate intraelite conflict leads to higher levels of violence, as was the case with electoral violence in 1922 and 1930. Acute elite competition in the post-1946 period led to the cataclysmic result of *La Violencia*.[30]

Institutional failure is also cited in a Colombian army publication, which presents the following list of causes for the political violence: "The coercive insufficiency of the State, operational deficiencies in the penal and judicial systems, the party confrontations, misunderstandings of the ideological contexts of the parties, and blind obedience to political leaders."[31]

Police and judicial institutions are commonly thought to be significant causes of the violence. The police, utilized as a repressive political force, are depicted as one of the main protagonists of the violence, and the judicial system is described as corrupt, inefficient, and often as the protector of criminals of determinate political affiliation. The end result of the aforementioned factors was, on the one hand, the impunity of some of those involved in the violence, and, on the other, gross injustices perpetrated by those responsible for the judicial system.[32]

The role of the state as an institution in fomenting and continuing the violence is generally considered to be an important factor. In addition to the allegations of official repression previously described, the state is commonly accused of having been instrumental in the reinitiation of the vio-

[30] Solaún, "*La Violencia*." Another nonpartisan political interpretation is contained in John Pollock, "The Violence in Colombia: A Challenge to Political Elites?" mimeographed (Stanford University, 1969). Pollock is of the opinion that the violence was due to the nonresponsiveness of the Colombian political system in which the elite was more interested in maintaining power than confronting distributive and participatory political demands from the populace.

[31] Republic of Colombia, Ejército, Octava Brigada, *De La Violencia a la Paz* (Manizales: Imprenta Departamental, 1965), pp. 16–20.

[32] Eduardo Umaña Luna, *El Ambiente Penal de la Violencia* (Bogotá: Ediciones Tercer Mundo, 1962), reprint from chap. 12, "Factores Socio-Jurídicos de la Impunidad," of Guzmán, Fals Borda, and Umaña Luna, *La Violencia*; Horacio Gómez Aristizábal, *Teoría Gorgona* (Bogotá: Editorial Iqueima, 1962); Jorge Enrique Gutiérrez Anzola, *Violencia y Justicia* (Bogotá: Ediciones Tercer Mundo, 1962).

lence in late 1954. The basic version is that Communist-influenced regions in Eastern Tolima that opposed the military dictatorship were invaded by the army. Peasants were massacred and a resistance movement was organized, but, as it became progressively stronger, the repression became more intense. In the end, the peasants were forced to emigrate from the area, which was declared a "zone of military operations." [33]

A completely different approach to the study of *La Violencia* is to be found in attitudinal and racial explanations.

Psychological, Cultural, and Racial Causes

One line of this type of interpretation stresses the importance of the learning of attitudes necessary to perpetrate violent acts. Robert G. Williamson presents an example of this approach. He writes, "Socialization was systematically devoted to aggression and sadism over the larger part of a generation, at least for some thousands of males in relevant geographical areas." [34]

Of course, socialization was not devoted to violence for the prior generation that taught the subsequent group how to kill, yet one cannot dismiss this type of argument. If killing has taken place, someone definitely has learned to kill. The problem is obviously that such arguments tend to become tautological.

Another interpretation with a heavily psychological component is Robert Dix's explanation of *La Violencia* as a superimposition of the crisis of modernization upon Colombia's traditional party hatreds. He argues that "underlying conditions of social and economic change in the Colombian countryside led certain kinds of men to seek in la violencia an outlet for the frustrations of modernization. In the absence of such conditions, it is doubtful that the old political calls to violence would have evoked the response they did." [35]

An explanation used to account for the ferocity of violence in the interior of the country has to do with sexual frustrations. The argument, used both by Williamson and by Dix, runs that in the principal violent areas there is closer adherence to monogamy and Catholic marriages. Con-

[33] James M. Daniel, *Rural Violence in Colombia since 1946* (Washington, D.C.: American University, 1965), p. 93; Francisco Leal Buitrago, *Estudio del Comportamiento Legislativo*, pp. 100–103; Montaña Cuéllar, *Colombia: País Formal y País Real*, pp. 206–208.

[34] Robert G. Williamson, "Toward a Theory of Political Violence: The Case of Rural Colombia," *Western Political Quarterly* 18 (March 1965): 42.

Another example of this approach is to be found in Marvin E. Wolfgang and Franco Ferracuti, *The Subculture of Violence* (London: Tavistock, 1967), pp. 275–279.

[35] Dix, *Colombia*, pp. 363–364.

siderable regional exceptions are recognized, but the contention is made that the intensity of the violence in some areas may be attributed to this factor. While not wishing to deny that monogamy has its frustrations, one must still demand some evidence for the underlying presupposition, that is, that monogamous people tend to be more violent than others. The authors cited fail to demonstrate this presupposition.[36]

Psychiatrist José Gutiérrez conceptualizes *La Violencia* as a case of social pathology based on "political passion." The latter may lead to irrational sentiments conducive to a bestial regression to destructiveness, hate, and bitterness. Part of "political passion" is the unrestricted acceptance of political leadership. He writes:

> Constituted as a protective, root emotion that man needs to transcend the drama of his individuality, loneliness, and fear, the submission to irrational authority is in and of itself a regressive passion. Since it cripples man and tends to regress him to bestiality, it is a spring from which crimes are born as well as the rest of the inhuman characteristics of the Colombian violence.[37]

The frustration of "status deprivation" leads to a "need for aggression" among Colombians in general. This is the viewpoint of Everett Hagen, who holds that political and economic explanations of the violence are insufficient to account for the persistence of the phenomenon in the 1960s. Hagen not only explains the violence with this hypothesis but also with economic development. During his 3-month stay in Colombia, this author further found that "The high need for aggression is manifested less spectacularly today in urban traffic, national beauty contests and the rate of prostitution."[38] In sum, Hagen's use of "status deprivation" resembles "poverty" as a catchall explanation for almost anything that happens in an underdeveloped country.

[36] Williamson, "Toward a Theory of Political Violence," pp. 35–44; Dix, *Colombia*, pp. 368–369.

[37] José Gutiérrez, *La Revolución Contra el Miedo* (Bogotá: Ediciones Tercer Mundo, 1964), esp. pp. 65—115 (the direct quotation is from p. 77). See also his other work, *La Rebeldía Colombiana* (Bogotá: Ediciones Tercer Mundo, 1972).

Psychologically oriented studies have also been undertaken of *Violencia* victims. See Alfredo Ardila, *Psicología y Problemas Sociales en Colombia* (Tunja: Universidad Pedagógica y Tecnológica de Colombia, 1971), pp. 41–44; Aaron Lipman and A. Eugene Havens, "The Colombian Violencia: An Ex-Post Facto Experiment," *Social Forces* 44 (December 1965): 238–245.

[38] Everett E. Hagen, *El Cambio Social en Colombia* (Bogotá: Ediciones Tercer Mundo, 1963). The "need for aggression" in Colombia is discussed on pp. 97–101. The direct quotation is from p. 99. The original reads: "La elevada necesidad de agresión se manifiesta menos espectacularmente hoy en el tráfico urbano en los concursos nacionales de belleza y en la tasa de prostitución." The original quotation is given inasmuch as it in turn is a translation from English. This book is a translation of Hagen's *On the Theory of Social Change* (Homewood, Ill.: The Dorsey Press, n.d.), chap. 15.

Cultural interpretations are often close to and/or combined with racist explanations. Typical of these arguments is the account attributed to "numerous observers" in the conclusions on *La Violencia* of an American University study for the United States Army.

> Some have advanced the theory that the ethnic mixture of the considerable majority, particularly in the countryside, predisposes to violence, or has a "low boiling point." . . . Still others adduce Spanish culture conditioning characterized by excessive and touchy individualism, which causes intolerance of opposition, the viewing of difference of opinion as an insult and the desire of each person or faction to be a law unto itself, finding security only in the extermination of opponents. Such qualities they find transmitted, without any inhibiting "civilized control," by the dominant culture to the masses of mixed blood.[39]

RATIONAL AND IRRATIONAL VIOLENCE

Closely linked to some of the cultural and psychological interpretations is the notion that *La Violencia* was largely an irrational phenomenon. It is also common in the literature in general to find sensationalistic attention devoted to irrational aspects of the violence. For both of these reasons it is necessary to examine this theme.

Violence may be either rational or irrational. This study of *La Violencia* in Colombia is primarily restricted to violence as a "means," that is to say "rational violence." Violence is considered rational if it is a means utilized in the pursuit of potentially realizable goals. Conversely, "irrational violence" is physical aggression or the credible threat of the same that is not oriented toward a goal, but that has violence itself as a goal (i.e., as in the case of psychological satisfaction derived from violence), or that does not have the potential to achieve the goal in question. Examples are a senseless killing, the elicitation of sadistic, masochistic, or cathartic satisfactions, violence employed in the pursuit of an impossible goal, or violence by which it is impossible to achieve a realistic objective. In sum, the violent conduct of psychotics, sadists, or *quijotes* ("rebels motivated by illusory causes") with tenuous relationships to reality constitutes "irrational violence."

Most instances of widespread, protracted social violence are not characterized by irrational violence. However, irrational violence does tend to

[39] United States, Department of the Army, *U. S. Army Handbook for Colombia* (Washington, D.C.: U.S. Army Headquarters, 1961), p. 387. These studies are prepared by Foreign Area Studies, American University. Other racist interpretations are to be found in: José Francisco Socarras and Luis López de Mesa cited in Guzmán, Fals Borda, and Umaña Luna, *La Violencia*, vol. 2, pp. 384–385; Lt. Col. Efraín Vivas García, "La Violencia en Colombia," in *Revista del Ejército*, vol. 4, no. 17 (February 1964); Daniel, *Rural Violence in Colombia Since 1946*, p. 12; Gutiérrez Anzola, *Violencia y Justicia*, p. 17.

accompany rational violence and increase in intensity with it. In war, sadistic killings, senseless slayings, and the destruction rather than the attainment of goals by the use of excessive violence are common. Likewise, in civil violence, the breakdown of the instruments of social control tends to lead to an incapacity to efficiently repress irrational violence, with a concomitant increase in its frequency.

Social life tends to have a rational basis. Irrational behavior, of course, is nearly always present and it is an important object of study, but it tends to be of less importance in structuring social relationships than rational behavior. We might hypothesize that rational actors with explicit goals and at least potentially efficient means have a tremendous strategic advantage relative to more irrational actors, given their relative rationality (although tactically the unpredictability of irrational behaviors may prove to be a short-run advantage). What concrete goals and means constitute a given rationality is subject to great sociohistoric variation. There are many rationalities, but the bare fact that social life responds to one or another of them, or set of them, is what makes potentially possible the explanation and prediction of social phenomena.

These general observations about rational behavior may also be argued for a social process as pervasive in human history as violence. Rational violence has been more important as a social process in structuring society than its irrational equivalent. On the other hand, irrational violence, like other forms of behavior that respond to the abnormal psychology of individuals responding to internal conflicts and satisfactions, is not *generally* significant in structuring society. The most important exception would seem to be the results of the attainment of great power by a psychopathic individual or group of individuals. More frequent in the structuring of most societies, most of the time, are the outcomes of social conflicts between goal-oriented groups attempting to maximize their interests by at least potentially efficient means.

Psychological approaches to the explanation of violence are not rejected in this study. However, it is maintained here that psychological processes that involve large numbers of individuals over protracted periods of time, as do most structuring social processes, cannot be referred exclusively to cognitive factors without adopting an idealist view of social dynamics. The other alternative is to refer the psychological variables to either social or biological bases.

The most common psychological approach to the study of violence is "frustration–aggression" theory.[40] The classical version of this position

[40] Much discussed recently has also been the "instinct" theory of aggression. Obligatory reading in this literature is Konrad Lorenz, *On Aggression* (New York: Harcourt, 1966). Lorenz considers aggression to be a highly functional instinct that contributes to survival.

posits that *aggression is always a consequence of frustration*.[41] While quite obviously much aggressive behavior, both rational and irrational, is preceded and accompanied by frustration and anger, it is very venturesome to state this position universally.

Some of the most violent of human events, such as wars of conquest or the massive repression of determinate groups, are realized by specialized "professionals" in violence. The application of "frustration–aggression" theory tends, however, to restrict the concept "violence" or cognate terms to illegitimate nongovernmental acts, thus adopting a unilateral view of violent interactions, which eliminates most "professionals" from consideration, by definition.[42] "In the end, the actions of frustrated dissidents are uniformly depicted as 'irrational,' expressive, aggressive, and violent, whereas the actions of political authorities are rational, instrumental, benevolent, and conflict-managing." [43] The categorization of physical coercion as irrational or rational is thus based on criteria of political legitimacy. It is doubtful whether the literature that suffers this bias is uniformly correct in terms of any nation. It is very clear that this type of theoretical presupposition would destine a study of *La Violencia* in Colombia to complete failure.

Even in instances where "frustration" patently accompanies violent behavior, it does not explain anything in and of itself. The question only resolves to what might one attribute the frustration in question. The position taken in this research is that social conflicts generally present the most promising avenue for research if one is interested in studying the role of violent behavior in structuring social relations.

In Colombia, the sociopolitical processes known as *La Violencia* were accompanied by much irrational violence. This is hardly surprising con-

[41] John Dollard, Leonard W. Dobb, Neal E. Miller, O. M. Mowrer, and Robert R. Sears, *Frustration and Aggression* (New Haven: Yale University Press, 1967).

[42] See Leonard Berkowitz, "The Study of Urban Violence: Some Implications of Laboratory Studies of Frustration and Aggression," in *When Men Revolt and Why*, ed. James Chowning Davies (New York: The Free Press, 1971), pp. 182–187; Leonard Berkowitz, ed., *Roots of Aggression: A Re-examination of the Frustration and Aggression Hypothesis* (New York: Atherton Press, 1968); Ted Gurr, "Psychological Factors in Civil Violence," in *Revolution and Political Change*, eds. Claude E. Welch, Jr., and Marvis Bunker Taintor (Belmont, California: Wadworth, 1972), pp. 91–121; Ted Robert Gurr, *Why Men Rebel* (Princeton, N.J.: Princeton University Press, 1970); Ivo K. Feierabend and Rosalind L. Feierabend, "Aggressive Behavior within Polities, 1948–1962: A Cross-National Study," *Journal of Conflict Resolution*, 10 (Sept. 1966): 240—271.

A similar theory applied to revolutions is maintained by James C. Davies. He holds that revolutions occur when rising expectations meet sharp frustrations. See his "Toward a Theory of Revolution," *American Sociological Review* 6 (Feb. 1962): 5–19, and his "Revolution and the J-Curve," in *Revolution and Political Change*, eds. C.E. Welch and M.B. Taintor, op. cit., pp. 122–153.

[43] Terry Nardin, "Violence and the State: A Critique of Empirical Political Theory," Sage Professional Paper No. 01-120 (Beverly Hills: Sage Publications, 1971), p. 62.

sidering the intensity of *La Violencia* and the degree to which the repressive capacity of the state was deflated.

The literature on *La Violencia* tends to be highly sensationalistic with regard to sadistic and other irrational aspects of the phenomenon.[44] These include sadistic torture, the mutilation of corpses, "not leaving the seed," sexual crimes and genocides, each of which are now briefly examined.

Within the extensive catalogue of irrational violence in Colombia, one finds most of the well-known forms of sadistic torture, ranging from psychological torment to intense physical pain, to dismemberment, to death. One form of investigation consisted of airborne questioning in which those who did not talk were thrown from the airplane one by one by the military authorities.

The mutilation of corpses took the form of quartering, sadistic machete cuts (scalping, the passing of the tongue from the bottom of the mouth over the throat, known as the "necktie cut," and the opening of the throat so as to hang victims from stakes), as well as the use of knives to open the victims like a fish or to cut them into small pieces (known as "dicing for tamales"). Ears were also cut off of some victims. There existed commandants that demanded ears from patrols as a macabre form of accounting for efficiency. Mutilation of sexual organs also took place.

"Not leaving the seed" of the enemy consisted of the assassination of children and pregnant women, some of whom had the fetus cut out of them by the aggressors.

Rapes and mass rapes, at times before relatives of the victims, were another aspect of the ferocity of *La Violencia,* with children often being the victims.

"Genocides" consisted of the slaying of entire families or villages. The objective would be to leave no one alive. On occasion these mass assassinations took the form of burning gasoline-drenched victims. Highwaymen also killed at times the totality of the occupants of the buses, cars, and trucks attacked.

The authors that posit psychocultural and/or racist interpretations also seek explanatory leverage by depicting the violence as pathological. Wolfgang and Ferracuti, for example, label the violence as senseless in their conclusions:

> Almost all of the brutal and senseless paraphenalia of slaying known to history have been exhibited in Colombia. The ever-present feeling of menace,

[44] This is especially the case with non-Colombian authors. The single source of much of their information is contained in Guzmán, Fals Borda, and Umaña Luna, *La Violencia,* vol. 1. Sensational photographs and detailed recompilation of the more prevalent forms of irrational violence are contained on pp. 176–177 and 203–214. The following summary of forms of irrational violence is based on extensive interviews, as well as on the Guzmán *et al.* account.

> fear, and death, the actual visual presentation of mangled bodies and other sadistic manifestations, together with a desire for revenge in those children whose parents or relatives have been victims of violence, all tend to perpetuate a situation which possibly has no equal in contemporary Western Civilization. . . . But nowhere in the Western world in recent times since the Second World War has senseless brutality, a genocidal pattern, and a non-war pattern of violence been nearly so total as in the Colombian tragedy.[45]

The emphasis on the irrational aspects of the violence combined with psychocultural and racist explanations has led to the discussion in Colombia of whether or not Colombians are a violent people.[46]

The approach used in this study considers that Colombians are neither more nor less prone to violence than other nationalities. One of the most notable characteristics of violence is its universality. All peoples have been violent in certain structural conditions and pacific in others. All nations continually confront irrational violence and all have experienced violent sociopolitical processes of a rational nature at different junctures in their histories.

This study argues that *La Violencia* may be explained by reference to rational socioeconomic and political processes, and that the irrational aspects of the phenomenon do not satisfactorily explain its origins or its intensity or its geographical distribution. To achieve an explanation of widespread, protracted, social violence, one must refer to the *social conflicts* that underlie such conduct and to the factors that condition whether a given conflict becomes violent or not.

A Critique

A question that arises in reference to the psychological and cultural explanations regards the presuppositions that underlie them. To what, in turn, might one attribute the psychocultural factors?

If further psychological or cultural elements are exclusively cited, one

[45] Marvin Wolfgang and Franco Ferracuti, *The Sub-Culture of Violence: Toward an Integrated Theory in Criminology* (London: Tavistock, 1967), pp. 276–277, 278–279.

[46] An interesting discussion of this same polemic, with reference to the United States, is found in the epilogue entitled: "The Violent People Myth," in Richard E. Rubenstein, *Rebels in Eden: Mass Political Violence in the United States* (Boston: Little, Brown, 1970), pp. 188–192. Rubenstein considers that the myth "locates the source of all violence in individual souls rather than in the way the political system works" (p. 189). "It begins by imposing upon all Americans an unbearable burden of personal responsibility for *all* violence, and ends by relieving most of us—and our system—of any responsibility for *political* violence" (p. 190). In Colombia, as in the United States, I would add, "Modern national self-denunciation ends with a new resolve to root out and exterminate violent men" (p. 190).

arrives at a view of social life similar to idealist ontological and epistemological positions, that is, a concept of society reduced exclusively to cognitive processes with no objective structural limit, be it natural or social on man's "will." This "voluntaristic" position leads to little explanatory leverage with regard to complex social processes.

If psychocultural factors are to be related to other elements, the options are basically two. Psychological or cultural explanations of the behavior of large aggregates of human beings over long periods of time reduce to either social or racial explanations. If collective psychocultural traits are not attributable to social-structure factors, then the explanation must be genetic (and thus collectively racial) or some mix of the two. Hybrid theories, however, are usually clearly social or racial in their basic assumptions.

In sum, if psychological or cultural variables are seen as socially influenced, they must be grounded by an analysis of the socioeconomic and political factors that structure society. If genetic criteria are selected, then the psychocultural arguments lead to racist explanations. If only further psychocultural factors are utilized, then the argument lapses into a classic idealist position by positing that only subjective, cognitive elements structure social life.

It is argued here that psychological or cultural explanations of violence are highly unsatisfactory if not referred to social-structure contexts. Racial arguments do not have any basis whatsoever. The reason for both of these assertions is that social violence is to be found within all racial and cultural groups given all of the collective psychological variations that are to be found within them. Germans, North Americans, and the British have all been violent given different social conflicts and peaceful in other structural conditions. The same may be said for Chinese, Japanese, Indonesians, Laotians, Nicaraguans, Congolese, Algerians, and South Africans. Any group that one can mention has resorted to violence in the past and may do so in the present or in the future, given certain structural circumstances. The interesting questions then, are the social conflicts that underlie group antagonisms and the factors that condition their becoming violent.

The institutional, socioeconomic, and political causes identified in the literature are all important for an understanding of *La Violencia*. There obviously were multiple collapses in the basic institutions of the country. Likewise, the socioeconomic and political explanations all contain crucial elements. Within these interpretations, however, there is great diversity as to how these factors are interrelated and as to how to depict the violence. The versions range from an armed conflict between political parties for bureaucratic posts to an aborted social revolution.

The studies that stress political factors tend to have a common failing in that they do not adequately explain the causes of the intraelite rivalries that fomented partisan violence. To stipulate merely an intraelite conflict for control of the state as a basic cause of the violence, without attempting to explain the same, leaves the interpretation at a very superficial level. Attempts to relate this conflict to economic factors often avoid the task of specifying the groups and leaders that correspond to different interests or encounter serious problems in the process. Those interpretations that stress interclass struggles to the point of ignoring Conservative–Liberal intraelite contradictions confront an even more serious problem, which is that the manifest motivation of a large portion of the participants in the violence was partisan.

In sum, the relationships between political and socioeconomic factors, and between interclass and intraclass conflicts, as well as the explanation of the causes of the latter, are crucial questions that are not satisfactorily answered in the literature on the Colombian *Violencia*. The lack of an integrated theory is a major lacunae in the existing knowledge of this phenomenon.

The Contribution of the Alternative Structural Explanation

One of the causes of the weaknesses in the literature may be a common presupposition that underlies most of the interpretations: that the violence was a unitary phenomenon susceptible to a single set of explanations for the entirety of the Republic of Colombia. It will be recalled that the alternative explanation summarized in Chapter 1 begins with the position that *La Violencia* consisted precisely of a series of social processes that occurred in different locations at different times. In some regions these processes took place simultaneously, in others sequentially, while still other areas experienced only a single process instead of several.

But if the violence is composed of various processes, of what do they consist, how are they interrelated, and what are the common elements that might explain their occurrence at practically the same point in Colombian history? These questions might best be handled by a structural analysis of Colombian society. This approach, hopefully, permits a clearer understanding of the mix between political and socioeconomic elements in the origins and development of the violence, of the violence producing conflicts within the political elite, and of the role of interclass as opposed to intraclass conflicts. This treatment of *La Violencia* as several processes requires an examination of local and regional, as well as national, socioeconomic and political processes. In order to achieve this, a structural regionalization of *La Violencia* is undertaken to study the various conflicts that led to violence.

The social structural theoretical framework for the study of violence utilizes a dialectical methodological procedure. It identifies: (1) the areas in which violence took place; (2) the social groups involved; (3) the conflicts and contradictory interests that underly physically coercive struggles; and (4) the factors that conditioned the maturation of contradictions into conflicts and those that condition their violent expression.

Different answers to these queries are to be found for different areas of Colombia. That is the basis of the structural regionalization.

The diversity of the phenomenon precludes the achievement of an adequate explanation without reference to the multiple conflicts that led to violence in different areas. This approach immediately leads to the question of why these conflicts almost simultaneously evolved into physically coercive struggles.

The answer forms one of the basic hypotheses of this study. It is that a partial collapse of the state occurred as a result of intense partisan conflicts. The political elite was divided to such an extent that state authority was deflated. This took place at the national, regional, and local levels. It is this partial collapse of the state that explains the nearly simultaneous evolution of numerous conflicts into violence. This dovetailing of various physically coercive struggles is what in turn explains the intensity of *La Violencia*. The duration is in part attributable to the difficulty of reasserting state authority in some areas. The importance of the hypothesis of the "partial collapse of the state" requires extensive treatment in the course of this study.

A historical, structural analysis is necessary to understand the reason for the intense, state-delibitating conflict within the political elite, the concrete manifestations and effects of the partial collapse of the state, and the reasons for the social explosions that followed the deflation of state authority.

The basic historical analysis employed in this study has analyzed the role of the state relative to other factors in the total structuring of society. These relationships were also examined in relation to previous instances of widespread social violence in Colombian history.

Spanish colonial society was characterized by a strong state embedded in a strong social structure. This describes a very stable society, which colonial Nueva Granada certainly was for centuries.

The nineteenth-century republic is described as a weak state in a strong social structure. Indeed, the latter was so resilient that the state collapsed partially, or nearly totally, a number of times without the social fabric undergoing major transformations. The nineteenth-century civil wars were, with few, but significant, exceptions, intraclass conflicts for the control of the state and the structure of domination within the society. Some of these wars concerned precisely the question of state organization (federalism versus centralism, limited parliamentary democracy versus dictatorships). Despite the frequency of the wars, these intense conflicts among the ruling class and the concomitant collapses of effective state power did not alter the basic socioeconomic relations of the society, or even the fundamental power relations, in that these were not highly "state-oriented."

The lower classes generally accepted without conflict the authority of the *latifundistas*, the local *caudillo*, and the priest. The dominated classes generally did not need to be coerced into obedience, as they were often ideologically in agreement with the prevailing social distribution of goods, services, privileges, and responsibilities. In addition, to the high degree of legitimacy characteristic of nineteenth-century Colombian society, the national government was a distant and abstract entity with little impact on day-to-day life. In those exceptional cases where popular rebellions occurred, generally the local power structure, and not the distant national government, forcefully maintained the existing social order.

Toward the late-nineteenth century and the beginning of the twentieth century there began in Colombia a series of socioeconomic processes that matured the potential social conflicts (i.e., contradictions) in Colombian society and spawned new ones. Concentrated economic and social change led to new forms of social consciousness and to the appearance of organized labor and political groups that were outside of the traditional ruling circles. Conflicts of diverse types developed both in the countryside and in the rapidly changing urban environments. These conflicts subsequently proved to have a high potential for violence.

During the 1920s, the political issue *par excellence* among the ruling, traditional party elites was the "social question," a relative novelty in Colombian politics. The solutions proposed to confront the new social ferment (which matured due to the dovetailing of several socioeconomic factors) were either to emphasize repressive measures or to adopt a more reformist tactic. In either event, the political strategies debated within the ruling class implied a common denominator, the strengthening of the state. In a situation of weakened social control, the state was fortified.

During the period of the 1920s and especially the 1930s, the contemporary Colombian state (whose foundations were laid by Rafael Núñez and his followers in 1886) was constructed. The state edifice that emerged was an interventionist, nonpluralist entity that either absorbs or represses the social forces and organizations that are political actors. The nonpluralist nature of the state not only encompassed control of the government by a small ruling class, but also the exclusion of part of the same on partisan, political grounds.

This tendency to exclude the opposing party from participation in state power was a continuation of nineteenth-century political processes, which were characterized by efforts to construct political party hegemonies. This political pattern was complicated by the tendency of the parties to be divided into political factions, due to the representation in each party of heterogeneous interests. Within the strategies designed to create hegemonies, alliances and coalitions were often formed with factions of the opposing party. These accords were designed to divide the partisan enemy, offset factional opponents in the same party, reduce the relative political power of opponents at critical junctures, or close ranks within the ruling elite in those rare but significant instances of threats to the common, fundamental interests of the ruling groups in the society (e.g., acute economic crisis, foreign interventions, popular rebellion).

The intricate politics of political party hegemonies took place in the context of a weak state within a strong social structure. The loss of state power did not present a given group with an absolutely critical situation because frequently their economic, social, political, and even military repressive powers were locally based and not subject to national government revocation. It was in this context that one must consider the intricate strategies and continual series of wars between the factions that struggled to control Colombian national politics.

With the weakening of social structure as a result of relatively rapid economic and social transformations, this situation swiftly changed. As previously mentioned, the state was fortified to compensate for the weakening of other elements in the social structure. From the 1920s through the 1940s the economy was rapidly "state-oriented," in terms of both governmental regulations and the role of the state as a key economic actor. The formation of militant agrarian movements and labor unions, and the appearance of strikes, land invasions, and other expressions of interclass social contradictions, reached the point where the central government buttressed by a strong army assumed a more important role in the maintenance of the social order. Other attempts to modernize the state by reformist measures led to the entrance of the state into areas of Colombian society where it had previously been absent.

The increasing "state-orientation" of the economy and the social order led to the point where it became impossible to conceive of any large-scale enterprise in any sector of activity without the protection and good-will of the state. Yet patterns of political relations had not altered with the socioeconomic realities. The basic partisan objective was still the erection of mutually exclusive party hegemonies. The alliances and coalitions between groups were still merely tactical maneuvers toward hegemonic goals.

Partisan, hegemonic policies were pursued under circumstances where it was inconceivable for any group within the propertied classes of society to accept being excluded from governmental contracts, regulatory decision making, tax favors, import privileges, control of the police, and the other "success or failure" benefits to be derived from "*palancas*" ("political pull"). For middle-level party activists, political patronage was also at stake, but for the powerful economic interest groups that controlled the traditional Colombian political parties, the increased economic importance of the state was the prime motivation for the intraelite political struggles.

These battles cut across class lines, factions of classes, income and wealth strata, and, indeed, across the entire society. Given the traditional hatreds and the intense party elite conflicts, almost everyone had an interest in the outcome of the conflict. The issue of security against repression affected the bulk of the society in this nonpluralistic contest to create absolutistic party hegemonies. The possibility of an opposition victory was considered catastrophic.

When party competition began to deflate state authority and effectiveness, some important party leaders sought continued coalitions to defend basic common interests of the dominant classes and/or to avoid a civil war. The dynamics of party competition proved unabateable, however, and the party struggle continued at all levels of society.

In sum, a division in Colombia's *clase dirigente* ("ruling class") occurred as a result of nonpluralistic, mutually exclusive partisan politics under socioeconomic circumstances where neither side would admit banishment from state power. The result of this conflict was a partial collapse of the state in a society with numerous potential social conflicts. The deflation, inefficacy, and, in some cases, absence of state power led to the exacerbation of these conflicts, and frequently to their violent expression. Many of these conflicts were of an interclass nature. This combination of different social processes in *La Violencia* accounts in good measure for the intensity of the phenomenon. Its geographical distribution was generally concentrated in those areas in which there occurred both the partial collapse of the state and the maturation of social contradictions into acute conflicts. In the absence of one or both of these factors the violence did not tend to occur or its presence was mild and transitory.

It is considered that the contribution of the social-structure explanation to the literature is that it provides a comprehensive position from which to analyze and perfect a more precise interpretation of *La Violencia*. Future research might thus benefit from and critique a view that considers *La Violencia* as having consisted of multiple social processes and therefore which posits diverse conditioning elements with regard to its origins, evolution, intensity, and geographical distribution. This approach also facilitates the simultaneous treatment of socioeconomic and sociopolitical factors and of interclass and intraclass conflict, as well as offers a structural explanation for the social contradictions involved.

For the development of this argument, we now turn to a consideration of, first, the hypothesis of the partial collapse of the state and, finally, the structural regionalization of *La Violencia*.

5

The Partial Collapse of the State

The Social Question

A reading of the Colombian press during the 1920s reveals that the obsessive political issue was termed *la cuestión social* ("the social question"). Indian rebellions, peons refusing to pay landlords rents or their part of the share crop, landlords evicting colonists, peasants refusing to cease to grow coffee on their plots and the landlords uprooting coffee plants, peasants migrating to the public works projects, and the landlords and local authorities impeding the migrations, organized groups of peasants challenging the land rights of large landowners, organized labor unions and socialist political activities, large-scale strikes, the army intervening in labor disputes, and jailings, house-burning, crop destruction, killings, and massacres were all part of the most heated public polemic of Colombia of the 1920s.

The importance of the emergence of acute interclass conflict and the enormous impact that it produced within the Colombian ruling groups must be placed in their proper historical context. First, the dominant class in Colombia was not accustomed to this type of conflict. The submissive masses of the nineteenth century did not represent a threat to the dominant groups in society. With the exceptions of the War of the Supremes and the military–artisan coup of 1854, there were practically no serious interclass conflicts in nineteenth-century Colombia. For nearly 75 years politics had been a game between different factions of the same class. Second, the conflicts involved were important because they formed the dynamic cutting edge that was defining and structuring social relationships in times of land scarcity,[1] industrialization, and the entrance of considerable foreign capital.

[1] In the central core areas of the country.

The 1930 presidential election presents a microcosm of the debate over the social question. The Conservative candidacy of General Alfredo Vásquez Cobo recommended certain changes in labor relations, but its basic solution was to violently repress all manifestations of social disorder. The candidacy of Guillermo León Valencia offered a mix of reform and a strong hand, as did that of Liberal Enrique Olaya Herrera. The latter candidate, however, stressed more vigorously the need to reform the country's socioeconomic and political structures so as to facilitate domestic industrialization, foreign investment, and the achievement of labor relations in accord with the new capitalist system that was rapidly replacing the traditional, paternalistic work relations that had characterized nineteenth-century Colombia. In sum, the candidates offered different mixes of "reform and repression as solutions to "the social question." Within the various positions there was a common denominator: Under conditions where the traditionally strong structure of domination in Colombia was rapidly weakening as a result of accelerated socioeconomic change, all of the candidates recommended an increase in the power of the state.

Religious, partisan ideological, and paternalistic economic relationships were no longer structuring relations between the Colombian bourgeoisie and significant portions of the working classes with their traditional effectiveness. The result had been a series of conflicts that demonstrated the progressive weakness of the structure of domination. Privately applied violence was utilized, but the working groups by then were often organized, and they had the capacity to resist. The landlords and the owners of industries began to rely on the state to structure and consolidate their relations with the rebellious groups. Whether by reform or repression, the state was beginning to assume a more important role in the structuring of Colombian society. Contrary to the colonial case of a strong state in a strong structure of domination, or the nineteenth-century republican case of a weak state within a strong structure of domination, twentieth-century Colombia came to be progressively characterized by an increasingly strong state within a weakened structure of social domination. The strengthening of the state was designed both to structure relations between the classes and to facilitate the transformation of the nation's socioeconomic structures to capitalistic modernity.

The Strengthening of the State

Within the first decades of this century, but particularly after 1930, the state vastly increased in importance as a structuring element in Colombian society. The weak state within a strong structure of social domination, which characterized nineteenth-century Colombia, had not ended with the proclamation of the 1886 constitution, which contemplated a strong, centralist state. Indeed, these constitutional precepts were still largely fictional as late as 1908, as demonstrated by Rafael Reyes's ill-fated confrontation with regional power structures over the centralization of monopolies.[2]

The strengthening of the state in the twentieth century basically coincided with the socioeconomic changes that began to affect the country beginning with World War I and the social conflicts accompanying those processes. The state was strengthened to accommodate Colombian society to capitalist socioeconomic structures, to accelerate integration into the world capitalist system, and to compensate for the decline of traditional mechanisms of social control.

The increase in the structural importance of the state consisted of numerous factors initiated at diverse points in time. The most important, however, were the increase in the importance of the armed apparatus of the state in structuring social relations, the increase in the state's control over the most strategic special-interest groups in Colombian society, and the state's emergence as the nation's prime economic actor.

The efficacy of the armed apparatus of the state was increased as a result of the permanent establishment of the National Military Academy in 1907, the arrival of Chilean and Swiss military missions, the acquisition of contemporary arms to replace antiquated stocks, and the general professionalization and modernization of the military.[3] The armed apparatus became more important because it assumed control over social conflicts, which had not been the case in the nineteenth century. During that century, repression generally was not used to maintain the existing social structure; when it was, directly applied local violence was more common than recourse to state control. The appearance of organized movements that sought to transform important aspects of existing socioeconomic structures led to conflicts that local and regional power structures could not handle. The result was an increased reliance on state repression. Thus, the police and the army confronted Indians, colonists, sharecroppers, and workers during agrarian and labor conflicts from 1914 onward.

The state also increased its control over the most strategic special-in-

[2] Reference is made here to the previously described attempts by Reyes to nationalize liquor, tobacco, and match monopolies. The move was resisted by regional, *latifundista*-backed *caudillos* in Huila and Magdalena. Reyes lost this battle and was forced to retreat in face of opposition from his own political base of support. See Malcolm Deas, "Algunas Notas sobre el Caciquismo en Colombia," *Revista de Occidente*, no. 127 (1973), p. 131. Deas states that "due to the weakness of its resources, the state remained in fact much less centralized than one would deduce from the letter of the 1886 constitution" (p. 12).

[3] Francisco Leal Buitrago, "Política e Intervención Militar en Colombia," in *La Dependencia Externa y el Desarrollo Político de Colombia*, ed. Rodrigo Parva Sandoval (Bogotá: Universidad Nacional de Colombia, 1970), pp. 5–18; Anthony Maingot, "The Colombian Military: A Case of Inconsistent Status," in *The Role of the Military in Latin America*, ed. Lyle N. McAlister (Gainesville: University of Florida Press, forthcoming), pp. 89–294.

terest groups in Colombian society. The most powerful group was and is the *Federación Nacional de Cafeteros* ("National Coffee Growers Federation"). Founded very late (1927), the federation was born with a state subsidy. The government was to collect a 10-cent (Colombian currency) tax on the export of every sack of coffee.[4] These funds were to be returned to the federation to finance its programs. In 1935, a higher tax was enacted, and the government began to be represented on the board of directors of the federation.[5] Very soon the federation began to assume functions that in most societies would be considered attributes of the state. It monopolizes legal coffee exports, largely controls the domestic coffee market, sets prices, and makes decisions that affect obtaining foreign exchange with regard to the nation's leading export. In addition, the huge capital managed by the federation makes it one of the nation's most important financial institutions.[6] At times it is difficult to determine whether the state controls the federation or the federation controls the state, at least with regard to coffee policy. At any rate, it is impossible to determine where the state ends and the federation begins.

The labor movement provides another example of the increase in interaction between the state and strategic special-interest groups. The Liberal governments of the 1930s began to attempt to ameliorate the highly conflictive labor situation by legally recognizing the labor movement and by actively supporting its development. The López Pumarejo administration sided several times with strikers in their confrontations with management. In addition, the López government firmly supported the establishment in 1936 of the *Confederación de Trabajadores de Colombia* (CTC, "Colombian Confederation of Workers"). In turn, organized labor (including the Communist unions) firmly supported the López government.[7]

[4] Ana Luz Londoño, "La Federación Nacional de Cafeteros" (Bogotá: unpublished essay, 1975), chap. 2. Direct State subsidies of special-interest groups continue to this day. The Rice Growers Association receives $1 Colombian peso from the government for each pound of rice produced in the country, and the Cereal Growers Association, among others, has similar arrangements. The National Cattlemen's Association receives the benefits of a tax collected by the state on each head of cattle slaughtered in the country. Government subsidies obviously impede active opposition to policies or recourse to partisan politics as a means to protect the interests of a given sector. For example, in the 1974 presidential campaign, Alfonso López Michelsen headed off a declaration by the cattlemen at their Ibagué Convention in favor of Alvaro Gómez Hurtado, by pointing out that a government-financed entity could not support a candidate.

[5] *El Tiempo*, Nov. 9, 1934, Jan. 6, July 2, Aug. 4, Oct. 4, 1935.

[6] Estanislao Zuleta and Asociación Nacional de Usuarios Campesinos (ANUC), *La Tierra en Colombia* (Bogotá: La Oveja Negra, 1973), p. 49.

[7] Miguel Urrutia, *Historia del Sindicalismo en Colombia* (Bogotá: Ediciones Universidad de Los Andes, 1969), chap. 8; Daniel Pecaut, *Política y Sindicalismo en Colombia* (Bogotá: La Carreta, 1973), chap. 2; Edgar Caicedo, *Historia de las Luchas Sindicales en Colombia* (Bogotá: Ediciones Suramérica, 1974), pp. 61–79.

The second annual labor congress of the CTC was financed by a subsidy that the Liberal government had pushed through Congress. A subsequent decree, issued in December 1937, led to government regulation of the unions' expenditures of government subsidies. This initiated government supervision of union assemblies and its involvement in union elections. Progressively the labor movement became an instrument of the Lopista wing of the Liberal party, which maintained a "popular front alliance" with the Communists in the labor movement. Thus, the once belligerent labor movement was institutionalized and controlled by the Liberal governments of the 1930s.[8]

In a manner similar to the coffee growers and the unions, existing special-interest groups in Colombia generally tend to be closely linked with the state, or harassed and repressed by it. The state has also played an important role in organizing special-interest groups. The *Asociación Nacional de Industriales* (ANDI, "National Association of Industrialists") was founded in 1944, largely at the insistence of Alfonso López Pumarejo, who was then serving his second term as president of the republic. Interlinking directorates were also formed between the state and the most important special-interest groups of the propertied classes. Thus, the National Federation of Coffee Growers, the Society of Agriculturalists, and the National Federation of Merchants began to have representation on the boards of economic regulatory agencies, such as the *Banco de la República* (Bank of the Republic) and the Office of Control of International Exchange, and the state in turn received representation on the governing boards of the special-interest groups.[9] The pluralist model of independent interest groups competing for policy decisions from a neutral state is hardly applicable to Colombia.[10]

[8] Caicedo, *Historia de las Luchas Sindicales*, p. 69; Pecaut, *Política y Sindicalismo*, pp. 153–155. A 1938 resolution stated that the National Department of Labor had the functions of maintaining permanent contact with the unions, supervising them, and assuring their correct functioning. See *El Siglo*, Feb. 19, 1938; *El Tiempo*, Feb. 1, 1938.

[9] Francisco Leal Buitrago, *Análisis Histórico del Desarrollo Político Nacional: 1930–1970* (Bogotá: Tercer Mundo, 1973), pp. 48—52.

[10] The pattern of relations between the state and special-interest groups still holds in Colombia. During the Carlos Lleras Restrepo administration (1966—1970), the Colombian State created and vigorously organized the *Associatión Nacional de Usuarios Campesinos* (ANUC, "National Association of Peasant Users of State Services"). This group came to have over 1 million peasant members. During the subsequent Pastrana Borrero administration, the ANUC became progressively radicalized, and it demanded the acceleration of the agrarian reform, which had been largely halted. The ANUC applied pressure politics, including land invasions, to achieve the reactivation and acceleration of the agrarian reform. The government responded by dividing the organization. The passive, official wing (*Línea Armenia*) continued to receive State support (and occupy offices and positions in the Ministry of Agriculture) while the independent wing (*Línea Sincelejo*) was vigorously repressed.

The increased importance of the state in the activities of special-interest groups is closely related to the emergence of the state as the nation's prime economic actor. For example, the state's relationship with both the Coffee Federation and organized labor increased its interventionist role in the economy. Coffee policy came to be formulated by the state and the federation rather than by the sum of individual decisions, which had characterized earlier laissez-faire epochs. The state thus began to regulate the nation's principal product. Likewise, the state became the most important factor in Colombian society in structuring relations between management and labor.

Labor legislation began to be enacted in Colombia as soon as "the social question" was defined as a major national crisis. The legislation of the 1910s and 1920s principally defined work relations.[11] Law 83 of 1931 recognized the legality of labor unions and collective bargaining,[12] and a series of decrees issued by Alfonso López Pumarejo in 1944 and 1945 expanded the protection and benefits afforded workers.[13]

The economic importance of the state in management–labor relations went beyond a normative role. In the 1920s, as was previously described (see Chapter 3), the state harassed unions and violently broke the most important strikes. During the first years of Liberal support for organized labor in the 1930s, the government began to support workers who collaborated closely with the Liberals. Groups that did not play the game by the government's rules were repressed. Thus, the government declared a state of siege in Antioquia to break a prolonged railway strike in 1934,[14] but it tilted the balance in favor of the workers in strikes against the Tropical Oil Company in Barrancabarmeja in the same year and against the United Fruit Company in Magdalena in 1935.[15] Government support for most strikes ended after December 1936, when the López administration, which was confronted by increased opposition within the bourgeoisie, announced a "pause" in its reformist measures. After that date most movements were labeled "crazy strikes" or Communist-inspired. Thus, the 1937 strike on the Pacific Railway was broken, as was the 1938 strike by river

[11] For a compilation of these laws, see Eduardo Santa, *Sociología Política de Colombia* (Bogotá: Editorial Iqueima, 1955), pp. 137–138.

[12] Caicedo, *Historia de las Luchas Sindicales*, p. 64; *Anales del Senado*, June 23, 1931.

[13] Caicedo, *Historia de las Luchas Sindicales*, pp. 75–76; Carlos Agudelo, "El Estado y los Partidos Políticos en Colombia 1930–1933", *Ideología y Sociedad*, no. 9 (Jan.–Mar. 1974), p. 77. These measures included the right to organize, the right to strike, termination pay (*cesantías*), the minimum wage, the prohibition to fire union organizers and officials, and tighter governmental control over union assemblies and finances.

[14] *El Tiempo*, June 5–7, July 27, Aug. 3, 18, Sept. 1, 1934.

[15] Pecaut, *Política y Sindicalismo*, p. 159; Caicedo, *Historia de las Luchas Sindicales*, p. 65

stevadores in Barrancabermeja.[16] The position of the government proved consistently decisive in determining the structure of labor relations in Colombia.[17] This is an important aspect of the increased economic importance of the newly interventionist state.

Other important aspects of the increase in state economic intervention include the Colombian state's expansion of the transport infrastructure in the 1920s, its facilitation of the entrance of foreign capital,[18] and its intervention in the agrarian conflicts of the 1930s by parceling out large haciendas and by passage of Law 200 of 1935.[19] In all of these spheres, the state was increasing its structuring role in society, However, perhaps the most transcendental changes were (*a*) the increase in state intervention in the nation's financial and foreign trade structures and (*b*) the expansion of the bureaucracy for the purpose of "rationalizing" the production and commercialization of basic goods and the delivery of basic services.

Colombia's financial system was transformed following the suggestions of the 1923 Kremmerer Mission from the United States. With part of the funds of the United States indemnification, a central bank was founded, the Banco de la República, which was to monopolize the issuance of currency, and the *Banco Agrícola Hipotecario* ("Agricultural Mortgage Bank") was also formed.[20] The most significant economic changes occurred as a

[16] *El Tiempo*, Mar. 11–14, 1937 (railway strike). A subsequent strike movement in various industries in Cali was also repressed. See *El Tiempo*, Sept. 17, 1937. For Barrancabermeja, see Pecaut, *Política y Sindicalismo*. The López government support for labor was always somewhat hedged. As early as Jan. 1936, the minister of government, Alberto Lleras Camargo, had urged a Frente National against communist labor agitation; see *El Tiempo*, Jan. 26, 1936.

[17] See Chapter 3 of this volume, pp. 111–114. This is the basic argument of Urrutia's study, *Historia del Sindicalismo*.

[18] The initial settlement of the Panama dispute was closely related to the activities of the Tropical Oil Company (a Standard Oil Company of New Jersey subsidiary). Although the Conservative governments generally encouraged foreign capital to enter the country (except for the British Tobacco Company, which would have competed with the Campañía Colombiana de Tabaco, an Antioquian monopoly), the Liberals were even more open to foreign investment.

Law 37 of 1931 suppressed the obligation of foreign oil companies to sell 20% of their stock to Colombian nationals and the requirement to hire 25% Colombian employees, as well as the obligation to renounce recourse to diplomatic channels in case of disputes. In a very real sense, this measure constituted a retreat from state intervention to control foreign capital, but it was at the same time the beginning of a policy, continued in the López Pumarejo administration, of discriminating against Colombian capital in favor of foreign capital. That policy is clearly seen in tax exemptions, which were utilized to attract foreign capital. See *El Tiempo*, Feb. 20, 1925. For the 1931 law, see Eduardo Peña, *Origen y Desarrollo de la Burgesía Colombiana* (Barranquilla: Tipografía Dovel, 1971), pp. 81, 96, 125—139; *El Tiempo*, Mar. 5, 12, 1931.

[19] See chapter 3 of this volume, pp. 89–99.

[20] Luis Ospina Vásquez, *Industria y Protección en Colombia 1810–1930* (Medellín: E.S.F., 1955), p. 347; Francisco Leal Buitrago, "Social Classes, International Trade and

result of the impact of the depression in Colombia. Antonio García comments:

> No one can deny that the truly directed economy—whether well or poorly directed, but operated through a series of State organs—did not begin in 1924, with the founding of the central bank; rather it began in 1932 with the creation of control on international exchange, and in 1935, with the policy of the first López administration.[21]

During the depression, the Olaya Herrera administration received extraordinary emergency powers from Congress (Law 99 of 1931). Controls over foreign exchange transactions were established, and the government enacted a protective tariff that made prohibitive the importation of Colombia's main industrial products (bakery goods, beer, shoes, textiles, soap, and tobacco products) and prohibited the importation of cement.[22] Subsequently, the state began to take an active role in determining what goods should and should not be imported. Tariffs had ceased to be purely fiscal measures and had become governmental mechanisms to protect certain industries, to control the flow of goods and prices in domestic markets, and to manage the nation's balance of payments.[23]

The state also initiated the policy of devaluating the Colombian peso. The politically critical export sector of the economy was protected against the depression by a series of devaluations that diminished the value of the peso by 70% over a period of 5 years.[24] With reference to a similar process in Brazil, Celso Furtado has termed this the "socialization of losses." [25]

With regard to fiscal policy, the López Pumarejo administration began the process of moving away from governmental dependence on import duties to finance the state and toward direct taxes on income and capital.

Foreign Capital in Colombia," Ph.D. dissertation, University of Wisconsin (Madison, 1971), p. 236.

[21] Antonio García, *Gaitán y el Problema de la Revolución Colombiana,* cited in Leal, *Social Classes,* p. 175.

[22] Oscar Rodríguez Salazar, *Los Efectos de la Gran Depresión en la Industria Colombiana* (Bogotá: n.p., 1974), pp. 34–35; *El Tiempo,* Aug. 21, Sept. 24–25, 1931.

[23] In 1931, the government forbade the importation of liquors and other luxury goods and increased tariffs on food stuffs by 100%; see *El Tiempo,* Sept. 18, 1931. To rationalize the supply of sugar the López administration confronted the domestic sugar industry in 1938 over the issue of its importation; see *El Tiempo,* Mar. 2–4, 1926; *El Siglo,* Mar. 2, 1936. For the explicit purpose of improving the balance of payments, the government restricted the importation of woolen and cotton goods in 1938; see *El Tiempo,* Apr. 26, 1938. These citations illustrate only one example of each of several different types of government intervention.

[24] Pecaut, *Política y Sindicalismo,* p. 117.

[25] Celso Furtado, *The Economic Growth of Brazil* (Berkeley and Los Angeles: The University of California Press, 1963), pp. 203–213, cited in Pecaut, *Política y Sindicalismo,* p. 117.

This adjusted the fiscal structure to the emerging capitalist economic relations. A progressive tax on capital was created (*impuesto de patrimonio*), the progressive tax on incomes was greatly increased, and an inheritance tax was established, as was a progressive tax on excess profits.[26] Apart from the express purpose of "rationalizing" the nation's fiscal structure, these direct taxes represented an increase in income that allowed the government to expand its programs. They also represented an increase in the government's ability to influence the total economy by fiscal means.

An article from the Constitutional Reform Act of 1936 states:

> The state may intervene by means of laws in the exploitation of industries or public and private enterprises, toward the end of rationalizing the production, distribution, and consumption of wealth, or to give the worker the just protection to which he is entitled.[27]

Eduardo Santos proclaimed that both interventionism and protectionism were no longer theories in Colombia but rather historical facts.[28] The concrete expressions of the new role of the state were the new legal norms, the adoption of new functions by existing bureaucratic entities, and the creation of new administrative units.

Apart from the previously mentioned creation of the Banco de la República, the state in the 1920s, 1930s, and 1940s was reorganized. In the 1930s the economic sector of the public administration was restructured in such a way as to produce more specialized ministries. Important new agencies were also created, such as the *Caja Agraria* ("Agrarian Credit Agency") (1932), which soon became the most important source of rural

[26] *El Tiempo*, Nov. 24, Dec. 1–2, 11, 1934, Feb. 7, Aug. 2, Oct. 19, 30, 1935, Sept. 27, 1936; *El Siglo*, Feb. 10, May 19, 1936.

The vast increase in the income tax as well as its importance within total State income may be appreciated from the following data:

Income Taxes Collected, 1934–1938

Year	Value	Percentage of total fiscal receipts
1934	2,026,925	4.45
1935	14,346,764	7.57
1936	12,906,674	18.45
1937	15,587,846	18.99
1938	19,888,987	24.03

Source: *Revista de la República*, Jan. 1939, as cited in Rodríguez, *Los Efectos de la Gran Depresión*, p. 42.

[27] *El Siglo*, Mar. 6, 1936.

[28] Ospina Vásquez, *Industria y Protección*, p. 471.

credit. During the Eduardo Santos administration (1938–1942), the capital of the Caja Agraria was expanded, a section for short- and long-term credit was added to the Caja, and the *Fondo de Fomento Ganadero* ("Cattleman's Development Fund") was founded. In addition, the *Fondo Nacional del Café* ("National Coffee Fund") was organized, from which there eventually emerged the *Flota Mercante Gran Colombiana* ("Great Colombian Merchant Fleet") and the *Banco Cafetero* ("Coffeeman's Bank"), and the infrastructure for processing and commercializing coffee was rationalized. Subsequently, the state created a national system for the distribution of agricultural products (INA) in 1945. In sum, agricultural credit became predominantly a state affair, and the state began to intervene in other aspects of the agricultural sector as well.[29]

During the Santos administration, the *Instituto de Crédito Territorial* (ICT, "Institute of Territorial Credit") was created, which, along with the official *Banco Central Hipotecario* (BCH, "Central Mortgage Bank") became the principal source of credit for the nation's housing industry. Also founded was the *Fondo de Fomento Municipal* ("Municipal Development Fund"), responsible for financing the construction of aqueducts, sewers, schools, and other public projects. When combined with the existing public works programs related to infrastructure development, these governmental entities became the most powerful and decisive elements in financing the construction industry in Colombia.[30]

The *Instituto de Fomento Industrial* (IFI, "Institute of Industrial Development") was organized to finance and undertake industrial ventures both in the public sector and in conjunction with private capital. In addition, numerous specific developmental programs were undertaken in the agricultural, industrial, transport, communications, and energy sectors.[31]

Luis Ospina Vásquez states that the sum total of all of these developments had given the state a "truly impressive panoply of action over the economic realm."[32] When compared with 1922 or even 1930, the state in 1942 had acquired an importance in the structuring of Colombian society without precedent since the demise of the Spanish colonial state. Concomitant to the strengthening of the state, struggles for the control of the expanded state had also vastly increased in importance with regard to basic interests of the political groups into which the Colombian nation was divided.

[29] Carlos Lleras Restrepo, "El Presidente Eduardo Santos," *El Tiempo*, March 30, 1975; Enrique Caballero, *Historia Económica de Colombia* (Bogotá: Italgraf, 1971), pp. 203–218; Salomón Kalmanovitz, "Evolución de la Estructura Agraria en Colombia," *Cuadernos Colombianos*, no. 3 (1974), pp. 368–374.

[30] Caballero, *Historia Económica*, pp. 203–218.

[31] Lleras Restrepo, "El Presidente Santos," *El Tiempo*, Mar. 30, 1975; Caballero, *Historia Económica*, pp. 203–218; Kalmanovitz, "Evolución de la Estructura Agraria"; pp. 368–374; Ospina Vásquez, *Industria y Protección*, pp. 470–479.

[32] Ospina Vásquez, *Industria y Protección*, p. 473.

An Explanation of the Partial Collapse of the State

The partial collapse of the Colombian state occurred due to a severe conflict between the two partisan elites into which the dominant class in Colombian society was divided. That conflict reached such an intensity that the functioning of the state was affected. Given the political events of the period 1946–1952 (summarized in Chapter 3), this point is fairly obvious. However, it does not constitute in and of itself a satisfactory explanation for the partial collapse of the state. Rather, it raises another question: Why did partisan conflicts reach the point where such a severe decrease in state power could occur? This question does not have an obvious answer. The disparate descriptive threads presented in preceding chapters need to be analytically woven together to formulate an explanation for this phenomenon.

Let us first consider certain possibilities that must be discarded. The partisan conflict may not be satisfactorily explained by exclusive reference to interclass contradictions. Both the Liberal and Conservative parties were (and are) multiclass in nature. Both leadership elites were drawn from the relatively small and partially closed social groups known as the oligarchy. Exceptions to this rule are to be found, but they would appear to have occurred as much in one party as another (for example, a Gaitán in the Liberal party or a Marco Fidel Suárez in Conservative ranks). Furthermore, issues related to interclass conflict were not at the heart of the discrepancies between the two parties in the period 1946–1953, particularly after April 9, 1948. Both parties represented the interests of the propertied classes and both parties welcomed the entrance of foreign capital. They had experienced conflicts over basic socioeconomic policies in the 1930s, but those disputes had declined, and, after the assassination of Gaitán and the loss of importance of his wing of the Liberal party, they had all but disappeared.

It will be recalled from Chapter 4 that several authors attempt to explain the violence by reference to intraclass, factional conflicts. This approach is not fruitful because both the Liberals and the Conservatives enjoyed the support of some *latifundistas*, some industrialists, some merchants, some professionals, and, indeed, some urban workers and some peasants. To be sure, there are sociopolitical differences between the parties with regard to the numerical importance of these groups in their ranks, and it is true that these dimensions aid greatly in understanding the different wings into which the political parties were divided. The salient point with regard to the violence, however, is the extent to which these disparate party factions with different social bases joined together as a *party* to engage in violent conflict with an opposing, heterogeneous conglomerate of partisan and class factions. To what do we attribute this intense party loyalty? Certainly, the idea of party loyalty in and of itself cannot begin to explain such intense conflict. Furthermore, the Colombian parties had participated in bipartisan coalitions such as Reyes's National Concord and Restrepo's Republican Union after the War of a Thousand Days, and they had also each yielded power to their adversary, given their own division, on one occasion. It is hard to explain the reversion to such intense conflict that could not even parallel the civil wars of the past century in terms of sectarianism since those conflicts, as shown in Chapter 2, were generally more related to differing socioeconomic policies and diverse class factional interests than party rivalry per se.

It is obvious that neither group in the period 1946–1952 was willing to let its adversary consolidate political control without a battle. This was not the case in the period 1930–1934 or during the Conservative hegemony prior to 1930. What had changed?

Indeed, many things were different. As was shown in preceding sections of this chapter, Colombian society beginning with World War I underwent processes of socioeconomic transformation that led to the reemergence of interclass conflict. Concomitantly, the state became progressively more important in Colombian society as a mechanism to facilitate capitalist socioeconomic development and maintain the basic structure of the nation's highly conflictive social relations. From the situation in the nineteenth century, when Colombia was characterized by a weak state within a strong structure of social domination, Colombian society was progressively typified by a strong state in a greatly weakened structure of social domination. As was argued in the section on the strengthening of the state, more and more areas of national life came under the purview of state supervision and state control. By 1946, the state had an impressive array of institutions and mechanisms by which to control most spheres of national life.

What had not changed was the sectarian nature of the partisan political culture. The basic goal of each of the two parties was to achieve absolute power to the exclusion of its partisan adversary. Even most coalitions were but tactical moves designed to further hegemonic ends. Thus, the National Union coalition was for the Conservatives their equivalent of the National Concentration that the Liberals utilized in their transition to hegemony in the period 1930–1934. For the Liberals, the National Union was their instrument to maintain power positions so as to guarantee the conservation of their electoral machine and, subsequently, the recapture of total power in 1950.

The survival of sectarianism under the new circumstances of the increased importance of the state in structuring social relations augmented the stakes involved in politics. Whether one's party controlled the state or not began to affect more and more aspects of one's life, more and more intensely. The sectarian nature of governmental practice made it essential that one's party control the state in order to have the opportunity to develop the contacts (*palancas*) that could assure economic success. Control of the state by the partisan adversary implied exclusion from access to state favors. This had always been the case.[33] What had changed was the importance of the newly interventionist state and the increase in the potential impact of exclusivistic, hegemonic politics in the lives of Colombians.

In 1936, President Alfonso López Pumarejo, in an address before the Senate, made the following assertion:

> It may be affirmed in generic form, subject naturally to exceptions, that there is no large enterprise, no rich and prosperous industry in the country that does not have the support of a law, decree, or contract which places it, to a certain extent, beneath the tutelage of the state.[34]

Let us examine in a more concrete fashion the types of interests that were at stake in the political struggles of the late 1940s given the circumstances of the newly interventionist yet still sectarian state.

For the large cattleman and farmer, credit from the Caja Agraria, technical assistance from the ministry of agriculture, marketing favors from INA, the backing of the police to avoid land invasions and colonists, and support from judges over land disputes were all at stake on a political basis.

[33] Carlos Lleras Restrepo stated in 1957:

> In order that the participation of the two parties in the public administration is not surrounded by reserves and so that it might function in harmony, it is necessary to radically uproot the barbarous concept that official positions are an instrument that may be used legitimately to modify with more or less violent pressure the political composition of the country or any of its sections. *This idea of liberalizing or conservatizing the country by means of the adjudication of employment and the undue utilization of the powers and opportunities that these posts offer has been the cancer of national politics* [emphasis added]. ("El Liberalismo y el Frente Nacional: Conferencia Leida por la Radio Orientación, 27 de Mayo de 1957," reproduced in Carlos Lleras Restrepo, *Hacia la Restauración Democrática y el Cambio Social* [Bogotá: Editorial Agras, 1964], vol. 1, p. 60).

In 1947, in a more partisan vein, Lleras stated the following: "The country must defend itself from the Conservative tendency that wishes to make all bodies, every bureaucratic and police organization, an instrument for the abusive imposition of its sectarian interest" ("Discurso Pronunciado a Nombre del DNL en el Banquete Ofrecido a los Ministros Liberales Dimitentes del Gobierno de Unión Nacional," Hotel Granada, Bogotá, May 8, 1949, reproduced in Lleras Restrepo, *De la Democracia a la Dictadura*, p. 133).

An example of open sectarianism was presented by the minister of government, Ignacio Andrade, in 1952, when he stated in Congress:

> I am alive to guard the fate of the Conservative party, and praise God, I will not attend its fall while I live. I was called to the Ministry as a party man, not as a man of state, and I will continue acting in this fashion. (*El Tiempo*, Nov. 14, 1952)

[34] Cited in Pecaut, *Política y Sindicalismo*, pp. 136–137.

For the industrialist, credit, import exemptions, tax breaks, government support in labor disputes, the state as a customer, and the outcomes of regulatory and judicial decisions all depended on whether one had *palancas* ("political connections") or not. *Palancas* were dispensed on the basis of party loyalities in nineteenth- and twentieth-century Colombia. Their importance, however, increased as the state came to be the backbone of the society.

Similar factors were at stake for merchants, lawyers, and quite obviously for bureaucrats, because the latter group's jobs at all levels were at stake in the political battle. Whether a Conservative hegemony was consolidated or whether the Liberals would regain power and construct their own hegemony was thus a matter that affected the interests of most Colombians, and especially the most powerful.

The stakes of the political game had been dramatically increased and the struggle for political power thus became more intense. In the period in which the National Union coalition began to become undone, it became apparent that either the Liberals or the Conservatives would be excluded from power in 1950. The increased partisan rivalry led to further sectarianism, which reenforced the fears of the evils that would result from the consolidation of the opponent's hegemony. The result of this vicious circle was an extreme sectarianism in which one's party brethren were to be given every advantage while the adversary was to be harassed at every opportunity.

Given the increased importance of the state, and the existence of extreme sectarianism, the point was reached in the late 1940s where *no important social group could conceive of being excluded from state power or access to it.* This was particularly the case of the powerful socioeconomic groups that controlled Colombia's two traditional political parties. By the late 1940s very few in Colombian society could conceive of undertaking large-scale enterprises without the support and favors to be derived from access to state power.[35]

Party affiliation had become an important fact of life in Colombian society. It cut across class, factional, and strata lines. It could divide people with otherwise identical interests. Consider, for example, Liberal and Conservative construction contractors. The outcome of the partisan struggle in the late 1940s would determine who would receive government road and bridge contracts and who would not, who would construct government buildings and who would not, who would enjoy credit favors from the government-controlled housing bank and who would not, who could count on favors in order to import equipment, who could use substandard building

[35] This point was made in latent form in dozens of interviews. Once the author became aware of it, the point was developed easily into manifest discussions. Without probing, however, it remained latent, but apparent, in the ideological discussions of the causes of the violence.

materials or even ignore building codes, and who would become the scapegoat to prove that the government was firmly controlling the construction industry in the public interest. In the end, the difference between which party consolidated hegemony over the interventionist state of the late 1940s could mean the difference between economic bonanza and depressed business, or even bankruptcy.

The partisan battle also affected the popular classes. For many peasants, which party controlled a particular locality and which party would eventually consolidate power nationally made the difference of whether they could live in a determinate area or not.[36] For those who had abandoned their lands, the outcome of the party struggle would determine whether there would be any hope of recovering the lost farms or not. Also, for peasants seeking lands for colonization in government projects, party identification was decisive in the late 1940s and early 1950s.[37]

In some areas, party identification became a requisite for conducting official business. Critical in this regard became the stamp on the *cédula de identidad,* which certified that one had voted in the November 27, 1949, presidential elections. Without this proof of Conservative support (the Liberals had abstained), it became very difficult to enter or leave the entire Eastern Plains region. In areas of open armed conflict, it is a fact that party identification often became a question of life or death. One's fate was often decided by a one-word answer to the question of which party one belonged to, and there was no such thing as neutrality.

In sum, party identification had come to determine fundamental socioeconomic interests and even personal security. Thus, the question of party

[36] A joint communiqué of the National Conservative Directorate and the National Liberal Directorate issued March 17, 1949, stated the following:

> For the shame of our political culture, there exist in some regions areas where the violence has obtained permanent and systematic characteristics to the point where members of the party, which appears to be in the minority in those localities, find it almost impossible to continue living there and have had to abandon their homes and goods. (Reproduced in Lleras Restrepo, *De la Democracia a la Dictadura* [Bogotá: Ediciones Agra, 1955], p. 117)

See also *El Siglo,* Feb. 13, Apr. 1, 1949; *El Tiempo,* Mar. 31, Apr. 27, May 24, 25, 1949. In *Informe del Registrador 1949,* see pp. 122, 137–138, and 236.

[37] Interesting in this regard is the archive of the *Division of Colonization of the Instituto Colombiano de Reforma Agraria* (INCORA), "Colombian Institute of Agrarian Reform." Two of many examples follow: (1) a document addressed to Sr. José Jaramillo Montoya, Manager of the Institute of Colonization, from the Comando Conservador of San Vincente Ferrer in Bosa, Cundinamarca—On a letterhead that reads "Junta Pro-Ciudad Ospina Pérez," the letter dated August 5, 1950, recommends a group of Conservatives for parcels in the Colonia Agricola de Sumapaz; (2) a letter from the Minister of Public Works dated Oct. 27, 1950, to Sr. José Jaramillo Montoya recommending a Sr. Miguel Letrado for the Colonia Agrícola de Sumapaz because he is "an honorable and industrious man and a great friend and defender of our government."

control of the state was an issue over which large numbers of Colombians were willing to fight. Ideologically, the important struggle for party predominance had a messianic flavor.[38]

IDEOLOGICAL ELEMENTS

The intensity of the ideological element of the violence was logical, given the importance of the stakes that most Colombians had in the outcome of the conflict. The two parties, however, argued their cases and justified their actions, before friends and foes, within very different ideological systems.

The Liberals conceptualized their resistance to Conservative hegemony and their goal of an all-Liberal government as a crusade to save democracy. Being a majority party in the twentieth century, the National Liberal Directorate appealed to the norm of majority rule[39]:

> Recently the most authorized organ of the Conservative party [*El Siglo*] declared that the country has undergone a civil war and that it had been won by Conservatism. That interpretation may be exact because it signifies that the current government derives its powers from a violent imposition and not from the pacific play of democratic mechanisms and because it indicates that political predominance in Colombia was decided by force rather than by law. But it is arbitrary and false in pointing out the origins of the conflict, and the same is true for its appreciation of the position of the two great Colombian parties. The pure and simple truth is that the Conservative party grasped the instruments of power so as to decide by violence what ought to be decided by suffrage; that in order to do this it did not vacillate in breaking the constitution with a true coup d'etat.
>
> And it is also obvious that it was not the acts of the present directors of Liberalism that provoked, as a defensive reaction, the violence of Conservatism and the government. This violence began long ago, it has been exercised with a terrifying intensity, and it has been the symptom of the decision, firmly adhered to by the Conservative party, to retain power at all cost. The system chosen has naturally varied in intensity . . . in the measure that the Conservatives confirmed in repeated elections the existence of the Liberal popular majority, and in the degree that the facts permitted the chiefs of that collectivity to implant the notion in official spheres that without recourse to force Conservatism would lose power irrevocably.[40]

The Conservatives, on the other hand, stressed their ties with the church and their defense of the fatherland from communism, with which they

[38] Mauricio Solaún, "La Violencia: Socio-Historical Determinants of Political Violence in Colombia" (unpublished manuscript, n.p., n.d.). This manuscript deals extensively with messianic aspects of *La Violencia.*

[39] It will be recalled from Chapter 2 that the Liberal party was a minority party in the nineteenth century and that it had serious misgivings about universal suffrage for that reason at that time.

[40] Dirección Nacional Liberal, *El Liberalismo Frente a la Dictadura,* pp. 5–6, 11.

closely associated liberalism.[41] The values of the Conservatives were seen as above and beyond the vindication to be obtained from passing electoral majorities or minorities. The eternal conception of Conservative values might be appreciated from the following speech of a member of the National Conservative Directorate:

> The church and the Conservatives are faced with the deceiving trilogy of "liberty, equality, fraternity." . . . Our doctrine confronts the revolutionary formula with a trilogy of concepts that does not pass away because it is touched with eternity: "God, Fatherland, and Liberty." . . . Our ideas not only cover the totality of contemporary preoccupations, but they also guard the secret of the adequate solution to all conflicts.[42]

The political participation of the Catholic Church in favor of the Conservative party was perhaps the most important "messianic element" of the Conservative cause. The long-standing feud between the church and Liberalism gave a strongly ideological flavor to the struggle for political party hegemony. Important sectors of the Conservative rank and file were mobilized for a Holy Crusade in defense of the church and against liberalism and communism. Very instructive in this regard are the pastoral letters of the hierarchs of the Catholic Church prior to the critical June 1949 congressional elections. Given the importance of this point, and its controversial nature, multiple pastorals are cited.[43]

The Most Excellent Archbishop and Primate of Colombia, Monseñor Ismael Perdomo, issued the following letter:

> On the occasion of the proximity of the upcoming elections, we have thought it convenient and opportune to inform the parish priests, and in general the venerable secular and regular clergy of our archdiocese, the instructions and norms that the Vatican has given on this delicate matter on repeated occasions. . . . The liberalism that the Church reproaches and that no true

[41] See especially the declaration of the Conservative Minister of War, Dr. José María Bernal, *El Siglo* and *El Tiempo*, Aug 30, 1952. Other important examples are to be found in *El Siglo*, Mar. 9, May 8, 1949, June 13, July 5, 1952; *El Tiempo*, Jan. 14, 1953.

[42] "Conferencia Doctrinaria Dictada por el Dr. Guillermo Salamanca a Nombre del Directorio Nacional Conservador en la Ciudad de Cali el 11 de Noviembre de 1950" (Bogotá: Tipografía Voto Nacional, n.d.), pp. 11, 15, 22.

[43] All of the following pastoral letters are cited in José María Nieto Rojas, *La Batalla contra el Comunismo en Colombia* (Bogotá: Empresa Nacional de Publicaciones, 1956), pp. 279–293. The Conservative press gave ample coverage to these pastoral letters, and it heavily stressed religion as an issue in the campaign for the June 1949 elections. See *El Siglo*, Feb. 27, Mar. 4–5, 7–13, Apr. 22, 25, 30, May 5, 7–9, 11–15, 19, 23, 29, 31, June 3, 19, 1949. The Liberal press would seem to have attempted to avoid the issue. It sought to evade a head-on collision with the church at all costs. Thus, it sought to look for "positive points" within the pastorals; see *El Tiempo*, Jan. 29, Apr. 23, 28, May 4, 6, July 14, 1949.

Catholic may profess or favor is characterized in the aforementioned letter "Plures e Colombie" with diverse degrees and shades, by the proclamation of the pretended independence and autonomy of human reason before the authority of God and the Church.[44]

The bishop of Tunja, later archbishop of Bogotá and cardinal, Crisanto Luque, wrote in a preelection pastoral:

Now, in a well-known declaration of the principles of the Colombian Liberal party approved August 14, 1935, the Convention of that party ratified one more time its permanent adhesion to the following principles as the basis of its program: the liberty of cults; indifference to religion; obligatory, singular, and lay schools; civil matrimony; vincular divorce. All of these principles are equally erroneous and expressly condemned by solemn pontificial documents.

From the foregoing it may be deduced that the three conclusions that follow are unavoidable and undeniable: (1) For no Catholic is it licit to vote in favor of persons affiliated with the present Colombian Liberalism. (2) Every Catholic has, within his conscience, the duty to vote in the elections for candidates whose programs are inspired and based on integrally Christian principles. (3) A Catholic who, due to one cause or another, has grave difficulty in voting for candidates whose programs are integrally Christian should at least abstain from voting so that he does not participate actively in damaging the Church.[45]

The most reverend bishop of Pasto, Emilio Botero, stated:

Next June 5th the elections will be held to choose representatives for Congress, deputies for the assemblies, and councilmen in all of the Republic of Colombia. This is a most vital event for our country and one which has a great transcendence for religion among us, because it is going to confront, on one side, all of the forces of good, to which belong the parties of order and justice, and, on the other side, the parties that have produced immense evils, such as the Ninth of April, which have been backed by the chiefs of the parties that have always antagonized the Church, calling themselves communists, leftists, democrats, liberals, or as they wish, inasmuch as the name is the least important thing in this case.[46]

The equation of liberalism with communism is a common theme in the pastorals. The archbishop of Popayán, Dr. Diego María Gómez, wrote:

It may be deduced that not only is it necessary to teach citizens that they ought to vote, but that they are also obliged to vote in conscience, that is to say, for candidates who for their good habits and religious convictions offer the best guarantees for the church and the circumstances, in that it is a matter of deciding if there are going to go to the legislative bodies friends of Christ and his Church, or those who work according to the inspirations of Moscow.[47]

[44] Nieto Rojas, *La Batalla*, pp. 279–281.
[45] *Ibid.*, pp. 284–285.
[46] *Ibid.*, p. 290.
[47] *Ibid.*, p. 283.

A joint pastoral letter that links Liberals with communism and summarizes numerous aspects of the prevailing electoral system was issued by the bishop of Pamplona and the bishop of Socorro and San Gil, Rafael Afanador y Cadena and Angel María Ocampo, respectively:

> 1. All Catholics of our jurisdiction are obliged in conscience, and under mortal sin, to vote for candidates who they are certain, before God, will not be dangerous to the Church or favor communism.
> 2. They mortally sin, those who vote for candidates that are dangerous to the Church, either directly or indirectly, due to their links with communism.
> 3. They gravely sin, those who, without attending their conscience, let themselves be guided by the orders of others, be they political chieftains, owners or administrators of haciendas or chiefs of unions, or those who in one form or another sell or violate their consciences in this delicate matter.
> 4. They gravely sin, those landowners or administrators, employers or political bosses, who oblige their sharecroppers to vote for candidates who are enemies of the Church.[48]

Finally, consider the following pastoral delivered by the bishop of Santa Rosa de Osos, Dr. Miguel Angel Builes, to Christians within his violence-ridden diocese:

> Yes, the battle in these moments in the entire world, and especially in Colombia, is against the powers of Hell, which seek to destroy it. It is the battle of Christ against Belial, of good against evil, of the truth against error, of light against darkness, of Rome against Moscow.
>
> An unavoidable dilemma of the entirety of humanity: We march with Christ whose Vicar resides in Rome, or with Belial, whose principal agent resides in Moscow. There is no middle ground. In the same fashion that the chiefs of armies deliver passionate speeches to teach and motivate their soldiers, I by the grace of God am at the head of a portion of soldiers of the militant Church. I direct to you my call for the next electoral battle, that is, the battle of the Church and the Fatherland.
>
> Today, the third of May, is the day of the Holy Cross. The current ideal of Colombian leftist Liberalism is to overthrow the cross, crush Christ, eliminate Religion. The ideal of Catholics is to sustain in high the sign of the cross of Calvary, on top of our temples and above the tombs of our dead. Our ideal is to defend Christ and our sacrosanct rights, sustain religion, although we might have to give up our lives in the defense. Our ideal is to die as the Master died, before we allow that the inheritance that He left us, and that our fathers transmitted to us, be taken away. To fight the battles of the faith is the duty of all believers. And to call you to combat is the objective of this pastoral.[49]

In sum, a potent combination of divergent fundamental interests and intense ideological mobilization, both related to partisan identification, divided Colombians to the point that the partial collapse of the state became

[48] *Ibid.*, p. 288.
[49] *Ibid.*, pp. 285–286.

possible. At no point, however, was this outcome inevitable. There were concrete attempts to achieve agreements. This is another aspect of the partial collapse of the state that must be examined in order to place the preceding explanation of the phenomenon in its proper perspective.

COMPROMISE ATTEMPTS

Some of the efforts to achieve a settlement between the parties were only tactical moves within the struggle for hegemony. However, other attempts were genuine, and they reflected internal political struggles within both parties. There existed groups among both the Liberals and Conservatives who sought to ameliorate the conflict and reach a compromise solution. The historical fact is that these groups lost. Their political positions were not even potentially feasible, and they failed. Belligerent sectarianism proved to have a continued political potency within Colombia's traditional parties.

In a certain sense, the idea of a National Union coalition government sought to diminish partisan conflict. It did not, however, constitute a revision of the notion of exclusivistic, hegemonic politics. Both parties attempted to use the National Union for their own hegemonic ends. During the first months of the Ospina Perez government, the coalition undoubtedly reduced the levels of conflict. In the end, sectarian competition reached crisis proportions despite the coalition government, and the conflict-reducing alliance was eventually destroyed.

The first formal truce between the two parties was reached in the wake of the April 9 riots. Signed by the directive committees of the two parties on April 18, 1948, this document condemned the looting, which genuinely affected the interests of the dominant groups of both parties. It called for cooperation, while at the same time paradoxically stating that moderation must be compatible with a "fervent defense of the ideals and programs of the two parties." The relevant parts of the document state:

> The directorates recognized equally that the acrimony with which political struggles have been undertaken for many years has had gravely perturbing effects for the national spirit and that it is necessary to change this for a tone of maturity fully compatible with the autonomy of the parties and with the fervent defense of the ideals and programs of each of them.
>
> As a consequence of the preceding conclusions, the two directorates have agreed to implement a political truce that will take effect immediately, which we hope to consolidate in the future, and whose effects should be extended to all of the municipalities of the republic.[50]

[50] "Pacto Firmado el 18 de Abril de 1948 en el Palacio de la Carrera, en Presencia del Presidente Ospina Pérez y Cuya Redacción Correspondió a los Doctores Carlos Lleras Restrepo y Jorge Uribe Márquez, a Nombre de la Dirección Liberal, y a Guillermo León Valencia y Augusto Ramírez Moreno, a Nombre del Directorio Conservador," cited in Lleras Restrepo, *De la Democracia*, p. 91. See also Dirección Nacional

Even when the parties were separately issuing vigorous denunciations, they still managed to produce joint documents calling for peace. The mixed nature of this situation is not so much attributable to individual vacillations as to the existence of "war" and "peace" wings within the parties. Compromises had to be reached within the parties and this led to "compromise documents" between the parties, even while they were simultaneously issuing militant documents and engaging in belligerent activities. Consider, for example, the following joint communiqué that was drafted 2 months before the definitive retirement of the Liberal party from the National Union in 1949.

> The National Directorates of the Liberal and Conservative parties, in a meeting with the Most Excellent President of the Republic, have closely examined the problems of public order and the situation created by the political violence present in the country and have recognized the need to undertake joint action destined to maintain the peace in all of the regions of the republic and guarantee to all citizens the exercise of their rights.
>
> The wave of homicidal violence that has castigated the country for long years constitutes a grave danger for Colombian democracy and leads to the vain illusions among those who stimulate it or use it that they can break by the force of felonies the indestructible ideals of the people. Violence cannot have a place in the ideals of the Conservative and Liberal parties and, in consequence, those who execute it betray their own cause and work against the sacred interests of the Fatherland.[51]

After the events of 1949, the "war" factions of the parties were openly hostile but conferences seeking to normalize relations were held between the official party organizations at the insistence of the "peace" factions.[52]

Liberal, *Quince Meses de Política Liberal,* for a series of documents that depict Liberal–Conservative relations in Apr. 1948.

[51] "Comunicado de los Directorios Nacionales del Partido Liberal y del Partido Conservador, el 17 de Marzo de 1949," reproduced in Lleras Restrepo, *De la Democracia,* pp. 115–116.

[52] During 1949 several desperate peace attempts failed. Guillermo León Valencia proposed the postponement of the violence-producing presidential elections, Ospina Pérez once again proposed a coalition cabinet, and finally Ospina Pérez proposed an accord by which elections would be suspended for 4 years with all elected officials remaining in their present posts while the presidency would be rotated annually from one party to the other for a total of four presidents, two Liberals and two Conservatives. In early November, the Liberals proposed a constitutional amendment to implement partisan parity in government, but important Conservative segments—including Laureano Gómez—opposed the plan. However, throughout 1949 peace committees (*comités de la paz*) were very active in some areas. All of the conciliation attempts were unsuccessful. See *El Tiempo,* Mar. 14, Apr. 1, 3, 5, 19, 22–23, Nov. 3–6, 1949; *El Siglo* Apr. 19–23, Nov. 2–20, 1949. See also Enrique Cuéllar Vargas, *Trece Años de Violencia* (Bogotá Editorial SIPA, 1960), chap. 7; Abelardo B. Patiño, "Political Ideas of the Liberal and Conservative Parties during the 1946–1953 Crisis," Ph.D. dissertation, American University (Washington, D.C., 1954), pp. 185–186.

For example, in October 1951, the party directorates issued a joint manifesto that condemned the violence. An excerpt of this document follows:

> If we reject the employment of violence as a means to attempt to conquer power or retain it, it obviously follows that we must reject and condemn in the most emphatic manner violence that is the blind fruit of sectarian passions that make one see as an enemy whoever does not think the same way one does; the violence which with the appearance of being an act of political intolerance hides the foulest motives of personal greed; the violence that is exercised against the conscience of others or to deny them liberty with regard to their political opinions; the violence that consists of merciless attacks on peaceful villages and results in the sacrifice of defenseless citizens; the atrocious reprisals and private vengeance; and the acts of repression that exceed the limits defined by the rights of the people, the constitution, and the laws or that are executed against people not involved in the events that one is attempting to repress.[53]

The negotiations that produced this document eventually led to trips by important Liberals to guerrilla areas to negotiate settlements, including one to the Eastern Plains by ex-President Alfonso López Pumarejo.[54] Truces were also achieved on occasion between guerrilla groups and the armed forces. The latter, however, considered the truce with the guerrillas of the Eastern Plains to have been tactically advantageous for the rebels.[55] In the end, the relations between the party directorates worsened once again and they were completely broken in 1952. The negotiations with the "war" Liberals failed as they began to doubt and to oppose the largely passive "peace" leadership of the National Directorate with its doctrine of "civil resistance." The truces invariably broke down as a result of violent incidents between the armed apparatus of the State and the rebel forces.[56]

All of the peace efforts eventually ended in failure. The dynamic of exclusivistic, hegemonic politics and the importance of the question of party control of the state for most Colombians led to mutual mistrust and mutual antagonisms, which outweighed peace efforts and led to the partial collapse of the state.

[53] "Manifiesto Suscrito por los Directorios Políticos el Día 6 de Octubre de 1951," reproduced in Lleras Restrepo, *De la Democracia*, p. 326.

[54] Eduardo Franco Isaza, *Las Guerrillas del Llano* (Bogotá: Librería Mundial, 1959), chap. 12.

[55] Col. Gustavo Sierra Ochoa, *Las Guerrillas en los Llanos Orientales* (Manizales: Tipografia Departmental, n.d.), p. 88.

[56] After the departure of the most important Liberal leaders as a result of the events of Sept. 6, 1952, the most important spokesman for the "peace" faction of the Liberal party was Abelardo Foredo Benavides; see *El Siglo*, Oct. 29, Nov. 29, 1949, Jan. 12, 1953. The "war" Liberals were led by the guerrilla chieftains of the Eastern Plains, Southern Tolima, and elsewhere. Conciliatory activities in 1952 are described in *El Tiempo*, Feb. 10, 22, Mar. 5, Apr. 20, May 6, 11–12, June 8–10, 12, July 3, Aug. 30, Sept. 4, 1952; *El Siglo* Apr. 27, May 3, 1952.

Concrete Manifestations of the Partial Collapse of the State

Diverse aspects of the partial collapse of the state have been examined in the course of this chapter. This section will illustrate different *concrete* manifestations of the phenomenon. Intense partisan rivalry led to an extreme decrease in state power, which was manifested by: (1) the breakdown of the nation's political institutions; (2) the loss of the legitimacy of the state for significant portions of the populàtion; (3) contradictions within the armed apparatus of the state; and (4) the physical absence of the state in certain areas of the country. Also examined in this section are: (5) the outcomes of the partial collapse.

BREAKDOWN OF ESTABLISHED INSTITUTIONS

The party confrontations reached the point where the normal operations of the Colombian state were seriously affected. The party crisis was institutionally expressed in battles between the Liberal-controlled legislative branch and the Conservative-controlled executive branch. The end result was the expulsion of Liberals from most government jobs and, finally, President Ospina's closing the Congress in what amounted to a genuine coup d'etat by which the executive branch of government assumed total power.

Another institution that did not survive the crisis was the nation's electoral system, which was seriously dislocated and subsequently discontinued.

A third crisis occurred in the judicial branch of government. Partisan favoritism was evident in violence-related cases. In addition, both the police and the judiciary were overwhelmed by the social convulsions affecting the country. The end result was the breakdown of the judicial system since most crimes met with impunity, while even those processed were often judged using political criteria.[57]

[57] The judicial impunity that formed part of the partial collapse of the state is discussed in the following works: Eduardo Umaña Luna, "El Ambiente Penal de la Violencia," in Germán Guzmán, Orlando Fals Borda, and Eduardo Umaña Luna, *La Violencia en Colombia*, vol. 2 (Bogotá: Tercer Mundo, 1963, 1964), pp. 271–359; Horacio Gómez Aristizábal, *Teoría Gorgona* (Bogotá: Editorial Iqueima, 1962); Jorge Enrique Gutiérrez Anzola, *Violencia y Justicia* (Bogotá: Ediciones Tercer Mundo, 1962); James M. Daniel, *Rural Violence in Colombia Since 1946* (Washington, D.C..: American University, Special Operations Research Office, 1965), pp. 209–210; Jorge E. Gaitán: *Antología de su Pensamiento Económico y Social* (Bogotá Ediciones Suramérica, 1968), p. 209; Lino Antonia Sevillano Quiñónes, *El Hombre Frente a la Violencia* (Bogotá: Editorial Aplicación Publicitaria, 1965).

The joint communiqué of the Liberal and Conservative National Directorates issued Mar. 17, 1949, stated: "If there is anything that is generalized in the country and

In sum, fundamental political institutions of Colombian society ceased to function as a result of intense partisan conflict. The most important consequence of these breakdowns was the loss of the legitimacy of the state for significant segments of the nation.

LOSS OF LEGITIMACY OF THE STATE

For the followers of the majority Liberal party, the Conservative government became a dictatorship designed to repress Liberals as part of the political objective of retaining power at all costs. This led to open armed conflict designed to overthrow the government, related coup d'etat conspiracies, the formation of armed groups that sought to resist local repression in some areas, subtle forms of civic resistance that resulted in the sabotaging of government programs, and on the part of the government the organization of paramilitary terrorist groups that further decreased the legitimacy of the regime and further disorganized social relations.

The government was at war with significant Liberal guerrilla groups in the Eastern Plains, Southern Tolima, Northern Cundinamarca, Caldas, Antioquia, and Santander. These groups had as one of their objectives the violent overthrow of the Conservative government. In addition, the government faced the resistance and harassment of armed groups of Liberal irregulars operating in many areas. These armed groups enjoyed the sympathy of large numbers of Liberals, and they presented the government with a serious challenge that decreased its efficacy, and which potentially threatened its very existence.

In addition to the obvious weakness of a government at war with armed groups supported by large segments of the population, one must also consider the passive incompliance of predominately Liberal areas. For millions of Colombians living in hundreds of municipalities, the government was illegitimate. Government orders were to be ignored, taxes evaded, and officials misled and harassed. To take but one example, in predominately Liberal Miraflores, Boyacá, the orders of the Conservative governor were simply ignored by a population that considered both the departmental government in Tunja and the national government in Bogotá illegitimate dictatorships. Hence, highly partisan police were sent to command respect. The result was the harassment of the police, who were treated as an invading army. The army was eventually sent to the region, which was an important staging area for the delivery of support to the Liberal guerrillas in the Eastern Plains. So blatant was the defiance of the military authorities that Miraflores was eventually cleared of all of its residents except the

---

which is of infinite gravity, it is the impunity which constitutes the best soil for the cultivation and proliferation of felonies" (Lleras Restrepo, *De la Democracia*, p. 119). See also *El Tiempo*, July 31, Nov. 8, 1949, for examinations of the topic of "impunity."

local beer distributor, whom the thirsty troops permitted to stay in the town.[58]

The Conservatives reacted to both the armed and passive resistance of the Liberals by implanting authority by repression where voluntary compliance was not to be found. However, the extensiveness of the resistance, combined with contradictions in the armed apparatus of the State (described below), made it impossible for the government to repress to the point that its fiats might be made effective. The government proceeded to attempt to induce compliance by means of terror. Thus, paramilitary Conservative counterguerrillas (*Guerrillas de la Paz*, "Peace Guerrillas") were organized, as well as terror Squads (*pájaros*, "birds"). With the support of Conservative authorities, and especially of the police and judiciary, these groups assassinated key leaders of the Liberal resistance and terrorized the Liberal population in general. In affected areas, and especially in Northern Valle and Western Caldas, assassinations of Liberal leaders occurred daily with complete impunity. As will be described in Chapter 6, the activities of the *pájaros* were also extended, in a Mafia fashion, into extortion and forced land abandonments.

The end result of the application of official terror was the decrease in the power of the state that the government was attempting to maintain. Inasmuch as terror is a source of social disorganization, this was the very thing the Conservative party was attempting to stem in its attempt to suffocate opposition and consolidate its hegemony.[59]

CONTRADICTIONS WITHIN THE ARMED APPARATUS OF THE STATE

One of the factors that diminished the power of the state and that limited the government's ability to consolidate its position was the existence of partisan rivalries and favoritism within the armed apparatus.

On April 9, large contingents of the police in Bogotá joined with the rioters. In other localities Liberal policemen participated in, and on occasion led, the mini–coup d'etats that followed the assassination of Gaitán.[60] A new police law was placed into effect in 1948. It led in practice to a purge of Liberals. The police thus became almost an all-Conservative armed body. The highly sectarian nature of the police and the use of this force to repress Liberal areas led to a loss of legitimacy of the police institution.[61] Liberals conceived the police as a political enemy, and they

[58] Numerous interviews, including one with the beer dealer in question.

[59] Daniel, *Rural Violence*, pp. 60, 171–172; Guzmán *et al.*, *La Violencia*, vol. 1, pp. 148–152, and interviews.

[60] República de Colombia, Policía Nacional, *Criminalidad en 1958*, "Orígenes de la Violencia," pp. 16–18; John D. Martz, *Colombia: A Contemporary Political Study* (Chapel Hill: University of North Carolina Press, 1962), p. 80.

[61] United States, Department of the Army, *U.S. Army Handbook for Colombia*, p. 390; Leal *Análisis Histórico*, p. 75; Diego Montaña Cuéllar, *Colombia: Pais Formal y*

were reticent to approach the authorities even with regard to cases that had nothing to do with politics. In some areas any contact whatsoever with the police placed Liberals in jeopardy. *Chulavita* is the name that Liberals gave to the Conservative police of the period. The name is derived from the locality of Chulavo in the *municipio* of Boavita in Boyacá. That locality symbolized the massive recruitment of police from arch-Conservative *minifundio* areas of Boyacá where absolute loyalty and obedience to the party and the church are strongly held values. Liberals feared and hated the "Chulavita police," who were implacable in the pursuit of what they considered to be a holy crusade against the Liberal infidel.

The partisan nature of the police, combined with the previously described sectarianism of the judiciary, led to an increase in the tendency to settle disputes directly without recourse to the state agencies generally responsible for these functions. In addition, the police became a primary source of crime and violence. Orlando Fals Borda has written in this regard:

> The police are no longer guards of order but rather agents of disorder and crime. . . . Some groups [the state, the national parties, and the local political machinery] have legitimized for the police agent a new role, a violent role, distinct from that contemplated in the codes. It would be prejudicial for the agent who did not respond to the slogans imparted. Thus the violent "chulavita" is institutionalized and positively sanctioned, within the formal police institution.[62]

The Liberals considered the persecution of the police to be the most onerous facet of the Conservative regime.[63] The National Liberal Directorate stated in its report to the Liberal convention of July 3, 1949:

> But the most scandalous thing in this process of official coercion is without doubt the utilization of the departmental and municipal police for this purpose.

País Real, p. 186. Examples of Liberal accusations of police persecution are to be found in *El Tiempo*, Feb. 17, 24, Mar. 6, 14, 31, Apr. 13, May 9, 24, 26–27, June 1, 9, 11, 14, July 6, 13, 18–19, 22, 1949. The Conservative press in turn accused the Liberals of premeditated attacks on the police; see *El Siglo*, May 10, June 9, Nov. 5, 1949. Meanwhile the Conservative government proceeded with its police reform measures; consult *El Siglo*, Jan. 3, Nov. 11, Dec. 15, 27, 1949, Jan. 4, Mar. 30, July 14, 1952.

[62] Fals Borda, chap. 13, "El Conflicto, La Violencia, y la Estructura Social de Colombia," in Guzmán *et al.*, *La Violencia*, vol. 1, p. 364.

[63] The National Liberal Directorate declared in 1951 that "the greatest of the sins of the government of Sr. Ospina Pérez was the composition that he gave the police bodies. From 1947 these bodies began to be integrated by well-known sectarian elements, and very soon this policy was converted into the recruitment of genuine criminals, thirsty for blood, feared and hated by pacific peoples" (Dirección Nacional Liberal, *El Liberalismo Colombiano Frente*, p. 41). See also Miguel Angel Gaitán, *El Por qué de un Asesinato y Sus Antecedentes* (Bogotá: Editorial Minera, 1949), p. 46.

> The mayors under whose direction the police have been placed in each district, as a result of the nationalization of the police, have not vacillated in using the force for persecution and mayhem. The results of all this are well known to the country: *departamentos* where the mere announcement of the arrival of the police in a *municipio* determines a mass exodus of the Liberal citizens. Threats, theft of identification cards, flagellations, abusive detentions, violation of the municipalities, and in many cases robberies and assassinations fill the annals of the departmental police in the last two years.[64]

Apart from their sectarian favoritism and their own direct contribution to the violence, the police also conditioned the partial collapse of the state by their inefficiency. The police and the judiciary could not begin to handle the case loads of even the level of common crime that the violence engendered. Impunity became pervasive as the probability that a given illegal act would be investigated, much less prosecuted, was greatly reduced. The dedication of the police to political repression reduced their capacity to undertake their normal tasks, and it also decreased their ability to elicit the collaboration of large portions of the population. The latter, of course, is essential to efficacious and efficient police operations.

A Conservative writer observed:

> The repressive action of the state against the violence signifies nothing more than two equally disheartening facts: (1) There does not exist sufficient preventive means to combat the violence and avoid its disasters and (2) belated State action in persecution of the bandits is nothing more than the classic impulse of vengeance transplanted from the individual to the collectivity.[65]

An official army document also makes reference to the partial collapse of the repressive capacity of the state:

> The insufficiency of state coercion, operative deficiencies in the penal and judicial systems, party confrontations, a misunderstanding of the ideological contexts of the parties, and blind acceptance of the orders of the political bosses were the political causes of the violence.[66]

An additional reason for the coercive insufficiency of the state was the fact that the army did not begin to actively repress the violence until it had reached crisis proportions. Even then, internal contradictions within the army, and between certain army officers and the police, reduced the efficiency of the armed apparatus of the state.

[64] Dirección Nacional Liberal (D.N.L.) "Informe de la D.N.L. a la Convención Nacional del Partido Reunida en Bogotá el 3 de Julio de 1949," in D.N.L., *Quince Meses*, under the subtitle "El Gobierno de Unión National y las Garantías Políticas."

[65] Sevillano Quiñónes, *El Hombre Frente a la Violencia* (Bogotá: Editorial Aplicación Publicitaria, 1965), p. 65.

[66] República de Colombia, Ejército, Octava Brigada, *De la Violencia a la Paz* (Manizales: Imprenta Departamental, 1965), pp. 16–20.

The political conflicts that began in 1946 followed 16 years of Liberal rule. In that period numerous Liberal officers had risen to positions of importance. The new government's attempt to favor Conservatives could not be undertaken too rapidly for fear of provoking a coup d'etat attempt. The 1946–1949 stalemate between the executive and legislative branches of government was reflected in the army by a stalemate between Liberal and Conservative officers. They were also fearful that the partisan struggle might destroy the unity of the military institution.[67] The net result was the army's refusal to play an active role in the first stages of *La Violencia*.

The army did actively repress the Ninth of April riots and it urged the president's resignation at that point in time, but it did not stage a coup when Ospina Pérez refused to relinquish his position.

The Liberals considered the army to be a guarantee of their well-being. They consistently demanded military mayors in tense areas.[68] The National Liberal Directorate observed:

> Despite the excessive cruelty that some units unleashed in Bogotá on April 9 and subsequent days, the presence of troops in any region of the country was, until May 1948 in most cases, a guarantee of tranquility, of moderation, and of order. When the policies of the sectarian governors did not interfere with the action of the army, the violence did not prosper.[69]

In areas where Liberal peasants confronted police forces, they painted slogans such as *Con el Ejército No* ("Not with the Army") and *No Queremos Pelear con el Ejército* ("We do not wish to fight the Army").[70]

The increase in the levels of conflict made it impossible for the army to remain on the sidelines. When large guerrilla forces began to threaten the security of the government itself on the Eastern Plains and in Southern Tolima, the army began to play a major role. In this process the Conservatives redoubled their attempts to make the army trustworthy, and the Liberals tested the feasibility of a military coup. The latter was not possible largely because such a movement would have divided the army, something most officers wished to avoid at all cost.

The National Liberal Directorate analyzed the Conservative actions:

> This situation [the impartiality of the army] influenced, in a significant manner, the Liberal belief that it would be possible for the authorities to put an end to the violence. And we are sure that the violence would not have

[67] Interview with a retired army colonel.

[68] There were 202 military mayors in 1946. This was symptomatic of the impending crisis of confidence in partisan, civilian authority. See *Ministro de Gobierno 1946*, pp. 19–20. For examples of Liberal requests for military mayors, consult *Informe del Registrador 1949*, pp. 127–130; *El Tiempo*, May 22, June 5, July 9–10, 1949.

[69] D.N.L., *El Liberalismo Colombiano Frente a la Dictadura*, p. 22.

[70] Guzmán *et al.*, *La Violencia*, vol. 1, p. 54.

> later reached the proportions that it did, and that the democratic and republican orders would not have been altered, if President Ospina and the present government had not dedicated themselves, with a tenacity worthy of a better cause, to robbing the army of its national character, introducing into it political sectarianism, and depriving it of the liberty to efficaciously guard public order. The series of maneuvers executed with this end began with the removal of Lt. Col. [*sic;* should be Lt. Gen.] Ocambo from the Ministry of War, a removal that constituted the prologue to the breakup of the National Union. There followed skyrocketing promotions of military officers known for their sectarianism, exclusion of those who had demonstrated impartiality and independence of character, discriminatory maneuvers in the admission of cadets to the military academy, sectarian selection of officers who were given the command of troops, and restriction of recruitments to areas characterized by the most crude Conservatism.[71]

The Liberal Directorate planned an armed movement in November 1949. The unsuccessful coup in Villavicencio, led by Captain Alfredo Silva and Hernando Durán Dussan, was part of the initial plot. The National Directorate, however, had decided to stage a nationwide general strike, which also failed.[72] The demise of the Villavicencio movement confirmed what had been expected: The correlation of forces within the army ran against the possibility of a coup. This was the case due to the partisan deadlock between the officers and the fear of losing corporate unity and unleashing a civil war within the army itself.[73]

Liberal officers, however, did not persecute their party brethren with the same enthusiasm as their Conservative counterparts. This is an important point in analyzing the contradictions within the armed apparatus of the

[71] D.N.L., *El Liberalismo Colombiano Frente a la Dictadura,* p. 23. The removal of Ocampo and other allegedly political dismissals are discussed in *El Tiempo,* June 14, July 13, 15, 1949.

[72] Interview with one of the principal protagonists of this coup attempt. See also Franco Isaza, *Las Guerrillas del Llano* (which also contains information related to other Liberal coup plots); Montaña Cuéllar, *Colombia País Formal,* pp. 192–193; Guzmán *et al., La Violencia,* pp. 62–64. The "peace" Liberals who controlled the National Liberal Directorate (D.N.L.) analyzed the events of Nov. 1949 as follows: "We knew that from the Conservative violence there was born our right to self-defense, and that from the violation of the juridical order there was born our right to reestablish it, but consciously and deliberately we eliminated recourse to the rebellion, which was already in the hearts of all Liberals" (D.N.L., *El Liberalismo Colombiano Frente a la Dictadura,* p. 98). With reference to the general strike, the D.N.L. stated: "The general strike initiated on November 25 was not a rebellion capable of leading us to victory, but an essentially pacific act, destined to exteriorize Liberal protest" (*El Liberalismo Frente a la Dictadura,* p. 99). The failure of this strike ruined the Liberal labor organization (CTC). With the subsequent repressions, this federation existed only in name throughout the Gómez administration; see Pecaut, *Política y Sindicalismo,* p. 250; Caicedo, *Historia de las Luchas Sindicales,* pp. 87–88. See also Caicedo, pp. 91–92, for accounts of assassinations of union leaders during the Gómez administration.

[73] Interviews with numerous retired army officers.

state that decreased the government's coercive capacity. Indeed, Liberal officers often reached "live and let live" agreements with guerrilla forces operating in their command areas. This allowed the guerrillas to concentrate their forces in other zones, especially those controlled by the hated Conservative police. In addition, Liberal officers appeared to be in control of their regions, given the low incidence of violence.[74]

The conflicts within the armed apparatus of the state were also expressed by antagonism between Liberal army officers and the highly sectarian police, which reduced the repressive capacity of the state. For example, a retired army colonel related to the author how he and other Liberal officers sent reenforcements to police posts under attack by the most indirect and difficult routes possible under the pretext of avoiding possible ambushes. The troops thus arrived to bury the Conservative police without having made contact with the Liberal guerrillas. They then returned to their bases by the main roads since the danger of ambushes supposedly had passed.[75] This type of noncollaboration presents a dramatic illustration of how party rivalries were reflected in contradictions within the armed apparatus of the state. There also occurred isolated armed clashes between the army and the police.[76]

In sum, partisan conflicts reduced the repressive capacity of the state, and this in turn formed an important element in the partial collapse of the state.

PHYSICAL ABSENCE OF THE STATE

The breakdown of political institutions, the loss of legitimacy of the state, the inadequacy of the state's repressive capacity, and the emergence of Liberal guerrilla groups led to the circumstance that the Colombian state ceased to have a physical presence in large areas of the national territory.

In many areas, all manifestations of the public administration disappeared, in some the only presence consisted of the police and the army on a transitory basis, and in still others government offices remained open formally, but their functions remained unfulfilled, given the circumstances of widespread violence.

In the Eastern Plains, over 90% of the territory was in rebel hands.[77] In Southern Tolima, Liberal and Communist guerrilla control precluded a gov-

[74] Interviews with a retired Liberal officer.

[75] Interview with a retired army colonel who later occupied several important political positions.

[76] Examples of such clashes include those in Cali, Medellín, Puerto Berrero, Puerto Perales, Santa Marta, and Girardot. See *El Siglo*, Jan. 3, Apr. 19, 1949; *El Tiempo*, Feb. 19, Apr. 17, 19, 1949, Apr. 1–18, 1950.

[77] The 90% figure is given by Colonel Gustavo Sierra Ochoa, *Las Guerrillas en los Llanos Orientales* (Manizales: Tipografía Departamental, 1954), p. 17.

ernment presence in vast zones, as was also the case in the Communist-controlled areas of Cundinamarca. Extensive rural areas of Northern Cundinamarca, Western Santander, Southern and Eastern Antioquia, Eastern Cauca, Western Caldas, and Northern Valle were also outside government control. In some of these areas alternative patterns of authority were instituted, in others local customs guided social relations, while in still others the breakdown encompassed not only formal authority relations but also basic social patterns, as situations of structural anomie developed.

In sum, the most conspicuous symptom of the partial collapse of the state was the inability of the government to maintain even a physical presence in large areas of Colombia's national territory.

Outcomes

The partial collapse of the state accentuated with the passage of time. After 1952, the break between the Conservative government and the "peace" Liberals was total. The "war" Liberals pursued their guerrilla activities independently of the political leadership of the "peace" or "civil resistance" faction of the party. The Conservative party became increasingly divided, and the followers of Laureano Gómez remained the sole unconditional supporters of the government, as the Ospina Pérez and Alzate Avendaño wings of the party began opposition activities.[78]

The army was increasingly overwhelmed by the surge in violent activity accompanying the partial collapse of the state. It began to concentrate on the highly organized guerrilla groups, while more diffuse movements and generalized civilian violence were made the responsibility of the police or simply left to run their course (a phenomenon examined in Chapter 6). Even given this restricted interpretation of its functions, all did not go well for the military. The army suffered several serious defeats in guerrilla areas, including the extermination of a 96-man motorized column in an ambush near Puerto López on the Eastern Plains.[79]

[78] For the Conservative division, consult: *El Tiempo*, Jan. 27 ("Represento al Sector del Partido que Busca Regresar a la Normalidad: Dice el Doctor Alzate Avendaño"), 28, Feb. 4, May 17, 25, June 24, July 8, Nov. 10, 19–20, Dec. 6, 1949; Jan. 2, 4, Feb. 24, Mar. 28, Apr. 12 ("Contra Gobiernos de Minorías Pronunció Ospina Pérez"), 1953; *El Siglo*, May 27 ("La Disidencia es una Traición al Partido" 31, June 2, Nov. 15, 1952. See also *Informe del Registrador 1954*, pp. 63–67; Martz, *Colombia*, pp. 161–167, 213–218, 229–236; Cuéllar Vargas, *Trece Años de Violencia*, chap. 9.

[79] Franco Isaza, *Las Guerrillas del Llano*, p. 283. For a polemical appreciation of the state of army operations and morale prior to the coup, consult: Juventudes del Movimiento Revolucionario Liberal (M.R.L.), *Plataforma Política: Porqué Liberales, Porqué Revolucionarios, Porqué Ni un Paso Atrás* (Bogotá: Ediciones Libres, n.d.), p. 22. Also disquieting for the armed forces was a suicidal attack by more than 300 peasants, led by Liberal guerrilla leaders from Northern Cundinamarca, against the Palenquero

It was in this political and military context that the coup d'etat led by Army Commander General Gustavo Rojas Pinilla on June 13, 1953, met with the political support of all of the political groups in the country, except the Laureanista wing of the Conservatives and the Communists.[80] Ex-President Mariano Ospina Pérez appeared publicly to pay homage to President Rojas Pinilla. Darío Echandía termed the military movement not a coup of force but rather a "coup of opinion"; Carlos Restrepo stated:

> The military movement of June 13 cannot be judged with the same criterion applicable to the barracks coups that unfortunately have been so frequent in Latin American republics. This movement is not an isolated movement but rather the culmination of a series of circumstances that necessarily led to it. The country could not return to peace, or stability, or the normal functioning of its institutions [by other means].[81]

The new military government aroused great expectations of a rapid end to the violence. In his first speech to the nation Rojas declared: "No more pillage, no more war, no more hatred, but peace, liberty, and justice for all Colombians."[82]

On June 19, 1953, a general amnesty was declared for all those involved in the violence except military deserters.[83] Those engaged in insurrectional

---

air base. Badly organized, poorly armed, and largely drunk, the peasants were slaughtered by scores and then 124 were taken as prisoners. Nonetheless, the size and audacity of this attack against a major base underscored the increasing political isolation of the army as a result of its support for the increasingly weaker Gómez–Urdaneta regime. Interviews with retired Army officers: *El Siglo*, Jan. 4–9, 1953; *El Tiempo*, Jan. 4–6, 1953.

[80] For the coup, see *El Tiempo*, June 14–18, 1953. The "trigger" of the military movement was an attempt by Laureano Gómez to relieve Rojas Pinilla of command of the army. The army had been deliberating and conspiring for months. Operationally, the formation of a secret political intelligence unit became the army's first patently political activity. Rojas Pinilla was to have left the country in Apr. for an extended trip to Germany. Army political intelligence advised against his departure and 100 army officers went to the airport to successfully demand that Rojas not travel. Interview with retired army officers once active in army intelligence and *El Tiempo*, Apr. 18, 1953 ("El Teniente General Gustavo Rojas P. Canceló Su Viaje a Alemania").

When the June government–military crisis unfolded, military intelligence proved superior to the information supplied by Laureano Gómez's civilian political police. One of the first steps taken by the military rulers was the jailing of the civilian political police.

[81] Carlos Lleras Restrepo, "Declaraciones Concedidas a la United Press, en México, el día 15 de Junio de 1953," in Lleras Restrepo, *De la Democracia a la Dictadura* (Bogotá: Ediciones AGRA, 1955), p. 435. See also *El Tiempo*, June 20, 1953 ("Colombia Saluda el Fin de una Situación que Era Intolerable").

For accounts of civic demonstrations of support, labor union declarations, etc., consult *El Tiempo*, June 14–28, July 4, Aug. 16, 1953.

[82] Cited in Patiño, "Political Ideas," p. 367.

[83] *El Tiempo*, June 20, 1953.

activities, or other forms of violence, had merely to surrender their arms in order to return to civilian normality. Large numbers of persons promptly began to take advantage of the amnesty.[84]

The combination of widespread political support for the government and the general amnesty dramatically, and nearly immediately, reduced the levels of violence.[85]

The new military regime erased in good measure the subjective aspects that contributed to the partial collapse of the state. Perceived as legitimate by most of the population, the army enjoyed considerable authority despite the fact that the state remained physically absent from many zones.

Both the army's political support and the decline of the violence were relatively short-lived. The fragility of the army's largely psychological influence over large areas affected by the partial collapse of the state was illustrated by the rapidity with which the violence was reignited. By late 1954, violence had returned to high levels in the *departamentos* of the Central Cordillera. This second period of *La Violencia*, or the late violence, corresponded more to socioeconomic conflicts than to traditional partisan rivalries. Indeed, the Liberals and the Conservatives came to be highly united. They were both against what they considered to be the military's usurpation of power. Deprived of party support, the military government attempted to develop its own independent political base and to repress its opposition.

The military regime's attempts to repress its political opposition accelerated its loss of authority in many areas. Furthermore, the amnesty program became less attractive to many guerrillas because many ex-combatants who surrendered their arms were subsequently assassinated.[86]

Repressive activities included a massacre of students in Bogotá in June 1954, and later that year violent incidents broke out between the army and peasants in Communist-controlled areas of Eastern Tolima and Sumapaz.[87] In April 1955, the army declared the following municipalities zones of "military operations": Villarica, Icononzo, Carmen de Apicalá, Cabrera, Cunday, Pandi, and the rest of the *municipios* of the Sumapaz region. In the first locality, the army was resisted and a full-scale military invasion ensued, backed by bombing raids. Large numbers of refugees began to leave this region and the fighting was rapidly extended to neighboring areas.

[84] *El Tiempo*, June 15, 17, July 3–4, 9, 12, 21, Aug. 4 ("711 Guerrilleros se Entregaron en los Llanos Antier"), 5 ("El Guerrillero Rafael Rangel y 105 Hombres se Entregaron"), 10, 26, Sept. 12, 18 ("6500 Hombres en 5 Días se Rindieron al General Duarte Blum"), Nov. 2, 19, 1953.

[85] The survey data on violence in this study (see Chapter 1, Table 1.2) estimate a minimum of 13,250 violence-related deaths in 1952, 8650 in 1953, and 900 in 1954.

[86] Joaquín Paredes Cruz, *Causas y Efectos de una Dictadura* (Cali: n.p., 1957), p. 99. This point was also stressed in numerous interviews.

[87] *El Tiempo*, June 9–11, 17–18, 30, July 20–21, Sept. 7, Dec. 5, 15, 1953.

In a matter of months, the army was engaged in open conflicts in all of Tolima, as well as in adjacent departments.[88]

The paramilitary groups known as *pájaros* ("birds") also resumed operations in Northern Valle and Western Caldas, this time in support of the military government as well as for their personal enrichment.[89] The situation of massive repression was soon extended to Liberals, as illustrated by the closure of the nation's most important daily newspaper, *El Tiempo,* and to Conservatives, as illustrated by the detention of Conservative leader Guillermo León Valencia.

The military government's populist policies met as early as 1954 with the resistance of important economic interest groups. This opposition increased in the course of 1955.[90] During that year the Conservatives and the Liberals began to demand a return to civilian government.[91] The increased political opposition led to an acceleration of the attempt to create an independent "Peronist-style" political base. This met with the resistance not only of the traditional political parties but also of the church.[92] In this political battle, the government resorted to strict press censorship. Both *El Tiempo* and *El Espectador* ceased to appear (*El Siglo* closed early in the

[88] Daniel, *Rural Violence,* pp. 87–95; Montaña Cuéllar, *Colombia: País Formal y País Real,* pp. 206–208; Gumán, *La Violencia,* vol. 1, pp. 92–99; Leal, *Análisis Histórico,* Rodrigo Parra, pp. 103–104; Leal, "Política e Intervención Militar en Colombia," in *La Dependencia Externa y el Desarrollo Político en Colombia,* (Bogotá: Imprenta Nacional, 1970), pp. 185–186; Comité de Solidaridad con los Presos Políticos, *El Libro Negro de la Represión: Frente Nacional 1958–1974* (Bogotá: Editorial Gráficas Mundo Nuevo, 1974). In October 1953, the military governor of Tolima, Colonel Cuéllar Velandia, stated that there was not a single center of violence remaining in the department; see *El Tiempo,* Oct. 20, 1953. One month later, armed clashes were occurring between the army and Communist peasants; see *El Tiempo,* Nov. 16–18, 1953.

The military invasion of Eastern Tolima in April 1955 was accompanied by an army press campaign characterizing the reemergence of the violence as due to Communist agitation; see *El Tiempo,* March 23, April 7, 1955. The military government outlawed the Communist party in 1954 by virtue of an act of the *Asamblea Nacional Constituyents ("National Constituent Assembly");* see *El Tiempo,* Sept. 8, 1954.

[89] Daniel, *Rural Violence,* p. 172.

[90] For conflicts between the Rojas Pinilla government and the National Industrialists Association (ANDI) as well as the national merchants group (FENALCO), see *El Tiempo,* Sept. 21, 24, 26. Oct. 1, 15, 19–20, 28–30, Nov. 1, Dec. 13, 15, 1954, Feb. 23, April 4, July 23, Sept. 28, Oct. 25, Nov. 8–9, 15, 19–20, Dec. 15, 1955.

[91] They began to attack the regime as an arbitrary dictatorship. See *El Espectador,* Sept. 8, Oct. 20–23, Nov. 24, Dec. 13, 15, 18, 30, 1955; *El Tiempo,* Jan. 2, 7, 13, April 30, June 13, July 3, July 20, 1955.

[92] For the opposition of the church, see *El Tiempo,* Jan. 10 ("El Episcopado Antioqueño Condena la C.N.T. por Peronista y Anti-Católica"), Feb. 18 ("Sobre Justicialismo y Socialismo se Pronuncia el Clero Colombiano"), Apr. 30, 1955. For examples of the general controversy surrounding the attempts to create a progovernment labor union, political movement, and finally political party, consult *El Tiempo,* Dec. 7, 1954, Jan. 10, 12, 14, 28, 1955.

regime), although their editorial houses brought out newspapers under different names.[93]

By late 1956, both Conservative and Liberal leaders began to express belligerent opposition to the government. Coordination between the two parties evolved in 1957 into agreements between them, negotiated by Alberto Lleras and Laureano Gómez in Spain. They formed a *Frente Civil* ("Civil Front"), which eventually became the Frente Nacional.[94]

The military regime had financed its populist policies out of the revenues produced by record coffee prices. The decline of coffee prices in 1956 led to a balance of payments crisis and a large government deficit.[95] Thus, the continuation of the populist policies began to directly affect the interests of the propertied classes in Colombian society. Opposition activities increased, and they were redoubled after the military administration began to consider the nationalization of the banking industry.[96]

By November 1956, both Liberals and Conservatives had announced belligerent opposition to the regime. An atmosphere of political crisis was

[93] The political battle between the government and the press was one of the major political issues during the military government. See *El Tiempo*, Sept. 28–29, Oct. 1–2, Nov. 3, Dec. 2, 8, 18, 1954, Feb. 3, Mar. 2, Aug. 1, 1955; *El Espectador*, Oct. 24, Nov. 2, 6, 19, Dec. 23–24, 1953; *Intermedio* (published by the editorial house *El Tiempo*), Feb. 21–22, Mar. 15, Apr. 4, May 6, 1956, Jan. 11–12, 1957.

[94] As early as 1954, serious attempts were made at party conciliation; see *El Tiempo*, Feb. 5, 8 ("Alzate Sugiere Bases para un Acuerdo de los Dos Partidos"), Mar. 26, Oct. 26, Dec. 12, 1954 ("Quiero ser el Animador de un Movimiento de Reconciliación, Declara el Dr. López"). In early 1956, the bipartisan movement reached the state of joint declarations; consult *El Tiempo*, Feb. 21, Mar. 2, 6, Apr. 12–22, Sept. 24, Oct. 2, 18, 1956. In 1957, the Frente Nacional coalition was consolidated. See *Intermedio*, May 15–16, 21, 31, 1957; *El Tiempo*, July 9, July 16–30 (Sitges meeting), Aug. 4, 9, 18, 20, Sept. 11, Oct. 1–5, Nov. 21–22, 29–30, Dec. 2, 1957; *El Siglo* May 11, 21, June 4, July 10, 22, 30, Aug. 24, Oct. 2–3, 17, Dec. 1–2, 1957.

[95] *Intermedio*, Jan. 3, 8, 11, 13, 18, Mar. 5, 1957 ("El Déficit Fiscal de la Nación Alcanza a 120 millones de Pesos"); *El Siglo*, May 22 ("Las Reservas del País se Redujeron a Su Más Bajo Nivel el Año Pasado"), 31 ("Dramática Situación de Bancarrota Económica"), June 20, July 16, 1957 ("A 368 Millones Ascendía la Deuda del Régimen de Rojas").

[96] For general considerations of the Rojas Pinilla regime, consult Vernon Lee Fluharty, *Dance of the Millions: Military Rule and Social Revolution in Colombia, 1930–1956* (Pittsburgh: University of Pittsburgh Press, 1957), chaps. 7–13; Martz, *Colombia*, chaps. 10–14; Cuéllar Vargas, *Trece Años de Violencia*, chaps. 9–10; Comité Central, Partido Comunista, *Treinta Años de Lucha*, chaps. 7–10; Paredes Cruz, *Causas y Efectos, passim;* Carlos Lleras Restrepo, *Hacia la Restauración, Democrática y el Cambio Social* (Bogotá: Editorial AGRA, 1964), vol. 2; Agudelo, "El Estado y los Partidios Políticos," pp. 88–91; Carlos Villar Borda, *Rojas Pinilla: El Presidente Libertador* (Bogotá: Editorial Iqueima, 1953); Pecaut, *Política y Sindicalismo*, pp. 250–257; Caicedo, *Historia de las Luchas Sindicales*, pp. 92–96; República de Colombia, Presidencia de la República, Dirección de Información y Propaganda, *Seis Meses de Gobierno* (Bogotá: Imprenta Nacional, 1953).

added to the nation's economic problems by the declaration by the minister of war that the armed forces wished General Rojas Pinilla to remain in the presidency for the period 1958–1962.[97]

Opposition activities were soon channeled in a Conservative–Liberal civil resistance campaign that included student strikes, street actions, and finally a general lockout by industrialists, bankers, and merchants, who closed the doors of their establishments on May 6, 1957.[98] Four days later, the Rojas Pinilla government fell and power was entrusted to a military junta whose function was to guide the political transition to the assumption of power by a Conservative–Liberal coalition known as the Frente Nacional.[99]

The Frente Nacional was designed to immediately return political power to the traditional political parties. It was also conceived as an instrument to ameliorate the contradictory interests that had led to the partial collapse of the state. Thus, the coalition stipulated that ministries, governorships, and, indeed, every government post in the country were to be evenly divided between the two traditional collectivities with each fraction within the parties being proportionately represented in the 50% that corresponded to its party. The presidency was to be rotated between the two parties and basic policies were to be negotiated by means of political accords between the directorates of the traditional parties. Both parties, and every faction within them, were to be guaranteed equal treatment, access to political

[97] *Intermedio*, Oct. 16, Nov. 3, 1956, Jan. 27 ("Que las Fuerzas Armadas Exigen a Rojas Seguir en el Poder del 58 al 62, Dice Ministro de Guerra"), 30, Feb. 6, Mar. 23, 1957. The last citation reports a joint communiqué by the Liberal and Conservative parties repudiating the determination of the armed forces and demanding elections.

[98] *Intermedio*, May 10–12, 1957. According to *Intermedio*, May 12, 1957, there were 89 deaths related to the movement ("Suben a 89 los Muertos de las Históricas Jornadas de Mayo").

[99] For considerations of the emergence of the Frente Nacional and its subsequent development, consult: Cuéllar, *Trece Años de Violencia*, chap. 11; Paredes Cruz, *Causas y Efectos de Una Dictadura*, pp. 71–86; Martz, *Colombia*, chaps. 15–16; Montaña Cuéllar, *Colombia: País Formal y País Real*, pp. 213–250; Comité Central, Partido Comunista, *Treinta Años de Lucha*, pp. 132–138; Agudelo, "El Estado y los Partidos Políticos," pp. 91–107; Robert H. Dix, *Colombia: The Political Dimensions of Change* (New Haven; Yale University Press, 1967), chap. 6; Bernardo Gaitán Mahecha, *Misión Histórica del Frente Nacional* (Bogotá: Editorial Revista Colombiana, 1966); Humberto Rojas Ruíz and Alvaro Camacho Guizado, *El Frente Nacional: Ideología y Realidad* (Bogotá: Punta de Lanza, 1974); Eduardo Santa, *Sociología Política de Colombia* (Bogotá: Ediciones Tercer Mundo, 1964), pp. 64–119; Urrutia, *Historia del Sindicalismo*, chap. 12; Lucía de Niño and Equipo de Investigaciones Sociológicas, "Estructura de Clases en Colombia," mimeographed (Bogotá: Universidad Nacional, 1971), chap. 3; Rodrigo Losada, *Elites Políticas Colombianas* (unpublished manuscript, *passim*.

The Frente Nacional from its very inception had important political support from the Catholic Church. The curiate declared that Catholics should vote affirmatively in the plecibite which inscribed the coalition in the National Constitution; see *El Tiempo*, Nov. 20, Dec. 1, 1957.

decision-making, and political posts. No one among the socioeconomically powerful groups controlling Colombia's traditional political parties would have to fear official discrimination. All would also have access to at least part of the benefits to be derived from political power.

Coalitions between the country's two traditional political parties were not new in Colombia, but the Frente Nacional had some very singular characteristics, compared to prior alliances.[100]

Most previous coalitions had been conceived within the context of hegemonic politics. Thus, there was nearly always a distinctively inferior "junior partner" in each coalition. Also, prior coalitions either were conceived to be short term or turned out to be so given the exclusivistic nature of Colombia's hegemonic politics. The Frente Nacional called for a genuine 16-year truce with regard to exclusivistic, hegemonic politics between the traditional parties, but it did not mark the end of this pervasive political pattern. Instead of representing the political hegemony of the Liberals *or* the Conservatives, the Frente Nacional was the exclusivistic hegemony of the Liberals *and* the Conservatives. Indeed, the referendum measure that inscribed the Frente Nacional in the country's constitution stated that other groups were to be excluded from all access to power.[101]

In sum, the Frente Nacional permitted the Conservatives and the Liberals to transcend the contradiction that had led to intense partisan rivalry.

[100] The Frente Nacional was preceded by a century of coalition experiments and it was immediately anticipated by intense alliance activity during the late 1940s. It will be recalled from Chapter 2 that there occurred a Conservative–Liberal coalition during the presidency of Mallarino after the demise of the artisan–military regime in 1854. The Conservative Independent–Liberal coalition that eventually emerged into Rafael Núñez's Nationalist party is another coalition example, as are Rafael Reyes's Concordia Nacional and Carlos E. Restrepo's Unión Republicana. In addition, one must add to the list Olaya Herrera's Liberal-led *Concentración Nacional* and Ospina Pérez's Conservative-led *Unión Nacional* between 1946 and 1949, with a few months interruption in 1948.

In the late 1940s Alfonso López Pumarejo proposed a coalition in the last months before his resignation; Alberto Lleras installed a coalition cabinet during his caretaker government; in 1946, López Pumarejo seconded by Darío Echandía proposed that the Conservatives choose the next president from a list to be elaborated by the Liberals; in 1949, Ospina Pérez proposed another coalition cabinet and finally a plan by which the presidency would be alternated annually between the parties; and Liberals advanced a similar plan rejected by the Laureanistas in Nov. 1949.

[101] This tenet increasingly became a legal fiction. For example, Gustavo Rojas Pinilla's *Alianza Nacional Popular* (ANAPO, "National Popular Alliance") participated in elections as an opposition movement to the Frente Nacional by presenting itself as a dissident faction within both the Conservative and Liberal parties. However, Alberto Lleras Camargo stated in a speech in the stadium "El Campín" shortly before the 1970 presidential election that a presidential electoral victory by Rojas Pinilla would be unconstitutional. It is not inconceivable that the tenet was allowed to become a fiction only to the extent that it did not threaten the political control of the Liberal–Conservative coalition.

It ameliorated the factor that had originally produced the partial collapse of the state and the subsequent maturation into violent conflicts of multiple social contradictions. Under circumstances where no powerful group could conceive of being excluded from state power or access to it, the Frente Nacional guaranteed all of them political representation and at least part of the benefits to be derived from it.[102] This solution, which would also have been possible in the late 1940s, did not prove politically viable until after the country had experienced the extreme protraction of apparently endless violence, the advent of intense, interclass conflicts (described in Chapter 6), and the attempt by the military to construct a praetorian regime that unsuccessfully sought to mobilize a populist political base.

The inauguration of the Frente Nacional did not automatically result in the reconstruction of the state in all areas of the country. The complex forms of nonpartisan violence that had developed after 1946 continued intensely within a reduced geographical area (see Chapter 6). Most forms of partisan violence were reduced. This, in and of itself, ended the violence in some areas, such as the Eastern Plains.

A new amnesty also reduced the number of those actively involved in the violence. However, in some areas of the country, prolonged, full-scale military operations were required to reinstate government control. The

[102] It may be argued that the National Federation of Coffee Growers was an antecedent to the Frente Nacional. Christopher Abel argues that the National Federation of Coffee Growers in turn was closely associated with Restrepo's Republican Union bipartisan coalition:

> Republican thinking was visible above all, in the National Federation of Coffee Growers, which held its first Congress in 1927 with Restrepo as President. The Federation had successfully sought to avoid party polarization and class antagonism within coffee production and marketing. ("Conservative Politics in Twentieth Century Antioquia," Occasional Paper no. 3 [Oxford: St. Anthony's College, Latin American Centre, 1973], p. 15).

In this same light, it is interesting to note that the National Federation of Coffee Growers was one of the few institutions in Colombian society that did not lose its effectiveness even at the height of the partisan division. The leaders of the Federation had been traditionally careful to keep party politics out of the organization so as not to endanger the nation's principal export activity. Consider, for example, a polemic that began to appear in the press in Apr. 1934, over whether the coffee industry had developed due to Liberal or Conservative initiatives. Begun by Silvio Villegas en *El País*, it was promptly stopped when Mariano Ospina Pérez requested, on behalf of the Federation, "a suspension of the political polemic about the institution that defends the interests of the coffee growers," inasmuch as the institution was "apolitical" (*El Tiempo*, Apr. 9, 1934).

The Federation thus marked an early example of an economic group largely transcending partisan sectarianism in order to better defend their instrumental interests. In this sense, the Federation is a definite antecedent of the Frente Nacional. Thus, the first thing in Colombian society so sacred as to be placed above partisan conflict was not the church, which on the contrary was highly sectarian, but rather the commercialization of the coffee bean.

largest of these operations was Plan LASO, a United States-financed and -advised full-scale invasion of Communist guerrilla areas in the Central Chain of The Andes.[103] Gradually, between 1958 and 1966, most areas were returned to direct State control. This process was largely completed by 1966, although some isolated areas (e.g., El Pato) continue beyond state control to this date. In other areas the power of the state is still at best tenuous (e.g., the Central Cordillera in Southern Tolima.) However, with regard to all strategic and central regions of the country, the state was reconstructed by the Frente Nacional governments, and the most important manifestations of violent socioeconomic and sociopolitical conflict were repressed.

A Comparative Note

It may be argued that most of the Latin American countries have experienced relatively high levels of intraclass conflict within the dominant groups, that nearly all have undergone social processes that have entailed the progressive accentuation of interclass conflict, and that all have undergone the strengthening of the state at some point in the course of the present century. What, then, differentiated Colombia from other countries with regard to the appearance of widespread, intense social violence?

The first factor is the degree to which the traditional political parties formed the center of the nation's political life in a persistent manner and the extent to which exclusivistic, hegemonic politics prevailed between the two parties. Despite, and perhaps because of, virtually unchallenged oligarchical control of national politics via the two parties, internal, partisan conflicts within the traditionally dominant class remained at high levels through midcentury and continued to form the central arena of national politics. In the cases of Argentina, Brazil, Chile, Mexico, and Uruguay, that pattern of politics clearly lost its importance decades earlier.

In addition, in these other countries the middle stratum of society achieved autonomous political expression early in the twentieth century. After relatively short periods of confrontational politics with the traditional ruling class, they were generally integrated into the prevailing political system. In the case of Colombia, the prevalence of an ossified, sectarian two-party system conspired against the emergence of independent middle-stratum political parties. To a certain extent they formed counterelite movements within the traditional parties (such as Gaitán's

[103] Maingot, "The Colombian Military," p. 333. For the most complete account of United States military aid to Colombia, consult Russell Ramsey, "The Modern Violence in Colombia 1946–1965," Ph.D. dissertation, University of Florida (Gainesville, 1970), passim.

faction of the Liberal party), which made intraparty conflict almost as intense and sectarian as the interparty struggles.

Finally, in the other Latin American countries, the emergence of intense interclass conflict led, imperfectly but generally, to an increase in the cohesiveness of the bourgeoisie and unified recourse to numerous mechanisms, most recently neofascist military dictatorships, to stem increases in the socioeconomic and sociopolitical power of the popular classes. In Colombia, on the contrary, the intraclass struggle for political party hegemony intensified simultaneously with the strengthening of the state, which in turn had been undertaken partly to compensate for the weakened social structure that resulted from the emergence of progressively more acute forms of class conflict. Thus, the following all occurred in a simultaneous and conflictive fashion: intensified intraclass conflict within the traditional oligarchy; conflict between those groups and middle-stratum counter-elites attempting to enter into a very closed political system; and the increase in interclass conflict between the dominant group and militant, organized urban laborers, rural peasants, and Indians.

In the other Latin American countries, intraclass disputes within the traditional oligarchy were generally attenuated prior to, or simultaneously with, the emergence of confrontations with the middle stratum. The integration of the latter groups into the operative political system was generally consolidated prior to the emergence of acute interclass conflict with the popular sectors.[104] However, in Colombia, all of these conflicts occurred simultaneously in the late 1940s. Thus, the interclass conflict did not occur within the framework of a consolidated and strengthened state adapted to the capitalist mode of production, as was the case in the other countries. On the contrary, in Colombia, not only did all of these sets of conflicts occur simultaneously, but they occurred precisely during the process of the strengthening of the state. In sum, the cumulative combination of social conflicts and the partial collapse of the state that resulted from this process led to a lack of political coherence in civil society simultaneously with a severe decrease in state power. Also, the armed apparatus of the state underwent much the same process as a result of partisan contradictions within its ranks, at least in the initial stages of *La Violencia.*

These are the factors that distinguish the Colombian experience from those of the other major Latin American countries. Even though the countries underwent much the same processes, they did not occur in the same sequence or in the same fashion. In Colombia, the social contradictions typical of the twentieth century accumulated and evolved into highly conflictive social processes nearly simultaneously, accompanied by the ossi-

[104] With regard to this point, Mexico is obviously an exception due to the revolutionary process that consolidated an early and solid middle sector hegemony, allied with an emergent bourgeoisie, with the latter eventually evolving into the dominant force of the alliance.

fied survival of the nineteenth century pattern of exclusivistic, hegemonic politics between the Liberal and Conservative expressions of the traditional oligarchy. The latter point also distinguishes Colombia from the other countries mentioned and suggests a research problem worthy of intensive comparative analysis: the incredible strength, resiliency, and persistence of the Conservative–Liberal party system in Colombia to the practical exclusion of other forms of partisan organization.

The lack of resolution, even partially, of basic conflicts and the policy of "muddling through" which led to the accumulation of fundamental contradictions, were made possible precisely because the traditional oligarchy in Colombia maintained a much higher degree of political control in the society than it did in the other major Latin American countries, despite acute division within their own ranks. The mechanism for this domination was two oligarchical-led, multiclass political parties that divided society into two hostile camps and that enjoyed between the two of them the near-universal allegiance of the Colombians, to the point that other organizational forms of political expression invariably failed to prosper.

A Concluding Note

The partial collapse of the state occurred in the context of the increased importance of the state in the structuring of Colombian society. The augmented structural impact of the state, within a political culture characterized by continued exclusivistic hegemonic politics, led to a radical division within a dominant socioeconomic class divided by traditional partisan rivalries. This division led to a virtual civil war between the parties and a concomitant decrease in state power. Also of importance in this process was the emergence of interclass conflicts in the countryside and in the industrial sector. The interclass conflicts, along with residual traditionalist contradictions, were intensified in turn by the partial collapse of the state. Thus, the notorious intensity of the Colombian *Violencia* was due to the simultaneous maturation into intense conflicts, with a high potential for violence, of multiple contradictions of diverse origin, which was conditioned by the partial collapse of the state. A consideration of some of the diverse forms of violent conflicts conditioned by the partial collapse of the state is given in Chapter 6, where a structural regionalization of the violence is presented.

6

A Structural Regionalization of *La Violencia*

What happens if the state collapses in a given area? The answer to that question depends a great deal on the social contradictions existent in the region and on the strengths or weaknesses of other factors that structure social life. Consider, for example, the simple illustration of the presence or absence of the armed apparatus of the state, which, of course, is but one aspect of the state.

In a small town in Iowa the local police might not have anything to do for days on end. Even if they left town one night to go to a nearby city, their absence might not lead, in and of itself, to forms of violence. A lack of acute contradictions among the residents combined with the strength of nonstate forms of social control would impede the development of a critical social situation even given the absence of the armed apparatus of the state. Consider, on the other hand, a city such as New York. There a lack of presence of the armed apparatus of the state for even a few hours would lead to massive looting, arson, robberies, rioting, and perhaps even a large-scale insurrection.

The principal difference is that New York is a caldron of socioeconomic, racial, and political contradictions. The contradictory interests of different groups are such, and the non-state structuring of society sufficiently weak, that the presence of the state, and particularly its armed apparatus, is essential to maintain the social structure of that city.

Likewise, in Colombia, there are areas that could experience a partial collapse of the state and yet undergo little or no violence. Indeed, there are outlying areas of Colombia where the nearest manifestation of the state, even under normal circumstances, is days away by river boat or mule. In these zones, an absolute anarchy does not reign. The neighbors in such regions arrange their own affairs and rarely make use of the State apparatus. In other areas, however, contradictory interests over land, over local political control, over religion, or over national political questions make the presence of the state necessary for the maintenance of the existing social structure.

Explicitly or implicitly, state policies contribute to the structuring of society by generally deciding disputed issues in favor of the groups that have greater power resources and more power in the control of the state itself. Such policies are often backed by the armed apparatus of the state. Under such circumstances, if voluntary compliance to state edicts is not elicited, the threat of violence or violence itself is applied to procure compliance.

The state also tends to intervene in severe and particularly violent social conflict even when it is not directly related to issues that have come to form part of the ongoing social policies backed by the state, or even when the interests of those groups influential in the state are not at stake. The state generally attempts to monopolize the use of physical coercion, and it is highly prone to intervene as a "third party" in disputes that are violent. For example, in battles between Indian tribes in remote areas of Colombia, the state will send troops even if it has no particular interest in defending one group at the expense of the other, even though the interests of those who control the state and their constituencies may not be at stake, and even though state officials may not understand how the violence began or even the issues involved.

In the partial collapse of the Colombian state during *La Violencia,* the state lost part of its capacity to back its fiats in favor of certain groups at the expense of others. Thus, the existing structures of certain aspects of society were determined by the immediate power resources of different groups. Under these circumstances, a particularly valuable resource was superiority in the employment of violence. Also, the state lost in good measure its capacity to intervene as a "third party" in disputes that did not impinge on the more immediate interests of those groups who controlled the state. Thus, some conflicts received a very low priority when compared to other types of conflicts that were occurring simultaneously in Colombian society. Many of the low-priority conflicts were simply left to run their violent course. In the latter instances, citizens began to form or reenforce groups that could permit them to defend their lives and other interests, in situations in which state intervention could not be expected, even in instances of severe violence. In other cases, these groups were designed to defend citizens against the government itself. The relations between such groups were highly unstructured. Conflicts between them had a high potential for violence. In a vicious circle, the mechanisms that were created to protect certain groups from violence in turn spawned further violence.

Intense, protracted violence tended to occur in areas that combined *both acute social contradictions and a partial collapse of the state.* In areas without imminent social crisis, and in areas in which state coherence was maintained, violence tended to be less intense or nonexistent. Examples of all of the different types of the most important *Violencia* situations are to be found in the analysis of selected violence regions contained in this chapter. *La Violencia* regions considered illustrate different socioeconomic and sociopolitical processes that turned violent given the common conditioning factor of the partial collapse of the state. The cases were chosen on the basis of the criteria that they represent forms of violence that are analytically important for an understanding of *La Violencia,* are highly prevalent forms of violence, and/or are important regions. The extensiveness of the violence impedes a treatment in this study of all of the relevant cases or even of the totality of aspects associated with *La Violencia* in the regions studied. Within some of the latter, intensive case studies were undertaken of specific localities considered to be particularly important in, or representative of, the violenf processes that affected the structural region in question.

What follows is the analysis of cases that form a "structural regionalization" of the violence, in that the regions selected are not geographical or administrative units, but rather areas that reflect the same types of social conflicts and generally the same social-structural relations. These structural regions at times bear resemblances to geographical or administrative areas, but they were not chosen on the basis of these criteria.

This chapter analyzes the following cases: (1) guerrilla civil wars; (2) traditional rivalries between villages; (3) violence for control of the local power structure; (4) violence for control of land; (5) coffee crop violence; and (6) areas of state coherence.

Guerrilla Civil Wars

One of the most significant violent processes following in the wake of the partial collapse of the state was the accentuation of widespread partisan violence, which assumed the proportions of a full-scale civil war. The Conservative governments gave first priority to the repression of this phenomenon, which placed large portions of the national territory under the control of alternative power and authority structures, and which potentially threatened the very existence of the regime itself.

Guerrilla groups began to form in late 1949, and by 1950 full-scale civil wars were being fought in various areas of the country. The Eastern Plains, Southern Tolima–Northern Huila, Eastern Cauca, Northern Cundinamarca, Northern Tolima, Sumapaz, Viotá, Western Caldas–Northern Valle, Santander, and Antioquia were all the scenes of protracted, organized guerrilla activity. The guerrillas mostly fought under the banners of the Liberal party, although Communist party guerrillas also fought in Southern Tolima, as well as in Sumapaz and Viotá. The government also organized counterguerrillas, known as *guerrilleros de la paz* ("peace guerrillas"), in Liberal- and Communist-controlled areas. Given the prevailing conditions of a partially collapsed state, numerous organized groups of bandits also emerged simultaneously with the politically motivated guerrillas, and the latter on occasion undertook actions indistinguishable from those of the bandits. This was also true with respect to the police and the army. Indeed, no one had a monopoly on larceny during *La Violencia*.

The guerrilla warfare in Communist zones was generally associated with socioeconomic conflicts, as well as combat involving government and bandit attacks on those areas. Examples of these socioeconomic and sociopolitical factors will be examined later in this chapter. The coffee zones, which also had very special characteristics, will also receive special attention. The principal interest in this section is to treat the violent conflicts between Liberal guerrillas and the Conservative government.

The events of the Liberal–Conservative conflict of the period 1946–1949 led to the emergence of "war" and "peace" factions within each of the two traditional political parties. Control of the National Liberal Directorate was retained by the "peace" faction of that party, which wished to avoid a general civil war. The "war" faction of the party was continually enlarged by direct victims of the violence. These tended to be country dwellers of middle and, more frequently, lower class extraction. They were desperate men, many of whom were outside of the law prior to joining the guerrillas.[1] The direct victims of the violence were reenforced by middleclass "war" Liberal intellectuals, few in number but important in their impact, who sought to mobilize and coordinate the Liberal guerrillas to overthrow the Conservative regime.[2]

By far the most important Conservative–Liberal civil war occured on the Llanos Orientales (Eastern Plains). In the course of 1949, organized Liberal

[1] Most guerrilla leaders were outside of the law *prior* to initiating their guerrilla activity. They tended to be men who had violently suffered traumatic personal grievances and/or who had attacked Conservative authorities. Some had also abandoned the ranks of the armed forces or police on April 9 or thereafter. This fact emerged from the near totality of interviews of Liberal ex-guerrillas. For written corroboration, consult: Eduardo Franco Isaza, *Las Guerrillas del Llano* (Bogotá: Librería Mundial, 1959), passim; Germán Guzmán, Orlando Fals Borda, and Eduardo Umaña Luna, *La Violencia en Colombia* (Bogotá: Universidad Nacional, 1962), Monografías Sociológicas No. 12, vol. 1, chap. 5; Velásquez Santos, *Buenos Días Guerrilleros* (Bogotá: Editorial Agra, 1954), p. 62 and passim. The latter citation deals with the guerrillas of Northern Cundinamarca. The leader of that guerrilla force, Saul Fajardo, is a prime example of the violence victim turned aggressor of the Conservative authorities, who eventually formed a guerrilla movement of kindred persons.

[2] In the important guerrilla armies of the Eastern Plains, numerous middle-class youths from Boyacá, mostly educated in the Colegio de Boyacá in Tunja and the Colegio Sugamuxi in Sogamoso, reenforced the movement; see Franco Isaza, *Las Guerrillas*, p. 52. In an interview, an ex–rank-and-file guerrilla stated, "Almost all of the chiefs were from Boyacá."

resistance to the Conservative police arose on the Plains in a sporadic fashion. Additional police units were sent to confront the latent Liberal rebellion in the region.[3] An immediate precedent to the rebelliousness had been the capture of Puerto López on April 9, 1948. Led by Eliseo Vásquez, Liberals there staged one of the many mini–coup d'etats which followed the Liberal insurrection in Bogotá.[4] The initiation of the guerrilla war itself was presaged by the capture of Villavicencio, the most important city on the Plains, by air force units led by Captain Alfredo Silva.

The November 25, 1949, attack on Villavicencio had originally formed part of a Liberal party plot to spark a military coup d'etat, to coincide with the Conservative party's unilateral election of Laureano Gómez as president of the republic. The coup plot had been changed to a general strike, but Silva and the Liberal Directorate liaison, Hernán Durán Dussan, followed the original plan in hopes that a general uprising might be provoked.[5] After the failure of the Villavicencio movement many of those involved emigrated to distant areas of the Plains where Eliseo Vásquez had once again rebelled, where influential Liberal cattlemen were supporting and financing the nascent guerrilla movement, and where refugees from all over the plains, and even from as far away as Andean Boyacá, were forming a full-fledged Liberal guerrilla army.[6]

The bulk of those involved in the Liberal guerrilla movements considered them as an instrument to defend themselves and/or their other interests and/or their region from the abuses of sectarian officials, while some further considered the guerrillas to be an instrument of revenge.[7] In simple language, one of the most important surviving guerrilla leaders stated in an interview: "The people wanted to be informed about and cooperate in the defense of their land, their children, and their lives. For that reason it was easy to find people who were determined to act."

Only secondarily did the bulk of the guerrillas consider their movement to be a route to political power for their party. This fact helps explain the initial disillusionment and frustration with the guerrilla groups and leaders expressed by the intellectual "war" Liberals involved in the movement.[8]

[3] *El Tiempo*, Jan. 23, 1949, "Se Ponen en Duda los Motivos de Envío de Policía a Casanare." The article states: "It is said that they are arriving to persecute rustlers but their mission is to destroy Liberalism."

[4] Interviews in Puerto López and Villavicencio.

[5] Guzmán *et al.*, *La Violencia*, vol. 1, pp. 62–64; interview with one of the principal protagonists of the coup plot.

[6] Interviews in Puerto López, Villavicencio, Puerto Gaitán, Orocué, and Yopal. See also Franco Isaza, *Las Guerrillas*, chaps. 2–6. For a descriptive chronology of the development of the Plains guerrilla movement, consult Russell Ramsey, *La Revolución Campesina 1950–1954* (Bogotá: Ediciones Libros de Colombia, 1973).

[7] Interview.

[8] Franco Isaza and his Boyacense colleagues form the prime example of the middle-class "war" Liberals. His statements of their efforts and frustrations in *Las Guerrillas del Llano* (passim) form the most important evidence for this point.

It also helps to account for the lack of political coherence of the guerrillas and the lack of coordination between the various Liberal guerrilla groups in different regions and even in the same area.

In sum, the crucial contradiction involved in the initiation of the guerrilla war was sectarian persecution. The Liberal's armed resistance presented the Conservative government with an acute instance of rebellion against established authority, which it attempted to dominate by organized police repression, large-scale military operations, and random terror. The events of November 1949, which accelerated the process of the partial collapse of the state, conditioned the maturation of this conflict to the point of a full-scale guerrilla war.

The Liberal guerrilla movement in the Llanos initially enjoyed regionwide, multiclass support. Indeed, the most prominent and prosperous Liberal cattlemen, such as the Delgados, felt the most threatened by the arbitrary Conservative authorities, and they were instrumental in organizing and financing the guerrillas in their first stage. The guerrillas were also backed, morally and materially, by the "peace" Liberal-controlled National Liberal Directorate.[9] This aid was given for tactical reasons. The "peace" Liberal leadership did not sanction the formation of the guerrillas, nor did it consider that the guerrillas could capture power, but it did initially reason that, since the guerrillas existed, they could be utilized to pressure the government or create the conditions for a favorable military coup. Later in the struggle, the Liberal Directorate ceased to support the guerrillas, while some prominent "peace" Liberals even disowned them as simple bandits.

The guerrillas, for their part, at times looked upon the National Liberal Directorate as their supreme mentor and potential savior, while at other times they considered the politicians of the capital to be comfortable hypocrites content with newspaper polemics while peasants were slaughtered by the police and the army.[10] The view of the National Liberal Directorate as

[9] In addition to the National Liberal Directorate's initial support of a Nov. 1949 coup plot of which Silva's capture of Villavicencio was a part, the National Liberal Directorate would also appear to have been involved in a Mar. 1950 coup movement that included an aborted attempt to capture arms from the National Military School. Interviews with a colonel who was once director of the military school and with an ex-chief of army intelligence. See also Franco Isaza, *Las Guerrillas*, pp. 63–64, 67, 144. In the first months of the Plains guerrilla movement, the National Liberal Directorate sent provisions, including munitions. Interview with a principal guerrilla leader; see also Franco Isaza, *Las Guerrillas*, p. 63.

[10] For example, Franco Isaza writes:

> The revolution was never made despite the fact that it was happily called revolution. Certainly, we never went beyond the organization of armed bands that heroically defended themselves against the terror of the regime, weakly illuminated by a libertarian idea but without the slightest basic formation.
>
> The mistake consisted simply in having sought to make a revolution in the name

traitors was attenuated whenever the national-level politicians gave attention to the guerrillas.[11]

The guerrillas were directed by lower- and middle-class leaders who emerged in the course of the struggle itself. Not one national political figure of the Liberal party took to the field during the civil war. The guerrillas were also highly isolated. In a reedition of the popular insurrections of the War of the Supremes (1839–1843), there was little communication and no coordination between the various guerrilla groups in the country.[12] It was only with enormous effort that some degree of coordination was achieved between the different guerrilla groups operating on the Eastern Plains. The isolated nature of the guerrilla forces contributed to their great receptivity to the National Liberal Directorate as a potential source of coordination, despite its lack of continued support for them. They also considered that National Liberal Directorate support would "legitimize" their struggle.[13]

The scale of the initial National Directorate-backed rebellion in the Eastern Plains and the widespread popular support for it, led to an immediate and massive army reenforcement of police activities in the region. In some zones the army adopted Draconian tactics, while in others pro-Liberal officers reached "live and let live" agreements with the rebels, and even sabotaged police operations at the cost of police mortalities. In the end, drastic "carrot or stick" anti-guerrilla tactics led to significant military advances for the government.[14]

In May 1950, the loosely interconnected guerrilla networks on the Eastern Plains stretched from Arauca on the Venezuelan border to Northern Caquetá. By August of the same year, the guerrillas had been clearly defeated, and they rapidly lost open adherents and gained turncoats. At the end of the year, the various movements had largely disbanded, and the surviving leaders were living clandestinely.[15] In the course of their rapid

---

of the Liberal party, which in a determinate moment of its history was directed by notoriously antirevolutionary and antipopular chiefs; more or less complascent partners with the Conservatives in the enterprise of sweeping away all beginnings of organization and progress for the masses in their difficult—due to their disorientation—but constant efforts to free themselves from the Conservative-Liberal yoke. (*Las Guerrillas*, p. 85)

[11] An example of this is the triumphal reception given Alfonso López Pumarejo during his visit to the war zone. See Franco Isaza, *Las Guerrillas*, chap. 12; *El Tiempo*, Jan. 3, Apr. 19, 1952.

[12] It will be recalled from Chapter 2 that the War of the Supremes was also led by second- and third-level political figures of popular origin, with a few highly significant exceptions.

[13] A view unanimously held by all of the ex-guerrillas interviewed in the region.

[14] Interviews with army officers and ex-guerrillas and Plains residents. For written examples of army collaboration with Liberal guerrillas, see Franco Isaza, *Las Guerrillas*, pp. 18, 67, 89–94, 144–145.

[15] Franco Isaza, *Las Guerrillas*, pp. 124, 152, 167.

demise, the guerrillas had lost the support of both the National Liberal Directorate and the influential Liberal cattlemen of the region. The ambiguous attitude of the Liberal leadership in Bogotá is summarized by a statement reputedly made by Carlos Lleras Restrepo upon receipt of a petition from the harassed guerrillas: "We do not authorize or disauthorize. Tell those boys that our hearts are with them." [16]

The Liberal cattlemen, on the other hand, were soon very much against the change in the local power structure that guerrilla authority ultimately represented, the disruption of the cattle business due to the war, and the reprisals that surely awaited them for their collaboration in a losing cause.[17] One of the most important ex-guerrilla leaders summarized the landlords' position in the following terms during an interview: "The Liberal landlords utilized the guerrillas to defend their ranches against the Conservative violence, but when the workers asked for social improvements, when they asked for contributions of cattle to support the guerrillas, and when the landlords saw the possibility of a change in the structure of property relations, things were turned upside down and the guerrillas who had been stimulated by the landlords were suddenly classified as 'bands of outlaws.' " [18]

The loss of support of the Liberal cattlemen and the Directorates weakened the guerrillas, but more important in their defeat was their own lack of organization and coordination, their inexperience, and quite simply the military superiority of the armed forces.

The government soon began to systematically repress the areas that had supported the guerrillas. This time the attack on the "bandits" enjoyed the support of the majority of the Liberal cattlemen of the region, who even installed police posts on their ranches. The imprimatur of "bandits" on ex-Liberal insurgents was formally accepted by Liberal cattlemen at a meeting in Sogamoso in which they called for government intervention against banditry on the Plains. They formally signed a document, some willingly and others under the duress of a statement by Army Colonel Luis A. Castillo, that those who did not sign would be considered bandits.[19] Areas in which the peasants resisted a return to their previous relations with the landowners, and Liberal smallholding areas which had supported the guerrillas, were constantly raided by the police, with some extensive areas even being evacuated and declared "bandit-infested" free-fire zones.[20]

[16] *Ibid.*, p. 153.

[17] Multiple interviews with army officers, ex-guerrillas, and cattlemen.

[18] Interview with ex-guerrilla leader. For a summary of the literature related to this point, consult Francisco Posada, *Colombia: Violencia y Subdesarrollo* (Bogotá: Universidad Nacional, 1968), pp. 153–157.

[19] Franco Isaza, *Las Guerrillas*, pp. 176–177.

[20] *Ibid.*, p. 174.

Under these circumstances, large groups were soon uprooted from their farms or from their places of employment. They and others who feared impending reprisals soon followed guerrilla advice and moved to isolated areas of the Plains. The guerrilla movement reemerged, and it prospered under these conditions much faster than it had been defeated. Furthermore, it was bolstered by a series of military victories during the period of its reemergence. By June 1951, the army had abandoned its small posts on farms and retired to larger installations. Truces also began to be called in the course of 1951. These were two types: cattle truces and political truces.

Cattle as the basis of the economy of the Plains was the prime economic element in *La Violencia* in that region. Important reasons for the Liberal cattlemen's change of position in the first phase of the struggle was the guerrilla's decision to impose a tax on cattle leaving the Plains (10% for Liberal cattle and 20% for the Conservatives) and the army's decision to prohibit the sale of the cattle of the insurgents and impede their receipt of supplies by means of an economic blockade of the region. Throughout the conflict, the army demanded safe-conduct passes for cattle leaving the area. Thus, Conservative cattle were free to pass. Liberal cattle had to be proven to belong to government collaborators, while insurgent Liberal cattle were theoretically vetoed. In practice, the latter were bought by Conservative businessmen or by army officers at discount prices. By representing the animals as their own, they "Conservatized" the cattle. Numerous large fortunes were made by these means, including the initial wealth of some of the richest families in contemporary Villavicencio. Another prevalent route to immediate wealth was cattle thievery. A major source of these bovines was the massive, violent displacement of the smallholders.[21]

The cattle truces were thus a mutual recognition by the government and the guerrillas of the need to maintain the Plain's basic economy despite the civil war.

The first cattle truce occurred during 1951 when the army proposed a cease fire in the Mani region, which the guerrillas accepted. This provided a hiatus in both the armed hostilities and the economic blockade. Thus, cattle left the region and supplies entered. The guerrillas were also provided a rest zone as a result of this measure.

However, once the cattle had been taken out of the area, the army promptly renewed hostilities. Implicit as well as explicit cattle truces ensued in other areas, including a large-scale cessation of hostilities in Villavicencio at the end of the year.[22] The cattle truces were achieved due to a dovetailing of interests between archenemies: the absentee cattlemen,

[21] Interviews throughout the Plains. For the guerrillas' tax resolutions, see Franco Isaza, *Las Guerrillas*, pp. 114–116, 258–259. The cattle of Liberals who had signed the Sogamoso Declaration paid double, as did those of the Conservatives.

[22] Interviews; Franco Isaza, *Las Guerrillas*, pp. 215–216.

whose influence in the government achieved acceptance of the measure, and the guerrillas, who in the end also had cattle as their economic base.

Political truces also began during 1951. José Gnecco Mozo, a Conservative lawyer, proposed a peace mission to the Plains. With a note from the minister of war, Dr. Roberto Urdaneta Arbeláez, he traveled to the guerrilla zone at the risk of his life. After surviving an initial armed attack, Gnecco established both contact and rapport with the guerrillas. The peace petition that Gnecco obtained from the guerrillas is an important document in that it reflects the emergence of ill-defined social concerns within a very heterogeneous set of demands.

The basic contradiction between the rank-and-file plainsmen and the government continued to be sectarian violence. The peace proposal requested "that all prisoners be released, that schools and farms be built, that rice seed be brought, that rural credit and savings banks be established, that barbed wire be less expensive, that troops be removed from the Plains with the army retaining only those posts that existed before the conflict, that the government name Dr. José Gnecco Mozo governor of the region (because he is the only one in whom we may trust), that salaries bear a relation to the profits of the landlords, that we might have rights over the land, that we not be called bandits, that we be treated as brothers, that roads be constructed and that free trade be established, that there be no more blockade, that the region be governed by people from the region, and that there be progress." The government ignored the petition and renewed hostilities. Gnecco Mozo was disauthorized, vilified, and even detained for a short period.[23]

The next peace mission was undertaken at the end of 1951 by ex-President Alfonso López Pumarejo, who visited the guerrillas with the authorization of the government. In the midst of a general cease-fire, the principal guerrilla leaders assembled in what they considered to be the most triumphant moment of their movement.[24] Despite their continual criticism of the National Liberal Directorate, the bulk of the guerrillas were not alienated from the party's leadership, but rather discouraged by its lack of support for them. Any sign of interest on the part of the Directorate was enthusiastically received. The López mission did not lead to concrete results, and it was played down by the government.[25]

Army Colonel Gustavo Sierra Ochoa blames the political truces for the guerrilla's expansion in 1952:

> The subversion on the Eastern Plains was stimulated by the visits and conferences with political chiefs of Liberalism which occurred at the end of the

[23] Franco Isaza, *Las Guerrillas*, p. 233.

[24] Interviews; Franco Isaza, *Las Guerrillas*, p. 233.

[25] *El Tiempo*, Jan. 3, Apr. 19, 1952; interview with a person who accompanied López Pumarejo on the trip; James M. Daniel, *Rural Violence in Colombia since 1946*, (Washington, D.C.: American University, SORO, 1965), pp. 67–74.

> second semester of 1951. They felt favored by the lifting of the blockade of the Plains. They received support from the suspension of military actions and the retreat from numerous posts that the army occupied in key sites. The rebels took advantage politically and militarily of these circumstances. It was the most decisive moment for the reenforcement of their morale, which was broken and dominated in some sectors during the campaign that the army undertook with great efficacy, but which was lost almost totally for the cause of the reestablishment of order. . . . The numbers of guerrillas of political banditry have increased considerably after the conference of the political chieftains with the guerrilla chieftains.[26]

The National Liberal Directorate did not support the guerrillas materially during their resurgence in 1951 or during their impressive offensive in 1952, but it did adopt an ambiguous attitude with regard to the movement. The guerrillas were, for example, frequently used as a pressure point by the "peace" Liberals of the capital in their polemics with government authorities and the Conservative press. Carlos Lleras Restrepo stated in a February 1952 speech:

> Peace is not that which may be defined only as the absence of protest, as the silent resignation of a mass of slaves subject to opprobrious conditions, but rather that which consists of the tranquil coexistence of citizens with equality of rights, backed equally by the law and defended in the exercise of their activities, in their lives, honor, and property by an impartial and efficacious authority.
>
> Thus, the question of the guerrillas has its origins in, and continues to be intimately related to, the problem of whether the country will return to a true judicial regime, return to be a country of laws, where the authorities do not persecute a fraction of the citizenry or permit that they be persecuted, and where the law sanctions, without discrimination, the authors of every outrage.[27]

Another example of references to the guerrillas, even when unfriendly, to make "peace" Liberal political points is illustrated by a celebrated letter from ex-President Alfonso López Pumarejo to ex-President Mariano Ospina Pérez in 1952:

> The Liberal Directorate has received a letter from the Central Command of the Guerrillas of the Casanare in which they frontally attack the policy of peace and concord. . . . The criticism of the revolutionaries of the Casanare to the Liberal Directorate would have less importance than I have given them, if they did not have the support of events that a great number of co-partisans

[26] Colonel Gustavo Sierra Ochoa, *Las Guerrillas en los Llanos Orientales* (Manizales: Tipografía Departamental, 1954), pp. 8–9.

[27] Carlos Lleras Restrepo, "Una Política Liberal Para la Nación," speech made by Dr. Carlos Lleras Restrepo in name of the National Liberal Directorate in the meeting held in the Hotel Granada on February 1, 1952, cited in Lleras Restrepo, *De la Democracia a la Dictadura* (Bogotá: Ediciones Agra, 1955), pp. 350–351.

feel and interpret in a similar fashion, and if, besides, they did not give me an exceptional opportunity to renew the defense of the policy of peace and concord, defining at the same time my position in the difficult situation Liberalism is living. . . . .

We have been willing to declare ourselves [the National Liberal Directorate] in recess if the government believes and manifests to us that by this means we may help to reestablish public tranquility. Many times we have felt the impulse to do this so as not to continue serving as a pretext for new attacks against the lives and property of Liberals; but in no case, for no motive, in order to use arrogantly the excuses which Colombian society still accepts for the overflow of sectarian passions, as would happen, without doubt, if we would adopt the indications of Messrs. Bautista, Franco, Salcedo, Fonseca, and their companions in arms [the principal guerrilla leaders].

I know very well that, from the epoch of independence through our times, those adhering to the constitution have invariably been the most apt to undertake the great enterprises of our historical collectivities. Now I am seeing how not to even the abundance of financial resources, or the abundance of elements of war, or the slogan of blood and fire, implacably executed, obtain for our governors the obedience to their orders that would be assured, if they proceeded in accordance with the norms enshrined by our laws and customs.[28]

The use of the guerrillas as a chip in political arguments and negotiations was rejected by the more vehement peace Liberals who categorized the rebels as "bandits," as did the Government. Such was the case of the Liberal newspapers *El Tiempo* and *El Espectador*. The owner of *El Tiempo*, ex-President Eduardo Santos, wrote his own newspaper from Paris, giving the following appraisal of the situation:

You cannot struggle against an organized army with shotguns, revolvers, and clubs. To attempt to do so only brings prejudice to the cause that one wants to defend. In Colombia, the work of the guerrillas, whatever their motives, has produced infinite pain and incalculable damage to thousands and thousands of Liberals and, besides this, that road leads nowhere. I openly wish that all of this cease, that these methods of struggle be abandoned, and that we concentrate only on civil action, which requires as much courage and perhaps more. By the roads of armed violence, guerrillas, and civil war, Liberalism has nothing to gain and much to lose.[29]

The political polemics in the capital gained in importance as the guerrillas progressed on the battlefields. In 1952, the army had to undertake an extremely casualty-ridden and costly full-scale operation to purge the guerrillas from the passes in Chita and El Cocuy in the high Andes.[30] This wider base of operations spread the army thinner and took pressure off

[28] *El Tiempo*, Sept. 4, 1952.

[29] *Ibid.*, March 3, 1953.

[30] Sierra Ochoa, *Las Guerrillas*, pp. 22–24; Franco Isaza, *Las Guerrillas*, pp. 275, 282, 333.

guerrilla units on the Plains themselves. After months of having played down the importance of the guerrillas, Minister of War José María Bernal declared in January 1952 that the government confronted a revolution.[31] A guerrilla offensive in July and August placed the government further on the defensive. Liberal rebel units attacked the army throughout the Plains, with significant victories in Orocué and in Cháviva, where a motorized army column was ambushed at El Turpial with 96 soldiers killed.[32]

Faced with a deteriorating situation, the army began to shoot guerrilla prisoners and sometimes mere suspects. There are confirmed instances of prisoners having been dropped from transport planes in flight. According to guerrilla leaders the Draconian tactics only served to justify the necessity of their struggle in the view of the Liberal population and to increase their resolve to perservere.

The key to the rebels' success, as is the case in most instances of guerrilla warfare, was their ability to mobilize the civilian population in favor of their movement. Army Colonel Sierra Ochoa asserted: "There is an organized resistance movement against the government which enjoys the sympathy and complicity of the greatest number of the inhabitants of the region." [33] Ochoa Sierra complained of the lack of presence of the public administration as one of the "fertilizers" of subversion, and he estimated that 90% of the Llanos were beyond government control.[34]

The guerrillas increased the quality of their control as they progressively consolidated alternative authority and power structures. Guerrilla legal codes, courts, and taxes replaced those of the national government. Another indicator of rebel control of the region was the organization of counterguerrillas by the armed forces as their principal strategy against the insurgents in 1952 and 1953.[35] Despite the fact that the army had been increasing military pressure on the guerrillas at the time of the June 9, 1953, military coup, the guerrillas had achieved their greatest level of organizational coherence.[36] In June 1953, the scope and quality of rebel con-

[31] *El Tiempo*, Jan. 15, 1952.

[32] *Ibid.*, July 18, 1952. After the ambush, the minister of war simply stated that the government would redouble its efforts to control public order and that the army would work without truces and without rest.

[33] Sierra Ochoa, *Las Guerrillas*, p. 24.

[34] *Ibid.*, pp. 17, 80.

[35] Sierra Ochoa (*Las Guerrillas*, pp. 24–121) was one of the main advocates of the counterguerrilla strategy. See also Franco Isaza, *Las Guerrillas*, pp. 253–254. For information about the army's effort to mount an offensive, see *El Tiempo*, Nov. 14, 1952, Jan. 29, Mar. 22, Apr. 17, 1953.

[36] On Sept. 11, 1952, the various guerrilla groups of the Plains subscribed to an administrative and legal code known as the "First Law of the Plains." A second, and much more complex, legal code was proclaimed on June 13, 1953. Both codes and an analysis of them are contained in Eduardo Umaña Luna, "Normas Propias y Actitudes

trol would seem to have indicated that a protracted stalemate had been created on the Plains.

Several of those interviewed for this study, including some army officers, consider that the prospect of prolonged, seemingly endless violence in several areas of the country, but especially on the Eastern Plains, conditioned the army's decision to undertake the June 1953 coup d'etat.

One of the first actions of the new military government was the proclamation of a general amnesty for all those who surrendered their arms. Some elements within the guerrilla movement of the Eastern Plains opposed an unconditional surrender, but, once certain key units began to accept, the amnesty became a *fait accompli*.[37]

The return to normality on the Plains occurred at an incredibly fast pace. Inasmuch as the principal contradiction had been government repression, the return of guarantees for Liberal citizens ended the basis of the conflict. When further government repression sparked violence in Communist-controlled areas of Eastern Tolima, igniting the "late violence," the Liberals of the Plains escaped both the repression and the subsequent violence. The reconstruction of state authority was thus very solid. There were several attempts to reorganize the guerrillas for social revolutionary purposes. One attempt to reestablish armed activities was led by the Castroite Tulio Bayer and by the veteran Plains guerrilla leader "Minuto" Colmenares. All such attempts failed.[38]

In sum, the Liberal guerrilla rebellion was primarily a resistance movement. It began in an unsystematic fashion during the course of the critical year 1949. The conditions of the partial collapse of the state accompanying the Gómez government led to the maturation of full-scale guerrilla activities and to extensive population and territorial control by the rebels. The resistance movement ended, as might be expected, shortly after the fall of the repressive government. Under these circumstances, the reconstruction of state power and authority proved to be a relatively simple task. This is the case of the Eastern Plains. In different guerrilla areas, where other socioeconomic and sociopolitical contradictions accompanied resistance to official repression, the origins, development, and outcomes of guerrilla activities were much more complicated, as will be illustrated in succeeding sections of this chapter.

---

del Conflicto," which is Part I of Germán Guzmán, Orlando Fals Borda, and Eduardo Umaña Luna, *La Violencia en Colombia*, vol. 2 (Bogotá: Tercer Mundo, 1964), pp. 55–202. On June 10, 1953, the guerrillas had assembled to elect a supreme command for all of their previously disperse movement; see Franco Isaza, *Las Guerrillas*, p. 311.

[37] Franco Isaza, *Las Guerrillas*, pp. 312–329.

[38] Interview with an ex-guerrilla leader involved in this movement. Daniel, *Rural Violence*, p. 118; Alfonso Moncada Abello, *Un Aspecto de la Violencia* (Bogotá: Promotora Colombiana de Editores, 1963), pp. 392–429.

Traditional Village Rivalries

If the civil war on the Plains clearly reflected the conflicts between a faction of the Liberal party and the Conservative government, the same cannot be said for many other conflicts which were purportedly over traditional party politics. Such is the case of the numerous village rivalries that dramatically added to the high death toll of *La Violencia*.

The sectarian spirit in Colombia, with historical roots running back to the recurrent civil wars of the nineteenth century, has led to a traditional tendency to live in clusters of party brethren. This is true of many rural areas and of some urban settings. Like political and religious attitudes lead to like social relations, organizational affiliation, matrimony, parentage, and residence patterns. Thus, partisan considerations have led to politically homogeneous municipalities,[39] while within heterogeneous units there also exists a similar tendency toward political segregation.

Rural muncipalities tend to be divided into heavily Liberal and Conservative *veredas* ("rural neighborhoods"). Some cities also display similar patterns. For example, Chiquinquirá, Boyacá; Ocaña, Norte de Santander; and Caicedonia, Valle are all politically segregated. In the latter case, the entire *municipio* is divided with the partisan boundary line also running through the urban area. Violence there was (and is) most common along the borderline, currently known as the Berlin Wall. In Ocaña the division between the two bands is such that the patron saint is given a procession and celebrated in the Liberal neighborhoods in August and in Conservative districts in December.

Rivalries between neighboring localities of different party affiliations have been highly conflictive, and even violent, in some areas. Many of these violent rivalries had their origins in the civil wars of the nineteenth century when one village fought against another as part of the national conflicts. Subsequently, various patterns of recurrent violence emerged, some related to national politics and others not. The experience of recur-

[39] For 878 municipalities with electoral returns in the key 1930 and 1946 presidential elections, 36% of the municipalities had an average vote in those two elections of over 80% for one or the other of Colombia's two traditional political parties. This vote of over 80% in two elections separated by 16 years is considered to be an indicator of the presence of the *hegemony* of one or another of the parties in these municipalities. Considering municipalities with over a 60% average vote for one or another of the parties in the two elections reveals that 77% of the municipalities fall into this category, which is considered to be an indicator of the clear-cut political *control* of one or another of the parties. Only 23% of the municipalities demonstrate average voting patterns with less than a 60–40 spread separating the parties. Thus, less than a quarter of the *municipios* may be said to have had a historical pattern of political party *competition* in the period 1930–1946. See Paul Oquist, "Las Elecciones Presidenciales 1930–1970," in *Boletín Mensual de Estadística*, ed. DANE, nos. 268–269 (Nov.-Dec. 1973), pp. 63–79.

rent violence further reenforced the segregation of local communities along party lines.

Village rivalries tended to be accentuated at election time or during processes of acute national political conflict. Indeed, violence between rival villages formed a large part of the electoral and transitional party violence of 1922, 1930–1932, and 1946–1948, and it reached epidemic proportions after April 9, 1948. Singularly explosive was the transitional situation in which there was a change of political party control of local government due to national political shifts. This was particularly the case, for example, when the governor named as mayor a member of the hated local opposition (especially when this party constituted a small minority) or a representative of a hated neighboring community.

Other instances of village violence, however, are very difficult to explain by reference to partisan politics. Within the villages a "vendetta" mentality has arisen that is capable of operating quite independently of partisan motivations. A striking sociological fact is that the vendetta villages tend to be found mostly in highly *minifundista* ("small landholder") regions of Colombia. This type of violence is most common in towns with heavy populations of small, independent farmers in Boyaca, Santander, Norte de Santander, Cundinamarca, Tolima, Caldas, and Antioquia.

One area with a high incidence of village conflicts is the "Northern Corredor" of Boyacá, which runs northeast from Sogamoso to the Venezuelan border and includes most of the adjacent province of García Rovira in the Department of Santander. This region is heavily polarized politically. Most *municipios* are overwhelmingly identified with one party or another, and those municipalities with a sizable minority group are generally politically segregated at the *vereda* ("rural ward") level.

In Santander, the region is politically divided into two strips, one Conservative and one Liberal. The Conservative strip consists of San Andrés (67.16% Conservative),[40] Málaga (70.13%), and Mologavita (78.38%). The Liberal strip consists of Cerrito (99.67% Liberal), Concepción (98.69%), Carcasí (77.38%), Enciso (77.42%), San Miguel (66.16%), Capitanejo (74.90%), and Macaravita (71.91%). On the Boyacá side of the departmental boundary, the Liberal strip continues with Chiscas (96.51%), Panqueba (66.48%), and El Cocuy (82.64%). The latter *municipio*, which is the last in the Liberal belt, is practically surrounded by arch-Conservative Boyacense municipalities in addition to containing a few all Conservative *veredas* within its own limits. The Boyacá Conservative belt contains Güicán (99.91%), El Espino (73.10%), Guacamayas (91.62%), San Mateo (92.82%), Boavita (96.82%), La Uvita (96.59%), and Chita (78.34%).[41]

[40] The party identification indicators are the mean vote for each party in the 1930 and 1946 presidential elections; see Oquist, "Las Elecciones Presidenciales." *passim.*

[41] This pattern of political segregation most probably leads to the further reenforcement of extreme sectarianism, given the absence of cross-cutting social relations and loyalties as would be expected by "traditional" social science theory.

Heavily Liberal El Cocuy, surrounded by some of the most arch-Conservative *munifundista* municipalities in Colombia, has had a long history of village rivalry violence.

In the civil war of 1876, Cocuy was the last battlefield of the Conservative's attempt to defeat the Liberal Radical–Independent coalition. Even though the war was already lost for all practical purposes, Conservative troops from the neighboring areas of Santander invaded Cocuy, where Generals Gabriel Vargas Santos and Pedro María Flores had encamped a Liberal army half the size of the Conservative attackers. In the battle, the Conservatives burned most of the town, but the Liberal army emerged victorious. The combat was fierce and Liberal historians call particular attention to the participation in the battle of the local population, including children and the elderly, which greatly facilitated the Liberal victory.[42]

During the period of national political rivalry, El Cocuy and its Conservative neighbors engaged in violent incidents and even minor battles. On such occasions, the departmental or national government would send police or troops to the region and name military mayors to remedy the situation and bring a return to normalcy. During the party hegemonies, the police and military mayors would favor the side that belonged to the dominant party. Thus, the structuring of local relations depended in part on who controlled the national government.

It is apparent that the partisan differences were often secondary in the conflicts themselves, although most important for understanding the way that the local population reacted to them. This is particularly clear in periods of conflict in which there was no national political battle under way. The phenomenon of acute nonpartisan conflict is also present, although less apparent, during periods of intense national political conflict. To make these points clearer, let us consider El Cocuy and its Conservative neighbors as a particularly important case study.

Quite often the initiation of the conflicts between rival villages had at their roots the types of conflicts characteristic of a rural society of smallholders: boundary disputes over plots of land; conflicts over the use of the water of streams; different points of view over transit rights over certain plots of land or along determinate trails or roads; conflicts over animals grazing in neighbors' fields; disputes over lost animals with accusations of thievery; commercial and credit disputes of innumerable types; altercations created or accentuated by alcohol; and conflicts over courtships, pregnancies, and marriages. Especially in La Uvita and El Cocuy, the latter were particularly accentuated by local taboos over inter-*municipio* relations between the sexes.[43]

When any of these types of disputes reached an acute stage or erupted into violence, the conflict became collectivized. Within the "vendetta" men-

[42] Milton Puentes, *Historia del Partido Liberal Colombiano* (Bogotá: Editorial Prag, 1961), pp. 329–331.

[43] Numerous interviews.

tality of the villages there was no such thing as an individual affront. The violent incident would invariably be interpreted as the latest in the century-long series of abuses committed by the hated neighbors which resulted in spirals of revenge and counterrevenge, vendetta violence. Given the local violence, the groups that controlled the state would send police reenforcements and troops or name a military mayor to return the villages to normalcy, despite the fact that the politically dominant groups at the national level had no direct interests in the conflicts involved. The state intervention would be simply as a "third person" to end the violence and to attempt to create a state monopoly on the use of organized violence, although this intervention was not neutral in that local co-partisans tended to be favored as a matter of sectarian principle. Sectarian intervention by the national police probably contributed more to the further collapse of the state than to the reconstruction of its authority in Liberal areas.

During 1949, the entire Northern Boyacá–García Rovira region was affected by vendetta violence.[44] Some of this was due to electoral politics, while other instances are more attributable to collectivized conflicts corresponding to nonpolitical contradictions. The latter readily turned violent when the persons in conflict belonged to different communities engaged in traditional rivalries. Under the progressively more antagonistic circumstances of 1949, political, nonpolitical, and revenge violence became increasingly indistinguishable.

In May 1949 a particularly intense vendetta was ignited in Chita, Boyacá, with the death of two Conservatives and the burning of five Conservative homes. Subsequently, a full-scale battle evolved between armed bands of both parties. *El Siglo* reports 40 deaths as the result of a single battle in one day.[45] At that time, Liberal elements from La Salina and El Cocuy were accused of supporting the Liberal minority of Chita in the persecution of the vendetta. On August 18, Conservatives from Chita attacked La Salina and six Liberals were killed.[46] Interview data reveal the continuation of this series of vendettas for several years thereafter. There is no further press information, however, because battles between *minifundistas* lost their interest to the national press once the guerrillas on the Eastern Plains and other regions provided more important news.

The vendetta violence soon became centered around the Liberal municipality of El Cocuy. This municipality became a hate symbol to the Conservatives, just as La Uvita and Boavita (with the *veredas* of Chulavo and Chulavita) became hate symbols to the Liberals.[47] They represented the

[44] *El Siglo*, Jan. 2, Mar. 13, 16, June 1, 1949; *El Tiempo*, Mar. 15, 25, 30, May 17, 23, 24, 26, Apr. 9, 17, 18, June 6, 1949.

[45] *El Siglo*, May 14–15, 18–20, 23–24, 1949; *El Tiempo*, May 15, 18, 1949.

[46] *El Tiempo*, Aug. 9, 1949.

[47] The Liberals called the sectarian Conservative police *policía Chulavita* in reference to heavy police recruitment in that region of obedient, unconditional Conservative peasants.

most organized and most aggressive of the vendetta municipalities of the region.

As early as January 1949, *El Tiempo* published reports from Capitanejo of plans in the Chulavita neighborhood of Boavita and in La Uvita to organize an invasion of El Cocuy.[48]

In April 1949, *El Siglo* related that the Liberal chief of El Cocoy had been arrested for arms traffic and, a few days later, that military material had been seized, and that the desolation of Northern Boyacá was largely due to the Liberals of this *municipio*.[49] Isolated vendetta incidents occurred throughout 1949 between El Cocuy and its neighbors. In December 1949, however, the vendettas escalated into a full-scale battle at El Cocuy between the majority Liberal and the minority Conservative districts, and then into a full-scale war as vendetta militias from La Uvita, Boavita, Chita, and other Conservative *municipios* invaded El Cocuy.

The Conservative forces suffered heavy losses at the beginning of the vendetta war, but they were soon reenforced by troops sent by the governor.[50] The Conservative government considered the Cocuy vigilantes to be in open rebellion. The well-organized Cocuy militia, led by the Villamarín brothers, inflicted numerous casualties in house-to house fighting before being forced to retreat to the 4000-m-high Rechíniga Páramo.[51] There they staged another defense, taking advantage of excellent natural fortifications. With the pressure on their positions constantly mounting, the Cocuy Liberals finally decided to retreat down the Andean canyons and join the guerrilla armies being formed on the Eastern Plains. Thus, Cocuy became a *municipio* virtually without Liberal men, except for the *parameros* ("high mountain men"), for the remainder of the early period of *La Violencia*.[52]

There still occur incidents between the *municipios* of the region, although now the violence is soon repressed by the arrival of police, troops, and military mayors. The potential for violence is extremely high in that

[48] *El Tiempo*, Jan. 20, 1949.

[49] *El Siglo*, Apr. 19, 21, 1949.

[50] *El Siglo* reported 82 Conservative deaths in El Cocuy in its edition of Dec. 14, 1949.

[51] *El Tiempo* inferred that hundreds of Liberals were being massacred in the government's Cocuy operation (Dec. 27, 1949).

El Siglo, Dec. 28, 1949, answered: "The information about events in El Cocuy are false; there were *only* 57 victims [emphasis added].

[52] Cocuy once again became a battlefield in Apr. 1952 when the army sought to cut off a supply line that the Plains guerrillas had erected, and whose High Andean terminal was the Rechíniga Páramo. Once again the area's excellent natural fortifications allowed the rebels to resist a full-scale military operation, inflicting heavy losses on the army, before finally retreating to the Plains. For written references to *La Violencia* in El Cocuy consult Franco, *Las Guerrillas*, pp. 6, 23, 275–282, 333; Sierra Ochoa, *Las Guerrillas*, pp. 22–24; Guzmán *et al.*, *La Violencia*, vol. 1, pp. 75–76; Diego Montaña Cuéllar, *Colombia: País Formal y País Real* (Buenos Aires: Editorial Platina, 1963), p. 191.

the *municipios* maintain vigilante military organizations.[53] In the rural districts there are locally named majors, captains, lieutenants, etc., and the local population is almost totally organized into these vigilante militias that conserve hidden arsenals of rustic arms. In La Uvita and Boavita there are rural districts (*veredas*) in which strangers cannot enter without the permission of the informal local authorities. Students leaving the region to study in Sogamoso or Tunja must ask permission to leave, and when they return they must report to their military superior. The military atmosphere is reenforced by the fact that nearly everyone in these *municipios* enters the army, has been a member of the national police, or has numerous relatives who are policemen or soldiers. Given the permanent military preparations, there remains a latent possibility that the village wars could be reignited in this corner of Boyacá. If that were to happen, the press in the capital would label the conflict as between Liberals and Conservatives, despite the fact that the violent conflicts themselves would probably have nothing to do with party politics and, due to the fact that the determination of the opposing bands within the prevailing vendetta system, would be based on hereditary political party identification. This was also largely the case during the acute violence that affected the region during the partial collapse of the state.

Violence for Control of the Local Power Structure

Another type of violence-prone conflict, somewhat related to the one just described, involves conflicts for control of the local power structure. These conflicts occur most frequently in *minifundista* municipalities, although on occasion there have been violent conflicts between large cattlemen or farmers over who would control the local power structure of some municipalities.

In localities where there is a single large landholder it is not difficult to predict who is the most influential socioeconomic and political force in the community. Typically, *latifundista* municipalities are controlled by one or more families that are the main sources of employment, the prime customers of the local merchants, the rulers of the municipal councils, the patrons of the police, the judge, and other officials, and the intermediaries of the community with the departmental and national parties and governments. This type of political arrangement is common to numerous Colombian municipalities.

But what of *municipios* in which nearly everyone is a smallholder and in which no one possesses markedly more socioeconomic power than his

[53] Confirmed and reconfirmed in numerous interviews.

neighbors? In these municipalities there are often complex local political processes that determine which groups control the local power structure. In these processes political cliques are formed that generally are identified (like everything else in Colombia) with one or another of the two traditional political parties. It is not uncommon, however, that in a single municipality there might be several such political cliques that identify with the same political party.

Political competition between such political cliques, either of the same or of different parties, has tended to be acute. National politics are important for determining the mayor and other officials, with the former being named by the governor, who is in turn named by the president. Thus, national elections, especially during periods of transfer of control from one party to another, have tended to be highly conflictive in these municipalities.

Local politics, however, tend to have their own dynamics conditioned by national factors to be sure, but largely independent of control either by the party hierarchs in Bogotá or by those in the departmental capitals. Furthermore, the local political struggles in *minifundista* communities tend to be ignored by higher level politicians, who smply do not perceive that anything of value is at stake in these complex and delicate political processes. The minimal funds, few ill-paid posts, and extremely limited decision-making capabilities of the municipal councils of poor, *minifundista* communities hold no attraction for higher-level politicians. With regard to votes, they are negotiated with the existing *gamonales* ("political bosses"), without the necessity of getting unduly involved in the intricate and often dangerous processes by which the local bosses obtain their power positions.

Within the *minifundista* municipalities themselves, local politics are extremely important. The minimal funds and few ill-paid posts of the municipalities, and especially the social prestige to be derived from control of them, are valued by the impoverished, independent farmers. In addition, which local clique controls the town has multiple secondary implications. To be politically "connected" or not can make the difference between getting a loan from the *Caja Agraria* ("Agrarian Credit Agency") or not; it can determine who wins a legal battle over land limits or water rights and who loses; and it can make the difference between who goes to jail and who goes home after an altercation or a drinking bout in town. Inasmuch as the *gamonales* of the local communities are generally the intermediaries between the community and the departmental and national governments, control of the local power structure determines who benefits from the distribution within the *municipio* of occasional benefits derived from superior government units. For example, local control may determine whether the new road that the *departamento* constructs runs down one side of the valley or the other, and this may make the difference between who can get their produce to market during the rainy season and who cannot.

In the most depressed areas, the total effect of all of these factors may even determine who may survive as a small, independent farmer and who must face the necessity of being converted into a local wage laborer, emigrant to urban areas, or migratory farm laborer. In sum, the local power structures of even the poorest *municipios* directly affect the lives of the local inhabitants. This fact, conditions of extreme scarcity of valued resources, and a lack of externally imposed solutions to the question of the distribution of local power have all led to highly conflictive local politics.[54]

Violent conflicts over the control of the local power structures in such municipalities have a long history and they have continued after the period of *La Violencia* to this day. When such violent processes arise, the departmental or national governments intervene with police, troops, military mayors, martial law, curfews, etc. During the period of the partial collapse of the state, however, the superior governmental units were much more preoccupied with more important processes and more important areas. From the viewpoint of the governing officials, struggles for control of the local power structure in *minifundista* municipalities had a very low priority. The small farmers were simply dismissed as partisan fanatics,[55] and the troops were not sent to these zones, but rather allocated to guerrilla areas, to areas in which the interests of powerful groups were at stake, and to areas with strategic economic and political importance.

Given the generalized absence of sufficient state control of highly conflictive situations, the contradictory interests in dispute came to be defended ever more violently. In a vicious circle of violence and less efficient state control, more violence, and still less efficient state control, the violence became epidemic. The low priority given by state officials to these conflicts amounted to letting them run their violent course.

A classic area of these types of conflicts is the strip of largely *minifundista* municipalities which begins in Western Boyaca and continues past Chiquinquirá to the Provincia Vélez region of the Department of Santander, and which includes the Boyacá municipalities adjacent to the Provincia Vélez.

Violence was accentuated in this area as a result of the change of the

[54] These conclusions are basically derived from extensive interviews with people from different social and political positions.

[55] Manuel Serrano Blanco expresses the commonly heard notion that violence in the areas being described was due to a lack of culture and civilization: "The barbarism. . .was produced with greatest intensity in the most distant countryside and towns, in the burghs and sites without communications or with poor communications with the centers of culture, and for these reasons it is necessary to conclude that the problem resides therein" (*Las Viñas del Odio* [Bucaramanga: Imprenta del Departamento, 1949], p. 145).

correlation of control of national political power in the period 1946–1947.[56] This violence was a resurgence of the acute transitional violence that affected this same region in the period 1930–1933. Violence further accelerated during and after the critical year of 1949.[57]

The principal factor that conditioned the increased violent expression of the contradictory interests of various political cliques over control of the local power structure was the partial collapse of the state. This was expressed in the area by a lack of state intervention, which was tantamount to letting violent conflicts run their own course.

Under these circumstances, the importance of the political cliques dramatically increased. They were transformed into organized armed bands of neighbors involved in political conflicts with other bands of armed neighbors. Affiliation with a powerful band was a prerequisite for protecting one's life and property, because one could not rely on the state for protection. Indeed, the local representatives of the state were often not a source of protection but rather the very source of aggression. Who effectively controlled the municipalities or different areas of them had become largely a military question.

A 1962 national police report diplomatically states the following about this region:

> There exists the possibility, not exactly determined yet, that there may be political groups and some administrative authorities stimulating the violent actions. There are frequent disputes between the authorities (priests against mayors, town managers [*personeros*] against the former, and so forth) that create a favorable environment for violence.[58]

One of the groups that competed for control of the municipal power structures was the parish priests, who were very prominent in *La Violencia* in this area. The same police report cited above continues: "The activity of the clergy is considered notably counterproductive in many of these *municipios* [i.e.; Puente Nacional, Jesús María and Albania in Santander, and Saboyá in Boyacá]."[59]

[56] *El Siglo*, July 17, Sept. 25, 1946; Mar. 1, Oct. 1, Nov. 4, 1947; *El Tiempo*, Dec. 28, 1946. See also the *Memoria* of the minister of government for 1947, p. xi, and the *Informes de Jefes de Sección del Ministerio de Gobierno 1948* (Bogotá: Imprenta Nacional, 1949), p. 33.

[57] For examples of the 1949 violence in these regions, see: *El Siglo*, Feb. 22, Mar. 12, Apr. 6, 22, May 8, 10, June 2, 22, 1949; *El Tiempo*, Apr. 27, 1949.

[58] República de Colombia, Policía Nacional, F-2, *Criminalidad en 1962* (Bogotá: Editorial "El Voto Nacional," 1963), p. 140.

[59] República de Colombia, Policía Nacional, F-2, *Criminalidad en 1962*, p. 140. There would appear to be a long tradition of violent, political participation by priests in Santander. The Conservative leader Manuel Serrano Blanco reports that priests had a predominant role in the violence in the 1930 presidential elections when they themselves were divided between the candidacies of the Conservatives Guillermo Valencia

There were pistol-carrying priests who directly led their own cliques in battles against opposing groups after inspiring Sunday masses. Others did not participate directly in the violence but rather employed agents to represent them in the more violent aspects of the political struggles. This was the political base of the folk hero, gunman Efraín González. His name is revered as a secular saint by many of the peasants of this region, and especially by the Conservatives. González, who was the violent agent of a series of priests in the Ubate-Chinquinquirá-Provincia Vélez corridor, had the town of Jesús María as his principal base of operations. He would arrive in a municipality and defend the interests of the Conservative priests in their battles with local political enemies. González was virtually uncapturable because he traveled from convent to church to the homes of devout peasants chosen by the priests to harbor the crusading gunman.[60]

---

and Alfredo Vásquez Cobo. See Manuel Serrano Blanco, *La Vida es Así* (Bucaramanga: Imprenta del Departamento, 1953), pp. 169–174.

[60] Extensive interviews, including one with a police official, another with a priest who knew González, and a third with a Jesús María resident who is now the head of a *departamento* for an important decentralized government agency.

By 1964, Efraín González, like numerous protagonists of the violence, had become politically radicalized. Eschewing their old party indentifications, these guerrillas and gunmen, who had emerged from *La Violencia*, began to make contacts with revolutionary political groups. González's near-mythical popular image made him highly effective in his new role. With regard to González's popular appeal, the same police report previously cited (*Criminalidad in 1962*, p. 140) states with obvious reference to Efraín González that "there exists within the people of the area an ancestral romantic sentiment toward bandits, which facilitates the easy development of banditry." The mythical image of Efraín González as a martyred saint for the peasants of the Provincia Vélez and the Chiquinquirá area was sealed in 1965 when he was slain by the powerful Brigada de Institutos Militares (B.I.M.) (Military Institutes Brigade) after being surrounded in a house in the "Barrio San José" on the south side of Bogotá in one of the most spectacular episodes of *La Violencia* in the capital. The B.I.M. unit commanded by Colonel José Joaquín Matallana attacked González, who defended himself single-handedly. The official report issued by Brigadier General Omar Gutiérrez Ospina, Commanding Officer of the Brigada de Institutos Militares, states:

2. In the development of the action, measures were taken to isolate the sector and effect the capture of the anti-social element [González]. Faced with the number of casualties suffered in our own troops in the first four attempts to capture the house, the troops were obliged to employ a 40-mm cannon to open the house and to dominate the refuge occupied by the anti-social element.
3. The results obtained in this action were the following:
   a. Troops
      i. Deaths [i.e., there follow four names of military personnel with short biographies]
      ii. Wounded [there follow the names of ten military personnel, including a captain, and of three civilians]
   b. Enemy
      i. Deaths

The anti-social element EFRAIN GONZALEZ TELLEZ. (See the Bogotá newspaper *La República*, June 10, 1965).

The violence continued in this area after the formation of the Frente Nacional in that the national party agreements that decided who was to control the government in Bogotá did not decide who was to control the local power structure, for example, of Jesús María or of Puente Nacional in Santander. Indeed, national partisan politics per se had little to do with the local power struggles. On some occasions the conflicts were between Liberal and Conservative cliques and on others between cliques of the same party. In some cases, two cliques would ally to eliminate a third only to begin competition among themselves once their mutual goal had been reached.

There are even rare examples, highly significant considering the national political environment, of tacit agreements between Liberal and Conservative cliques in the area. Reinstating state authority in the region was difficult given the ongoing conflicts of clique rivalries and revenge violence. The reconstructed state began to have the capability to once again manage and repress the conflicts, but not to eliminate them. Local political violence continues periodically to this date in many municipalities of the area. For example, in Jesús María (Efraín González's old center of operations), there were at least 14 clearly political assassinations and several other murders of doubtful origin in the first half of 1974.[61] The state was managing the conflict by means of extra police reenforcements and the imposition of a military mayor who adopted strong, public order policies. During the period of the partial collapse of the state, such violence was left to run its own course, and the struggle for control of the local power structure left hundreds of deaths each year in the Velez province and in similar areas throughout Colombia.

Violence for Control of Land

Land formed the basis of one of the socioeconomic contradictions that frequently matured into conflicts with a high potential for violence, given the circumstances of the partial collapse of the state. These highly violent conflicts were basically of two varieties: first, the aggravation of the historically contradictory interests between Indians, large landowners, and colonists for control of land; second, the premeditated utilization of the existence of *La Violencia* to dispossess and dislocate small landowners.

The historical conflicts between Indians, large landowners, and colonists for control of land in Colombia were described in Chapters 2 and 3

See also J. Tito Alba, *Vida, Confesión y Muerte de Efraín González* (Bogotá: Tipografía Bermúdez, 1971). Even today one may observe candles burning at the South Botogá site where González was slain.

[61] The date of field research in the region.

of this work. It will be recalled that agrarian conflicts notoriously increased during the first decades of the twentieth century and that the state began to assume a more important and direct role in the definition and maintenance of the structure of land tenure. Thus, when the state partially collapsed, and the police and army no longer backed official land decisions, the structure of land tenure began to become undone in many areas. In some of these cases, highly violent conflicts began to directly determine the distribution of land.

In the Tirradentro region of Cauca, the partial collapse of the state resulted in acute conflict over disputed lands. In some cases, the landlords dislocated Indians, while in others Indians reclaimed lands from landowners and colonists. In the Ríochiquito area, with leadership from the Communist party, Indians completely sealed off a large area from all landowner or governmental influence. These conflicts soon became connected with the violence taking place in Southern Tolima and Northern Huila, on the other side of the watershed of the Central Chain of the Andes.

In Southern Tolima and Northern Huila, political conflicts led to the organization of Liberal and Communist resistance groups which confronted the Conservative authorities. These groups soon evolved into organized guerrilla bands, and they increased their potency due to an alliance between the Liberals and the Communists. The police and the army were reduced to the principal urban areas, and other aspects of the public administration ceased to function altogether under these circumstances.[62]

This area had been the scene of numerous conflicts over land. Important groups of Indians of the area had long been organized by the Communist party and by the traditionalist Indian movement of Manuel Quintín Lamé. Attempts to reestablish *resguardos* ("reservations") had been undertaken, and some de facto occupations of lands had proven successful. In addition, culturally assimilated ex-Indians had pursued a century-long battle, both in the courts and in the fields, to obtain title to lands held by *latifundistas* who had purchased large plots from their Indian ancestors at ludicrously low prices by allegedly fraudulent means.[63] Still a third source of conflict was the contradiction between *latifundistas* and numerous small-landholder colonists who had squatted on uncultivated lands in relatively inaccesible areas, to which the former held title in tracts which covered thousands of acres.[64]

[62] Jacobo Arenas, *Diario de la Resistencia de Marquetalia* (Bogotá: Abejón Mono, 1972), pp. 110–115; Ciro Trujillo, *Páginas de Su Vida* (Bogotá: Abejón Mono, 1974), pp. 8–12, 35–36. The Communist party had long had important influence among the Indians of Cauca and Tolima. Its 1934 presidential candidate, Eutiquio Timoté, was an Indian from Tolima; see *El Tiempo*, Jan. 7, 1934.

[63] Manuel Marulanda, *Cuadernos de Campaña* (Bogotá: Abejón Mono, 1973), pp. 11–16, 29–30, 46; interview with an ex-participant in the Liberal guerrilla movement.

[64] Pierre Gilhodes, *Las Luchas Agrarias en Colombia* (Bogotá: La Carreta, 1972), pp. 27, 43, 58–59, 70. The Chaparral region of Southern Tolima had long been very

Because of the partial collapse of the state, provoked by national and local political circumstances, all of these types of land conflicts became exacerbated. The structure of land tenure that the courts and the armed apparatus of the state had backed became undone. The result was generally the inability of the large landowners to control their haciendas.

The Communist party mobilized its base of support in the area principally on the basis of the agrarian conflicts. This led to political contradictions between the Liberal and Communist guerrillas, because the former were backed and oriented by important landowners while the latter proposed agrarian reform to the peasants.[65]

The guerrilla situation became extremely complicated. The Conservatives answered their lack of governmental control in the area by the organization of counterguerrillas (*guerrilleros de la paz,* "peace guerrillas"), principally from Huila, who made terrorist incursions against the Liberals and the Communists. In addition, the contradiction between the Liberal and Communist guerrillas led to armed conflicts between them. The state of chaos was also exploited by armed groups of bandits that began to

---

important. It was one of the principal cattle centers for Bogotá in the mid-nineteenth century and the bread basket of the Ambalema tobacco boom (Camacho Roldán, *Memorias,* p. 124). Politically, Chaparral was the home of Presidents Murillo Toro and Melo (Puentes, *Historia del Partido Liberal,* pp. 124, 293). Thus, the pressure by the Liberal reformers on the lands of the Páez Indians was particularly intense and protracted in the region. The historical background of these struggles for land in the Central Andean Chain is to be found in Juan Friede, *El Indio Lucha por la Tierra* (Bogotá: Editorial La Chispa, 1944).

[65] The Indians mobilized in Ríochiquito had been pushed off their land (Ciro Trujillo, *Páginas de Su Vida,* pp. 8–12). In Southern Tolima, the Communist guerrillas were formed from peasant groups which had long been oriented by the Party in land invasions, the refusal to pay land rents, and other socioeconomic movements (Alape, *Diario de un Guerrillero* [Bogotá: Abejón Mono, 1973], pp. 8–11). The clearest indications of the agrarian base of the movement are the issues by which the peasants of the region were mobilized. The political program issued by the "Guerrilla Forces of the Central Chain" in 1953 had as its principal objectives the following points:

> Democratic agrarian reform that puts in practice the principle of land for he who works it. . . . The movement is for the betterment of the living conditions of agricultural workers, for the 8-hour day in the countryside, for social benefits and complete medical service, and for sufficient and easy credit for peasants and farmers in general. . . . The movement defends the interests of the Indians, the integrity of their communities, the autonomy of their assemblies, and advocates the betterment of their living conditions and the return of their usurped lands. (Manuel Marulanda, *Cuadernos de Campaña* [Bogotá: Abejón Mono, 1973], pp. 98–99).

Likewise, the Guerrillas of Marquetalia issued, in 1964, a seven-point agrarian program; see Jacobo. Arenas, *Diario de la Resistencia de Marquetalia* (Bogotá: Abejón Mono, 1972), pp. 130–134. These documents confirm the subjective impression of interviews in the area that the general ideological sophistication of the Communist peasants is very low when compared to their motivation for an agrarian reform that would yield control of land.

operate in the region. At one point *La Violencia* consisted of a four-cornered, all-against-all contest between Conservative forces—both official and vigilante—and liberals, Communists, and nonpolitical bandits.[66] Raids on the settlements of the supporters of the opposing groups with house-burnings, cattle rustling ("expropriations" according to the side benefited), and crops seizures (especially of coffee) were carried out by all sides, including the army. Numerous military officers acquired fortunes through these raids.

The Conservatives tactically reduced the pressure on the Liberals somewhat during the latter group's battles with the better organized and more militarily formidable Communist forces, but they did not at any point leave them completely alone. The battles between the Liberals and the Communists soon proved so counterproductive to their respective situations against the common Conservative enemy, and with regard to their ability to resist the bandits, that a tacit cease fire was achieved. The Liberals and Communists did not reestablish their military alliance, nor did they undertake further joint military operations, but they did cease to attack one another.[67]

In the interim of the political conflicts, land was effectively appropriated in the area according to the correlation of politicomilitary forces.

With the military coup of June 1953 and the subsequent amnesty offer, the Liberal guerrillas of the region began to surrender their arms and return to their normal activities. Some, however, passed over to the Communist ranks, a phenomenon that took place throughout the conflict. This tendency occurred even with regard to leaders, particularly in the areas affected by acute agrarian conflicts (i.e., Chaparral and Río Blanco).[68] The Communist forces did not surrender, and they continued to control extensive areas in which alternative authority structures were erected. Land in these areas was distributed among the peasant inhabitants of what Conservative Senator Alvaro Gómez Hurtodo came to describe as "Independent Republics," due to their high level of socioeconomic and sociopolitical organization and their existence outside the influence of state authority.

Attempts at military forays into the Communist-controlled areas, known as "Marquetalia" and "Ríochiquito" in the Central Chain of the Andes, failed until a full-scale military operation, involving thousands of troops

[66] The most important guerrilla groups in these struggles were led for the Communists by Jacobo Prías Alope, "Charro Negro," and later by Manuel Marulanda Vélez, "Tirofijo"; for the Liberals they were led by the Loaiza family, Leopoldo García, "General Peligro," and "General Mariachi"; for the Conservatives, by the counterguerrilla Olivera brothers.

[67] Marulanda, *Cuadernos*, pp. 46–47, 59, 60, 67; Eric Hobsbawn, *Rebeldes Primitivos* (Barcelona: Ariel, 1968), p. 230.

[68] Such important Communist leaders as Manuel Marulanda and Ciro Trujillo began to struggle under Liberal banners.

backed by air strikes and advised and supplied by the United States armed forces, entered the area in 1964 and 1965. The territorial control of the Communist forces was broken. Their political influence did not decline, however, and their military force did not disappear. Rather, they reverted to mobile guerrilla tactics with the organization of the *Fuerzas Armadas Revolucionarias de Colombia* (FARC, "Revolutionary Armed Forces of Colombia") commanded by Manuel Marulanda Vélez, also known as "Tirofijo" (Sure-shot). This politicomilitary force continues to operate to this date, and it continues politically, although not directly territorially, to control important segments of that region.[69]

The continuation of *La Violencia* in the Central Andean departments even after the fall of the Conservative government in 1953, and its continuation to this date, was and is due to the fact that the conflicts involved in *La Violencia* in the region were and are based on conflicts over land, in addition to partisan political considerations.

Other land-linked violence also occured in the Sumapaz region, the scene of classical colonist conflicts, and in the Viotá region, with its history of coffee sharecropper, agrarian disputes. In both of these cases, as well as in Southern Tolima, the Communist party politically channeled these socioeconomic conflicts.

Areas of recent colonization were particularly prone to land violence. For example, in Antioquia, high rates of violence follow the railway to Puerto Berrío with its numerous colonist settlements. Such is also the case of the Antioquian corridor to the sea, a recent area of intensive settlement. Internal conflicts among colonists and between them and large landlords attempting to remove the colonists from the land also evolved into violence.

Another source of violence over land was the use of physical coercion, or the credible threat of the same, to push farmers off the land in order to obtain title to their holdings or simply de facto occupation of them. This phenomenon assumed massive proportions, and it represents one of the most important socioeconomic consequences of *La Violencia*. Given the partial collapse of the state, those who could not directly defend their lives or property were subject to coercion by the "guerrillas of the registry offices," who are analyzed in the next section of this chapter.

The survey information used in this study estimates a total of 393,648

[69] Arenas, *Diario de la Resistencia, passim*; Arturo Alape, *Las Muertes de Tirofijo* (Bogotá: Abejón Mono, 1972), p. 16; Comité de Solidaridad con los Presos Políticos, *El Libro Negro de la Represión* (Bogotá: Editorial Gráficas Mundo Nuevo, 1974), pp. 44–54, passim; Antonio Zapata, "Etapas y Coyunturas de la Lucha Guerrillera en Colombia," in *Diez Años de Insurrección en América Latina*, ed. Vania Bambirra (Santiago, Chile: Prensa Latinoamericana, 1971), vol. 2, pp. 198–199; Marulanda, *Cuadernos*, pp. 79–88; Regis Debray, *¿Revolución en la Revolución?* (México: Era, 1969), pp. 171–177.

TABLE 6.1
Departmental Distribution of Agricultural Parcels Lost due to *La Violencia*

Department	Agricultural parcels lost
Antioquia	16,200
Boyacá	26,400
Bogotá	0
Antiguo Caldas	36,800
Cauca	3,000
Cundinamarca	50,400
Huila	27,100
Meta	800
Norte de Santander	38,400
Santander	26,600
Tolima	54,900
Valle	98,400
Other departments and intendencies	14,648
	393,648

Source: Dr. Carlos Lemoine of the Compañía Colombiana de Datos. For the methodological procedures employed in this 1-year survey research project that employed my municipal-level violence data for sampling purposes, consult Chapter 1. n. 4.

land parcels "lost" as a result of violence. The geographical distribution of these parcels is given in Table 6.1. These parcels were lost by simple abandonment due to the violence in general, by abandonment due to direct threats or acts of violence against their owners, or by coerced land sales at ludicrous prices. In Tolima, a particularly prevalent way to evict peasants from the land was house-burning.[70] A study by the Department of Agriculture of that *departamento* estimates a total of 34,304 houses burned there during the period of *La Violencia*.[71]

It would appear that the social group most affected by the coerced loss of land, and the subsequent necessity to emigrate, was the smallholding peasants who could least defend themselves.[72] It has also been argued that the increase in the regressive concentration of wealth that occured as a result of this process was also extended to the commercial sector where small merchants, who furnished the small farmers with goods on credit

[70] Interview with ex-governor of the *departamento* who served during the "late violence."

[71] Secretaría de Agricultura del Departamento, *La Violencia en el Tolima* (Ibagüé: Imprenta Departamental, n.d.), p. 31.

[72] Alonso Tobón, *La Tierra y la Reforma Agraria en Colombia* (Medellín: La Oveja Negra, 1972), pp. 46–65.

TABLE 6.2
Migrations, Fatalities, and Land Parcels Lost due to *La Violencia*

Department	Migrations	Fatalities	Parcels lost
Antioquia	116,500	26,150	16,200
Bogotá, D.E.	31,200	2,585	0
Boyacá	123,000	5,363	26,400
Antiguo Caldas	179,500	44,255	36,800
Cauca	In others	1,236	3,000
Cundinamarca	265,700	4,033	50,400
Huila	112,000	4,111	27,100
Meta	16,800	5,842	800
Norte de Santander	174,400	20,885	38,400
Santander	290,500	19,424	26,600
Tolima	224,700	30,912	54,900
Valle	368,900	13,106	98,400
Others	100,400	2,386	14,648
	2,003,600	180,253	393,648

Source: Dr. Carlos Lemoine of the Compañía Colombiana de Datos. For the methodological procedures employed in this 1-year survey research project that employed my municipal-level violence data for sampling purposes, consult Chapter 1, n. 4.

until harvest time, were ruined simultaneously with their debtors.[73] It is on the basis of these processes that some authors have interpreted *La Violencia* as a process related to the formation of capitalism in the Colombian countryside, since massive numbers of direct producers were separated from the means of production.[74]

The coerced transfer of agricultural plots would also appear to be closely associated with the massive internal migrations accompanying the phenomenon of *La Violencia*. Table 6.2 presents comparative departmental indicators for *La Violencia* migrations, fatalities, and land parcels lost based on the survey research data employed in this study. "Migrations due to *La Violencia* does not, as one might expect, correlate with "*Violencia* fatalities" (r^2=.07). Neither is there a correlation between "Fatalities" and "Parcels lost" ($r^2 = .08$). However, there is a significant correlation between "land Parcels lost" and "Migrations due to *La Violencia*" ($r^2 = .76$).[75]

[73] Hermes Tovar, *El Movimiento Campesino en Colombia* (Bogotá: Ediciones Libres, 1975), pp. 121–124.

[74] A prime example of the "formation of capitalism" position is to be found in Estanislao Zuleta, *La Tierra en Colombia* (Medellín: Editorial La Oveja Negra, 1973), pp. 108–109.

[75] Bogotá "and others" were excluded from the calculations of the correlations so as not to vitiate the coefficients. Where x is migrations, y fatalities, and z parcels lost, the correlation are the following:

The loss of a peasant's or a landowner's means of subsistence as a result of the violence would appear to be more important in migrations than the proximity of intentional deaths, per se. Those who could defend their land and crops or those who were receiving the land and crops of those who left remained in the violent areas. Some of the latter groups apparently even migrated to violent areas to acquire land. It might be inferred tentatively that peasants without land felt the pressure of *La Violencia* less than those who possessed land, crops, livestock, and other goods. The individuals who lost their parcels of land appear to have been highly propense to migrate.

These data provide important evidence of the enormous social impact of violence over land and coffee crop violence within the total phenomenon of *La Violencia*. The coerced dislocation of hundreds of thousands of peasants would seem to be confirmed.

The mechanisms by which peasants were dispossessed of land, and the groups which benefited from this process, are essentially the same as those involved in the coffee crop violence analyzed in the next section.

In sum, competition over land formed an important contradiction that matured into conflicts with an extremely high potential for violence in several areas of Colombia, given the conditioning circumstances of the partial collapse of the state.

Coffee Crop Violence

Given the partial collapse of the state, banditry in every conceivable form prospered in Colombia during the period of *La Violencia*. In addition to the theft of land, described in the previous section, extortion and robbery of goods of every variety flourished. The greatest wealth in Colombian society is produced by coffee. With regard to this product, complex and violent social processes arose over the effective appropriation of the coffee crop. This contradiction formed one basis for the extreme prolongation of the violence. *La Violencia* study of the secretary of agriculture of the department of Tolima states:

> Political violence was superseded by violence as a prodigious commercial enterprise, as a new source of rights and obligations, as a new means to acquire property to things. While this enterprise produces dividends capable of guaranteeing its own existence, with the protection of vices with very profound roots, and while there remain the advantages to be obtained from

$r_{xy} = .26$ $(r^2 = .07)$, $r_{xz} = .87$ $(r^2 = .76)$, $r_{yz} = .28$ $(r^2 = .08)$

A simple regression with parcels lost (z) as the independent variable and migrations (x) as the dependent variable yields a t value of 2.83. For 9 degrees of freedom ($n-2$), this t value indicates that the hypothesis $B = 0$ (i.e., that z does not influence x) may be rejected with 99% probability.

crime and the situation of public disorder, this enterprise will wage its last battles, trying futilely in the long run, to sustain its opprobrious empires.[76]

During the entirety of the violence, but especially during the "late violence," bloodshed and robbery swept the central core region of Colombia two times a year, coinciding with the two coffee crops.[77] The Frente Nacional agreement and the end of Liberal–Conservative violence did not end the coffee crop violence or result in an immediate reconstruction of the state in the rural areas of the coffee region. On the contrary, apart from the Communist guerrilla zones, the coffee regions of Valle, Tolima, Antiguo Caldas, and Antioquia were the last parts of the country in which state authority was reasserted and the last areas to be affected by virulent violence. [78] Indeed, the phenomenon persists to this date in some areas.[79]

The coffee crop had to be commercialized in an armed fashion in violent areas or it might be stolen several times on the way to market. This violence did not represent national economic losses, but it did imply changes in the appropriation of the economic benefits of the crop. The coffee always got to market.

Key figures in the coffee crop violence were the administrators *(mayordomos)* of the large coffee farms. The prosperous landowners generally did not risk travel to violent areas, and thus they were placed in the hands of the lower class managers. The latter were obviously in a position to enormously profit from these circumstances. Eric Hobsbawn writes:

> This aspect of *La Violencia* developed forms that remind one extraordinarily of the Sicilian Mafia, especially in Caldas, the coffee-producing department par excellence. There is a replica of the Sicilian *gabellotti,* the administrators of the farms and the bourgeois have managed to establish a formal organization in order to blackmail the proprietors and terrorize the peasants—the "Confraternity of Majordomos." In these areas the violence has become economically institutionalized.[80]

The necessity to protect the coffee crop by force of arms led to the administrators' and the landlords' utilization of organized groups of gun-

[76] Secretaría de Agricultura, *La Violencia en el Tolima,* p. 5.

[77] Interview with an ex-governor of Tolima.

[78] The author compiled a list of *municipios* affected by the late violence, the majority of which are coffee producers. Other lists of areas affected by the violence after 1953 are to be found in: Republic of Colombia, Policía Nacional, *Criminalidad en 1958,* pp. 16–37; *Criminalidad en 1959,* pp. 25–37; *Criminalidad en 1962,* pp. 120–140; *Criminalidad en 1965,* pp. 25–27; Guzmán *et. al., La Violencia,* vol. 2, pp. 301–326.

[79] Examples of the persistence of this type of violence, with political protection, are to be found in La Celia and Balboa in the Department of Risaralda; interviews with persons affected.

[80] Eric Hobsbawn, *Rebeldes Primitivos* (Barcelona: Ediciones Ariel, 1968), p. 229.

men to protect their interests. Not infrequently, the groups that protected one group of farms were the predators of another group. The armed bands themselves were often criminal mutations of the armed groups of Liberals and Conservatives who had fought in the earlier, traditional partisan phase of *La Violencia.* Many of these groups enjoyed police, judicial, and political protection due to their partisan connections, even after the establishment of the Frente Nacional. This was the case because politically powerful groups often participated in the profits generated by the armed bands and/or relied on them to protect their own interests. This was particularly the case of the *pájaros* ("birds") who had assassinated political enemies with official sanction during the more political phase of the violence, and who progressively expanded their violent activities into more remunerative areas. Another source of armed bands were dislocated *Violencia* victims who resorted to the violence itself to achieve their subsistence. *La Violencia* eventually reached the point where the process itself reproduced the human resources necessary for its own continuation.[81]

A national police report summarizes the situation in coffee growing areas as follows:

> The appearance of the bandits coincides with the coffee crops. The harvesters and driers of the crop are assassinated and the crop stolen. Many landowners are forced to contract the "services" of bandits for the protection of their farms, others in order to settle personal vengeances or for the purchase of properties at ridiculous prices.
>
> The *majordomos* [administrators] of farms maintain the environment of anxiety and propitiate the violence in order to avoid the presence of the landowners, something which would deprive them of enormous earnings. Rivalries between ambitious administrators and aspirants who wish to replace the favored have caused hundreds of deaths.[82]

This chaotic situation was further complicated by the political support of influential persons and the sanction of the local officials. As is the case in the Eastern Plains, huge fortunes were both lost and made during, and as a result of, *La Violencia.* The individuals who initially accumulated their fortunes via violence-related enterprises today benefit from a collective amnesia of the immediate past in such cities as Pereira, Armenia, Caicedonia, and Sevilla.[83] These individuals also enjoy the respectability that huge fortunes proffer.

[81] Lists of bandit and political groups, their leaders, areas of operations, and activities are to be found in: Republic of Colombia, Policía Nacional, *Estudio Criminalístico del Año 1958,* pp. 16–37; *Criminalidad en 1962,* pp. 124–140; *Criminalidad en 1965,* pp. 34–47; Guzmán *et al., La Violencia,* vol. 2, pp. 287–297.

[82] República de Colombia, Policía Nacional, *Criminalidad Colombiana 1959,* p. 29.

[83] Of course, this collective amnesia is very functional to the maintenance of peace because, given recent history, the continual evocation of past grievances would lead to endless chains of vengeance violence. However, a subjective appreciation by the

Eduardo Santa summarizes this aspect of *La Violencia:*

> The political motive begins to disappear bit by bit among the executors of the official violence, inasmuch as many of them discover that the violence which they undertake against defenseless people produces juicy economic dividends. Police, detectives, and "birds" in the services of political directorates or of sectarian *caciques* find that the robbery of haciendas and farms, the seizure of the coffee crops, the murder of peasants who travel to the city to sell the coffee, and the purchase at a lower price of urban and rural properties from defenseless victims threatened with death established them as beneficiaries of the violence. Frequently political bosses patronize the violence economically for the benefits that might be derived from the same.[84]

The latter, the political bosses, often formed the "registry office guerrillas" who benefited from *Violencia*-induced transactions, without directly participating in the violence themselves.

By the early 1960s, *La Violencia* was reduced almost exclusively to the coffee zone. Intensive army and police campaigns sought to eliminate the bandit gangs and reestablish state authority in the most economically strategic region of the country.[85] By the mid-1960's the gangs were fewer and fewer, and they enjoyed dramatically less political support. The decline of the bandit gangs implied the reentry of the armed apparatus of the state and other state mechanisms in the structuring of land and commercial relations in the coffee areas. The demise of the gangs reached the point where the survivors were forced to abandon the countryside. They began to emigrate to urban settings and contributed to a dramatic increase in the index of urban crime, particularly kidnappings, which coincided precisely with the decline of coffee crop violence, a subject further developed in the last section of this chapter.

The organized *Violencia* gangs were responsible for much of the sadistic, "irrational" violence associated with *La Violencia* throughout its existence, but, in the period of their decomposition, there was a sharp increase in the use of macabre machete cuts against the corpses of victims as well as in genocides committed against entire families, by now without any political motivations, as well as mass sexual assaults, especially against minors. To take but one example there were hold-ups of buses on highways, in which after the larceny was committed all of the occupants

---

author, based on extensive interviewing, is that the topic of economic benefits derived from the violence is *much* more taboo than discussions of participation in violent acts per se.

[84] Eduardo Santa, *Sociología Política de Colombia* (Bogotá: Tercer Mundo, 1964), p. 65.

[85] República de Colombia, Ejército, Octava Brigada, *De la Violencia a la Paz* (Manizales: Imprenta Departamental, 1965); Evelio Buitrago, *Zarpazo: La Otra Cara de la Violencia* (Bogotá: Imprenta de las Fuerzas Armadas, 1967).

including women and children would be slain, with there being no apparent reason for the mass murders.

The effective "pacification campaigns" in the coffee areas were as violent as the conflicts that preceded them. In the coffee zone, as in the areas of the Liberal guerrillas and the areas of land conflicts channeled by the Communist party, the Colombian army and police adopted Draconian tactics to eliminate the armed groups. Torture and summary executions of captured enemies as well as those who aided or abetted the armed groups were all normal procedures. Inasmuch as some of the armed groups, particularly the bandits, operated in the same fashion, the peasants of the areas in which pacification campaigns were conducted were placed in impossible positions. Some were literally faced with "slain if you do and slain if you don't" dilemmas with regard to providing information to the groups involved in the combats, and their families and property were in continual danger.

These official pacification tactics proved largely successful. During the early violence Carlos Lleras Restrepo characterized these campaigns:

> And they are as grave and as perturbing as the actions of the guerrillas, and indeed much graver, the methods of repression employed by the authorities and the armed forces, the procedures employed that it has been thought possible to arrive at in order to obtain what has been called "pacification," cost what it may.[86]

In sum, the partial collapse of the state placed in a condition of flux the appropriation of the main source of wealth in Colombian society. The direct application of violence, or the credible threat of the same, came to determine the distribution of the proceeds of significant portions of the coffee crop. This fact constitutes yet another discrete process in the explanation of how the partial collapse of the state conditioned the maturation of numerous contradictions into conflicts with a high potential for violence.

Areas of State Coherence

In those areas in which state coherence was maintained, violence did occur, but it was sporadic and unsystematic. This was largely the case in urban areas, in selected regions which were not seriously affected, and in certain localities which managed to escape the full impact of the violence, despite their location in violent zones. Consideration is now given to the

[86] Carlos Lleras Restrepo, "Exposición Hecha por el Doctor Carlos Lleras Restrepo a Nombre de la Dirección Nacional Liberal, en la Reunión Celebrada en el Hotel Granada, Febrero 1, 1952," in Carlos Lleras Restrepo, *De la Democracia a la Dictadura* (Bogotá: Ediciones Agra, 1955), p. 350.

matter of how these "exceptions" affect the partial collapse of the state hypothesis.

La Violencia was primarily a rural rather than an urban phenomenon, precisely because the partial collapse of the state affected the countryside more than the cities. The public administration in general and the armed apparatus of the state in particular were concentrated in the metropolitan areas, and it was there that they maintained their greatest effectiveness. Furthermore, in the urban areas, the breakdown of relations within the political elite tended to be less severe because the "peace" faction of the Liberal party, which controlled the National Liberal Directorate, had its greatest political influence in the cities.

Violence did occur in the cities. April 9, 1948, was the date of violence in a context of leader-less anarchy in the capital and of violent processes of less intensity in almost every city of the republic. Assassinations and occasional mob violence continued in the capital and in other cities throughout *La Violencia*, but they generally represented sporadic and unsystematic processes not comparable by any standard to the violent processes affecting the rural areas.

The most violent urban areas were the small and medium-sized cities of the coffee region, particularly Northern Valle and Antiguo Caldas. There political and economic assassinations reached the point of systematic terrorism. The Conservative party first, and the military government second, relied on armed bands, known as *pájaros,* to intimidate a militant opposition. The *pájaros* and their political backers within the region soon extended their activities, within both urban and rural settings, to the land thievery, extortion, and coffee crop violence described in previous sections. The salient point with regard to the *pájaros* is that they could operate within the cities because they had the protection of key authorities. Thus, the most important prolonged violence within urban settings was *official* violence. In sum, the maintenance of the coherence and effectiveness of the state in urban areas generally reduced violence, except for that violence backed by state officials.

Urban Colombia was perhaps most massively affected by violence when the phenomenon began to decline in the countryside. There was more violence in urban *municipios* during the late period compared to the early stage. The highest crime rates of the late 1960s are to be found in those cities located in violent areas (see Table 6.3). The differences are enormous between those cities which were the stage for urban violence and/or which received violence refugees and those cities not affected by the violence, which received few refugees. Compare, for example, low-violence areas such as Cartagena and Pasto with the top cases of urban crime, all of which are located in violent areas.

The urban crime rate was particularly accelerated by the arrival in the cities of the remains of the armed bands that could no longer operate

TABLE 6.3
Urban Crime Index, 1968

City and rank order in urban crime index	Felonies (*delitos*) known to the police (per 10,000 inhabitants)
High-violence areas	
Ibagué, Tolima	230.8
Tuluá, Valle	155.9
Bucaramanga, Santander	140.3
Neiva, Huila	122.5
Girardot, Cundinamarca	121.1
Cartago, Valle	116.6
Armenia, Quindío	115.3
Bogotá, D.E.	105.8
Low-violence areas	
Pasto, Nariño	23.58
Magangué, Bolívar	18.42
Cartagena, Bolívar	12.25

Source: República de Colombia, Policía Nacional, *Criminalidad en 1968* (Bogotá: 1969), Chart 5, p. 19.

with impunity in the countryside due to the reestablishment of state authority.[87]

The high rates of urban crime that characterize contemporary Colombia are due to a complex set of social factors, one of which undoubtedly is the survival of residual effects of *La Violencia*. It is interesting to compare the collective insecurity of daily life in Colombia today with the depiction that José María Samper gave of the Colombia of the late nineteenth century:

> The mail is carried without escort, even when there are shipments of precious metals. Cattle are raised in absolute liberty on vast plains. Also, the police almost do not exist in any part of the country, and the methods for repressing crime are limited and diffuse. . . . The spirit of obedience is even manifested in penal and detention institutions because our masses are essentially submissive.[88]

In less than a century, intensive processes of socioeconomic change and sociopolitical conflicts led to a diametrically opposed situation with regard to public security, which was exacerbated as a result of the partial collapse of the state and the violent social processes of *La Violencia*. In

[87] See also Paul Oquist, "Una Aproximación Descriptiva del Crimen en Colombia," *Revista Cámara de Comercio de Bogotá* 3 (Mar. 1973): 103–133.

[88] José María Samper, *Ensayo sobre las Revoluciones Políticas* (Bogotá: Universidad Nacional de Colombia, 1969), pp. 267–268.

a very real sense, *La Violencia* survives today in the common violent crime that affects most Colombian cities.

Certain regions of Colombia largely escaped *La Violencia*. This was the case along the Caribbean Coast and in the Department of Nariño, on the Ecuadorean border, although the latter did experience significant partisan violence in the period 1946–1949. In both cases, it would appear that the regional power structure maintained its coherence. The local Liberal and Conservative political elites actively worked to remain united despite the breakdown in political relations at the national level. On the coast, the violence of April 9, 1948, was followed by peace parlays, as elsewhere, with the difference being that the regional political agreements proved effective.[89] Thus, the state did not resort to massive, systematic terror to obtain compliance to its fiats because they were peacefully observed. The public administration and the armed apparatus of the state could function normally and, finally, the contradictions within the armed institutions did not negatively affect the situation of public order in that there was no armed challenge to the government. The net result of these factors was that the state did not collapse on the Caribbean Coast or in Nariño. The levels of political violence were kept low here, and other sociopolitical and socioeconomic processes did not turn violent because the state continued to structure social relations with regard to them.

Similar conditioning factors help account for the extraordinarily low levels of relative violence in some *municipios* located in *Violencia* areas. A striking case of this is presented by the *municipio* of Aguadas in the Department of Caldas. Surrounded by highly violent municipalities in Northern Caldas and Southern Antioquia, Aguadas was an island of relatively little violence in a sea of bloody encounters. Political violence was minimal and even coffee crop violence was significantly less than in adjoining areas.

What separated Aguadas from its neighbors was that the local Liberal and Conservative elites nearly unanimously worked for the union of the two parties in the *municipio* despite the national civil war. Considered traitors to their parties by sectarians in neighboring communities, the majority Conservatives and minority Liberals periodically renewed their mutual allegiance in ceremonious meetings conducted in the public square with massive attendance.[90] The net result of this was that political violence was kept to a minimum, political institutions functioned, and even coffee crop violence proved more manageable.[91]

The examples of both the regions and the isolated localities in violent areas that largely escaped *La Violencia* would seem to indicate that re-

[89] Interviews.

[90] The average presidential election vote in Aguadas, Caldas, for the 1930 and 1946 elections was 74.66% Conservative and 25.32% Liberal.

[91] Interview with a historian from the region who has studied the municipality.

gional and local power structures were still sufficiently significant for the structuring of social relations in mid-twentieth-century Colombia that they could function independently of a national structural breakdown.

In sum, the "exceptions" to the rule of the "partial collapse of the state" hypothesis would also appear to provide positive evidence for it. Levels of partisan conflict conditioned whether the state maintained its coherence or not, and the latter factor conditioned the appearance of acute sectarian violence and the maturation into violent conflicts of other nonpartisan sociopolitical and socioeconomic processes. Thus, areas of state coherence form another structural region for the analysis of *La Violencia,* along with the areas affected by diverse socioeconomic and sociopolitical process that had a high potential for violence as a result of the partial collapse of the state.

7

A Concluding Note

The violence of the 1946–1966 period is explained in this study as having *begun* due to intensive partisan rivalries. These sectarian conflicts were particularly acute since hegemonic, exclusivitic party politics had survived into an era in which the state had acquired such an importance in national life that no sector within the dominant groups of society would accept exclusion from state power and its benefits. The sectarian conflicts led to a decrease in the efficacy of the state to the point that one may speak of a partial collapse of the state. This in turn conditioned the simultaneous maturation into violent conflicts of an entire series of different types of social contradictions in those areas that were affected by the partial collapse of the state. This is what accounts for the *intensity* of the violence.

The *geographical distribution* of the intensity of the violence was largely determined by two factors. First, whether there were intense local contradictions and, second, whether the partial collapse of the state affected the area or not.

The areas of maximum violence, such as Tolima, combined almost the entire gambit of violent social processes with an acute reduction in the power of the state. Thus, the origins, intensity, and geographical distribution of the violence are all susceptible to explanation by social-structural analysis.

It has been argued in this work that social violence is best explained by social-structural factors. That position implies that different races or nationalities are neither more nor less violent than others. It also implies that men in general are violent under certain social-structural circumstances and peaceful in others.

It might seem ludicrous to argue, as has been done in this work, that Colombians are neither more nor less violent than other peoples, considering the importance of violence as a structuring process throughout Colombian history. However, similar histories of violent social processes could be compiled for other nations as well, perhaps with the variation for European countries that international wars have played a greater relative role than domestic conflicts when compared with Latin American nations.

It is neither possible to argue that the violence in European cultures and their extensions throughout the globe are principally matters of the distant past. Indeed, the most violent episodes of all have occurred within the lifetimes of persons now living.

Despite its historical pervasiveness, social violence is not inevitable. Man's ability to transform his social environment intentionally, within the limits of structural restraints, which are themselves dynamic, implies the capacity to attain social structures that might minimize violence, both internationally and within nations. In a progressively integrated world community in a nuclear age, the future of human civilization will eventually depend on turning that possibility into a high probability. In that process, social science research must certainly attempt to make a significant and politically committed contribution. It has been the contention of this research, based on the concrete case of *La Violencia* in Colombia, that social-structural analysis is the most promising analytical tool for that task.

It is logical to assume by a projection of the structural analysis that the continued increase in the importance of interclass conflicts in Colombian politics will lead to continued violent social processes. Violence will not occur only if the working classes of Colombia indefinitely deny themselves resources in the struggle for power that the propertied classes of Colombia have repeatedly employed to defend their general class interests and, indeed, even their diverse factional interests.

A structure of social domination that denies the overwhelming majority of the population access to socioeconomic and political power, and thus to the ability to satisfy, even minimally, their most basic necessities, presages the continued maturation of existing social contradictions and the creation of new ones. The political expressions of these conflicts will have a high potential for violence as the dominated groups in Colombian society attempt to achieve positions of power that the dominant classes will violently deny them.

Bibliography

Books, Manuscripts, and Dissertations

Abella, Arturo. *Don Dinero en la Independencia.* Bogotá: Ediciones Lerner, 1966.

———. *El Florero de Llorente.* Bogotá: Editorial Antares, 1960.

Alape, Arturo. *Diario de un Guerrillero.* Bogotá: Abejón Mono, 1973.

———. *Las Muertes de Tirofijo.* Bogotá: Abejón Mono, 1972.

Alba, J. Tito. *Vida, Confesión y Muerte de Efraín González.* Bogotá: Tipografía Bermúdez, 1971.

Ardila, Alfredo. *Psicología y Problemas Sociales en Colombia.* Tunja, Colombia: Universidad Pedagógica y Tecnológica de Colombia, 1971.

Arenas, Jacobo. *Diario de la Resistencia de Marquetalia.* Bogotá: Abejón Mono, 1972.

Arrubla, Mario, ed. *Estudios sobre el Subdesarrollo Colombiano.* Bogotá: El Tigre de Papel, 1971.

Azula Barrera, Rafael. *De la Revolución al Orden Nuevo: Proceso y Drama de un Pueblo.* Bogotá: n.p., 1956.

Bejarano, Jesús. *El Capital Monopolista y las Inversiones Privadas Norteamericanas en Colombia.* Bogotá: Círculo Rojo Editores, 1972.

Bemis, Samuel Flagg. *The Latin American Policy of the United States.* New York: Harcourt, Brace, and World, 1943.

Bergquist, Charles Wylie. "Coffee and Conflict in Colombia 1886–1904: Origins and Outcome of the War of a Thousand Days." Ph.D. dissertation, Stanford University, 1973.

Berkowitz, Leonard, ed. *Roots of Aggression: A Re-examination of the Frustration and Aggression Hypothesis.* New York: Atherton Press, 1968.

Bienen, Henry. *Violence and Social Change: A Review of Current Literature.* Chicago: University of Chicago Press, 1968.

Boulding, Kenneth. *Conflict and Defense: A General Theory.* New York: Harper & Row, 1962.

Buitrago, Evelio. *Zarpazo: La Otra Cara de la Violencia.* Bogotá: Imprenta de las Fuerzas Armadas, 1967.

Bushnell, David. *El Régimen de Santander en la Gran Colombia.* Bogotá: Coediciones Tercer Mundo–Universidad Nacional, 1966.

Caballero, Enrique. *Historia Económica de Colombia.* Bogotá: Italgraph, 1971.

Caballero, Lucas. *Memoria de la Guerra de Mil Días.* Bogotá: Editorial Aguila Negra, 1939.

Caicedo, Edgar. *Historia de las Luchas Sindicales en Colombia.* Bogotá: Ediciones Suramérica, 1974.

Calle Restrepo, Arturo. "Conflictos Familiares y Problemas Humanos." Unpublished manuscript, mimeographed. Pereira, Colombia, 1963.

Camacho Roldán, Salvador. *Memorias.* Medellín: Editorial Bedout, n.d.

Canal Ramírez, Gonzalo. *9 de April de 1948.* Bogotá: Canal Ramírez, n.d.

Caputo, Annie. "Las Luchas Agrarias del Sumapaz." "Licenciatura" thesis, Universidad de Los Andes (Bogotá), 1974.

Cardona, Ramiro. *Migración, Urbanización y Marginalidad.* Bogotá: Asociación Colombiana de Facultades de Medicina (ASCOFAME), 1968.

Caro, Miguel Antonio. *Estudios Constitucionales.* Bogotá: Editorial Biblioteca Popular, 1951.

Castrillón, Alberto. *120 Días Bajo el Terror Militar.* Bogotá: Tercer Mundo, 1973.

Castrillón Arboleda, Diego. *El Indio Quintín Lame.* Bogotá: Tercer Mundo, 1973.

Chaves, Milciades. *Apropiación de la Tierra y Reforma Agraria.* Bogotá: Instituto Colombiano de Reforma Agraria (INCORA), 1965.

Colmenares, Germán. *Historia Económica y Social de Colombia.* Cali: Universidad del Valle, 1974.

———. *Partidos Políticos y Clases Sociales.* Bogotá: Universidad de Los Andes, 1968.

Comité de Solidaridad con los Presos Políticos. *El Libro Negro de la Represión: Frente Nacional 1958–1974.* Bogotá: Editorial Gráficas Mundo Nuevo, 1974.

Cortés Vargas, Carlos. *Los Sucesos de las Bananeras.* Bogotá: Imprenta La Luz, 1929.

Coser, Louis. *Continuities in the Study of Social Conflict.* New York: The Free Press, 1967.

———. *The Functions of Social Conflict.* Glencoe, Ill.: The Free Press, 1956.

Costa Pinto, Luis A. *Voto y Cambio Social: El Caso Colombiano en el Contexto Latinoamericano.* Bogotá: Ediciones Tercer Mundo, 1971.

Crow, John A. *The Epic of Latin America.* Garden City, N.Y.: Doubleday, 1952.

Cuéllar Vargas, Enrique. *Trece Años de Violencia.* Bogotá: Editorial SIPA, 1960.

Dahrendorf, Ralf. *Class and Class Conflict in Industrial Society.* Stanford, Calif.: Stanford University Press, 1959.

Daniel, James M. *Rural Violence in Colombia since 1946.* Washington, D.C.: American University, Special Operations Research Office (SORO), 1965.

Davies, James Chowning, ed. *When Men Revolt and Why.* New York: The Free Press, 1971.

Debray, Regis. *¿Revolución en la Revolución?* México City: Era, 1969.

Delgado, Alvaro. *La Colonia.* Bogotá: Editorial Colombia Nueva, 1974.

Dirección Nacional Liberal. *El Liberalismo Colombiano Frente a la Dictadura: Informe que Rinde la Dirección Nacional del Liberalismo a la Convención del Partido.* Bogotá: n.p., 1951.

Directorio Nacional Conservador. *Los Programas Conservadores de 1849 a 1949.* Bogotá: n.p., 1945.

Dix, Robert H. *Colombia: The Political Dimensions of Change.* New Haven: Yale University Press, 1967.

Dollard, John; Doob, Leonard W.; Miller, Neil E.; Mower, O. M.; and Sears, Robert R. *Frustration and Aggression.* New Haven: Yale University Press, 1967.

Eckstein, Harry, ed. *Internal War: The Problem of Anticipation.* New York: Macmillan, 1964.

Escalante, Aquiles. *El Negro en Colombia.* Bogotá: Universidad Nacional de Colombia, 1964.

Estrada Monsalve, Joaquín. *Así Fue la Revolución del 9 de Abril al 27 de Noviembre.* Bogotá: n.p., 1950.
———. *El Nueve de Abril en Palacio: Horario de un Golpe de Estado.* Bogotá: Editorial ABC, 1968.
Fals Borda, Orlando. *Subversion and Social Change in Colombia.* New York: Colombia University Press, 1969.
———. *La Subversión en Colombia.* Bogotá: Tercer Mundo, 1967.
Fandiño Silva, Francisco. *La Penetración Sovietica en América y el Nueve de Abril.* Bogotá: Editorial ABC, 1949.
Feierabend, Ivo; Feierabend, Rosalind; and Gurr, Ted Robert; eds. *Anger, Violence, and Politics: Theories and Research.* Edinburgh: Oliver and Boyd, n.d.
Fluharty, Vernon Lee. *Dance of the Millions: Military Rule and Social Revolution in Colombia, 1930–1956.* Pittsburgh: University of Pittsburgh Press, 1957.
Franco Isaza, Eduardo. *Las Guerrillas del Llano.* Bogotá: Librería Mundial, 1959.
Friede, Juan. *El Indio Lucha por La Tierra.* Bogotá: Editorial La Chispa, 1972.
———. *Invasión del País de los Chibchas.* Bogotá: Ediciones Tercer Mundo, 1966.
———. *Los Quimbayas Bajo la Dominación Española.* Bogotá: Banco de la República, 1963.
Furtado, Celso. *The Economic Growth of Brazil.* Berkeley: University of California Press. 1963.
Gaitán, Jorge Eliécer. *Antología de Su Pensamiento Económico y Social.* Bogotá: Ediciones Suramérica, 1968.
———. *La Masacre de las Bananeras: Documentos, Testimonios 1928.* Bogotá: Ediciones Libres, 1972.
Gaitán, Miguel Antonio. *El Por Qué de un Asesinato y Sus Antecedentes.* Bogotá: Editorial Minera, 1949.
Gaitán Mahecha, Bernardo. *Misión Histórica del Frente Nacional.* Bogotá: Editorial Revista Colombiana, 1966.
García, Antonio. *La Dialéctica de la Democracia.* Bogotá: Ediciones Cruz del Sur, 1971.
———. *Gaitán y el Problema de la Revolución.* Bogotá: Editorial W.S.C., 1955.
García, Carlos. *Características de los Migrantes en Cinco Ciudades Colombianas.* Bogotá: Universidad de Los Andes, CEDE, n.d.
Gibbens, T. C. N., and Ahrenfeldt, R. H. *Cultural Factors in Delinquency.* London: Tavistock, 1966.
Gilhodes, Pierre. *Las Luchas Agrarias en Colombia.* Bogotá: La Carreta, 1972.
Gómez Aristizábal, Horacio. *Teoría Gorgona: Causación de la Violencia y Estructuración de un Sistema para Erradicarla.* Bogotá: Editorial Iqueima, 1962.
Gómez Dávila, Ignacio. *Viernes Nueve.* México City:n.p., 1953.
Gómez Lorena, Pedro. *El Nueve de Abril.* Bogotá: n.p., 1951.
González, Florentino. *Memorias.* Medellín: Editorial Bedout, 1971.
González, Margarita. *El Resguardo en el Nuevo Reino de Granada.* Bogotá: Universidad Nacional, 1970.
González Ochoa, Gustavo. *Frente a la Violencia.* Medellín: Editorial Bedout, 1960.
Guillén Martínez, Fernando. *El Poder: Los Modelos Estructurales del Poder Político en Colombia.* Bogotá: Universidad Nacional, Centro de Investigaciones del Desarrollo (CID), 1973.
———. *Raíz y Futuro de la Revolución.* Bogotá: Ediciones Tercer Mundo, 1963.
Gurr, Ted Robert. *Polimetrics: An Introduction to Quantitative Macropolitics.* Englewood Cliffs, N.J.: Prentice Hall, 1972.
———. *Why Men Rebel.* Princeton, N.J.: Princeton University Press, 1970.
Gutiérrez, José. *La Rebeldía Colombiana.* Bogotá: Tercer Mundo, 1962.
———. *La Revolución Contra el Miedo.* Bogotá: Tercer Mundo, 1964.
Gutiérrez Anzola, Jorge. *Violencia y Justicia.* Bogotá: Ediciones Tercer Mundo, 1962.

Guzmán, Germán; Fals Borda, Orlando, and Umaña Luna, Eduardo. *La Violencia en Colombia.* 2 vols. Bogotá: Tercer Mundo, 1963, 1964.

Hagen, Everett E. *El Cambio Social en Colombia.* Bogotá: Ediciones Tercer Mundo, 1963.

———. *On the Theory of Social Change.* Homewood, Ill.: Dorsey Press, 1964.

Havens, Eugene, and Usandizaga, Elsa. *Tres Barrios de Invasión.* Bogotá: Universidad Nacional, Facultad de Sociología, 1965.

Hernández Rodríguez, Guillermo. *De los Chibchas a la Colonia y a la República.* Bogotá: Universidad Nacional, 1949.

———. *La Alternación ante el Pueblo como Constituyente Primario.* Bogotá: Editorial America Libre, 1962.

Hibbs, Douglas A., Jr. *Mass Political Violence: A Cross National Causal Analysis.* New York: Wiley, 1973.

Hobsbawn, Eric. *Rebeldes Primitivos.* Barcelona: Ediciones Ariel, 1968.

Huntington, Samuel P. *Political Order in Changing Societies.* New Haven: Yale University Press, 1968.

Jaramillo Uribe, Jaime. *Ensayos Sobre Historia Social Colombiana.* Bogotá: Universidad Nacional, 1968.

———. *El Pensamiento Colombiano en el Siglo XIX.* Bogotá: Editorial Temis, 1964.

Johnson, Chalmers. *Revolutionary Change.* Boston: Little, Brown, 1966.

Juventudes del Movimiento Revolucionario Liberal. *Plataforma Política: Por Qué Liberales, Por Qué Revolucionarios, Por Qué Ni un Paso Atrás.* Bogotá: Ediciones Voces Libres, n.d.

Kirkham, James F.; Levy, Sheldon G.; and Crotty, William J. *Assassination and Political Violence: A Staff Report to the National Commission on the Causes and Prevention of Violence.* New York: Bantam Books, 1970.

Kossok, Manfred. *El Virreynato del Río de la Plata.* Buenos Aires: Editorial Futuro, 1959.

Lasswell, Harold D., and Kaplan, Abraham. *Power and Society.* New Haven: Yale University Press, 1950.

Leal Buitrago, Francisco. *Desarrollo Político Colombiano 1930–1970.* Estudio del Comportamiento Legislativo en Colombia, vol. 1. Bogotá: Ediciones Tercer Mundo, 1972.

———. "Social Classes, International Trade, and Foreign Capital in Colombia: An Attempt at Historical Interpretation of the Formation of the State." Ph.D. dissertation, University of Wisconsin (Madison), 1974.

Lemaitre, Eduardo. *Biografía de un Gran Colombiano: Rafael Reyes.* Bogotá: n.p., 1967.

———. *Panamá y Su Separación de Colombia.* Bogotá: Banco Popular, 1973.

Lieuwen, Edwin. *Arms and Politics in Latin America.* New York: Praeger, 1969.

Liévano Aguirre, Indalecio. *Los Grandes Conflictos Sociales y Económicos de Nuestra Historia.* 3 vols. Bogotá: Ediciones Nueva Prensa, 1954.

———. *El Proceso de Mosquera ante el Senado.* Bogotá: Editorial Revista Colombiana, 1968.

———. *Rafael Núñez.* Lima: Editora Latinoamericana, n.d.

Lleras Restrepo, Carlos. *De la Democracia a la Dictadura.* Bogotá: Ediciones Agra, 1955.

———. *Hacia la Restauración Democrática y el Cambio Social.* 2 vols. Bogotá: Editorial Agra, 1964.

López,, José Hilario. *Memorias.* Medellín: Editorial Bedout, 1969.

López Michelsen, Alfonso. *Cuestiones Colombianas.* México City: n.p., 1955.

López Toro, Alvaro. *Migración y Cambio Social an Antioquia Durante el Siglo XIX.* Bogotá: Ediciones Universidad de Los Andes, 1970.

Lorenz, Konrad. *On Aggression.* New York: Harcourt, Brace and World, 1966.

Losada, Rodrigo. "Elites Políticas Colombianas." Unpublished manuscript, Bogotá, 1972.
Manrique, Ramón. *A Sangre y Fuego.* Barranquilla: n.p., 1948.
Martz, John D. *Colombia: A Contemporary Political Study.* Chapel Hill: University of North Carolina Press, 1962.
———. *Colombia: Un Estudio de Política Contemporánea.* Bogotá: Universidad Nacional de Colombia, 1969.
Marulanda, Manuel. *Cuadernos de Campaña.* Bogotá: Abejón Mono, 1973.
McGreevey, William Paul. *An Economic History of Colombia.* Cambridge: Cambridge University Press, 1971.
———. "The Economic Development of Colombia." Ph.D. dissertation, Massachusetts Institute of Technology, 1965.
Mellafe, Rolando. *La Esclavitud en Hispanoamérica.* Buenos Aires: EUDEBA, 1964.
Mendoza Neira, Plinio, and Camacho Angarita, Alberto. *El Liberalismo en el Gobierno.* Bogotá: Prag, n.d.
Mesa, Darío. *El Problema Agrario en Colombia: 1920–1960.* Bogotá: El Tigre de Papel, 1972.
Molina, Gerardo. *Las Ideas Liberales en Colombia: 1849–1914.* Bogotá: Ediciones Tercer Mundo, 1972.
Moncada Abello, Alfonso. *Un Aspecto de la Violencia.* Bogotá: Promotora Colombiana de Editores, 1963.
Montaña Cuéllar, Diego. *Colombia: País Formal y País Real.* Buenos Aires: Editorial Platina, 1963.
Needler, Martin C. *Latin American Politics in Perspective.* Princeton, N.J.: Van Nostrand, 1963.
———. *Political Development in Latin America: Instability, Violence, and Evolutionary Change.* New York: Random House, 1968.
Nieburg, H. L. *Political Violence: The Behavioral Process.* New York: St. Martin's Press, 1969.
Nieto, Eduardo. *Economía y Cultura en la Historia de Colombia.* Bogotá: Librería Siglo XX, 1944.
Nieto Rojas, José María. *La Batalla Contra el Comunismo en Colombia.* Bogotá: Empresa Nacional de Publicaciones, 1956.
Niño, Lucía de, and Equipo de Investigaciones Sociológicas. "Estructura de Clases en Colombia." Mimeographed. Bogotá: Universidad Nacional, 1971.
Niño, Alberto. *Antecedentes y Secretos del 9 de Abril.* Bogotá: n.p., 1949.
Núñez, Rafael. *La Reforma Política.* Bogotá: Empresa Imprenta de la Luz, 1882.
Obando, José María. *Apuntamientos para la Historia.* Medellín: Editorial Bedout, n.d.
Ocampo, José Fernando. *Dominio de Clase en la Ciudad Colombiana.* Medellín: La Oveja Negra, 1972.
Orrego Duque, Gonzalo. *El Nueve de Abril Afuera de Palacio.* Bogotá: Editorial Patria, 1949.
Osorio, Abraham. *Por Qué Mataron a Gaitán.* Bogotá: Editorial Iqueima, 1948.
Ospina Vásquez, Luis. *Industria y Protección en Colombia (1810–1930).* Medellín: E.S.P., 1955.
Palza, Humberto. *La Noche Roja de Bogotá.* Buenos Aires: Editorial López, 1949.
Paredes Cruz, Joaquín. *Causas y Efectos de Una Dictadura.* Cali: n.p., 1957.
Parsons, James J. *Antioqueño Colonization in Western Colombia.* Berkeley: University of California Press, 1949.
Partido Comunista de Colombia. *Treinta Años de Lucha del Partido Comunista en Colombia.* Bogotá: Ediciones Paz y Socialismo, 1960.
Patiño, Abelardo. "Political Ideas of the Liberal and Conservative Parties during the 1946–1953 Crisis." Ph.D. dissertation, American University (Washington, D.C., 1954).

Payne, James L. *Patterns of Conflict in Colombia.* New Haven: Yale University Press, 1968.

Pecaut, Daniel. *Política y Sindicalismo en Colombia.* Bogotá: La Carreta, 1973.

Pena, Eduardo. *Origen y Desarrollo de la Burguesía Colombiana.* Barranquilla: Tipografía Dovel, 1971.

Pérez, Luis Carlos. *Delitos Políticos: Interpretación Jurídica del Nueve de Abril.* Bogotá: Editorial Iqueima, 1949.

Pombo, Manuel Antonio, and Guerra, José Joaquín. *Constituciones de Colombia.* Bogotá: Biblioteca Popular de Cultura Colombiana, 1951.

Posada, Francisco. *Colombia: Violencia y Subdesarrollo.* Bogotá: Tercer Mundo, 1969.

———. *El Movimiento Revolucionario de los Comuneros.* México City: Siglo XXI, 1971.

Posada Gutiérrez, Joaquín. *Memorias Histórico-Políticas.* 3 vols. Medellín: Editorial Bedout, 1971.

Puentes, Milton. *Historia del Partido Liberal Colombiano.* Bogotá: Editorial Prag, 1961.

Quintín Lame, Manuel. *En Defensa de Mi Raza.* Bogotá: La Rosca, 1971.

———. *Las Luchas del Indio que Bajó de la Montaña al Valle de la Civilización.* Bogotá: La Rosca, 1971.

Ramsey, Russell. "The Modern Violence in Colombia 1946–1965." Ph.D. dissertation, University of Florida (Gainesville), 1970.

———. *La Revolución Campesina 1950–1954.* Bogotá: Ediciones Libros de Colombia, 1973.

Reichel-Dolmatoff, Gerardo. *Colombia.* London: Thames and Hudson, 1963.

Restrepo, Roberto. *Nueve de Abril: Quiebra Cultural y Política.* Bogotá: n.p., 1948.

Rippy, J. Fred. *The Capitalists and Colombia.* New York: Vanguard Press, 1931.

———. *El Capital Norteamericano y la Penetración Imperialista.* Medellín: La Oveja Negra, 1971.

Rivas, Medardo. *Los Trabajadores de Tierra Caliente.* Bogotá: Biblioteca Popular de Cultura Colombiana, 1946.

Rodríguez Acosta, Hugo. *Elementos Críticos para una Nueva Interpretación de la Historia Colombiana.* Bogotá: Editorial Tupac Amaru, 1971.

Rodríguez Piñeres, Eduardo. *Diez Años de Política Liberal: 1892–1902.* Bogotá: Editorial Antena, 1945.

Rodríguez Salazar, Oscar. "Las Constituciones del Siglo XIX y Su Contenido de Clase." Unpublished manuscript. Bogotá, 1976.

———. *Efectos de la Gran Depresión en la Industria Colombiana.* Bogotá: n.p., 1974.

Rubenstein, Richard. *Rebels in Eden: Mass Political Violence in the United States.* Boston: Little, Brown, 1970.

Russet, Bruce M.; Alker, Hayward R.; Deutsch, Karl M.; and Lasswell, Harold. *World Handbook of Political and Social Indicators.* New Haven: Yale University Press, 1964.

Samper, José María. *Ensayo Sobre las Revoluciones Políticas.* Bogotá: Universidad Nacional de Colombia, 1969.

Santa, Eduardo. *Arrieros y Fundadores.* Bogotá: Editorial Cromos, 1961.

———. *Rafael Uribe Uribe.* Medellín: Editorial Bedout, n.d.

———. *Sociología Política de Colombia.* Bogotá: Editorial Iqueima, 1955.

———. *Sociología Política de Colombia.* Bogotá: Ediciones Tercer Mundo, 1964.

Santos Forero, Enrique. *Yo Vi Huir al Verdadero Asesino de Jorge Eliécer Gaitán.* Bogotá: Gráficas Atenas, 1959.

Serrano Blanco, Manuel. *La Vida Es Así.* Bucaramanga: Imprenta del Departamento, 1953.

———. *Las Viñas del Odio.* Bucaramanga: Imprenta del Departamento, 1949.

Sevillano Quiñones. *El Hombre Frente a la Violencia.* Bogotá: Editorial Aplicación Publicitaria, 1965.

Short, James F., Jr., and Wolfgang, Marvin E., eds. *Collective Violence.* Chicago: Aldine–Atherton, 1972.

Sierra, Luis Fernando. *Tabaco en la Economía Colombiana del Siglo XIX.* Bogotá: Universidad Nacional de Colombia, 1971.

Sierra Ochoa, Col. Gustavo. *Las Guerrillas en los Llanos Orientales.* Manizales: Tipografía Departamental, 1954.

Simmel, Georg. *Conflict and the Web of Group Affiliations.* New York: The Free Press, 1955.

Skolnik, Jerome H. *The Politics of Protest: Report to the National Commission of the Causes and Prevention of Violence.* New York: Ballatine Books, 1969.

Smelser, Neil. *Theory of Collective Behavior.* New York: The Free Press, 1962.

Smith, T. Lynn. *Colombia: Social Structure and the Process of Development.* Gainesville: University of Florida Press, 1967.

Solaún, Mauricio. "*La Violencia:* Socio-Historical Determinants of Political Violence in Colombia." Unpublished manuscript. N.p., n.d.

Solaún, Mauricio, and Quinn, Michael A. *Sinners and Heretics: The Politics of Military Interventions in Latin America.* Urbana: University of Illinois Press, 1973.

Stinchcombe, Arthur. *Constructing Social Theories.* New York: Harcourt, Brace and World, 1968.

Tamayo, Joaquín. *La Revolución de 1899.* Bogotá: Editorial Cromos, 1938.

Tirado Mejía, Alvaro. *Introducción a la Historia Económica de Colombia.* Bogotá: Universidad Nacional, 1971.

Tisnes, Roberto María. *Movimientos Pre-Independientes Grancolombianos.* Bogotá: Academia Colombiana de la Historia, 1962.

Tobón, Alfanso. *La Tierra y la Reforma Agraria en Colombia.* Medellín: La Oveja Negra, 1973.

Torres García, Guillermo. *Historia de la Moneda Colombiana.* Bogotá: Banco de la República, 1945.

Torres Giraldo, Ignacio. *Los Inconformes: Historia de la Rebeldía de Masas en Colombia.* 5 vols. Bogotá: Editorial Margen Izquierdo, 1973–1974.

———. *María Cano: Mujer Rebelde.* Bogotá: La Rosca, 1972.

———. *Síntesis de la Historia Política de Colombia.* Bogotá: Editorial Margen Izquierdo, 1972.

Tovar, Hermes. *El Movimiento Campesino en Colombia.* Bogotá: Ediciones Libres, 1975.

Trujillo, Ciro. *Páginas de Su Vida.* Bogotá: Abejón Mono, 1974.

Umaña Luna, Eduardo. *El Ambiente Penal de la Violencia: Factores Socio-Jurídicos de la Impunidad.* Bogotá: Ediciones Tercer Mundo, 1962.

Urrutia, Miguel. *Historia del Sindicalismo en Colombia.* Bogotá: Ediciones Universidad de Los Andes, 1969.

Urrutia, Miguel, and Castellanos, Luis. *Estudio Económico Social de la Población de Bogotá.* Bogotá: CAR, 1962.

Urueta, Carlos Adolfo. *Documentos Militares y Políticos Relativos a la Campaña del General Rafael Uribe Uribe.* Bogotá: Imprenta de Vapor, 1904.

Valcárcel, Daniel. *La Rebelión de Tupac Amaru.* México City: Fondo de Cultura Económica, 1965.

Vargas Martínez, Gustavo. *Colombia 1854: Melo, los Artesanos, el Socialismo.* Bogotá: Editorial Oveja Negra, 1972.

Velásquez Santos, Jorge. *Buenos Días Guerrilleros.* Bogotá: Editorial Agra, 1954.

Vidales, Luis. *La Insurrección Desplomada.* Bogotá: Editorial Iqueima, 1949.

Vieira, Gilberto. *Nueve de Abril: Experiencia del Pueblo.* Bogotá: Ediciones Sudamérica, 1973.

Villar Borda, Carlos J. *Rojas Pinilla: El Presidente Libertador.* Bogotá: Editorial Iqueima, 1953.

Weber, Max. *The Theory of Social and Economic Organization.* New York: The Free Press, 1947.

Wolfgang, Marvin E., and Ferracuti, Franco. *The Subculture of Violence: Towards an Integrated Theory in Criminology.* London: Tavistock, 1967.

Zuleta, Angel Eduardo. *El Presidente López.* Medellín: Editorial Albon-Intrprint, 1968.

Zuleta, Estanislao, and Asociación Nacional de Usuarios Campesinos (ANUC). *La Tierra en Colombia.* Bogotá: La Oveja Negra, 1973.

Articles, Monographs, and Occasional Papers

Abel, Christopher. "Conservative Politics in Twentieth Century Antioquia 1910–1953." Occasional Paper No. 3. Oxford: St. Anthony's College, Latin American Centre, 1973.

Agudelo, Carlos. "El Estado y los Partidos Políticos en Colombia 1930–1973." *Ideología y Sociedad,* no. 9 (January–March 1974).

Anderson, Charles W. "La Violencia in Colombia." In *Issues of Political Development,* edited by Charles W. Anderson, Fred R. Von Der Meliden, and Crawford Young. Englewood Cliffs, N.J.: Prentice Hall, 1967.

Asociación Nacional de Usuarios Campesinos (ANUC). "Consideraciones sobre la Lucha en el Campo Colombiano." In *La Tierra en Colombia,* Estanislao Zuleta and ANUC. Medellín: Editorial Oveja Negra, 1973.

Bay, Christian. "Violence as a Negation of Freedom." *The American Scholar* 40 (1971): 634–641.

Benalcázar Saavedra, Enrique, and Martínez Rave, Gilberto. "La Violencia in Colombia." In *Proceedings of the 12th International Course in Criminology.* Jerusalem: Conference on the Causation and Prevention of Crime in Developing Countries, 1963.

Berkowitz, Leonard. "The Study of Urban Violence: Some Implications of Laboratory Studies of Frustration and Aggression." In *When Men Revolt and Why,* edited by James Chowning Davies. New York: The Free Press, 1971.

Borah, Woodrow C. "America as Model: The Demographic Impact of European Expansion upon the Non-European World." Berkeley: University of California, Center for Latin American Studies, n.d.

Botero, Camila, and Gómez de Martínez, Angela. "La Huelga de las Bananeras." Unpublished essay. Bogotá: Universidad de Los Andes, 1972.

Bustamante, Darío. "Efectos Económicos del Papel Moneda Durante la Regeneración." Bogotá: Universidad Nacional, Centro de Investigaciones de Desarrollo (CID), 1973.

Bwy, Douglas P. "Dimensions of Social Conflict in Latin America." In *Riots and Rebellions: Civilian Violence in the Urban Community,* edited by Louis H. Maselti and Don R. Bowen. Beverly Hills, Calif.: Sage Publications, 1969.

Comisión Católica Internacional de Migración and Caritas Internationalis. "Informe de Misión Venezuela y Colombia." Geneva and Rome: n.p., 1972.

Currie, Elliot, and Skolnik, Jerome H. "A Critical Note on Conceptions of Collective Behavior." *The Annals of the American Academy of Political and Social Science,* no. 391 (1970), pp. 340–345.

Davies, James Chowning. "Revolution and the J-Curve." In *Revolution and Political Change,* edited by Claude E. Welch and Marvis Bunker Taintor. Belmont, Calif.: Wadsworth, 1972.

———. "Toward a Theory of Revolution." *American Sociological Review* 6 (1962): 5–19.

Deas, Malcolm. "Algunas Notas sobre el Caciquismo en Colombia." *Revista de Occidente,* no. 127 (1973).

———. "Una Finca Cundinamarquesa entre 1870 y 1910." Bogotá: Universidad Nacional, Centro de Investigaciones del Desarrollo, 1974.

Fajardo Montaña, Darío. "Ayer y Hoy de Los Indígenas Colombianos." In *Ayer y Hoy de los Indígenas Colombianos,* edited by Departamento Administrativo Nacional de Estadística (DANE), República de Colombia. Bogotá: DANE, 1971.

———. "Los Sectores Indígenas en el Desarrollo del Capitalismo en Colombia." In *Indigenismo y Aniquilamiento de Indígenas en Colombia,* edited by Juan Friede, Nina S. Friedemann, and Darío Fajardo. Bogotá: Universidad Nacional de Colombia, 1975.

———. "Tenencia de la Tierra y Producción en el Valle de Chisaca." Bogotá: Universidad Nacional, Centro de Investigaciones del Desarrollo, 1974.

Fals Borda, Orlando. "Violencia and the Breakup of Tradition in Colombia." In *Obstacles to Change in Latin America,* edited by Claudio Veliz. London: Oxford University Press, 1965.

Feirabend, Ivo F., and Rosalind L. "Aggressive Behavior within Polities, 1948–1962: A Cross National Study." *Journal of Conflict Resolution* 10 (1966): 240–271.

Feirabend, Ivo F.; Feierabend, Rosalind; and Nesvold, Betty A. "Social Change and Political Violence." In *Violence in America: Historical and Comparative Perspectives,* edited by Hugh Davis Graham and Ted Robert Gurr. New York: Bantam Books, 1969.

Firestone, Joseph M. "Three Frameworks for the Study of Violence." Binghamton, N.Y.: SUNY, Center for Comparative Research, 1971.

Galtung, Johan. "Violence, Peace, and Peace Research." *Journal of Peace Research* 6 (1969): 172–192.

Garver, Newton. "What Violence Is." *The Nation* 206 (1968): 819–822). In Rose, T., ed. *Violence in America.* New York: Vintage, 1970.

Gude, Edward F. "Batista and Betancourt: Alternative Responses to Violence." In *Violence in America: Historical and Comparative Perspectives,* edited by Hugh Davis Graham and Ted Robert Gurr. New York: Bantam Books, 1969.

———. "Political Violence in Venezuela: 1958–1964." In *When Men Revolt and Why,* edited by James Chowning Davies. New York: The Free Press, 1971.

Gurr, Ted Robert. "Psychological Factors in Civil Violence." In *Revolution and Political Change,* edited by Claude Welch, Jr., and Marvis Bunker Tainter. Belmont, Calif.: Wadsworth, 1972.

———. "Sources of Rebellion in Western Societies: Some Quantitative Evidence." *The Annals of the American Academy of Political and Social Science* 391 (1970): 126–144.

Gurr, Ted Robert, with Ruttemberg, Charles. "The Conditions of Civil Violence: The First Tests of a Causal Model." Research Monograph No. 28. Princeton, N.J.: Princeton University, Center for International Studies, 1967.

Hudson, Michael C. "Conditions of Political Violence and Stability: A Preliminary Test of Three Hypotheses." Beverly Hils, Calif.: Sage Publications, Professional Papers, 1971.

Huntington, Samuel. "Patterns of Violence in World Politics." In *Changing Patterns of Military Politics,* edited by Samuel Huntington. New York: The Free Press, 1961.

Kalmanovitz, Salomón. "A Propósito de Arrubla." *Ideología y Sociedad,* no. 10 (April–June 1974), pp. 39–74.

———. "Evolución de la Estructura Agraria en Colombia." *Cuadernos Colombianos,* no. 3 (1974).

———. "Sobre Algunas Teorías del Imperialismo en Colombia." *Ideología y Sociedad,* no. 8 (December 1973), pp. 27–47.

Kling, Merle. "Toward a Theory of Power and Political Instability in Latin America." *Western Political Science Quarterly* 9 (1956): 24–35.

Leal Buitrago, Francisco. "Política e Intervención Militar en Colombia." In *La Dependencia Externa y el Desarrollo Político de Colombia,* edited by Rodrigo Parra Sandoval. Bogotá: Universidad Nacional de Colombia, 1970.

Lipman, Aaron, and Havens, Eugene. "The Colombian Violence: An Ex Post Facto Experiment." *Social Forces* 44 (December 1965).

Londoño, Ana Luz. "La Federación Nacional de Cafeteros." Unpublished essay. Bogotá: Universidad del Rosario, 1975.

López Toro, Alvaro. "Nota Sobre los Fenómenos Migratorios en el Valle del Cauca." *Razón y Fabula: Revista de la Universidad de Los Andes* (May–June 1969).

Machado, Absalón. "Estudio de la Economíca Cafetera de Colombia." Medellín: Universidad de Antioquia, Centro de Investigaciones Económicas, 1975.

Maingot, Anthony. "The Colombian Military: A Case of Inconsistent Status." In *The Role of the Military in Latin America,* edited by Lyle N. McAlister. Gainesville: University of Florida Press, forthcoming.

Melo, Jorge Orlando. "Colombia 1880–1930: La República Conservadora." Unpublished article. Calif.: Universidad del Valle, 1974.

Mesa, Darío. "Treinta Añas de Historia Colombiana." In *Colombia: Estructura Política y Agraria,* edited by Darío Mesa. Bogotá: Ediciones Estrategia, 1972.

Midlarsky, Manus, and Tanter, Raymond. "Toward a Theory of Political Instability in Latin America." *Journal of Peace Research* 3 (1967): 207–209.

Molano, Alfredo. "Cultura y Educación en el Siglo XIX." Bogotá: Instituto Colombiano de Pedagogía (ICOLPE), 1973.

Nardin, Terry. "Conflicting Conceptions of Political Violence." *Political Science Annual* 4 (1973): 75–126.

———. "Violence and the State: A Critique of Empirical Political Theory." Beverly Hills, Calif.: Sage Publications, 1971.

Nesvold, Betty A. "A Scalogram Analysis of Political Violence." *Comparative Political Studies* 2 (1960): 77–194.

Nordlinger, Eric. "Conflict Regulation in Divided Societies." Cambridge: Harvard University, Center for International Affairs, Occasional Papers, 1972.

North, Robert G.; Koch, Harold E.; and Zinnes, Dina A. "The Integrative Functions of Conflict." *The Journal of Conflict Resolution* 4 (1960).

Oquist, Paul. "Una Aproximación Descriptiva del Crimen en Colombia." *Revista Cámara de Comercio de Bogotá* 3 (1973).

———. "Las Elecciones Presidenciales, 1930–1970." In *Boletín Mensual de Estadística,* edited by Departamento Administrativo Nacional de Estadística (DANE), República de Colombia, nos. 268–269 (1973), pp. 63–79.

Parsons, Talcott. "Some Reflections on the Place of Force in Social Processes." In *Internal War: The Problem of Anticipation,* edited by Harry Eckstein. New York: The Free Press, 1964.

Partido Conservador. "Conferencia Doctrinaria Dictada por el Dr. Guillermo Salamanca a Nombre del Directorio Nacional Conservador en la Ciudad de Cali el 11 de Noviembre de 1950." Bogotá: Tipografía Voto Nacional, n.d.

Payne, James. "Perú: The Politics of Structured Violence." *The Journal of Politics* 27 (1965): 362–374.

Pineda, Robert. "El Impacto de la Violencia en el Tolima: El Caso de Líbano." Monografía Sociológica No. 6. Bogotá: Universidad Nacional de Colombia, 1960.

Pollock, John. "The Violence in Colombia: A Challenge to Political Elites?" Unpublished paper. Stanford, Calif.: Stanford University, Workshop on Crises in Political Development, 1969.

Prieto, Rafael. "Causas del Desempleo y la Movilidad de la Fuerza del Trabajo en

Bogotá." In *Empleo y Desempleo en Bogotá,* edited by Centro de Estudios para el Desarrollo (CEDE), Universidad de Los Andes. Bogotá: Universidad de Los Andes, 1969.

Putnam, Robert D. "Toward Explaining Military Intervention in Latin American Politics." *World Politics* 29 (1967): 83–110.

Quimbaya, Anteo. "Formación del Capitalismo en Colombia." *Revista Estudios Marxistas,* no. 4 (September 1975), pp. 43–97.

Revista Javeriana. "La Publicidad de La Violencia" (unsigned article). *Revista Javeriana* 11 (1960).

Reyes, Marco F. "Estudio Socio-Económico del Fenómeno de la Inmigración a Bogotá." *Revista de Economía Colombiana* (October 1964).

Rothlisberger, Dora, and Oquist, Paul. "Algunos Aspectos de la Abstención Electoral." *Boletín Mensual de Estadística,* nos. 268–269 (1973).

Rummel, Rudolph J. "Dimensions of Conflict Behavior within and between Nations." *General Systems Yearbook* 8 (1963).

———. "Dimensions of Conflict between Nations." *The Journal of Conflict Resolution* 10 (March 1966): 65–77.

———. "A Field Theory of Social Action and Political Conflict within Nations." *General Systems Yearbook* 10 (1965).

Smelser, Neil. "Two Critics in Search of a Bias: A Response to Currie and Skolnik." *Annals of the American Academy of Political and Social Science,* no. 391 (1970), pp. 46–55.

Solaún, Mauricio, and Aguero, Manuel S. "Socialización y Compromiso por Medio de *La Violencia.*" *Razón y Fábula* 10 (1968): 61–76.

Stokes, William S. "Violence as a Power Factor in Latin American Politics." *Western Political Science Quarterly* 5 (1952): 443–459.

Stone, Lawrence. "Theories of Revolution." *World Politics* 18 (1966): 159–176.

Tanter, Raymond. "Dimensions of Conflict within and between Nations, 1958–1960." *The Journal of Conflict Resolution* 10 (March 1966): 44–65.

Tilly, Charles. "The Changing Place of Political Violence." In *Essays in Theory and History,* edited by Melvin Richter. Cambridge, Mass.: Harvard University Press, 1970.

———. "Collective Violence in European Perspective." In *Violence in America: Historical and Comparative Perspective,* edited by Hugh Davis Graham and Ted Robert Gurr. New York: Bantam Books, 1969.

———. "Revolutions and Collective Violence." In *Handbook of Political Science,* edited by Fred Greenstein and Nelson W. Polsby. Reading, Mass.: Addison-Wesley, 1972.

Tilly, Charles, and Rule, James. "Measuring Political Upheaval." Research Monograph No. 19. Princeton, N.J.: Princeton University, Center for International Studies, 1966.

Tirado Mejía, Alvaro. "La Tierra en Colombia." *Revista de Divulgación Popular de la Universidad Nacional,* no. 7 (December 1970).

Torres Restrepo, Camilo. "La Violencia y los Cambios Socio-Culturales en las Areas Rurales Colombianas." In *Cristianismo y Revolución.* México City: Era, 1970.

Tovar Pinzón, Hermes. "Estado Actual de los Estudios de Demografía Histórica en Colombia." *Anuario Colombiano de Historia Social y de La Cultura,* no. 5 (1970).

Uribe Uribe, Rafael. "El Socialismo de Estado." Bogotá: Editorial Stella, n.d.

Valencia Betancourt, Captain Antonio. "Causas y Soluciones de La Violencia en Colombia." *Revista de La Policía Nacional de Colombia,* no. 86 (March–April 1961).

Vivas García, Lt. Col. Efraín. "La Violencia en Colombia." *Revista del Ejército* 4 (February 1964).

Wilkenfield, Jonathan. "Domestic and Foreign Conflict Behavior of Nations." *Journal of Peace Research* 5 (1968): 58–69.

Williamson, Robert C. "Toward a Theory of Rural Violence: The Case of Rural Colombia." *Western Political Science Quarterly* 18 (March 1965).

Wolff, Robert Paul. "On Violence." *Journal of Philosophy* 66 (1969): 601–616.

Wolin, Sheldon. "Violence and the Western Political Tradition." *American Journal of Orthopsychiatry* 33 (1963): 15–28.

Zapata, Antonio. "Etapas y Coyunturas de la Lucha Guerrillera en Colombia." In *Diez Años de Insurrección en América Latina*, vol. 2, edited by Vania Bambirra. Santiago, Chile: Ediciones Latinoamericana S.A., 1971.

Documents

Colombia, República de, *Actos Legislativos de la Constitutión de Ríonegro*. Bogotá: Imprenta Nacional, n.d.

———, *Informe del Registrador*, Annual Report of the Registrar's Office for the Years 1949, 1952, and 1954. Bogotá: Imprenta Nacional.

———, Departamento Administrativo Nacional de Estadística, *13th Censo Nacional de Población: Resumen General*. Bogotá: Imprenta Nacional, 1967.

———, Departamento del Tolima, Secretaría de Agricultura, *La Violencia en el Tolima*. Ibagué: Imprenta Departamental, 1958.

———, Dirección de Información y Propaganda, *Seis Meses de Gobierno*. Bogotá: Imprenta Nacional, 1953.

———, Ejército, Octava Brigada, *De La Violencia a La Paz*. Manizales: Imprenta Departamental, 1965.

———, Ministerio de Eduación Nacional, "Primer Seminario sobre la Educación en las Zonas de Violencia." Ibagué: n.p., 1963.

———, Ministerio de Eduación Nacional, "Segundo Seminario sobre la Educación en las Zonas de Violencia." Cali: n.p., 1963.

———, Ministerio de Gobierno, *Informes de Jefes de Sección del Ministerio de Gobierno, 1948*. Bogotá: Imprenta Nacional, 1949.

———, Ministerio de Gobierno, *Memorias*, Annual Report of the Activities of the Ministry of Government for the Years 1930, 1931, 1932, 1933, 1934, 1936, 1939, 1942, 1944, 1945, 1946, and 1947. Bogotá: Imprenta Nacional.

———, Policía Nacional, *Criminalidad*, Annual Report of Criminal Statistics for the Years 1958–1975, Bogotá: Policía Nacional.

———, Presidencia de La República, *Documentos Relacionados con la Renuncia del Presidente López y el Orden Público*. Bogotá: Imprenta Nacional, 1945.

———, Presidencia de La República, *Un Año de Gobierno (1950–1951)*. Bogotá: Imprenta Nacional, 1952.

———, Presidencia de La República, *Un Año de Gobierno, 1945–1946: Discursos y Otros Documentos*. Bogotá: Imprenta Nacional, 1946.

———, Senado, *Anales del Senado*, for the following dates: June 23, 1931, and November 12, 1935.

Comité Interamericano de Desarrollo Agrícola (CIDA), *La Estructura Agraria: Formas de Tenencia*. Washington, D.C.: CIDA, 1966.

United Nations, *Demographic Yearbook*, vol. 8, 1961.

United States, Department of the Army, *U.S. Army Area Handbook for Colombia*, Department of the Army Pamphlet No. 550–26, 1964.

———, Department of State, *Papers Related to the Foreign Relations of the United States 1928*. Washington, D.C.: United States Government Printing Office, 1943.

———, National Advisory Commission on Civil Disorders, *Report*. New York: Bantam Books, 1968.

Newspapers

El Espectador (Bogotá daily), 1928, 1931, 1934, 1939, 1955.
Intermedio (Bogotá daily), 1957.
El Nuevo Tiempo (Bogotá daily), 1928.
La República (Bogotá daily), 1965.
El Siglo (Bogotá daily), 1935, 1936, 1937, 1938, 1939, 1946, 1947, 1948, 1949, 1950, 1951, 1952, 1953, 1957.
El Tiempo (Bogotá daily), 1920, 1921, 1922, 1923, 1924, 1925, 1926, 1927, 1928, 1929, 1930, 1931, 1932, 1933, 1934, 1935, 1936, 1946, 1947, 1948, 1949, 1950, 1951, 1952, 1953, 1954, 1955, 1956, 1957, 1975.

Index

STUDIES IN SOCIAL DISCONTINUITY

Under the Consulting Editorship of:

CHARLES TILLY
University of Michigan

EDWARD SHORTER
University of Toronto

In preparation

David J. Rothman and Stanton Wheeler (Eds.). Social History and Social Policy

Published

Samuel Kline Cohn, Jr. The Laboring Classes in Renaissance Florence

Richard C. Trexler. Public Life in Renaissance Florence

Paul Oquist. Violence, Conflict, and Politics in Colombia

Fred Weinstein. The Dynamics of Nazism: Leadership, Ideology, and the Holocaust

John R. Hanson II. Trade in Transition: Exports from the Third World, 1840–1900

Evelyne Huber Stephens. The Politics of Workers' Participation: The Peruvian Approach in Comparative Perspective

Albert Bergesen (Ed.). Studies of the Modern World-System

Lucile H. Brockway. Science and Colonial Expansion: The Role of the British Royal Botanic Gardens

James Lang. Portuguese Brazil: The King's Plantation

Elizabeth Hafkin Pleck. Black Migration and Poverty: Boston 1865-1900

Harvey J. Graff. The Literacy Myth: Literacy and Social Structure in the Nineteenth-Century City

Michael Haines. Fertility and Occupation: Population Patterns in Industrialization

Keith Wrightson and David Levine. Poverty and Piety in an English Village: Terling, 1525-1700

Henry A. Gemery and Jan S. Hogendorn (Eds.). The Uncommon Market: Essays in the Economic History of the Atlantic Slave Trade

Tamara K. Hareven (Ed.). Transitions: The Family and the Life Course in Historical Perspective

Randolph Trumbach. The Rise of the Egalitarian Family: Aristocratic Kinship and Domestic Relations in Eighteenth-Century England

Arthur L. Stinchcombe. Theoretical Methods in Social History

Juan G. Espinosa and Andrew S. Zimbalist. Economic Democracy: Workers' Participation in Chilean Industry 1970-1973

Richard Maxwell Brown and Don E. Fehrenbacher (Eds.). Tradition, Conflict, and Modernization: Perspectives on the American Revolution

Harry W. Pearson. The Livelihood of Man by Karl Polanyi

Frederic L. Pryor. The Origins of the Economy: A Comparative Study of Distribution in Primitive and Peasant Economies

Charles P. Cell. Revolution at Work: Mobilization Campaigns in China

Dirk Hoerder. Crowd Action in Revolutionary Massachusetts, 1765-1780

David Levine. Family Formations in an Age of Nascent Capitalism

Ronald Demos Lee (Ed.). Population Patterns in the Past

Michael Schwartz. Radical Protest and Social Structure: The Southern Farmers' Alliance and Cotton Tenancy, 1880-1890

Jane Schneider and Peter Schneider. Culture and Political Economy in Western Sicily

Daniel Chirot. Social Change in a Peripheral Society: The Creation of a Balkan Colony

Stanley H. Brandes. Migration, Kinship, and Community: Tradition and Transition in a Spanish Village

James Lang. Conquest and Commerce: Spain and England in the Americas

Kristian Hvidt. Flight to America: The Social Background of 300,000 Danish Emigrants

D. E. H. Russell. Rebellion, Revolution, and Armed Force: A Comparative Study of Fifteen Countries with Special Emphasis on Cuba and South Africa

John R. Gillis. Youth and History: Tradition and Change in European Age Relations 1770-Present

Immanuel Wallerstein. The Modern World-System I: Capitalist Agriculture and the Origins of the European World-Economy in the Sixteenth Century; II: Mercantilism and the Consolidation of the European World-Economy, 1600-1750

John W. Cole and Eric R. Wolf. The Hidden Frontier: Ecology and Ethnicity in an Alpine Valley

Joel Samaha. Law and Order in Historical Perspective: The Case of Elizabethan Essex

William A. Christian, Jr. Person and God in a Spanish Valley